学ぶ人は、変えてゆく人だ。

目の前にある問題はもちろん、

人生の問いや、

社会の課題を自ら見つけ、

挑み続けるために、人は学ぶ。

「学び」で、

少しずつ世界は変えてゆける。

いつでも、どこでも、誰でも、

学ぶことができる世の中へ。

旺文社

JN036236

▌壁越えトレーニング
シリーズ③

TOEIC® L&Rテスト 壁越えトレーニング Part 7

大里秀介 著

Osato Shusuke

旺文社

本書を手に取ってくださり，ありがとうございます。

本書で対策するTOEIC® L&RテストのPart 7とは「長文読解問題」です。つまり，まとまった文章を読んで，解くパートです。こう書くとシンプルですが，限られた時間で大量の文章を読んで解くのは大変なことです。リーディング・セクションで450点以上のハイスコアを取得する方でも「正解が見つからない！」「最後まで解き終わらずに試験時間が終了してしまった…」という経験があるパートではないでしょうか。

本書は，そんなPart 7に対して皆さんが感じている「壁」を「越える」ためのヒントや処方薬として執筆しました。10年以上前になりますが，私自身も皆さんと同じように「壁」にぶつかっていたことがあります。そのときに感じていた，わからない，解けない，時間が足りない，悔しいという気持ちを思い出しながら，皆さんが壁を攻略するために必要なポイントの検討を重ねました。

TOEIC® L&Rテストは出題される範囲がある程度決まっています。ビジネスや日常生活に関する内容について，限定された範囲での語彙や文法を用いて出題されるため，パターンを押さえ，制限時間内に解くための戦略を立てることができます。特にPart 7では文書や設問の種類にパターンがあり，文書の読み方と解答のアプローチをつかんでおけば，効率的に解答することができます。

本書では「診断テスト」の結果をもとに，文書［設問］タイプ別に解くためのコツを学んでいきます。どれくらいのスピードで読む必要があるか，速く読むにはどうすればいいか，そのトレーニング方法なども盛り込みました。本書をしっかり学習すれば，自分が苦手とするポイントを克服し，今まで感じていた「壁」を越えられるだけでなく，さまざまなシーンで役立つ英語力が身に付けられると思います。

本書を通じて皆さんが「Part 7を最後まで解くことができた！」「スコアアップにつながった！」という喜びを感じ，レベルアップされることを心より願っています。

大里秀介

もくじ

Chapter 1 文書タイプ別攻略法

Chapter 2 設問タイプ別攻略法

編集協力：日本アイアール株式会社，鹿島由紀子，鎌田賀津子，久島智津子，Michael Joyce

問題作成協力：株式会社 メディアビーコン

装丁デザイン：ごぼうデザイン事務所　　装丁写真：荒川潤，平賀正明

本文デザイン：伊藤幸恵，尾引美代　　本文イラスト：矢戸優人

録音：ユニバ合同会社　　ナレーション：Howard Colefield, Ann Slater（以上，米），Christiane Brew（英）

本書の構成は以下の通りです。効果的な学習法はp.8の「濵﨑潤之輔&大里秀介のパワーアップ学習法」をご覧ください。

診断テスト

自分の得意・苦手な文書［設問］タイプを把握するために，診断テストを最初に解きます。その後，各タイプの正答数・誤答数を確認し，「濵﨑潤之輔&大里秀介のトレーニング・カウンセリング」を参考にして学習計画を立てましょう。

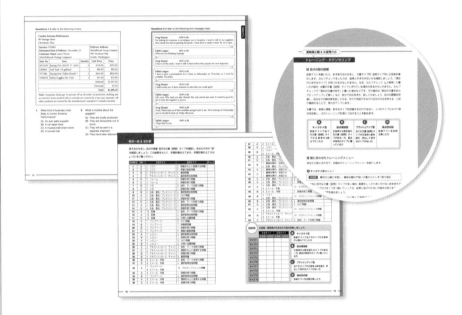

濵﨑潤之輔&大里秀介のパワーアップ対談

本書の巻頭・中間・後半に，濵﨑潤之輔先生と大里秀介先生の対談があります。読んで，モチベーションを上げましょう。

※濵﨑潤之輔先生は，本シリーズのPart 1-4（うち，Part 1と2），Part 5-6を執筆しています。

文書［設問］タイプ別攻略法

Part 7の文書［設問］タイプ別の攻略法です。各自の学習計画に従って進めましょう。もちろん，最初から順番に始めても構いません。

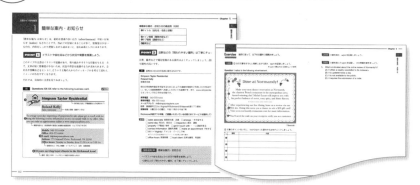

Final Test

学習計画を終えたら，Final Testで仕上げをしましょう。本番の試験のつもりで取り組んでください。解説のページには文書［設問］タイプが振られていますので，診断テストのように自分の得意・苦手を分析し，もう一度攻略法に戻って学習を深めましょう。

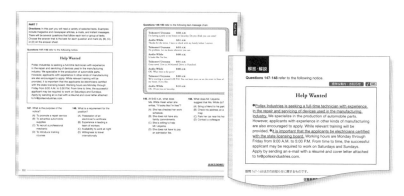

■■ 自動採点サービスについて

診断テストとFinal Testは自動採点サービスに対応しています。パソコンやスマートフォン，タブレットなどからオンラインマークシートで解答すると，結果が自動採点され，また，得意・苦手の分析も行うことができます。以下のサイトにアクセスしてご利用ください。

https://toeic.obunsha.co.jp

（右のQRコードからもアクセスできます）

※本サービスは無料でご利用いただけますが，通信料金はお客さまのご負担となります。
※本サービスは予告なく終了することがあります。

本書は，まず「診断テスト」で現状を把握し，「文書［設問］タイプ別攻略法」でトレーニングをし，「Final Test」で総仕上げをする，という3段階で構成されています。それぞれの目的をしっかり認識して学習計画を立て，問題を解くことで，より効果的に力をつけることができます。

1 現状を把握する

（1）セルフチェック

診断テストを解く前に，セルフチェックをしましょう。ノートなどに自分がPart 7で得意・苦手と思う点を書き出してみます。

【記入例】

> Part 7
> 得意：文章量が少ない広告，メモ，メール
> 苦手：記事，ダブル・トリプルパッセージ

なお，一度も受験したことがない方，得意・苦手を把握していない方，すでにリーディング・セクションのスコアを450点以上取得している方（またはPart 7で54問中50問程度正解できるレベルの方）は，このステップは飛ばしてください。

（2）診断テストを解く

できる限り本番と同じように邪魔をされない環境で，診断テストに挑戦してください。どうしてもまとまった時間が確保できない場合は，シングルパッセージ（設問1～29）とダブル・トリプルパッセージ（設問30～54）に区切るか，設問数×1分を目安に区切って解いても構いません。

TOEIC L&Rテストはマークシート形式なので，わからない問題でも勘で正解してしまう可能性もあります。診断テストは実力を測ることが目的なので，勘で解かないようにしてください。また，自信がない問題は「？」や「△」などの記号を付けておくとよいでしょう。

（3）答え合わせをし，自分の現状の型を診断する

セルフチェック・診断テストの結果を受けて，自分の現状を診断します。単純に「得意・苦手なタイプ」を把握するだけではなく，本書では，4つの型に分けて現状を診断し，次のトレーニング計画につなげることを勧めます。詳しくは，p.100からの

「トレーニング・カウンセリング」をご覧ください。

診断テストがそれほど苦労なく解けた場合は，解答時間を普段の8割くらいに短縮し，負荷をかけてもう一度解いてみましょう。そうすることで解けなくなったり，正解したものの，正解の根拠があいまいになったりしたものは，実は苦手かもしれない問題，または残り時間がなくなってきて焦った場合にミスをする可能性のある問題です。

2 トレーニング計画を立て，実行する

自分の型がわかったら，試験までに学習にかけられる時間，それまでにするべきことを考え，トレーニングの計画を立てます。それぞれの型に合わせたトレーニングメニューや，各文書［設問］タイプの攻略にかかる時間の詳細は「トレーニング・カウンセリング」をご覧ください。

計画を立てたら，とにかく実行します。始めてみたら思っていたより時間がかかる場合もあると思います。適宜，メニューを組み直してください。

3 Final Testで仕上げる

計画を一通り終えたら，仕上げとしてFinal Testにチャレンジします。本番と同じように邪魔されない環境で，時間を取って行ってください。解答時間は1問1分，すなわち54問＝54分としましょう。解答後は答え合わせをするだけでなく，解説をしっかり読み，間違えた箇所は「なぜ間違えたか」もしっかり分析しましょう。また，最初に行った診断テストと同様に分析を行い，苦手な文書タイプや設問タイプがあるようなら，各攻略法に戻って再度学習してください。Final Testを全問正解できるようになるまで，何度も復習しましょう。

Final Testを全問正解できるレベルの実力がついたら，他の模試や問題集に挑戦しましょう。別の問題を解くことで，実は苦手だったタイプが発見できたり，新たに克服すべきポイントを見つけたりすることができます。他の問題集を解きながら，「苦手だったものが克服できていない」と感じたら，本書に戻って再度学習しましょう。しばらく時間が経過することで，忘れかけていた内容を思い出すことができ，内容がより一層，定着します。また，実際の試験で似たような文書が出た場合に「こんなストーリーを読んだことがあるな」と感じられ，余裕を持って問題を解くことができるでしょう。

TOEIC® L&R テストについて

✂TOEIC® L&Rテストとは？

TOEIC（Test of English for International Communication）とは，英語によるコミュニケーション能力を測定する世界共通のテスト。このテストは，アメリカにある非営利のテスト開発機関であるETS（Educational Testing Service）によって開発・制作されています。TOEIC L&R（TOEIC Listening and Reading Test）では「聞く」「読む」という２つの英語力を測定します。受験者の能力は合格・不合格ではなく，10～990点の５点刻みのスコアで評価されるのが特徴です。解答方法は，正解だと思う選択肢番号を塗りつぶすマークシート方式。解答を記述させる問題はありません。

申し込み方法・受験に関する詳細は公式サイトをご覧ください。

https://www.iibc-global.org

✂TOEIC® L&Rテストの構成

以下のように，ListeningとReadingの２つのセクションで構成されています。2時間で200問に解答し，途中休憩はありません。

Listening （約45分・100問）	Part 1	写真描写問題		6問
	Part 2	応答問題		25問
	Part 3	会話問題		39問
	Part 4	説明文問題		30問
Reading （75分・100問）	Part 5	短文穴埋め問題		30問
	Part 6	長文穴埋め問題		16問
	Part 7	読解問題	1つの文書	29問
			複数の文書	25問

●問い合わせ先　一般財団法人 国際ビジネスコミュニケーション協会

IIBC 試験運営センター	〒100-0014 東京都千代田区永田町2-14-2　山王グランドビル 電話：03-5521-6033／FAX：03-3581-4783 （土・日・祝日・年末年始を除く10:00～17:00）
名古屋事業所	電話：052-220-0286 （土・日・祝日・年末年始を除く10:00～17:00）
大阪事業所	電話：06-6258-0224 （土・日・祝日・年末年始を除く10:00～17:00）

※このページの情報は2020年6月現在のものです。詳細や変更は実施団体のホームページなどでご確認ください。

本書の音声の利用方法は以下の通りです。

▟▙ 旺文社リスニングアプリ「英語の友」（iOS/Android）

❶「英語の友」公式サイトより，アプリをインストール
（右のQRコードから読み込めます）

https://eigonotomo.com

❷ ライブラリより「TOEIC L&Rテスト 壁越えトレーニング
Part 7」を選び，「追加」ボタンをタップ

※本アプリの機能の一部は有料ですが，本書の音声は無料でお聞きいただけます。詳しいご利用
　方法は「英語の友」公式サイトまたはアプリ内のヘルプをご参照ください。なお，本サービス
　は予告なく終了することがあります。

▟▙ パソコンで音声ファイル（MP3）をダウンロード

❶ パソコンから以下のサイトにアクセスし，書籍を選択する

https://www.obunsha.co.jp/service/kabegoe

❷ パスワードを入力

xf3wa

❸ ファイルを選択してダウンロードする
音声ファイル（MP3）はZIP形式にまとめられた形でダウンロードされます。
展開後，デジタルオーディオプレーヤーなどでご活用ください。

※本サービスは予告なく終了することがあります。

本書をさらに活用するために以下のものを上記サイトよりダウンロードできます。

- 診断テスト・Final Testの解答用紙
- 設問タイプ別攻略法Practiceのwpm記録表

切磋琢磨しあった
2人の力が詰まったシリーズ誕生

切磋琢磨しながら990点を目指す

編集部（以下，編）：お二人のこれまでの TOEIC学習歴，交流歴を教えてください。

大里秀介（以下，大）：出会いのきっかけは ナンパですね。

濱﨑潤之輔（以下，濱）：どういうことです か，それ。

大：あの池袋のオフ会ですよ（笑）。僕たち は二人とも2006年にTOEICを受け始めた ので，学習歴は近いですね。でも，その当 時は全く会ったことがありませんでした。 僕がTOEICの学習を始めたのは，会社で留 学するためにTOEICの点数が必要だった からです。念願かなって留学し，帰国後， 2008年1月の受験でTOEICは最後にしよ うと思っていたのですが，このころ，神崎 正哉先生のTOEICのインターネットラジ オをたまたま聞いたんです。このラジオが 面白くて，この後もTOEICを続けて受ける ことになりました。そして，いろんな先生 のブログを見ているうちに，濱崎さんのブ ログを見つけて意識するようになりました。 2008年7月以降，僕もそのラジオに出演す るようになったのですが，出演前のオフ会 で初めて濱崎さんとお会いしました。僕は 800点前半で伸び悩んでいるころで，一方， 濱崎さんは970点くらいを取っていた。講 師じゃない一般の学習者が900点後半を取 っているのを見て，この差は何なんだと思 ったんです。筋肉が違うのかなとか（笑）。

濱：思い出した！池袋のオフ会が始まる前 にカフェに行ったら，たまたま大里さんに 会ったんですよ。いきなり声をかけられて， すごく書き込まれたノートを見せられまし た。「何だこの人？」ってドン引きしてその ときは終わったんですけど（笑）。

大：2009年ごろからは週1回，新宿で会う ようになりました。900点を超えると TOEICをやめる人が多いんですが，僕らは ずっと満点の先生たちと一緒にラジオに出 てたんです。2009年はまだ僕は900点前 半，濱崎さんは980点から985点を取れて るけど，満点ではないので，答え合わせす ると何個か間違っている。

濱：僕らだけ間違ってるんですよね。

大：「何で990点を取れないんだろう」って いうその悔しさを毎週木曜日に新宿で集ま って，話をする。100％英語学習の話で，そ のうち99％はTOEICの学習の話をしてい ました。

濱：今って，情報がたくさんありますが，当 時はほとんどなかったので，どういう学習 をしていけば上に行けるのかなっていつも 考えていました。とにかく何でもやる感じ ですね。大里さんは外を歩いているときも 勉強してるんですよ。危ないですよね。交 差点で信号を待つ1分ももったいないの で，ポケットからレシートを出して，英文 を書いてぶつぶつしゃべる。そんな感じで したね。

著者紹介：写真左から
濱﨑潤之輔 …「壁越え Part 1-4」（うち Part 1 と 2），「壁越え Part 5-6」著者
大里秀介 …「壁越え Part 1-4」（うち Part 3 と 4），「壁越え Part 7」著者

大：とにかく上に行くためにやれることはやりました。

濱：で，2010年に僕が，翌年に大里さんが990点を取りました。

編：お二人が切磋琢磨して990点を目指されたんですね。共通点もある一方，お互いの学習スタイルに違いがあったからこそ毎週会うようになったのかなと思います。それぞれ「良い」と思った点，お聞かせください。

大：濱﨑さんは謙虚で，ストイックなところです。僕は満点を取ったその先があまり見えていなかったんですが，濱﨑さんは満点を取った後，人に教えたいというビジョンがあったんですよ。1つの物事に対してしっかり取り組むっていうところがすごいなと。

濱：大里さんは，集中力や，短期・長期の目標を設定してそれをなるべく速くこなしていける点です。僕は，目の前のことを一生懸命やるっていうのはまあまあ長けていると思うんですが，あんまり目標設定をしてそれを達成していく方ではないので，それができている大里さんはすごいなと思います。例えば，朝3時に起きて勉強しているところとか，真似しようとしたんですが，僕は挫折しました。

学習者の「壁」

編：学習者の感じる「壁」とはどのようなものでしょうか。ご自身の経験も踏まえて，お聞かせください。

大：文法の理屈を理解する，語彙の知識を吸収する，音を聞き取れるようになる，そして，ある程度量をこなしてTOEICの問題パターンを押さえれば，実はある程度のスコアは取れるんです。このポイントは，本書の「タイプ別攻略法」に入っています。濱﨑さんはTOEICをメインで勉強して順調に800点まで取ったんですが，その後はたくさん問題を解いたりセミナーに行ったりしたのに900点に届かず，伸び悩んだんですよね。

濱：そうですね。

大：僕も，最初の壁は感じずに860点くらいまでトントントンと進みましたが，伸び悩んだのは「自分はわかってる，できてる」っていう風に思い込み始めてから（笑）。そこからトリッキーな問題に対応できる力をつける必要が出てくるんです。単語をただ知っているだけでなく，使い方まで知らないといけないというか。その状態で多くの問題を解こうとすると，自分が引っかかるポイントを一つ一つきちんと覚えていないから，結局同じような問題で間違うんです。間違えた理由を「語法上こうだから」と考えながら英文を分析するなど，苦手なタイプを見つけたら一つ一つ克服する必要があります。次にそれが出題されるかわからないけど，間違えた問題をちゃんと磨いておけば，出たときに解けるようになる。地道

にやっていく必要があります。

僕はリスニングが伸び悩んでいたんですけど，分析してみるとオーストラリア人の発音が苦手でした。例えば，theyをアメリカ人やオーストラリア人はたまに「ネイ」って発音するんです。これに気付かずに「次，次」と解いてしまうと，実は同じところで間違ってしまうんですが，聞こえ方を理解すれば克服できるんです。

おそらく濵﨑さんもそうなんですが，1セットの模試で84％正解した場合，「16％を間違えないためにどうするか」だけでなく，「正解した84％は，自分が本当に理解して正解したのか，エイ！と選んでたまたま正解したのか」まで一問一問丁寧に復習しました。で，それをやって860点でストップしていたのが，970点までパコーンっていった。

濵：うん，うん。

大：最後の壁は990点でした。ここを突破できたときはたぶん，スピードと，正確さと緻密さが全部つながったときだったと思いますね。

編：自分でも気付かない，間違ってしまう問題のタイプに気付くという目的で，本書は診断テストがありますね。本書をご執筆している中で注意した点はありますか。

濵：そうですね，上級者でも引っかかる知識を極力入れるようにしています。上級になってくると，先ほど大里さんが言ったように足りない知識を一つ一つ入れていかなきゃいけないので。経験上，上級者でもここが足りていない人が多いと思う知識を入れました。

大：Part 3, 4は「聞き方」，Part 7は「読み方」のポイントを意識して入れています。今まではただ聞いて，読んで解いていた人に，もっとこうやった方がいいよって教えてあげるサポート機能，上にあがるための背中を押す要素を詰め込みました。

編：最後に，これから学習を始める読者へのメッセージをお願いします。

大：このシリーズを手に取っていただいた，ということはリスニングやリーディングに何かしら苦手意識を感じているのでは，と思っています。私も濵﨑さんも一学習者だった時代を思い出し，試行錯誤してきた経験を活かして「こうすれば克服できる」という攻略法をまとめることができました。ぜひ取り組んでいただき，皆さんの一助になれば幸いです。頑張りましょう！

濵：本書を手に取っていただきまして本当にありがとうございます。心より感謝申し上げます。細部まで一切無駄なく仕上げた自信作です。僕たちがTOEICに対し，一途な思いを持って研究し続けてきたエッセンスを集約したこの本。本書があなたの今後の人生のさらなる飛躍の一助になることを願っています。頑張っていきましょう，応援しています。

診断テスト

まずは今の実力を確認しましょう。
本番と同じように邪魔をされない環境で
一気に解いてください。

●

目標時間：54分

Questions 1-2 refer to the following invoice.

Cordon Extreme Performance
98 Vantage Street
Cleveland, Ohio

Invoice: I732891 **Estimated Date of Delivery:** December 23 **Customer Name:** Laura Turner (Mitchelbrook Tuning Company)			**Delivery Address:** Mitchelbrook Tuning Company 992 Voorhees Way Seattle, Washington	
Item No.	**Item**	**Quantity**	**Unit Price**	**Price**
HG1039	Racing Tire (265/55 17- inch)	4	$138.00	$552.00
LK9863	Fuel Tank (19 gallons)	1	$96.50	$96.50
YT7482	Racing Seat (Tullox Brand) *	2	$410.00	$820.00
VN6478	Safety Goggles (No Tint)	1	$33.00	$33.00
			Subtotal	$1,501.50
			Discount	$3.30
			Total	**$1,498.20**

Note: Corporate clients get 10 percent off on all orders of protective clothing and accessories. Items marked with an asterisk are covered by a two-year warranty. All other products are covered by the manufacturer's standard 12-month warranty.

1. What kind of business most likely is Cordon Extreme Performance?

    (A) An auto parts supplier
    (B) A computer repair shop
    (C) A musical instrument store
    (D) A concert hall

2. What is implied about the goggles?

    (A) They are locally produced.
    (B) They are temporarily out of stock.
    (C) They will be sent in a separate shipment.
    (D) They have been discounted.

Questions 3-4 refer to the following text-message chain.

> **Greg Harper**   8:50 A.M.
> I'm looking for someone to accompany me to Scranton. I need to talk to our suppliers there about how they're packing the goods. I want them to make it easier for us to open.

> **Edith Langos**   8:51 A.M.
> When are you thinking of going?

> **Greg Harper**   8:52 A.M.
> It has to be this week. I want to talk to them before they prepare the next shipment.

> **Edith Langos**   8:53 A.M.
> I have to give a presentation for a client in Milwaukee on Thursday, so I won't be available, I'm afraid.

> **Greg Harper**   8:54 A.M.
> I didn't mean you. Is there someone in sales that you could spare?

> **Edith Langos**   8:59 A.M.
> OK, sorry. Why don't you take Glenda? She only started last week. It would be good for her to meet the suppliers in person.

> **Greg Harper**   9:02 A.M.
> Great. Please find out if she's available and get back to me. We're leaving on Wednesday, and we should be back on Friday afternoon.

> **Edith Langos**   9:03 A.M.
> I'll get back to you.

3. At 8:52 A.M., what does Mr. Harper most likely mean when he writes, "It has to be this week"?

(A) He would like a shipment urgently.
(B) He would like to leave soon.
(C) He is not in charge of the situation.
(D) He is not sure of the exact date.

4. What is true about Glenda?

(A) She is a senior employee.
(B) She has been to Scranton before.
(C) She works in the sales department.
(D) She will give a presentation on Thursday.

Name: Norma Walsh _____ (Optional)

Thank you for holding your event at the Normandy Symphony Hall.

Please take a few minutes to fill out the following survey and let us know about your experience at Normandy Symphony Hall. Place a ✔ in the box that best matches your impression.

	Strongly Disagree	Disagree	Agree	Strongly Agree
The facilities are modern.			✔	
The staff is helpful.			✔	
The location is convenient.		✔		
The hall is clean.	✔			

Comments: Despite the issue indicated above, I was extremely pleased with Normandy Symphony Hall overall. Nevertheless, we have been looking into other venues recently and keeping in mind the reduced budget we will have next year, I hope you will be open to negotiating on price.

5. What aspect of the facility was Ms. Walsh least impressed with?

(A) Its equipment
(B) Its employees
(C) Its position
(D) Its cleanliness

6. What does Ms. Walsh hope to do?

(A) Use another hall for next year's event
(B) Receive a partial refund on the rental cost
(C) Rent the hall at a better rate
(D) Attract more people to her event

MEMO

To All Tenants,

Yesterday evening, some repairs were carried out on the pipes that deliver water to the building. Unfortunately, the workers accidentally cut the high-speed Internet line. We were only made aware of the problem this morning. A team of cabling specialists has arrived, and they predict that the Internet will be reconnected by 3:00 P.M.

The Internet café in the next building has offered to provide tenants with access to their wireless Internet until the work is carried out. This may be an attractive offer for businesses that rely heavily on their Internet connection. If you would like to take advantage of this generous offer, please call me at 555-8482, or if you are in a hurry, you can visit Slater Office Tower building management on the first floor.

Sincerely,

Ren Walters
Building Manager
Slater Office Tower

7. What is the memo mainly about?
   (A) Increased rental rates
   (B) An interruption to a service
   (C) Updates to a Web site
   (D) A change to a delivery schedule

8. According to the memo, why might tenants contact Mr. Walters?
   (A) To request an invitation
   (B) To reserve some equipment
   (C) To arrange a service
   (D) To extend a deadline

JOB VACANCY

The Ferguson Museum is a small museum on Baker Street in Central Silverton. The museum's exhibits all center on the clothing of the early settlers of the region. We have perfectly preserved boots, suits, and women's garments, some of which are nearly 200 years old. We have a vacancy for a museum guide. It is not necessary to have specific knowledge of local history or the items in our collection. We have an excellent training program to prepare the successful candidate. We are, however, looking for someone with experience as a tour guide. The applicant will also need to have a valid bus driver's license, as we are sometimes called upon to give guided tours of Silverton. As Saturdays and Sundays are our busiest times, applicants must be prepared to work on both days.

If you require a more detailed job description or have any specific questions, contact the head curator at 555-8489 or by e-mail at curator@ fergusonmuseum.com. All applications must be submitted online by visiting our Web site and following the links to the employment section.

9. What is stated about the Ferguson Museum?

(A) It is a publicly-owned institution.

(B) It specializes in period clothing.

(C) It provides employees with uniforms.

(D) It was founded very recently.

10. What is NOT a requirement of the position?

(A) Qualifications as a curator

(B) Experience as a tour guide

(C) A license to drive a bus

(D) Willingness to work on weekends

11. How can people apply for the position?

(A) By calling the museum curator

(B) By sending an e-mail

(C) By accessing a Web site

(D) By visiting the museum in person

Daly Events, Inc.

Ignatius Yates
Chief of Event Management
Daly Events, Inc.
(712) 555 8392
iyates@dalyeap.com

FOR IMMEDIATE RELEASE

Durant Fairgrounds will host
the York Motor Show

York (May 2)—Daly Events is proud to announce that it will be organizing and promoting the tenth annual York Motor Show at its traditional location. It will take place over three days starting on June 3. Gates open at 11:00 A.M. and close at 9:00 P.M. on each day of the show. Tickets are available on the official Web site or the usual ticket sellers.

Representatives of more than 30 automobile manufacturers will be operating booths, where they will be demonstrating their latest vehicles. Among the most highly anticipated vehicles are the VFV Thundercat and the Stratton Stallion, both of which will have their public debut at the show. A number of very popular international celebrities will be there for the opening, including comedian Joe Eaton and the host of Channel 4's *Mighty Machines*, Talia Newman. On the evening of June 5, York Mayor Rhonda Grimes will be addressing the attendees and announcing the winner of this year's Car-of-the-Show Award.

Interested people can learn more by visiting www.yorkmotorshow.com.

12. What is one purpose of the press release?

(A) To announce the dates of a sporting event

(B) To encourage people to watch a special broadcast

(C) To promote the expansion of a well-known business

(D) To publicize an upcoming trade fair

13. What is implied about the event?

(A) It has been held at Durant Fairgrounds before.

(B) Tickets for the first day have already sold out.

(C) It will be larger than it was in previous years.

(D) Advertisements will appear on television.

14. Who is Rhonda Grimes?

(A) An event organizer

(B) An entertainer

(C) A commentator

(D) A city official

Cincinnati Business News

June 23—Halliday's Ice Cream has announced that it will be moving its headquarters next month. — [1] —. The company has purchased a building in Cincinnati and will be having its staff set up the office there in the coming weeks. While no announcement had been made, it seems that the company president, Maddie Harmer, has been planning this for several years and the staff has been making preparations. — [2] —. A spokesperson for the company said that they were taking advantage of some tax breaks and other benefits that the State of Ohio was offering.

— [3] —. The president has indicated that this will be her final major decision before she hands over control of the company to her niece, Chloe Davis, in August this year. In August, Halliday's Ice Cream will have been in business for 100 years. This is a significant milestone in the company's history. It is likely that the changes have been scheduled to coincide with the company's celebration. There is certainly a lot to be proud of. — [4] —. Shareholders surely have high expectations for the company's future.

15. What is the article about?

(A) The relocation of a business
(B) The activities of a charity organization
(C) A community's hard work
(D) A council program's benefits

16. What is suggested about Ms. Harmer?

(A) She will retire soon.
(B) She has purchased a new home.
(C) She was recently promoted.
(D) She founded Halliday's Ice Cream.

17. In which of the positions marked [1], [2], [3], and [4] does the following sentence best belong?

"In the last four years, its market share has grown by some 15 percent."

(A) [1]
(B) [2]
(C) [3]
(D) [4]

http://www.bradandtomsdiy.com/about

Brad and Tom's DIY

Welcome to Brad and Tom's DIY Online Video Channel. This is where we post previews of our latest videos, sell T-shirts, hats, and stickers associated with our show, and stay in touch with our fans on the bulletin boards.

Brad and Tom's DIY Online Video Channel has been running for 10 years now and to mark the anniversary, we are releasing the first issue of our quarterly magazine. It will be available on Nileways Online Bookstore as well as in most regular bookstores and newsstands from September 17.

On the day of the release, we will have an event at Bryant and Milton Bookstore in Chicago to launch the magazine. Ted Frasier from the popular television show, *Ted's Tools* has contributed an article and he will also be there to help publicize the event.

Scroll down for links to other sections.

18. What is NOT a purpose of the Web page?

(A) Providing reviews of new products

(B) Selling official merchandise

(C) Communicating with viewers of online content

(D) Offering samples of upcoming programs

19. The word "regular" in paragraph 2, line 4, is closest in meaning to

(A) constant

(B) traditional

(C) systematic

(D) satisfactory

20. What new aspect of the business is being announced?

(A) A 24-hour helpline

(B) A periodical publication

(C) A range of tools

(D) A live performance

21. What will happen on September 17?

(A) The grand opening of a bookstore will occur.

(B) Instructional videos will be sold at a bookstore.

(C) A celebrity will make an appearance.

(D) Some people will visit a workshop.

Questions 22-25 refer to the following customer review.

Customer: Sigmund Reeves   **Date:** 11:34 A.M., Saturday, August 1

Yesterday, I took a group of guests visiting from Sweden to Alphonso's for dinner. — [1] —. Although I made the reservation at the last minute, I was surprised to find that the staff was not only able to offer us a table, but also provide a delicious meal in a reasonable amount of time. I didn't realize that one of the people in our party was a vegetarian, and when we got there, I found that the restaurant didn't have a vegetarian menu. — [2] —. When I mentioned the situation to the server, she introduced us to one of the chefs who came and discussed some ideas he had for substituting ingredients. In the end, my vegetarian guest was extremely pleased with her meal and said that she'd like to dine there again before she goes home next Thursday.

If you're looking for somewhere to entertain guests, I can't recommend Alphonso's highly enough. — [3] —. The menu is innovative and exciting, the staff is extremely helpful, and the interior is clean and modern. — [4] —. They're closed on Wednesdays and Sundays, but they're open for lunch and dinner for the rest of the week. I think I was lucky to get a booking at such short notice. I suggest calling them a week in advance.

22. What is implied about
Mr. Reeves?

(A) He expected Alphonso's to
be fully booked.
(B) He often dines at Alphonso's.
(C) He cannot eat dishes with
meat in them.
(D) He will take a trip to Sweden
in the future.

23. When did Mr. Reeves visit
Alphonso's?

(A) On Thursday
(B) On Friday
(C) On Saturday
(D) On Sunday

24. What aspect of the restaurant is
NOT praised in the review?

(A) The location
(B) The menu
(C) The furnishings
(D) The employees

25. In which of the positions marked
[1], [2], [3], and [4] does the
following sentence best belong?

"It was something I should have
checked in advance."

(A) [1]
(B) [2]
(C) [3]
(D) [4]

Questions 26-29 refer to the following online chat discussion.

Joan Getz [3:29 P.M.]
Hi, everyone. I'm in the parking garage. I've reserved the office car from 3:30, but it's not here. Does anyone have any idea who has it?

Hans Mertaug [3:30 P.M.]
Priti took it at lunchtime. She was going shopping for some office supplies. Did anyone see her come back?

Priti Singh [3:31 P.M.]
I'm back. I've been in the office since 1:30. I left the car in the usual location. Has anyone looked at the online reservation system? I would but I'm in the conference room preparing for tomorrow's event.

Hans Mertaug [3:32 P.M.]
Sorry, Priti, I didn't see you come in.

Priti Singh [3:33 P.M.]
That's OK. I came straight to the conference room.

Steve Tanner [3:33 P.M.]
Joan, it looks like the car was booked in for maintenance today. I think the mechanics must have come and picked it up.

Joan Getz [3:34 P.M.]
I see. Well, I have to get to a client's office in Ascot. Is there anyone who can give me a ride?

Steve Tanner [3:35 P.M.]
I've called you a taxi. You'd better go to the front of the building and wait.

Joan Getz [3:38 P.M.]
Thanks, Steve. Can I get my money back if I bring back the receipt?

Steve Tanner [3:45 P.M.]
Sure. Just leave it on my desk.

26. Why did Ms. Getz start the online chat discussion?

(A) To gain entry to the building
(B) To suggest that some maintenance be carried out
(C) To find out the location of a vehicle
(D) To suggest a venue for a presentation

27. Where did Ms. Singh most likely go at lunchtime?

(A) To a restaurant
(B) To a client's office
(C) To an auto repair garage
(D) To a stationery store

28. Why does Mr. Tanner suggest going to the front of the building?

(A) Some guests will arrive.
(B) A taxi has been ordered.
(C) Some food will be delivered.
(D) A key has been found.

29. At 3:45 P.M., what does Mr. Tanner mean when he writes, "Just leave it on my desk"?

(A) He will pay a mechanic's bill later.
(B) He will reimburse an employee.
(C) He cannot fill out a form right now.
(D) He does not need his book at the moment.

Rudolph's Carpet Kingdom

177 Baker Street
San Francisco, CA 94103
(415) 847-7587

Ms. Glenda Drexel
734 Dobbs Creek Road
San Carlos, CA 94070

April 28

Dear Ms. Drexel,

I placed a suggestion box at the front of our store when I was promoted to store manager 12 years ago. Although I check the box every day, it is very rare that we find a suggestion from customers. I would like to express my sincerest appreciation to you for taking the time to compose a message. I am in complete agreement with you and will be making the suggested changes immediately. I will write on the store's Web site about some of the changes we are making in the next few days, and I will be listing your suggestion first as I believe it will benefit the most customers.

As a token of our appreciation for sharing this excellent idea with us, I would like to offer you a membership card which will allow you to receive 15 percent off on every purchase you make at Rudolph's Carpet Kingdom. You can pick up the card at the counter next time you come to the store.

Sincerely,

Terry Wells

Terry Wells
Store Manager

Rudolph's Carpet Kingdom

We're making some changes this month!

Starting this Monday, May 1:

- We are offering free home delivery for purchases over $300. If you make your purchase before noon, we can even guarantee same-day delivery.
- We are extending our weekend hours. From now on, the store will be open from 9:00 A.M. to 5:00 P.M. seven days a week.
- We are expanding our range to include top European brands known for their high quality and timeless designs.
- We are offering free classes on carpet protection and cleaning once a month at our main store at 23 Sapphire Lane in San Francisco.

If you are in the market for a great carpet, excellent customer service, and fantastic prices, you really need to check us out.

30. Why is Ms. Wells writing to Ms. Drexel?

(A) To offer her a position
(B) To thank her for her input
(C) To ask her to carry out some research
(D) To offer her some advice on a project

31. What is indicated about Ms. Wells?

(A) She is a patron of Rudolph's Carpet Kingdom.
(B) She has spoken directly with Ms. Drexel in the past.
(C) She is in charge of marketing for Rudolph's Carpet Kingdom.
(D) She has been in her current position for over a decade.

32. Which change resulted from Ms. Drexel's suggestion?

(A) Free home delivery
(B) New opening hours
(C) The addition of new products
(D) Classes on cleaning techniques

33. What does Ms. Wells offer Ms. Drexel?

(A) A discount card
(B) Some sample products
(C) Interior decorating advice
(D) An invitation to an event

34. What is implied about Rudolph's Carpet Kingdom?

(A) It has moved to new premises.
(B) It has multiple locations.
(C) It closes early on weekdays.
(D) It is hiring new staff members.

Questions 35-39 refer to the following e-mail and program.

From:	Soya Tsubota <stsubota@silvertonp.com>
To:	Norma Waters <nwaters@megaweba.com>
Subject:	Welcome!
Date:	June 2

Dear Ms. Waters,

We are so glad that you have agreed to join our amateur painters' group. We were all very excited when we learned you were moving to the area. Of course, we debated whether or not we should reach out to you. Considering your status, we were concerned that you may not be interested in collaborating with an amateur group. So, when you contacted us, we were excited, to say the least. I have already registered you as an honorary member and sent you a package with relevant information including our yearly schedule. Honorary members receive free lifetime membership as well as other benefits. You may be asked to speak at special events or help judge competitions but we will understand if you are too busy to do so.

We will be holding our annual awards ceremony at the end of this month, and I was wondering if you would mind presenting one of the awards. Actually, we would very much appreciate it if you could take my place as a presenter.

Sincerely,

Soya Tsubota
Silverton Painters

Tentative Program for
the Silverton Painters Annual Awards Ceremony

7:30 P.M.   **Opening Address**
Ray Huttenmeister (Group Founder)

7:40 P.M.   **Hanson Art Supplies Award for Best Portrait**
Presented by Joe Hanson, Hanson Art Supplies

7:50 P.M.   **Members' Award for Most Popular Artwork**
Presented by Soya Tsubota (Chairperson)

8:00 P.M.   **Lipton Paints Award for Best Landscape**
Presented by Jane White, Lipton Paints

8:10 P.M.   **Dinner and Entertainment**

9:00 P.M.   **Gladwell Gallery Award for Highest Selling Piece**
Presented by Randolph Garden (Curator)

9:10 P.M.   **Closing Remarks**
Seth Wiseman (Group President)

35. Who most likely is Ms. Waters?

(A) A professional artist
(B) A financial advisor
(C) A politician
(D) An architect

36. What does Mr. Tsubota indicate that he has done?

(A) Moved into a new house
(B) Purchased a piece of works
(C) Designed a building
(D) Mailed a parcel to Ms. Waters

37. What is implied about Ms. Waters?

(A) She may be requested to make speeches.
(B) She must perform as a judge at contests.

(C) She will pay yearly fees.
(D) She must renew her membership yearly.

38. When will the ceremony commence?

(A) At 7:30 P.M.
(B) At 7:40 P.M.
(C) At 9:00 P.M.
(D) At 9:10 P.M.

39. Which award does Mr. Tsubota ask Ms. Waters to present?

(A) Hanson Art Supplies Award
(B) Members' Award
(C) Lipton Paints Award
(D) Gladwell Gallery Award

The New England Gardening Society needs new members!

For over 100 years, the New England Gardening Society (NEGS) has been promoting gardening as a hobby and a way of life for the people of New England. We have organized annual contests and events, which have attracted visitors from near and far. In recent years, our membership numbers have been falling. Despite this, the number of entrants in our contests and attendance at our events has been increasing steadily. We are strictly a volunteer group and therefore, we are unable to offer much in the way of reward for those who dedicate their time.

Nevertheless, there are certain benefits which you may want to consider: NEGS members receive 20 percent off on all gardening items from Green Fingers Nurseries, free transportation to and from society events, and a magazine subscription to *New England House and Garden*.

Interested people can contact the secretary of the society by calling 555-8432 or by sending an e-mail to secretary@negs.org.

Membership Agreement
New England Gardening Society

By signing the following membership agreement, you agree to fulfill the requirements of the society. In return, you will be able to take advantage of all the benefits membership affords. At the end of each year, your eligibility for continued membership will be determined by a review of your contributions to the society.

Requirements

Members are required to pay a one-time membership fee to cover processing. This will become payable again if there is any type of discontinuation in membership.

Additionally, you must carry out at least two of the following duties:
• Assist the society with at least one annual society event
• Act as a judge at the New England Annual Gardening Contest
• Vote in yearly elections for society president

Signed:

Max Dunkirk

Max Dunkirk
Applicant

Sandy Polanski

Sandy Polanski
President — New England Gardening Society

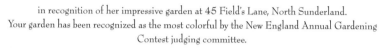

The New England Gardening Society

presents this

Award of Excellence
to
Enid Butler

in recognition of her impressive garden at 45 Field's Lane, North Sunderland.
Your garden has been recognized as the most colorful by the New England Annual Gardening
Contest judging committee.

Max Dunkirk, Chief Organizer and Head of the Judging Committee

40. What is the purpose of the advertisement?

(A) To attract new members to an association

(B) To encourage people to enter a contest

(C) To publicize the services of a local store

(D) To promote a new magazine

41. What is indicated about NEGS?

(A) It receives financial support from the city.

(B) It is closed during winter.

(C) It is looking to hire a new secretary.

(D) It was established more than a century ago.

42. What is suggested about Ms. Polanski?

(A) She will retire as president of the society at the end of the year.

(B) She is entitled to a discount on some gardening goods.

(C) She has contributed an article to *New England House and Garden*.

(D) She is a founding member of NEGS.

43. In the membership agreement, the word "return" in paragraph 1, line 2, is closest in meaning to

(A) compensation

(B) recovery

(C) revenge

(D) addition

44. What is implied about Mr. Dunkirk?

(A) His garden was entered in the New England Annual Gardening Contest.

(B) He was chosen for his position by a vote of members.

(C) His membership will be renewed at the end of the year.

(D) He has volunteered his home as a location for society meetings.

GORDON VOCATIONAL SCHOOL
Upcoming Courses for the Local Community

Every February, Gordon Vocational School offers short courses for interested members of the local community.

All courses related to cooking will be provided at the Stanton campus. Courses related to the repair of vehicles and electrical goods will be provided at the Clarendon campus. This year, graphic design courses will be offered at the Lasseter campus only. All other courses are provided at our main campus at Beaumont Point.

● **Intermediate Flower Arrangement**
Mondays – February 1 to February 29, 10:00 A.M. to 12:00 noon
Instructor: Miwa Takatsuka
This is a course for students who took part in last year's introductory course.

● **An Introduction to French Cuisine**
Tuesdays - February 2 to February 23, 7:00 P.M. to 9:00 P.M.
Instructor: Pierre DuPont
Learn the basics of preparing food in the traditional French style.

● **Diagnose and Repair Engine Problems**
Wednesdays – February 3 to February 24, 7:00 P.M. to 10:00 P.M.
Instructor: Otto Mendez
Learn to find and fix minor engine problems in standard passenger vehicles.

● **Air-conditioner Installation**
Thursdays – February 4 to February 25, 1:00 P.M. to 3:00 P.M.
Instructor: Leslie Carlisle
People who complete this course are certified to work as installers of domestic air-conditioners.

Information about other courses is available on our Web site at www.gordonvs.edu.

*We are currently in urgent need of a highly qualified individual to teach our course on databases and spreadsheets. Please call our human resources department at 555-4823 to discuss job requirements and necessary qualifications.

To:	Lisa Taylor
From:	Harry Dean
Subject:	RE: Application approved
Date:	February 1

Dear Ms. Taylor,

Thank you for accepting my last-minute application for the course on engine maintenance. I am writing because I have not yet received an invoice for my tuition fees. Please let me know how much they will be and how I should pay them. I would like to take care of this as soon as possible. I am also wondering about what books, equipment, and clothing I will be expected to bring to class.

Sincerely,

Harry Dean

GORDON VOCATIONAL SCHOOL
Student Identification

Name: Peta Love
Classification: Short Course Enrollment
Course: An Introduction to French Cuisine
Student Number: SC430
Campus: Stanton
Valid through: February 29

45. What topic is NOT taught at Gordon Vocational School?

(A) Graphic design
(B) Appliance repair
(C) Interior decorating
(D) Food preparation

46. According to the information, how should people apply for a position at Gordon Vocational School?

(A) By calling the personnel department
(B) By visiting the office in person
(C) By filling out an online form
(D) By sending an e-mail

47. Which campus of Gordon Vocational School will Mr. Dean attend?

(A) Stanton campus
(B) Beaumont Point campus
(C) Lasseter campus
(D) Clarendon campus

48. What does Mr. Dean write that he is waiting for?

(A) An employment contract
(B) Information on what to prepare
(C) An application form
(D) Permission to use the parking lot

49. When does Ms. Love's course begin?

(A) On February 1
(B) On February 2
(C) On February 23
(D) On February 24

Questions 50-54 refer to the following job advertisement, e-mail, and text message.

Dunhill Advertising is seeking an experienced writer to create advertisements for its clients in the Cavendish region. Applicants must have experience in magazine and newspaper advertising. You are required to submit examples of previous work along with your résumé. As we are a small firm, employees are expected to carry out a number of responsibilities in addition to those associated with their position. You may need to come to agreements with publishers regarding their fees, make presentations to prospective clients, and even take photographs of products for publication. In recent years, we have been expanding into Internet advertising so applicants with a good knowledge of online advertising techniques will have an advantage. We offer a competitive salary and benefits package including a company car.

Visit the Dunhill Advertising Web site at www.dunhilladvertising.com to download an application form and submit the required documents. The deadline is January 16.

To:	Ichiho Fukazawa <ifukazawa@redbird.com>
From:	Fred Scaramouch <fscaramouch@dunhilladvertising.com>
Subject:	Vacant position
Date:	January 17

Dear Ms. Fukazawa,

Thank you very much for your application. I was most impressed with your résumé. However, you seem to have forgotten to send the other documents mentioned in the advertisement. Unfortunately, we cannot consider your application without all the necessary documents. The official cutoff date for applications was yesterday. However, as we already have your résumé, you may send the outstanding documents by this evening.

My secretary will be scheduling the interviews tomorrow morning. Provided you contact us today, you can expect a telephone call from him tomorrow morning. We plan to hold interviews on January 30. Please let him know what time you will be available.

Sincerely,

Fred Scaramouch
Managing Director, Dunhill Advertising

To: Ichiho Fukazawa

From: Fred Scaramouch

Thanks for coming in to discuss the position at Dunhill Advertising today. I was impressed with many of your ideas and excited to hear more about your experience in both radio and online advertising. You have been put on a shortlist for the position. My secretary will be in touch in the coming days to schedule another interview.

Sent at 5:20 P.M., January 30

50. What is suggested about Dunhill Advertising?

(A) It has offices in numerous capital cities.

(B) It is broadening its range of services.

(C) It allows employees to work flexible hours.

(D) It will soon hire a new managing director.

51. What is NOT a responsibility of the advertised position?

(A) Writing reports on sales performance

(B) Negotiating advertising rates with publishers

(C) Attracting new clients to the firm

(D) Photographing clients' products

52. What required item has Ms. Fukazawa forgotten to attach to her e-mail?

(A) Her résumé

(B) A letter of reference

(C) Her portfolio

(D) A copy of her driver's license

53. When did Ms. Fukazawa probably respond to Mr. Scaramouch's e-mail?

(A) On January 16

(B) On January 17

(C) On January 18

(D) On January 30

54. What is the purpose of the text message?

(A) To recommend that Ms. Fukazawa obtain some additional qualifications

(B) To advise Ms. Fukazawa of some changes to the position's requirements

(C) To inform Ms. Fukazawa that she has cleared the first round of interviews

(D) To request that Ms. Fukazawa provide a full list of her previous works

Questions 1-2 refer to the following invoice.

リスト 🎵 001

---

❶Cordon Extreme Performance
98 Vantage Street
Cleveland, Ohio

Invoice: I732891	**Delivery Address:**
Estimated Date of Delivery: December 23	Mitchelbrook Tuning Company
Customer Name: Laura Turner	992 Voorhees Way
(Mitchelbrook Tuning Company)	Seattle, Washington

Item No.	Item	Quantity	Unit Price	Price
HG1039	❷Racing Tire (265/55 17- inch)	4	$138.00	$552.00
LK9863	Fuel Tank (19 gallons)	1	$96.50	$96.50
YT7482	❸Racing Seat (Tullox Brand) *	2	$410.00	$820.00
VN6478	❹Safety Goggles (No Tint)	1	❺$33.00	$33.00
			Subtotal	$1,501.50
			❻Discount	$3.30
			Total	**$1,498.20**

Note: ❼Corporate clients get 10 percent off on all orders of protective clothing and accessories. Items marked with an asterisk are covered by a two-year warranty. All other products are covered by the manufacturer's standard 12-month warranty.

設問1-2は次の請求書に関するものです。

Cordon Extreme Performance社
Vantage通り98番地
Ohio州Cleveland市

請求書：I732891	配送先住所：
配送予定日：12月23日	Mitchelbrook Tuning社
お客さま氏名：Laura Turner	Voorhees Way 992番地
(Mitchelbrook Tuning社)	Washington州Seattle市

商品番号	品目	数量	単価	金額
HG1039	レース用タイヤ（265/55 17インチ）	4	138.00 ドル	552.00 ドル
LK9863	燃料タンク（19ガロン）	1	96.50 ドル	96.50 ドル
YT7482	レース用シート（Tullox社製）*	2	410.00 ドル	820.00 ドル
VN6478	安全ゴーグル（色なし）	1	33.00 ドル	33.00 ドル
			小計	1,501.50 ドル
			割引額	3.30 ドル
			合計	**1,498.20 ドル**

備考：法人のお客さまは，防護用衣服や用品の全てのご注文が10パーセント割引になります。アステリスクの付いた商品は2年保証が付いています。その他の商品は製造会社の標準である1年保証です。

語句 □ estimated date of delivery 配送予定日　□ item 品目，細目
□ racing レース用の　□ gallon ガロン（液量の単位）　□ safety goggles 安全ゴーグル
□ tint 色，色合い　□ subtotal 小計　□ corporate client 法人の顧客
□ protective 保護用の　□ accessories 付属品　□ mark 〜に印を付ける
□ asterisk アステリスク，*の印

1.

情報をもとに推測する問題

What kind of business most likely is Cordon Extreme Performance?
(A) An auto parts supplier
(B) A computer repair shop
(C) A musical instrument store
(D) A concert hall

Cordon Extreme Performance社はおそらくどんな業種ですか。
(A) 自動車部品供給会社
(B) コンピューター修理店
(C) 楽器店
(D) コンサート会場

正解 (A)

解説 Cordon Extreme Performance社が何を扱う会社か問われています。❶よりこの請求書を発行したのがCordon Extreme Performance社だとわかります。明細には，❷，❸「レース用のタイヤやシート」があることから，自動車関連の部品を取り扱っていると推測できます。以上から正解は(A)となります。

語句 □ auto parts supplier 自動車部品供給会社　□ musical instrument 楽器

2.

情報分散型問題

What is implied about the goggles?
(A) They are locally produced.
(B) They are temporarily out of stock.
(C) They will be sent in a separate shipment.
(D) They have been discounted.

ゴーグルについて何が示唆されていますか。
(A) 地元で製造されている。
(B) 一時的に品切れである。
(C) 別送される。
(D) 割引されている。

正解 (D)

解説 ゴーグルに関して示唆されていることが問われています。請求書の備考欄❼を見ると，「防護用衣服や用品の全てのご注文が10パーセント割引」とあります。明細にあるゴーグルの商品名が❹「安全ゴーグル」となっていることから，これは防護用品だと見当がつきます。さらに❻の割引額が3.3ドルで，❺にあるゴーグル価格の10パーセントであることから，この商品が割引対象の商品だと確認できます。よって，正解は(D)となります。

語句 □ locally 地元で　□ temporarily 一時的に　□ out of stock 在庫切れで
□ separate 分けた，分かれた

Questions 3-4 refer to the following text-message chain.

Greg Harper   8:50 A.M.
I'm looking for someone to accompany me to Scranton. I need to talk to our suppliers there about how they're packing the goods. I want them to make it easier for us to open.

Edith Langos   8:51 A.M.
❶When are you thinking of going?

Greg Harper   8:52 A.M.
It has to be this week. ❷I want to talk to them before they prepare the next shipment.

Edith Langos   8:53 A.M.
I have to give a presentation for a client in Milwaukee on Thursday, so I won't be available, I'm afraid.

Greg Harper   8:54 A.M.
I didn't mean you. ❸Is there someone in sales that you could spare?

Edith Langos   8:59 A.M.
OK, sorry. ❹Why don't you take Glenda? She only started last week. It would be good for her to meet the suppliers in person.

Greg Harper   9:02 A.M.
Great. Please find out if she's available and get back to me. We're leaving on Wednesday, and we should be back on Friday afternoon.

Edith Langos   9:03 A.M.
I'll get back to you.

設問3-4は次のテキストメッセージのやりとりに関するものです。

Greg Harper   午前8時50分
Scrantonまで私に同行してくれる人を探しているんだ。そこの納入業者と品物の梱包方法について打ち合わせが必要でね。先方には我々がもっと簡単に開けられるようにしてほしいんだ。
Edith Langos   午前8時51分
いつ行こうと考えているの？
Greg Harper   午前8時52分
今週でなくてはならない。彼らが次の発送品を準備する前に打ち合わせをしたいんだ。
Edith Langos   午前8時53分
私は木曜日にMilwaukeeのお客さまにプレゼンをしなくてはならないの。だから申し訳ないけど、

私は行けそうにないわ。

Greg Harper　　　午前8時54分

君に頼むつもりはなかったよ。営業部で誰か派遣できそうな人はいるかい？

Edith Langos　　　午前8時59分

ああ，そうか，ごめんなさい。Glendaを連れて行ったら？　彼女は先週仕事を始めたばかりなの。直接納入業者に会うのは彼女にとってもいいことだと思うわ。

Greg Harper　　　午前9時02分

良かった。彼女が行けるかどうか確認して，折り返し連絡を頼むよ。水曜日に出発して，金曜日の午後に戻る予定だ。

Edith Langos　　　午前9時03分

また連絡するわ。

語句　□ accompany ～について行く　□ pack ～を荷造りする，詰める
　　　　□ spare（時間・人など）を割く　□ Why don't you ～? ～してはどうか
　　　　□ in person 自ら，直接　□ get back to ～ ～に後で連絡する

3.

意図問題

At 8:52 A.M., what does Mr. Harper most likely mean when he writes, "It has to be this week"?
(A) He would like a shipment urgently.
(B) He would like to leave soon.
(C) He is not in charge of the situation.
(D) He is not sure of the exact date.

午前8時52分に，Harperさんが"It has to be this week"と書いているのはおそらく何を意図していますか。
(A) 至急発送してもらいたい。
(B) 速やかに出発したい。
(C) この件の担当ではない。
(D) 正確な日付がわからない。

正解　(B)

解説　Harperさんが下線部で「今週でなくてはならない」と書いた意図が問われています。この前後を見てみると，❶いつ行くのか→今週でなければならない→❷次の発送の前に打ち合わせをしたいから，という流れになっているので，次に品物が発送される前に急いで納入業者に会って打ち合わせをしたい，ということがわかります。以上から，正解は(B)です。

語句　□ urgently 緊急に　□ be in charge of ～ ～を担当している　□ exact date 正確な日付

4.

選択肢照合型問題

What is true about Glenda?
(A) She is a senior employee.
(B) She has been to Scranton before.
(C) She works in the sales department.
(D) She will give a presentation on Thursday.

Glendaさんについて何が正しいですか。
(A) 上級社員である。
(B) 以前Scrantonに行ったことがある。
(C) 営業部で働いている。
(D) 木曜日にプレゼンをする。

正解　(C)

解説　Glendaさんについて正しいことが問われています。Harperさんが❸で「営業部の誰かを派遣できないか」と打診したのに対して，Langosさんが❹で「Glendaを連れて行ってはどうか」と提案しているので，LangosさんがHarperさんの希望する営業部員の中からGlendaさんを推薦したことがわかります。以上から正解は(C)となります。

語句　□ senior employee 上級社員

フォーム ♪ 003

Name: Norma Walsh _____ (Optional)

Thank you for holding your event at the Normandy Symphony Hall.

Please take a few minutes to fill out the following survey and let us know about your experience at Normandy Symphony Hall. Place a ✔ in the box that best matches your impression.

	Strongly Disagree	Disagree	Agree	Strongly Agree
The facilities are modern.			✔	
The staff is helpful.			✔	
The location is convenient.		✔		
❶The hall is clean.	❷✔			

Comments: Despite the issue indicated above, I was extremely pleased with Normandy Symphony Hall overall. Nevertheless, we have been looking into other venues recently and keeping in mind the reduced budget we will have next year, ❸I hope you will be open to negotiating on price.

設問5-6は次の調査票に関するものです。

氏名：___ Norma Walsh ___ （任意）
Normandyシンフォニーホールにてイベントをご開催いただき，ありがとうございます。

少しお時間を割いて以下の調査票にご記入いただき，Normandyシンフォニーホールでの体験を私どもにお聞かせください。あなたの印象に最も合う欄にチェックマークを付けてください。

	全く当てはまらない	当てはまらない	当てはまる	とても当てはまる
設備が最新だ			✓	
スタッフが協力的だ			✓	
場所が便利だ		✓		
ホールが清潔だ	✓			

コメント：上記の問題があったにもかかわらず，全般的にNormandyシンフォニーホールにとても満足しました。ですが，最近，他の開催場所も検討しており，来年度は予算が削減されることを考えると，料金の交渉に応じていただけたらと思います。

語句 □ optional 任意の　□ impression 印象　□ despite ～にもかかわらず
□ indicated above 上述の　□ extremely とても　□ overall 全体として
□ nevertheless それにもかかわらず　□ venue 開催場所
□ keep in mind 心に留めておく　□ reduced 削減された
□ be open to ～（提案など）を受け入れる　□ negotiate on price 料金について交渉する

5.

詳細を問う問題

What aspect of the facility was Ms. Walsh least impressed with?
(A) Its equipment
(B) Its employees
(C) Its position
(D) Its cleanliness

Walshさんは施設のどの点について一番印象が良くないと感じましたか。
(A) 設備
(B) 従業員
(C) 場所
(D) 清潔さ

正解 (D)

解説 調査票の回答者であるWalshさんが施設で一番印象が良くないと感じた点が問われています。❶の「ホールが清潔だ」という項目で唯一「全く当てはまらない」という欄に❷のチェックが入っていることから，正解は(D)です。

語句 □ aspect（物事の）側面　□ least 最も～でなく
□ be impressed with ～ ～に（好ましい）印象を受ける

6.

詳細を問う問題

What does Ms. Walsh hope to do?
(A) Use another hall for next year's event
(B) Receive a partial refund on the rental cost
(C) Rent the hall at a better rate
(D) Attract more people to her event

Walshさんは何を希望していますか。
(A) 来年のイベントに別のホールを使う
(B) 賃貸料に関して一部払い戻しを受ける
(C) より良い料金でホールを借りる
(D) イベントにもっと多くの人を誘致する

正解 (C)

解説 Walshさんが望んでいることは何か問われています。Walshさんは調査票のコメント欄で，❸「料金の交渉に応じてほしい」と述べています。ここからホール使用料の見直しを求めていることが読み取れるので，それをat a better rateと言い換えた(C)が正解です。

語句 □ partial 部分的な　□ at a better rate より良い料金で

Questions **7-8** refer to the following memo.

MEMO

To All Tenants,

Yesterday evening, some repairs were carried out on the pipes that deliver water to the building. Unfortunately, the workers accidentally cut the high-speed Internet line. ❶We were only made aware of the problem this morning. A team of cabling specialists has arrived, and they predict that the Internet will be reconnected by 3:00 P.M.

The Internet café in the next building has offered to provide tenants with access to their wireless Internet until the work is carried out. This may be an attractive offer for businesses that rely heavily on their Internet connection. ❷If you would like to take advantage of this generous offer, please call me at 555-8482, or if you are in a hurry, you can visit Slater Office Tower building management on the first floor.

Sincerely,

Ren Walters
Building Manager
Slater Office Tower

設問7-8は次のメモに関するものです。

メモ

テナント各位

昨晩，ビルの配水管の修理が行われました。残念なことに，作業者が誤って高速インターネット回線を切ってしまいました。弊社も今朝知らされたばかりです。現在配線の専門チームが到着し，午後3時までにはインターネットは再接続されると見込んでおります。

作業終了までの間，隣のビルにあるインターネットカフェからテナントの皆さまに無線インターネット接続をご提供いただくお申し出を受けました。インターネット接続に依存するところが大きい事業者さまには魅力的な提案かと存じます。この寛大なお申し出のご利用をご希望の方は私宛てに555-8482までお電話いただくか，お急ぎの場合はSlater Office Tower 1階のビル管理課にお越しいただいても結構です。

敬具

Ren Walters
ビル管理者
Slater Office Tower

語句 □ tenant テナント，居住者　□ carry out ~ ~を実施する　□ pipe 導管，パイプ
□ accidentally 誤って　□ be made aware of ~ ~に気付かされる
□ cabling ケーブル設置［配線］　□ reconnect ~に再接続する　□ wireless 無線の
□ attractive 魅力的な　□ rely heavily on ~ ~に大きく頼る，依存する
□ take advantage of ~ ~を利用する　□ generous 寛大な，気前のよい
□ be in a hurry 急いでいる

7.

目的・テーマを問う問題

What is the memo mainly about?

(A) Increased rental rates
(B) An interruption to a service
(C) Updates to a Web site
(D) A change to a delivery schedule

メモは主に何についてですか。

(A) 値上げされた賃料
(B) サービスの中断
(C) ウェブサイトの更新
(D) 配送予定の変更

正解 (B)

解説 何についてのメモか問われています。第1段落で工事中に誤ってインターネット回線が切断されたことを伝えた後に，❶で「今朝の段階でわかったばかりで，午後3時までにはインターネットが再接続される見込み」と述べており，当面インターネットが使えないことがわかります。以上からインターネット接続サービスをa serviceと表した(B)が正解となります。

語句 □ interruption 中断，中止

8.

詳細を問う問題

According to the memo, why might tenants contact Mr. Walters?

(A) To request an invitation
(B) To reserve some equipment
(C) To arrange a service
(D) To extend a deadline

メモによると，テナントはなぜWaltersさんに連絡する可能性がありますか。

(A) 招待を要請するため
(B) 設備を予約するため
(C) サービスを手配するため
(D) 期限を延長するため

正解 (C)

解説 このメモを見ているテナントがWaltersさんに連絡する理由が問われています。メモの書き手であるWaltersさんは第2段落で，当面のインターネット回線の代替サービスについて触れ，その後❷で「この寛大な申し出を利用するには私にお電話を」と述べているので，紹介された代替サービスを利用するためにWaltersさんに連絡する可能性があることがわかります。以上から，それを言い換えた(C)が正解となります。

語句 □ extend ~を延長する

Questions 9-11 refer to the following advertisement.

JOB VACANCY

The Ferguson Museum is a small museum on Baker Street in Central Silverton. ❶The museum's exhibits all center on the clothing of the early settlers of the region. We have perfectly preserved boots, suits, and women's garments, some of which are nearly 200 years old. We have a vacancy for a museum guide. It is not necessary to have specific knowledge of local history or the items in our collection. We have an excellent training program to prepare the successful candidate. ❷We are, however, looking for someone with experience as a tour guide. ❸The applicant will also need to have a valid bus driver's license, as we are sometimes called upon to give guided tours of Silverton. ❹As Saturdays and Sundays are our busiest times, applicants must be prepared to work on both days.

If you require a more detailed job description or have any specific questions, contact the head curator at 555-8489 or by e-mail at curator@ fergusonmuseum.com. ❺All applications must be submitted online by visiting our Web site and following the links to the employment section.

設問9-11は次の広告に関するものです。

求人

Ferguson博物館はCentral SilvertonのBaker通りにある小さな博物館です。博物館の展示品は全てこの地域における初期の開拓者の衣服が中心です。私どもはブーツやスーツ，女性用衣服を完全な状態で保存しており，それらの一部はほぼ200年前のものです。現在博物館ガイドに欠員があります。地元の歴史や当館の収蔵品に関する特定の知識は必要ありません。当博物館には採用された方に学んでいただく優れた教育プログラムがあります。ただし，見学ガイドとしての経験がある方を探しています。また，有効なバスの運転免許証も必要です。というのは，時折Silvertonのガイド付きツアー開催の依頼があるためです。土日は繁忙日ですので，応募者には両日とも働くことをご理解いただく必要があります。

より詳細な仕事内容が知りたい，または具体的な質問がある場合は，学芸員長宛てに電話555-8489か，メール curator@fergusonmuseum.com までご連絡ください。ご応募はウェブサイトにアクセスいただき，雇用部門のリンクからオンラインでのみ受け付けます。

語句 □ vacancy 欠員，空き　□ exhibit 展示品　□ center 中心とする　□ clothing 衣服
□ early settler 初期の開拓者　□ preserve ～を保存する　□ garment 衣類
□ nearly ほぼ　□ specific 特定の，具体的な　□ applicant 応募者　□ detailed 詳細な
□ job description 職務説明（書）　□ curator（博物館の）学芸員

9.

|---|---|
| What is stated about the Ferguson Museum?
(A) It is a publicly-owned institution.
(B) It specializes in period clothing.
(C) It provides employees with uniforms.
(D) It was founded very recently. | Ferguson博物館について何が述べられていますか。
(A) 公営機関である。
(B) 年代物の衣類に特化している。
(C) 従業員に制服を支給している。
(D) ごく最近設立された。 |

正解 (B)

解説 Ferguson博物館について述べられていることが問われています。❶に「博物館の展示品はこの地域の初期の開拓者の衣服が中心だ」とあるので，「特定の年代の服装」を意味するperiod clothingを用いた(B)が正解です。その他の選択肢は本文に記載がないため，いずれも不正解です。言い換えられた表現が難しい場合は，消去法で残ったものを選ぶ方法もあります。この問題では，なじみのないperiod clothingという表現が含まれる選択肢をとりあえず保留にし，他の選択肢についての記載が本文にないことを確認するという方法です。

語句 □ publicly-owned institution 公共（で所有されている）機関　□ period 年代物の
□ found 〜を設立する

10.

What is NOT a requirement of the position? (A) Qualifications as a curator (B) Experience as a tour guide (C) A license to drive a bus (D) Willingness to work on weekends	その職の要件ではないものは何ですか。 (A) 学芸員の資格 (B) 見学ガイドの経験 (C) バスを運転するための免許証 (D) 快く週末に仕事をすること

正解 (A)

解説 NOT問題で，募集している職の要件ではないものが問われています。❷「見学ガイドとしての経験がある方を探している」が(B)と，❸「バスの運転免許証が必要」が(C)と，❹「土日両日ともに働く必要あり」が(D)に合致するので，残った(A)が正解です。博物館で働くと考えると，一見学芸員の資格が必要であるように思えますが，本文にはそのような記載はありません。「なんとなく」で解くのではなく，しっかり文書の内容を踏まえて解答しましょう。

語句 □ qualification 資格　□ willingness 進んでやること［気持ち］

11.

How can people apply for the position? (A) By calling the museum curator (B) By sending an e-mail (C) By accessing a Web site (D) By visiting the museum in person	職にはどのように応募できますか。 (A) 博物館の学芸員に電話することによって (B) メールを送付することによって (C) ウェブサイトにアクセスすることによって (D) 博物館を直接訪問することによって

正解 (C)

解説 職の応募方法について問われています。❺に「応募はオンラインでのみ受け付ける」とあるので，それを言い換えた(C)が正解です。本文中のvisit a Web siteのように，visitは目的語が「ウェブサイト」のような言葉の場合は「〜にアクセスする」という意味になります。また，visitを含む(D)に引っ掛からないようにしましょう。

Questions 12-14 refer to the following press release.

Daly Events, Inc.

Ignatius Yates
Chief of Event Management
Daly Events, Inc.
(712) 555 8392
iyates@dalyeap.com

FOR IMMEDIATE RELEASE

❶Durant Fairgrounds will host
the York Motor Show

York (May 2)—❷Daly Events is proud to announce that it will be organizing and promoting the tenth annual York Motor Show at its traditional location. It will take place over three days starting on June 3. Gates open at 11:00 A.M. and close at 9:00 P.M. on each day of the show. Tickets are available on the official Web site or the usual ticket sellers.

Representatives of more than 30 automobile manufacturers will be operating booths, where they will be demonstrating their latest vehicles. Among the most highly anticipated vehicles are the VFV Thundercat and the Stratton Stallion, both of which will have their public debut at the show. A number of very popular international celebrities will be there for the opening, including comedian Joe Eaton and the host of Channel 4's *Mighty Machines*, Talia Newman. ❸On the evening of June 5, York Mayor Rhonda Grimes will be addressing the attendees and announcing the winner of this year's Car-of-the-Show Award.

Interested people can learn more by visiting www.yorkmotorshow. com.

設問12-14は次のプレスリリースに関するものです。

Daly Events社

Ignatius Yates
イベント管理部長
Daly Events社
(712) 555 8392
iyates@dalyeap.com

即日発表

Durant博覧会場にて
Yorkモーターショーを開催

York市（5月2日）—Daly Events社は，第10回年次Yorkモーターショーを恒例の場所にて開催することをお知らせできてうれしく思います。モーターショーは6月3日から3日間開催されます。ショーの期間は毎日，午前11時開場，午後9時閉場です。チケットは公式ウェブサイトまたは通常のチケット販売店でお求めいただけます。

30社以上の自動車メーカーの代表者がブースを開設し，最新型車両を出展します。最も大きな期待を集めているものにVFV ThundercatとStratton Stallionがあり，いずれもこのショーで初めて一般公開されます。オープニングの際にはとても人気のある国際的な著名人も大勢来場し，その中にはコメディアンのJoe Eaton氏やChannel 4の『Mighty Machines』の司会を務めるTalia Newman氏も含まれています。6月5日の夕方にはYork市のRhonda Grimes市長が来場者に向けてあいさつし，今年のカー・オブ・ザ・ショー賞の受賞者を発表します。

ご興味のある方はwww.yorkmotorshow.com.をご覧いただくと，より詳しくおわかりいただけます。

語句　□ immediate release 即日発表　□ motor show 自動車展示会
□ anticipated 期待された　□ public debut 初公開　□ a number of ～ たくさんの～
□ celebrity 著名人　□ mayor 市長　□ address ～に話をする，演説する
□ attendee 参加者，出席者 □ interested 興味のある

12.

What is one purpose of the press release?	プレスリリースの目的の1つは何ですか。
(A) To announce the dates of a sporting event	(A) スポーツイベントの日程を知らせること
(B) To encourage people to watch a special broadcast	(B) 特別番組の視聴を推奨すること
(C) To promote the expansion of a well-known business	(C) 有名な事業の拡大を促進させること
(D) To publicize an upcoming trade fair	(D) 来る展示会を宣伝すること

正解 (D)

解説 プレスリリースの目的が問われています。❶に「Durant博覧会場にてYorkモーターショーを開催」とあるので，ビジネス用途の展示会について発表していることがわかります。よって正解は(D)となります。正解の選択肢ではmotor show「モーターショー」がtrade fair「展示会」と言い換えられています。

語句 □ special broadcast 特別放送番組　□ expansion 拡大，拡張
□ well-known よく知られた　□ publicize ～を宣伝する，一般に知らせる
□ upcoming 来るべき　□ trade fair 展示会

13.

What is implied about the event?	イベントについて何が示唆されていますか。
(A) It has been held at Durant Fairgrounds before.	(A) 以前Durant博覧会場で行われたことがある。
(B) Tickets for the first day have already sold out.	(B) 初日のチケットはすでに売り切れている。
(C) It will be larger than it was in previous years.	(C) 過去の開催よりも大規模になる。
(D) Advertisements will appear on television.	(D) 広告がテレビに出る。

正解 (A)

解説 イベントに関して示唆されていることは何か問われています。❷で「Daly Events社は第10回年次Yorkモーターショーを恒例の場所にて開催する」と述べており，❶からその場所がDurant博覧会場だとわかるので，(A)が正解です。このように「地名+host+イベント」で「ある場所がイベントの開催地となる」という表現は時折使用されるので押さえておきましょう。本文では，主催者がDaly Events社で，開催地がDurant博覧会場となります。

語句 □ appear 現れる，登場する

14.

Who is Rhonda Grimes?	Rhonda Grimesさんとは誰ですか。
(A) An event organizer	(A) イベント企画者
(B) An entertainer	(B) 芸能人
(C) A commentator	(C) コメンテーター
(D) A city official	(D) 市職員

正解 (D)

解説 Rhonda Grimesさんは誰か問われています。❸に「York市のRhonda Grimes市長」という表現が出てくるので，Grimesさんは「市長」，つまり「市のために働く人」であることがわかります。以上から，mayorを言い換えた(D)が正解です。市長をこのように言い換える場合があることを押さえておきましょう。

語句 □ entertainer 芸能人，もてなす人　□ commentator コメンテーター，解説者
□ city official 市職員

Cincinnati Business News

June 23—❶Halliday's Ice Cream has announced that it will be moving its headquarters next month. —[1]—. The company has purchased a building in Cincinnati and will be having its staff set up the office there in the coming weeks. ❷While no announcement had been made, it seems that the company president, Maddie Harmer, has been planning this for several years and the staff has been making preparations. — [2] —. A spokesperson for the company said that they were taking advantage of some tax breaks and other benefits that the State of Ohio was offering.
— [3] —. ❸The president has indicated that this will be her final major decision before she hands over control of the company to her niece, Chloe Davis, in August this year. In August, Halliday's Ice Cream will have been in business for 100 years. This is a significant milestone in the company's history. It is likely that the changes have been scheduled to coincide with the company's celebration. There is certainly a lot to be proud of. — [4] —. Shareholders surely have high expectations for the company's future.

設問15-17は次の記事に関するものです。

Cincinnati ビジネスニュース

6月23日—Halliday's Ice Cream社は来月本社を移転すると発表した。—[1]— 社はCincinnatiにあるビルを購入しており，今後数週間以内に社員に現地で事務所を開設させる予定だ。発表されてはいなかったが，社長のMaddie Harmer氏は本件を数年前から計画しており，社員も準備を進めてきたようだ。—[2]— 広報担当者によると，会社はOhio州が提供している法人税の優遇措置やその他の利点にあずかっているという。

—[3]— 社長はこれが自身で下す最後の大きな決断になると述べ，今年8月には会社の経営権をめいのChloe Davis氏に譲渡する。8月にHalliday's Ice Cream社は創業100周年を迎える。これは会社の歴史において非常に大きな節目だ。この会社の祝賀行事に合わせて変革が計画されていたようだ。確かに誇るべきことがたくさんある。—[4]— 株主は確実に会社の未来に期待を寄せている。

語句 □ headquarters 本社　□ spokesperson 広報担当者
　　　□ take advantage of ～ ～を利用する　□ tax break 税の軽減，優遇措置
　　　□ hand over control of ～ ～の管理権を譲渡する　□ niece めい
　　　□ be in business 営業している　□ significant 重要な，重大な
　　　□ milestone 重要な段階，画期的なこと　□ It is likely that ～ ～のようだ
　　　□ coincide with ～ ～と同時に起こる，一致する　□ certainly 確かに
　　　□ shareholder 株主　□ surely 確実に　□ high expectations 高い期待

15.

What is the article about?	記事は何についてですか。
(A) The relocation of a business	(A) ある会社の移転
(B) The activities of a charity organization	(B) ある慈善団体の活動
(C) A community's hard work	(C) ある共同体の勤労
(D) A council program's benefits	(D) ある評議会プログラムの利点

正解 (A)

解説 この記事の目的が問われています。記事の冒頭❶で「Halliday's Ice Cream社は来月本社を移転すると発表した」と述べているので，これを言い換えた(A)が正解となります。

語句 □ charity organization 慈善団体

16.

What is suggested about Ms. Harmer?	Harmerさんについて何が示されていますか。
(A) She will retire soon.	(A) 間もなく引退する。
(B) She has purchased a new home.	(B) 新居を購入した。
(C) She was recently promoted.	(C) 最近昇進した。
(D) She founded Halliday's Ice Cream.	(D) Halliday's Ice Cream社を設立した。

正解 (A)

解説 Harmerさんについて示されていることが問われています。まず❷からHarmerさんはこの会社の社長であることがわかります。次に❸の「社長はこれが自身で下す最後の大きな決断になると述べ，今後会社の経営権をめいに譲渡する」という文から，Harmerさんは社長を引退する意向であることがわかります。以上より(A)が正解となります。

語句 □ found 〜を創立する，設立する

17.

In which of the positions marked [1], [2], [3], and [4] does the following sentence best belong?

"In the last four years, its market share has grown by some 15 percent."

(A) [1]
(B) [2]
(C) [3]
(D) [4]

以下の文は[1], [2], [3], [4]のどの位置に入るのが最も適していますか。

「直近の4年間で，市場占有率は約15パーセント増加した」

(A) [1]
(B) [2]
(C) [3]
(D) [4]

正解 (D)

解説 文挿入位置問題です。問われている挿入文は「直近の4年間で市場占有率が15パーセント成長した」と，会社の業績を説明する内容です。[1], [2], [3]の前後はいずれも「会社の移転」についての説明であり，挿入文の内容はうまくつながりません。残った[4]の前後を見ると「確かに誇るべきことがたくさんある→[4]→株主は会社の今後に期待している」となっており，「直近4年間の業績が好調なので，株主が期待を寄せている」と考えると文脈がつながります。以上から正解は(D)となります。

語句 □ market share 市場占有率

ウェブページ ♪ 008

http://www.bradandtomsdiy.com/about

Brad and Tom's DIY

Welcome to Brad and Tom's DIY Online Video Channel. ❶This is where we post previews of our latest videos, sell T-shirts, hats, and stickers associated with our show, and stay in touch with our fans on the bulletin boards.

Brad and Tom's DIY Online Video Channel has been running for 10 years now and to mark the anniversary, ❷we are releasing the first issue of our quarterly magazine. It will be available on Nileways Online Bookstore as well as in most regular bookstores and newsstands from September 17.

❸On the day of the release, we will have an event at Bryant and Milton Bookstore in Chicago to launch the magazine. Ted Frasier from the popular television show, *Ted's Tools* has contributed an article and he will also be there to help publicize the event.

Scroll down for links to other sections.

設問18-21は次のウェブページに関するものです。

http://www.bradandtomsdiy.com/about

Brad and Tom's DIY

Brad and Tom's DIYオンラインビデオチャンネルにようこそ。ここでは最新ビデオの予告編のアップやショーに関連したTシャツ，帽子，ステッカーの販売，また掲示板ではファンの皆さまとの交流を行っています。

Brad and Tom's DIYオンラインビデオチャンネルはこれまで10年間にわたって配信してきており，それを記念して季刊誌の創刊号を発行します。創刊号は9月17日からほとんどの通常の書店や新聞売り場だけではなくNilewaysオンライン書店でもお求めいただけます。

発売日当日には，創刊に当たってChicagoのBryant and Milton書店でイベントを行います。人気テレビ番組『Ted's Tools』のTed Frasier氏が寄稿してくださり，イベントのPRの支援に書店にもお越しくださいます。

他のコーナーへのリンクは画面を下にスクロールしてください。

語句 □ DIY（= Do It Yourself）日曜大工　□ preview 予告編　□ latest 最新の
□ sticker ステッカー　□ associated with ～ ～に関連した
□ stay in touch with ～ ～と連絡を取り合う　□ anniversary 記念日
□ first issue 創刊号　□ newsstand 新聞・雑誌売り場
□ contribute（記事など）を寄稿する
□ scroll down（パソコン画面を）下にスクロールする

18.

What is NOT a purpose of the Web page?	ウェブページの目的ではないものは何
(A) Providing reviews of new products	ですか。
(B) Selling official merchandise	(A) 新商品のレビューの提供
(C) Communicating with viewers of online	(B) 公式商品の販売
content	(C) ネットコンテンツ閲覧者との交流
(D) Offering samples of upcoming programs	(D) 今後の番組の視聴サンプルの提供

正解 (A)

解説 NOT問題で，ウェブページの目的ではないものが問われています。冒頭❶でどのようなウェ
ブページかについて触れており，その中の「最新ビデオの予告編」が(D)に，「ショーに関連し
たTシャツ，帽子，ステッカーの販売」が(B)に，「掲示板でのファンの皆さまとの交流」が
(C)に言い換えられているので，残った(A)が正解となります。

語句 □ upcoming 来るべき

19.

The word "regular" in paragraph 2, line 4, is closest in meaning to	第2段落・4行目にある"regular"に最も意味が近いのは
(A) constant	(A) 絶え間ない
(B) traditional	(B) 従来の
(C) systematic	(C) 組織的な
(D) satisfactory	(D) 満足のいく

正解 (B)

解説 同義語問題です。問われている語を含む文には「ほとんどの通常の書店や新聞売り場はもちろ
んオンライン書店でも…」とあり，オンラインショップと対比して「以前からあるリアル店
舗」という意味で使われているので，同様の意味を表す(B)が正解です。

語句 □ constant 絶え間ない，一定の　　□ traditional 従来の，伝統的な
□ systematic 組織的な，体系的な　　□ satisfactory 満足のいく

20.

What new aspect of the business is being announced?	事業のどのような新たな展望が発表されていますか。
(A) A 24-hour helpline	(A) 24時間の電話相談
(B) A periodical publication	(B) 定期刊行物
(C) A range of tools	(C) さまざまなツール
(D) A live performance	(D) 実演

正解 (B)

解説 事業展望について何が発表されているか問われています。❷に「(配信10周年の) 記念として季刊誌の創刊号を発行する」とあるので，定期的に刊行される雑誌を意味する(B)が正解とわかります。

語句 □ helpline 電話相談　□ periodical publication 定期刊行物
　　　□ a range of 〜 さまざまな〜

21.

What will happen on September 17?	9月17日に何が起きますか。
(A) The grand opening of a bookstore will occur.	(A) 書店が盛大にオープンする。
(B) Instructional videos will be sold at a bookstore.	(B) 教育用ビデオが書店で販売される。
(C) A celebrity will make an appearance.	(C) 有名人が現れる。
(D) Some people will visit a workshop.	(D) 人が講習会に来る。

正解 (C)

解説 9月17日に何が起きるか問われています。❷に「雑誌を新たに創刊し，発売日は9月17日」，❸に「創刊号発売日に書店でイベントを行う。イベントのPRの支援にテレビ番組出演者が登場する」とあり，イベントに有名人が参加することがわかります。正解は有名人をA celebrityと表現した(C)となります。

語句 □ instructional video 教育用ビデオ　□ celebrity 有名人
　　　□ make an appearance （人前に）現れる，登場する

Questions 22-25 refer to the following customer review.

Customer: Sigmund Reeves   ❶**Date:** 11:34 A.M., Saturday, August 1

❷Yesterday, I took a group of guests visiting from Sweden to Alphonso's for dinner. — [1] —. ❸Although I made the reservation at the last minute, I was surprised to find that the staff was not only able to offer us a table, but also provide a delicious meal in a reasonable amount of time. ❹I didn't realize that one of the people in our party was a vegetarian, and when we got there, I found that the restaurant didn't have a vegetarian menu. — [2] —. When I mentioned the situation to the server, she introduced us to one of the chefs who came and discussed some ideas he had for substituting ingredients. In the end, my vegetarian guest was extremely pleased with her meal and said that she'd like to dine there again before she goes home next Thursday.

If you're looking for somewhere to entertain guests, I can't recommend Alphonso's highly enough. — [3] —. ❺The menu is innovative and exciting, the staff is extremely helpful, and the interior is clean and modern. — [4] —. They're closed on Wednesdays and Sundays, but they're open for lunch and dinner for the rest of the week. I think I was lucky to get a booking at such short notice. I suggest calling them a week in advance.

設問22-25は次のお客さまレビューに関するものです。

お客さま氏名：Sigmund Reeves　　　　**日時**：8月1日 土曜日 午前11時34分

昨日，スウェーデンから来ているお客さま一行をAlphonso'sへ夕食に連れて行きました。—[1]— 直前で予約したにもかかわらず，スタッフに席を用意してもらえただけではなく，おいしい食事を妥当な時間内に出してもらえたことに驚きました。私は一行の中の1人がベジタリアンとは知らず，着いてからこの店にはベジタリアン向けのメニューがないとわかりました。—[2]— 給仕の方にそのことを伝えると，シェフの1人を呼んでくれて，代わりの材料について案を出して相談してくれました。最終的にはベジタリアンのお客さまは食事に大満足して，来週木曜日に帰国する前にもう一度ここで食事をしたいと言っていました。

もしお客をもてなす場所を探しているのであれば，Alphonso'sは言葉に尽くせないほどお薦めします。—[3]— メニューは革新的かつ刺激的，スタッフは非常に協力的で，内装は清潔感があり近代的です。—[4]— お店は水曜日と日曜日はお休みですが，それ以外の日はランチ，ディナーともやっています。私が直前に連絡して予約が取れたのはラッキーだったと思います。行く際は1週間前には電話するといいですよ。

語句　　□ at the last minute　間際になって，土壇場で
　　　　　□ in a reasonable amount of time　妥当な時間内で
　　　　　□ vegetarian　菜食主義者，ベジタリアン　□ server（レストランなどの）給仕係
　　　　　□ substitute　代わりになる　□ ingredient　材料　□ extremely　極めて
　　　　　□ dine　食事をする　□ innovative　革新的な　□ interior　内装
　　　　　□ be lucky to *do*　幸運にも〜する　□ at such short notice　それほど急に
　　　　　□ in advance　前もって，事前に

22.

What is implied about Mr. Reeves?	Reevesさんについて何が示唆されていますか。
(A) He expected Alphonso's to be fully booked.	(A) Alphonso'sは予約でいっぱいだと思っていた。
(B) He often dines at Alphonso's.	(B) よくAlphonso'sで食事をする。
(C) He cannot eat dishes with meat in them.	(C) 肉料理が食べられない。
(D) He will take a trip to Sweden in the future.	(D) 将来スウェーデンに旅行する予定だ。

正解 (A)

解説 Reevesさんについて示唆されていることは何か問われています。レビューを書いたReeves さんは❸で「間際に予約したが，スタッフが席を用意し，食事も妥当な時間で提供されたことに驚いた」と述べていることから「直前だったので予約でいっぱいだろうと思っていた」ということが示唆されています。以上から(A)が正解となります。Alphonso'sに行く頻度については述べられていないので，(B)は不正解です。

語句 □ take a trip 旅行する　□ in the future 将来

23.

When did Mr. Reeves visit Alphonso's?	ReevesさんはいつAlphonso'sを訪問しましたか。
(A) On Thursday	(A) 木曜日
(B) On Friday	(B) 金曜日
(C) On Saturday	(C) 土曜日
(D) On Sunday	(D) 日曜日

正解 (B)

解説 ReevesさんがAlphonso'sを訪問した曜日が問われています。❶，❷に，このレビューが書かれたのは土曜日で，書き出しに「昨日訪問した」とあることから，訪問したのは金曜日とわかります。以上から(B)が正解です。

24.

What aspect of the restaurant is NOT praised in the review?	レストランについてレビューで褒められていないことは何ですか。
(A) The location	(A) 場所
(B) The menu	(B) メニュー
(C) The furnishings	(C) 家具
(D) The employees	(D) 従業員

正解 (A)

解説 NOT問題で，レビューの中でレストランについて褒めていないことが問われています。❺の中の「メニューは革新的で刺激的」が(B)に，「スタッフが非常に協力的」が(D)に，「内装は清潔感があり近代的」が(C)に該当します。よって，残った(A)が正解となります。

25.

In which of the positions marked [1], [2], [3], and [4] does the following sentence best belong?	以下の文は[1]，[2]，[3]，[4]のどの位置に入るのが最も適していますか。
"It was something I should have checked in advance."	「それは私が事前に確認しておくべき事柄でした」
(A) [1]	(A) [1]
(B) [2]	(B) [2]
(C) [3]	(C) [3]
(D) [4]	(D) [4]

正解 (B)

解説 文挿入位置問題です。挿入文は，「私が事前に確認しておくべき事柄だった」と何かについて確認しなかったことを後悔する内容です。確認しなかったため，何かを「知らなかった」と推測できます。❹で「一行の中の1人がベジタリアンだと知らなかった，レストランにベジタリアン向けのメニューがないことも店に行ってから知った」と述べており，その後にレストランのシェフがベジタリアンの客のために対応してくれたと言っています。以上から，[2]に挿入文を入れると文脈に合致するので，正解は(B)となります。

語句 □ in advance 事前に

Questions 26-29 refer to the following online chat discussion.

テキストメッセージ・チャット　　♪ 010

✕

Joan Getz [3:29 P.M.]
❶Hi, everyone. I'm in the parking garage. I've reserved the office car from 3:30, but it's not here. Does anyone have any idea who has it?

Hans Mertaug [3:30 P.M.]
❷Priti took it at lunchtime. She was going shopping for some office supplies. Did anyone see her come back?

Priti Singh [3:31 P.M.]
I'm back. I've been in the office since 1:30. I left the car in the usual location. Has anyone looked at the online reservation system? I would but I'm in the conference room preparing for tomorrow's event.

Hans Mertaug [3:32 P.M.]
Sorry, Priti, I didn't see you come in.

Priti Singh [3:33 P.M.]
That's OK. I came straight to the conference room.

Steve Tanner [3:33 P.M.]
Joan, it looks like the car was booked in for maintenance today. I think the mechanics must have come and picked it up.

Joan Getz [3:34 P.M.]
❸I see. Well, I have to get to a client's office in Ascot. Is there anyone who can give me a ride?

Steve Tanner [3:35 P.M.]
❹I've called you a taxi. You'd better go to the front of the building and wait.

Joan Getz [3:38 P.M.]
Thanks, Steve. ❺Can I get my money back if I bring back the receipt?

Steve Tanner [3:45 P.M.]
Sure. Just leave it on my desk.

設問26-29は次のオンラインチャットの話し合いに関するものです。

Joan Getz [午後3時29分]
こんにちは，皆さん。今立体駐車場にいます。3時半に社用車を予約したんだけど，ここにないんです。誰が使っているか知っている人，いますか。

Hans Mertaug [午後3時30分]
Pritiさんが昼休みに車を使ったよ。事務用品を買いに行こうとしていた。誰か彼女が戻るのを見たかい？

Priti Singh [午後3時31分]
私は戻っているわよ。1時半から事務所にいるわ。車はいつもの場所に戻したわよ。オンライン予約システムを見た人はいるかしら。私がそうしようと思ったんだけど，明日のイベントの準備で会議室にいるので。

Hans Mertaug [午後3時32分]
Pritiさん，ごめん。戻ってきたのに気付かなかったよ。

Priti Singh [午後3時33分]
大丈夫よ。私は直接会議室に来たの。

Steve Tanner [午後3時33分]
Joanさん，どうやら社用車は今日整備の予定が入っていたようだ。整備士が取りに来ていたに違いないよ。

Joan Getz [午後3時34分]
そうですか。ええと，私はAscotのクライアントの事務所に行かなくちゃいけないんです。誰か車に乗せてくれないかしら？

Steve Tanner [午後3時35分]
タクシーを呼んであげたよ。ビルの前に行って待っているといいよ。

Joan Getz [午後3時38分]
ありがとう，Steveさん。領収書を持ってくればお金は戻ってきますか。

Steve Tanner [午後3時45分]
もちろんだ。私の机の上に領収書を置いておいてくれ。

語句 □ office supplies 事務用品 □ usual location いつもの場所
□ online reservation system オンライン予約システム
□ conference room 会議室 □ come straight to ～ ～に直行する
□ give ～ a ride ～を車に乗せる

26.

Why did Ms. Getz start the online chat discussion?	Getzさんはなぜオンラインチャットの話し合いを始めたのですか。
(A) To gain entry to the building	(A) ビルの入館許可を得るため
(B) To suggest that some maintenance be carried out	(B) 整備の実施を提案するため
(C) To find out the location of a vehicle	(C) 乗り物のある場所を調べるため
(D) To suggest a venue for a presentation	(D) プレゼンのための場所を提案するため

正解 (C)

解説 Getzさんがオンラインチャットの話し合いを始めた理由が問われています。冒頭の❶で「予約した社用車があるはずのところにない」と問題提起しており，それを言い換えた(C)が正解です。なお，(B)は〈suggest that S＋動詞の原形〉という形になっています。動詞suggestやrecommendの後にthat節が続く場合，that節の中は仮定法現在（動詞の原形）になるという点はPart 5でも出題される文法事項の1つなので，押さえておきましょう。

語句 □ gain entry 入場許可を得る，入る　□ venue 開催場所

27.

Where did Ms. Singh most likely go at lunchtime?	Singhさんは昼休みにおそらくどこへ行きましたか。
(A) To a restaurant	(A) レストラン
(B) To a client's office	(B) クライアントの事務所
(C) To an auto repair garage	(C) 自動車修理工場
(D) To a stationery store	(D) 文具店

正解 (D)

解説 Singhさんが昼休みに行った場所はどこか問われています。チャット中にMertaugさんが❷で「Priti（Singh）さんが昼休みに事務用品を買いに行こうとしていた」と述べていることからSinghさんは文房具を取り扱っている店に行ったと推測できます。よって，正解は(D)です。

語句 □ auto repair garage 自動車修理工場　□ stationery store 文具店

28.

Why does Mr. Tanner suggest going to the front of the building?
(A) Some guests will arrive.
(B) A taxi has been ordered.
(C) Some food will be delivered.
(D) A key has been found.

Tannerさんはなぜビルの前に行くよう勧めているのですか。
(A) 客が到着するから。
(B) タクシーが呼ばれているから。
(C) 食べ物が配達されるから。
(D) 鍵が発見されたから。

正解 (B)

解説 Tannerさんがビルの前に行くよう勧めている理由が問われています。Getzさんが❸で「誰かAscotまで乗せてくれないかしら」と打診したのに対し，Tannerさんが❹で「タクシーを呼んだから，ビルの前に行って待つといい」と応じていることから，タクシーを待つためにビルの前に行くよう勧めているとわかります。よって，正解は(B)です。

29.

At 3:45 P.M., what does Mr. Tanner mean when he writes, "Just leave it on my desk"?
(A) He will pay a mechanic's bill later.
(B) He will reimburse an employee.
(C) He cannot fill out a form right now.
(D) He does not need his book at the moment.

午後3時45分に，Tanner さんが "Just leave it on my desk" と書いているのは何を意図していますか。
(A) 後で整備士の費用を支払う。
(B) 従業員に経費を返金する。
(C) 今すぐフォームに記入できない。
(D) 今は本を必要としていない。

正解 (B)

解説 意図問題で，Tannerさんが「机の上にそれを置いておいてくれ」と書いた意図が問われています。直前の❺に「領収書を持ってくればお金（＝タクシー代）は戻ってきますか」とあり，それに対してもちろんだと答えて「私の机の上にそれ（領収書）を置いておいてくれ」と書いています。つまり，TannerさんはGetzさんの領収書を受理して精算するプロセスを担っていることがわかるので，ここから「返金する」という意味のreimburseを使った(B)が正解となります。

語句 □ fill out ～ ～に記入する　□ at the moment 現在のところ

Eメール・手紙 ♪ 011

Rudolph's Carpet Kingdom

177 Baker Street
San Francisco, CA 94103
(415) 847-7587

Ms. Glenda Drexel
734 Dobbs Creek Road
San Carlos, CA 94070

April 28

Dear Ms. Drexel,

❶I placed a suggestion box at the front of our store when I was promoted to store manager 12 years ago. Although I check the box every day, it is very rare that we find a suggestion from customers. ❷I would like to express my sincerest appreciation to you for taking the time to compose a message. I am in complete agreement with you and will be making the suggested changes immediately. ❸I will write on the store's Web site about some of the changes we are making in the next few days, and I will be listing your suggestion first as I believe it will benefit the most customers.

As a token of our appreciation for sharing this excellent idea with us, ❹I would like to offer you a membership card which will allow you to receive 15 percent off on every purchase you make at Rudolph's Carpet Kingdom. You can pick up the card at the counter next time you come to the store.

Sincerely,

Terry Wells

Terry Wells
Store Manager

ウェブページ ♪ 012

www.rudolphsck.com

Rudolph's Carpet Kingdom

We're making some changes this month!
❺Starting this Monday, May 1:

- ❻We are offering free home delivery for purchases over $300. If you make your purchase before noon, we can even guarantee same-day delivery.
- We are extending our weekend hours. From now on, the store will be open from 9:00 A.M. to 5:00 P.M. seven days a week.
- We are expanding our range to include top European brands known for their high quality and timeless designs.
- ❼❸We are offering free classes on carpet protection and cleaning once a month at our main store at 23 Sapphire Lane in San Francisco.

If you are in the market for a great carpet, excellent customer service, and fantastic prices, you really need to check us out.

設問30-34は次の手紙とウェブページに関するものです。

Rudolph's Carpet Kingdom社
Baker通り177番地
郵便番号94103 California州San Francisco市
(415) 847-7587

Glenda Drexel様
Dobbs Creek通り734番地
郵便番号94070 California州San Carlos市

4月28日

Drexel様

私どもの店の前に投書箱を設置したのは，私が12年前に店長に昇進したときでした。毎日箱を確認していますが，お客さまからご提案を頂くのはとてもまれです。このたびはお時間を割いてメッセージをお書きいただき，心から感謝申し上げます。あなたのご意見には完全に同意しており，早急にご提案いただいた変更を行うつもりです。数日のうちに店のウェブサイトに行う予定の変更点を掲載しますが，あなたのご提案が最も多くのお客さまのためになると思われるので，最初に載せるつもりです。
弊社に素晴らしいアイデアをくださったお礼の印として，Rudolph's Carpet Kingdom社での毎回のお買い上げで15パーセント割引になる会員証を差し上げたいと思います。次回ご来店の際に，カウンターでカードをお受け取りください。

敬具

Terry Wells（署名）
Terry Wells
店長

語句 □ be promoted to ～ ～に昇進する　□ express *one's* appreciation to ～ ～に感謝の意を示す　□ compose ～を書く，作る　□ be in agreement with ～ ～に同意している　□ benefit ～のためになる　□ as a token of ～ ～の印として

---

www.rudolphsck.com
Rudolph's Carpet Kingdom社
今月，いくつか変更を行います！

今週月曜日5月1日より，
- 300ドル以上のお買い上げでご自宅への配送を無料で提供いたします。正午前にご購入いただければ，即日のお届けも保証します。
- 週末の営業時間を延長します。今後は，毎日午前9時から午後5時まで営業します。
- 商品の幅を拡張し，高品質と時代を超越したデザインで知られているヨーロッパ随一のブランドを加えます。
- San Francisco市Sapphire通り23番地にある本店にて，カーペットの保護とクリーニングに関する無料講習会を開催します。

素晴らしいカーペットと優れたお客さまサービス，そして驚くような値段をお求めであれば，ぜひ当店をチェックしてみてください。

語句 □ guarantee 〜を保証する □ from now on 今後 □ expand 〜を拡張する
□ range 範囲 □ timeless 時代を超越した □ in the market for 〜 〜を買おうとして

30.

Why is Ms. Wells writing to Ms. Drexel?
(A) To offer her a position
(B) To thank her for her input
(C) To ask her to carry out some research
(D) To offer her some advice on a project

WellsさんはなぜDrexelさんに手紙を書いていますか。
(A) 職を提示するため
(B) 意見提供にお礼を言うため
(C) 調査をするよう依頼するため
(D) 企画について助言するため

正解 (B)

解説 WellsさんがDrexelさんに手紙を書いた理由が問われています。❷で「時間を割いてメッセージを書いてもらってとても感謝している」と述べているので，このmessageをinputと言い換えた(B)が正解です。

語句 □ input（提供された）意見，アイデア □ carry out 〜 〜を実行する

31.

What is indicated about Ms. Wells?
(A) She is a patron of Rudolph's Carpet Kingdom.
(B) She has spoken directly with Ms. Drexel in the past.
(C) She is in charge of marketing for Rudolph's Carpet Kingdom.
(D) She has been in her current position for over a decade.

Wellsさんについて何が述べられていますか。
(A) Rudolph's Carpet Kingdom社の得意客である。
(B) Drexelさんと過去に直接話をしたことがある。
(C) Rudolph's Carpet Kingdom社のマーケティング担当である。
(D) 10年以上現在の職位に就いている。

正解 (D)

解説 Wellsさんについて何が示されているか問われています。❶でWellsさんは12年前にRudolph's Carpet Kingdom社のstore manager（店長）になったと述べています。そして手紙の最後にある肩書もstore managerであることから，Wellsさんは10年以上同じポジションで仕事をしていることがわかります。以上から正解は12年をover a decade（10年以上）と表現した(D)となります。

語句 □ patron 得意客，後援者 □ in charge of 〜 〜を担当して □ current 現在の
□ decade 10年

32.

Which change resulted from Ms. Drexel's suggestion?
(A) Free home delivery
(B) New opening hours
(C) The addition of new products
(D) Classes on cleaning techniques

Drexelさんの提案からどんな変更が生まれましたか。
(A) 無料自宅配送
(B) 新しい開店時間
(C) 新商品の追加
(D) クリーニング技術に関する講習会

正解 (A)

解説 Drexelさんの提案から生まれた変更は何か問われています。Wellsさんは❸で「ウェブサイトに挙げる変更点の中でDrexelさんからの提案を最初に掲載する」と述べています。❺で最初の変更点が述べられており，「300ドル以上の購入に対し無料宅配を始める」とあります。ここから(A)が正解とわかります。この問題は，❸の「最初にあなたの提案を掲載する」という箇所を読み取り，ウェブページで最初に述べられている変更点を探して解答するクロスリファレンス問題（両文書参照型問題）です。

語句 □ result from ～ ～によって生じる

33.

詳細を問う問題

What does Ms. Wells offer Ms. Drexel?

(A) A discount card
(B) Some sample products
(C) Interior decorating advice
(D) An invitation to an event

Wellsさんは Drexel さんに何を提供しますか。

(A) 割引カード
(B) いくつかのサンプル製品
(C) 室内装飾のアドバイス
(D) イベントの招待券

正解 (A)

解説 WellsさんがDrexelさんに提供しているものが問われています。Wellsさんは❹で「アイデアのお礼として，買い物の際に割引を受けられる会員証を提供する」と述べているので，割引ができる会員証をdiscount cardと言い換えた(A)が正解です。

語句 □ interior decorating 室内装飾，内装

34.

選択肢照合型問題

What is implied about Rudolph's Carpet Kingdom?

(A) It has moved to new premises.
(B) It has multiple locations.
(C) It closes early on weekdays.
(D) It is hiring new staff members.

Rudolph's Carpet Kingdom社について何が示唆されていますか。

(A) 新しい店舗に引っ越した。
(B) 複数の店舗がある。
(C) 平日は早く閉店する。
(D) 新しい従業員を採用予定である。

正解 (B)

解説 Rudolph's Carpet Kingdom 社について示唆されていることが問われています。❻に「本店で講習会を開催する」とあることから，本店以外の店があることが推測できるので，複数の店舗があるという(B)が正解です。営業時間の変更については書かれていますが，平日に早く閉めるとは述べていないので(C)は不正解です。

語句 □ premises 店舗，敷地　□ multiple 複数の

Questions 35-39 refer to the following e-mail and program.

From:	Soya Tsubota <stsubota@silvertonp.com>
To:	Norma Waters <nwaters@megaweba.com>
Subject:	Welcome!
Date:	June 2

Dear Ms. Waters,

❶We are so glad that you have agreed to join our amateur painters' group. We were all very excited when we learned you were moving to the area. Of course, we debated whether or not we should reach out to you. Considering your status, we were concerned that you may not be interested in collaborating with an amateur group. So, when you contacted us, we were excited, to say the least. ❷I have already registered you as an honorary member and sent you a package with relevant information including our yearly schedule. Honorary members receive free lifetime membership as well as other benefits. ❸You may be asked to speak at special events or help judge competitions but we will understand if you are too busy to do so.

❹We will be holding our annual awards ceremony at the end of this month, and I was wondering if you would mind presenting one of the awards. Actually, we would very much appreciate it if you could take my place as a presenter.

Sincerely,

Soya Tsubota
Silverton Painters

Tentative Program for
the Silverton Painters Annual Awards Ceremony

❺7:30 P.M.　**Opening Address**
Ray Huttenmeister (Group Founder)

7:40 P.M.　**Hanson Art Supplies Award for Best Portrait**
Presented by Joe Hanson, Hanson Art Supplies

7:50 P.M.　**Members' Award for Most Popular Artwork**
❻Presented by Soya Tsubota (Chairperson)

8:00 P.M.　**Lipton Paints Award for Best Landscape**
Presented by Jane White, Lipton Paints

8:10 P.M.　**Dinner and Entertainment**
9:00 P.M.　**Gladwell Gallery Award for Highest Selling Piece**
Presented by Randolph Garden (Curator)

9:10 P.M.　**Closing Remarks**
Seth Wiseman (Group President)

設問35-39は次のメールとプログラムに関するものです。

送信者: Soya Tsubota <stsubota@silvertonp.com>
宛先: Norma Waters <nwaters@megaweba.com>
件名: ようこそ！
日付: 6月2日

Waters様

わがアマチュア画家団体への参加に同意してくださり，大変うれしく思います。この地域に引っ越してこられると聞き，私たちは皆とても興奮しました。もちろん，Watersさんに連絡すべきかどうか思案しました。社会的な地位を考えると，Watersさんはアマチュア団体と協同することにご興味がないかもしれないと心配でした。ですので，Watersさんからご連絡をいただいたとき，控えめに言っても私たちは興奮しました。私の方ですでにWatersさんを名誉会員として登録させていただき，年間の予定表を含む関連の情報が入った小包をお送りしています。名誉会員は生涯年会費無料やその他の特典が受けられます。特別イベントでのスピーチやコンテストの審査をお願いするかもしれませんが，ご多忙でできないとしても，それは承知しております。

今月末に年次表彰式を開催する予定ですが，差し支えなければ，表彰の1つを贈呈していただけないでしょうか。実は，私の代わりにプレゼンターになっていただければ大変ありがたく存じます。

敬具
Soya Tsubota
Silverton Painters

語句 □ amateur アマチュアの，素人の □ painters' group 画家の団体
□ debate 〜を熟慮する □ whether or not 〜か否か □ reach out to 〜 〜に接触する，
連絡する □ status 立場，地位 □ be concerned that 〜 〜ということを懸念する
□ collaborate with 〜 〜と協同する □ to say the least 控えめに言っても
□ honorary member 名誉会員 □ relevant information 関連情報 □ yearly 毎年の
□ lifetime membership 終身会員権 □ judge 〜を審査する
□ competition コンテスト □ I was wondering if 〜 〜でしょうか
□ take *one's* place 〜の代わりを務める

Silverton Painters年次表彰式暫定プログラム

午後7時30分 **開会の辞**
Ray Huttenmeister（団体創設者）

午後7時40分 **Hanson画材社賞：最優秀肖像画**
贈呈者 Joe Hanson氏，Hanson画材社

午後7時50分 **会員向け表彰：最優秀人気作品**
贈呈者 Soya Tsubota（議長）

午後8時00分 **Lipton絵具店賞：最優秀風景画**
贈呈者 Jane White氏，Lipton絵具店

午後8時10分 夕食と余興

午後9時00分 **Gladwellギャラリー賞：最高額販売画**
贈呈者 Randolph Garden氏（学芸員）

午後9時10分 **閉会の辞**
Seth Wiseman（団体会長）

語句 □ tentative 暫定の，仮の　□ opening address 開会の辞　□ founder 創設者
□ portrait 肖像画　□ artwork 美術作品　□ landscape 風景画
□ curator 学芸員，美術館員　□ closing remarks 閉会の辞

35.

情報をもとに推測する問題

Who most likely is Ms. Waters?	Watersさんとはおそらく誰ですか。
(A) A professional artist	(A) プロの画家
(B) A financial advisor	(B) 金融関係のアドバイザー
(C) A politician	(C) 政治家
(D) An architect	(D) 建築家

正解 (A)

解説 Watersさんとは誰か問われています。Watersさんに宛てられたメールを読むと，❶から「アマチュア画家団体に参加してもらえるとうれしい存在」「アマチュア団体と協同することを喜ばない可能性のある存在」ということがわかります。ここからアマチュアではなくプロの画家であることが推測されるので，正解は(A)です。

36.

詳細を問う問題

What does Mr. Tsubota indicate that he has done?	Tsubotaさんは何をしたと述べていますか。
(A) Moved into a new house	(A) 新居へ引っ越した
(B) Purchased a piece of works	(B) 作品を1つ購入した
(C) Designed a building	(C) 建物を設計した
(D) Mailed a parcel to Ms. Waters	(D) Watersさんへ小包を送った

正解 (D)

解説 Tsubotaさんは何をしたと述べているか問われています。メールの❷で「私の方でWatersさんを名誉会員として登録し，小包を送った」と述べているので，「小包を送付した」をmail a parcelと言い換えた(D)が正解です。なお，mailは「～を郵送する」という意味で「Eメール送付」ではないので注意しましょう。

語句 □ mail ～を郵送する　□ parcel 小包

37.

選択肢照合型問題

What is implied about Ms. Waters?	Watersさんについて何が示唆されていますか。
(A) She may be requested to make speeches.	(A) スピーチをするよう求められるかもしれない。
(B) She must perform as a judge at contests.	(B) コンテストの審査員をしなくてはいけない。
(C) She will pay yearly fees.	(C) 年会費を支払うことになる。
(D) She must renew her membership yearly.	(D) 会員証を毎年更新しなくてはいけない。

正解 (A)

解説 Watersさんについて示唆されていることが問われています。メールの❸でTsubotaさんはWatersさんに「特別イベントでのスピーチや協議会の審査をお願いするかもしれません」と伝えています。この前半にあるスピーチに言及した(A)が正解です。必ず審査をするよう依頼されているわけではないので，(B)は不正解です。

語句 □ renew ～を更新する

38.
詳細を問う問題

When will the ceremony commence?	式典は何時に始まりますか。
(A) At 7:30 P.M.	(A) 午後7時30分
(B) At 7:40 P.M.	(B) 午後7時40分
(C) At 9:00 P.M.	(C) 午後9時00分
(D) At 9:10 P.M.	(D) 午後9時10分

正解 (A)

解説 式典が何時に始まるか問われています。プログラムの❺で，開会の辞が午後7時30分となっているので，正解は(A)です。❺で使われているaddressは「あいさつ，スピーチ」という意味で，公式な場でのあいさつなどに用いられる言い回しです。

語句 □ commence ～を開始する

39.
クロスリファレンス問題

Which award does Mr. Tsubota ask Ms. Waters to present?	Tsubotaさんはどの賞の贈呈をWatersさんに依頼していますか。
(A) Hanson Art Supplies Award	(A) Hanson画材社賞
(B) Members' Award	(B) 会員向け表彰
(C) Lipton Paints Award	(C) Lipton絵具店賞
(D) Gladwell Gallery Award	(D) Gladwellギャラリー賞

正解 (B)

解説 TsubotaさんがWatersさんにプレゼンターを依頼する賞が何か問われています。Tsubotaさんはメールの❹で「当団体表彰の1つを贈呈してほしい」「私の代わりにプレゼンターになってほしい」と言っています。次にプログラムの❻を見ると，Tsubotaさんは「会員向け表彰」のプレゼンターになっています。ここから，Watersさんはこの賞の贈呈を依頼されていることがわかるので，正解は(B)となります。

広告・宣伝／プレスリリース ♪ 015

❶ The New England Gardening Society needs new members!

❷ For over 100 years, the New England Gardening Society (NEGS) has been promoting gardening as a hobby and a way of life for the people of New England. We have organized annual contests and events, which have attracted visitors from near and far. In recent years, our membership numbers have been falling. Despite this, the number of entrants in our contests and attendance at our events has been increasing steadily. We are strictly a volunteer group and therefore, we are unable to offer much in the way of reward for those who dedicate their time.

Nevertheless, there are certain benefits which you may want to consider:
❸ NEGS members receive 20 percent off on all gardening items from Green Fingers Nurseries, free transportation to and from society events, and a magazine subscription to *New England House and Garden.*

Interested people can contact the secretary of the society by calling 555-8432 or by sending an e-mail to secretary@negs.org.

簡単な案内・お知らせ ♪ 016

Membership Agreement
New England Gardening Society

By signing the following membership agreement, you agree to fulfill the requirements of the society. In return, you will be able to take advantage of all the benefits membership affords. ❹ At the end of each year, your eligibility for continued membership will be determined by a review of your contributions to the society.

Requirements
Members are required to ❺ pay a one-time membership fee to cover processing. This will become payable again if there is any type of discontinuation in membership.
❻ Additionally, you must carry out at least two of the following duties:
• Assist the society with at least one annual society event
• Act as a judge at the New England Annual Gardening Contest
• Vote in yearly elections for society president

Signed:

Max Dunkirk   *Sandy Polanski*
_____   _____
Max Dunkirk   Sandy Polanski
❼ Applicant   ❽ President — New England Gardening Society

設問40-44は次の広告，会員同意書，賞状に関するものです。

New Englandガーデニング協会は新会員を求めています！

100年以上にわたって，New Englandガーデニング協会（略称NEGS）は，New England住民の皆さまに趣味としての，また生活様式の1つとしてのガーデニングを奨励してきました。当協会は毎年コンテストやイベントを開催し，方々からお客さまを引き付けています。近年，当協会の会員数は減少しています。にもかかわらず，コンテストの参加者やイベント出席者の数は堅調に増加しています。当協会は厳密なボランティア団体であるため，時間を提供していただいた方に報酬という点ではあまり報いることができません。

ですが，ご検討いただけるかもしれない特典もあります。NEGS会員はGreen Fingers園芸店の全てのガーデニング用品が20パーセント割引となり，協会のイベントへの無料送迎と『New England House and Garden』誌の購読が受けられます。

ご興味がありましたら，協会秘書宛てに555-8432までお電話いただくかsecretary@negs.orgまでメールをお送りください。

語句 □ society 協会，団体 □ promote 〜を促進する □ a way of life 生活様式
□ from near and far 方々から □ fall 落ちる，下がる □ despite 〜にもかかわらず
□ entrant 参加者 □ attendance 参加者（数） □ steadily 堅調に □ strictly 厳密には
□ therefore 従って □ in the way of 〜 〜の点で □ reward 褒賞 □ dedicate 〜をささげる □ nevertheless それにもかかわらず □ certain benefit 一定の特典
□ nursery 園芸店，保育所 □ subscription 定期購読 □ interested 興味のある

会員同意書
New Englandガーデニング協会

以下の会員同意書に署名することにより，協会要件を満たすことに同意することになります。返礼として，会員に与えられる全ての特典をご利用いただけるようになります。毎年年末に協会への貢献度を検討し，会員継続の資格があるかどうかを決定します。

要件

会員は手数料として一度払いの会費を支払う必要があります。何らかの理由で会員権を失った場合は，再度お支払いいただくことになります。
加えて，以下の職務のうち少なくとも2つを行わなければなりません。
・最低1つの年次イベントの運営を支援する
・年次New Englandガーデニングコンテストの審査員を務める
・毎年の協会会長選挙で投票する

署名欄：

Max Dunkirk（署名）	Sandy Polanski（署名）
Max Dunkirk	Sandy Polanski
お申込者氏名	New England ガーデニング協会会長

語句 □ fulfill 〜を満たす □ requirement 要件 □ take advantage of 〜 〜を利用する
□ afford 〜を与える □ eligibility 適格であること □ continued 継続した
□ determine 〜を決定する □ contribution to 〜 〜への貢献 □ one-time 1回限りの
□ processing 処理 □ payable 支払われるべき □ discontinuation 停止
□ carry out 〜 〜を実行する □ act as 〜 〜（の役）を務める

The New England Gardening Society

presents this

Award of Excellence

to

Enid Butler

in recognition of her impressive garden at 45 Field's Lane, North Sunderland.
Your garden has been recognized as the most colorful by the New England Annual Gardening
Contest judging committee.

Max Dunkirk

❾ Max Dunkirk, Chief Organizer and Head of the Judging Committee

New Englandガーデニング協会は
この**優秀賞**を
Enid Butler氏に贈呈します。
North Sunderland市Field's通り45番地にある氏の素晴らしい庭園をたたえます。貴殿の庭園は
年次New Englandガーデニングコンテスト審査委員会により最優秀色彩賞に認定されました。
Max Dunkirk（署名）
Max Dunkirk．組織委員長兼審査委員長

語句 □ present ～を贈呈する □ in recognition of ～ ～をたたえて
□ impressive 感銘を与えるような □ recognize ～を認める
□ chief organizer 組織委員長 □ head of the judging committee 審査委員長

40.

What is the purpose of the advertisement?	広告の目的は何ですか。
(A) To attract new members to an association	(A) 協会に新会員を勧誘すること
(B) To encourage people to enter a contest	(B) コンテストへの参加を奨励すること
(C) To publicize the services of a local store	(C) 地元の店のサービスを宣伝すること
(D) To promote a new magazine	(D) 新雑誌のプロモーションをすること

正解 (A)

解説 広告の目的は何か問われています。❶で「New England ガーデニング協会は新会員を求めています！」と会員を勧誘しているので，これを言い換えた(A)が正解です。このように文書のタイトルがヒントになっていると，意外に正解を見つけられない人も出てきます。「灯台下暗し」にならないように気を付けましょう。

語句 □ association 協会　□ enter a contest コンテストに参加する
□ publicize 〜を宣伝する

41.

What is indicated about NEGS?	NEGS について何が述べられていますか。
(A) It receives financial support from the city.	(A) 市の財政支援を受けている。
(B) It is closed during winter.	(B) 冬季は閉まっている。
(C) It is looking to hire a new secretary.	(C) 新しい秘書を雇おうとしている。
(D) It was established more than a century ago.	(D) 100年以上前に設立された。

正解 (D)

解説 NEGS について述べられていることが問われています。広告の❷に「100年以上にわたってNEGS はガーデニングを奨励してきた」とあるので，設立されてから100年以上経過していることがわかります。この100年以上をmore than a century と言い換えた(D)が正解となります。

語句 □ financial support 財政支援　□ look to do 〜しようとしている
□ establish 〜を設立する

42.

What is suggested about Ms. Polanski? (A) She will retire as president of the society at the end of the year. (B) She is entitled to a discount on some gardening goods. (C) She has contributed an article to *New England House and Garden*. (D) She is a founding member of NEGS.	Polanskiさんについて何が示されていますか。 (A) 年末に協会会長を引退する。 (B) ガーデニング商品の割引を受ける権利がある。 (C) 『New England House and Garden』誌に寄稿したことがある。 (D) NEGSの設立メンバーである。

正解 (B)

解説 Polanskiさんについて示されていることが問われています。会員同意書の❽からPolanskiさんがNEGSの会長、つまりNEGS会員だとわかります。次に、広告の❸に「NEGSメンバーは園芸店のガーデニング全商品が20パーセント割引などの特典を受けられる」とあるので、これを言い換えた(B)が正解です。(A)会長引退、(C)記事寄稿、(D)設立メンバーについては本文に記載がないので、いずれも不正解です。

語句 □ be entitled to ～ ～の権利がある　□ contribute an article 記事を寄稿する
□ founding member 設立メンバー

43.

In the membership agreement, the word "return" in paragraph 1, line 2, is closest in meaning to (A) compensation (B) recovery (C) revenge (D) addition	会員同意書の第1段落・2行目にある"return"に最も意味が近いのは (A) 報酬 (B) 回復 (C) 復讐 (D) 追加

正解 (A)

解説 同義語問題です。問われている語の前後を見てみると、「会員同意書に署名すると協会規約に同意することになる。その返礼として、会員特典を利用できる」という文脈になっているので、このreturnは「返礼、報酬」を意味しています。以上より(A)が正解となります。

44.

What is implied about Mr. Dunkirk?

(A) His garden was entered in the New England Annual Gardening Contest.
(B) He was chosen for his position by a vote of members.
(C) His membership will be renewed at the end of the year.
(D) He has volunteered his home as a location for society meetings.

Dunkirkさんについて何が示唆されていますか。

(A) 庭園が年次New Englandガーデニングコンテストに出品された。
(B) 会員の投票によって役職に選出された。
(C) その年の年末に会員資格が更新される。
(D) 協会の会合場所として自宅を提供したことがある。

正解 (C)

解説 Dunkirk さんについて示唆されていることは何か問われています。まず、Dunkirkさんは誰かというと、会員同意書の❼からNEGSに新たに入会した会員だとわかります。会員同意書には、会員について以下の記載があります。

❹毎年年末に貢献度を審査した上で会員資格の継続が決まる
❺一度払いの会費を支払う必要がある

さらに、❻に「次のうち2つ以上の任務を果たすこと」とあり、その選択肢に「年次イベントへの協力」「コンテスト審査員を務める」が挙げられています。賞状の❾に、コンテストの組織委員長兼審査委員長としてDunkirkさんの名前があることから、規約にある会員資格継続の条件を満たしていると判断できます。以上より、正解は(C)となります。少し正解にたどり着きにくいクロスリファレンス問題でしたが、本文を読みながらもう一度根拠を確認してみましょう。

語句 □ renew 〜を更新する □ volunteer 〜を自発的に提供する

広告・宣伝／プレスリリース ♪ 018

GORDON VOCATIONAL SCHOOL
Upcoming Courses for the Local Community

Every February, Gordon Vocational School offers short courses for interested members of the local community.

❶ All courses related to cooking will be provided at the Stanton campus. ❷ Courses related to the repair of vehicles and electrical goods will be provided at the Clarendon campus. ❸ This year, graphic design courses will be offered at the Lasseter campus only. All other courses are provided at our main campus at Beaumont Point.

● **Intermediate Flower Arrangement**
Mondays – February 1 to February 29, 10:00 A.M. to 12:00 noon
Instructor: Miwa Takatsuka
This is a course for students who took part in last year's introductory course.

● ❹ **An Introduction to French Cuisine**
Tuesdays - February 2 to February 23, 7:00 P.M. to 9:00 P.M.
Instructor: Pierre DuPont
Learn the basics of preparing food in the traditional French style.

● **Diagnose and Repair Engine Problems**
Wednesdays – February 3 to February 24, 7:00 P.M. to 10:00 P.M.
Instructor: Otto Mendez
Learn to find and fix minor engine problems in standard passenger vehicles.

● **Air-conditioner Installation**
Thursdays – February 4 to February 25, 1:00 P.M. to 3:00 P.M.
Instructor: Leslie Carlisle
People who complete this course are certified to work as installers of domestic air-conditioners.

Information about other courses is available on our Web site at www.gordonvs.edu.

❺ *We are currently in urgent need of a highly qualified individual to teach our course on databases and spreadsheets. Please call our human resources department at 555-4823 to discuss job requirements and necessary qualifications.

設問45-49は次の案内，Ｅメール，学生証に関するものです。

Gordon職業訓練学校
地域コミュニティー向けの近日開講予定の講座

毎年2月Gordon職業訓練学校は，ご興味をお持ちの地域の方々に短期講座を提供しています。

料理関連の全ての講座はStantonキャンパスで行われます。車両と電気製品の修理に関する講座はClarendonキャンパスで行われます。今年，グラフィックデザインの講座はLasseterキャンパスでのみ行われる予定です。他の全ての講座はBeaumont Pointのメインキャンパスにて行われます。

●中級者向けフラワーアレンジメント
2月1日から2月29日までの月曜日開催，午前10時から正午まで
講師：Miwa Takatsuka
昨年度の入門講座に参加された方向けの講座です。

●フランス料理入門
2月2日から2月23日までの火曜日開催，午後7時から午後9時まで
講師：Pierre DuPont
伝統的なフランス流調理法の基礎を学びましょう。

●エンジン故障の診断と修理
2月3日から2月24日までの水曜日開催，午後7時から午後10時まで
講師：Otto Mendez
標準的乗用車における軽度のエンジン故障の発見と修理について学びましょう。

●エアコンの設置
2月4日から2月25日までの木曜日開催，午後1時から午後3時まで
講師：Leslie Carlisle
本講座修了者は国産エアコンの設置者として働く資格が与えられます。

その他の講座に関する情報は，当校ウェブサイトwww.gordonvs.edu.でご覧いただけます。

*私どもは現在，データベースや表計算の講座を指導する高度な資格を持った方を急募しています。職務要件や必要な資格については人事部555-4823までお電話ください。

語句　□ vocational 職業に関する　□ upcoming 来るべき　□ course 講座
□ local community 地域コミュニティー　□ interested 興味を持った
□ related to ～ ～に関連した　□ electrical goods 電気製品　□ intermediate 中級の
□ instructor 講師　□ take part in ～ ～に参加する　□ introductory 入門の，初めの
□ introduction 入門，紹介　□ cuisine 料理（法）　□ diagnose ～を診断する
□ be certified to *do* ～することを認定される　□ domestic 国内の
□ be in need of ～ ～を必要とする　□ urgent 早急な
□ highly qualified 高い技能を持つ　□ individual 個人　□ database データベース
□ spreadsheet 表計算プログラム，スプレッドシート

To:	Lisa Taylor
From:	Harry Dean
Subject:	RE: Application approved
Date:	February 1

Dear Ms. Taylor,

❻Thank you for accepting my last-minute application for the course on engine maintenance. I am writing because I have not yet received an invoice for my tuition fees. Please let me know how much they will be and how I should pay them. I would like to take care of this as soon as possible. ❼I am also wondering about what books, equipment, and clothing I will be expected to bring to class.

Sincerely,

Harry Dean

GORDON VOCATIONAL SCHOOL
Student Identification

❽**Name:** Peta Love
Classification: Short Course Enrollment
❾**Course:** An Introduction to French Cuisine
Student Number: SC430
Campus: Stanton
Valid through: February 29

宛先：Lisa Taylor
送信者：Harry Dean
件名：RE：お申し込み承認
日付：2月1日

Taylor様

エンジン保守整備講座へのぎりぎりの申し込みを受理していただきありがとうございました。受講料の請求書をまだ受け取っていないので，今これを書いています。いくらになるか，また支払い方法についてお知らせください。できるだけ早く処理したいと思います。それから，講座にはどんな本や用具，服を持って行けばいいでしょうか。
敬具
Harry Dean

語句 □ last-minute 直前の，間際の □ tuition fees 受講料
□ wonder about 〜 〜についてどうかと思う

Gordon職業訓練学校
学生証

氏名：Peta Love
分類：短期講座受講
講座：フランス料理入門
学生番号：SC430
キャンパス：Stanton
有効期限：2月29日

語句 □ enrollment 受講，登録，入学

45.

NOT問題

What topic is NOT taught at Gordon Vocational School?

(A) Graphic design
(B) Appliance repair
(C) Interior decorating
(D) Food preparation

Gordon職業訓練学校で教えられていない科目は何ですか。

(A) グラフィックデザイン
(B) 電気製品の修理
(C) 室内装飾
(D) 食品の調理

正解 (C)

解説 NOT問題で，Gordon職業訓練学校で教えていない科目が問われています。案内の❶，❷，❸に「料理関連，車と電気製品の修理，グラフィックデザインの講義」とありますが，(C)の室内装飾は出てこないので，これが正解となります。

語句 □ interior decorating 室内装飾

46.

According to the information, how should people apply for a position at Gordon Vocational School?
(A) By calling the personnel department
(B) By visiting the office in person
(C) By filling out an online form
(D) By sending an e-mail

案内によると，Gordon職業訓練学校での職にはどのように応募すればよいですか。
(A) 人事部に電話することによって
(B) 直接事務局を訪ねることによって
(C) インターネットのフォームに記入することによって
(D) メールを送付することによって

正解 (A)

解説 案内から，Gordon職業訓練学校の求人への応募方法について問われています。❺に「データベースや表計算の講座を指導する高度な資格を持った方を急募中。人事部555-4823までお電話を」とあり，ここから人事部に電話をすればよいとわかります。人事部（human resources department）をthe personnel departmentと言い換えた(A)が正解です。

語句 □ in person 直接

47.

Which campus of Gordon Vocational School will Mr. Dean attend?
(A) Stanton campus
(B) Beaumont Point campus
(C) Lasseter campus
(D) Clarendon campus

Deanさんが通うのはGordon職業訓練学校のどのキャンパスですか。
(A) Stantonキャンパス
(B) Beaumont Pointキャンパス
(C) Lasseterキャンパス
(D) Clarendonキャンパス

正解 (D)

解説 Deanさんが通うキャンパスはどこか問われています。メールの❻でDeanさんは「エンジン保守整備講座」への申し込み受理のお礼を述べています。次に案内の❷を見ると，「車両修理に関する講義はClarendonキャンパスで」とあります。以上から(D)が正解です。2つ目の文書を読んでから1つ目に戻って場所を検索する，というクロスリファレンス問題でした。

48.

What does Mr. Dean write that he is waiting for?	Deanさんは何を待っていると書いていますか。
(A) An employment contract	(A) 雇用契約書
(B) Information on what to prepare	(B) 準備するものについての情報
(C) An application form	(C) 申込用紙
(D) Permission to use the parking lot	(D) 駐車場の使用許可

正解 (B)

解説 Deanさんが待っているものは何か問われています。メールの❼で「講座にはどんな本，用具，服を持って行けばよいか」と尋ねており，講座に出席する際に何を準備するかという情報を待っていることがわかるので，正解はこれを言い換えた(B)となります。

語句 □ employment contract 雇用契約　□ permission 許可

49.

When does Ms. Love's course begin?	Loveさんの講座はいつ始まりますか。
(A) On February 1	(A) 2月1日
(B) On February 2	(B) 2月2日
(C) On February 23	(C) 2月23日
(D) On February 24	(D) 2月24日

正解 (B)

解説 Loveさんの講座はいつ始まるか問われています。❽・❾からこの学生証がLoveさんのものであり，かつフランス料理の講座を履修することがわかります。また，案内の❹にフランス料理の講座に該当する情報があり，この講座は2月2日から始まることがわかります。以上から(B)が正解となります。

Questions 50-54 refer to the following job advertisement, e-mail, and text message.

Dunhill Advertising is seeking an experienced writer to create advertisements for its clients in the Cavendish region. Applicants must have experience in magazine and newspaper advertising. ❶You are required to submit examples of previous work along with your résumé. As we are a small firm, employees are expected to carry out a number of responsibilities in addition to those associated with their position. ❷You may need to come to agreements with publishers regarding their fees, make presentations to prospective clients, and even take photographs of products for publication. ❸In recent years, we have been expanding into Internet advertising so applicants with a good knowledge of online advertising techniques will have an advantage. We offer a competitive salary and benefits package including a company car.

Visit the Dunhill Advertising Web site at www.dunhilladvertising.com to download an application form and submit the required documents. The deadline is January 16.

To:	Ichiho Fukazawa <ifukazawa@redbird.com>
From:	Fred Scaramouch <fscaramouch@dunhilladvertising.com>
Subject:	Vacant position
❹Date:	January 17

Dear Ms. Fukazawa,

Thank you very much for your application. ❺I was most impressed with your résumé. However, you seem to have forgotten to send the other documents mentioned in the advertisement. ❻Unfortunately, we cannot consider your application without all the necessary documents. The official cutoff date for applications was yesterday. However, as we already have your résumé, you may send the outstanding documents by this evening.

❼My secretary will be scheduling the interviews tomorrow morning. Provided you contact us today, you can expect a telephone call from him tomorrow morning. We plan to hold interviews on January 30. Please let him know what time you will be available.

Sincerely,

Fred Scaramouch
Managing Director, Dunhill Advertising

設問50-54は次の求人広告，Eメール，テキストメッセージに関するものです。

Dunhill Advertising 社はCavendish地域のお客さま向けの広告制作に当たる熟練の広告制作者を求めています。応募者は雑誌や新聞広告での経験があることが必要です。履歴書とともに過去の制作物をご提出ください。弊社は小さい会社なので，従業員は自分の担当業務に加え，複数の任務を担うことになります。料金に関して出版社と合意したり，仕事を依頼してくれそうなクライアントにプレゼンを行ったり，掲載用の商品写真を撮影したりすることもあります。近年はインターネット広告にも進出しているので，オンラインでの広告技術に関する知識がある応募者が有利です。弊社では水準以上の給与と社用車を含む福利厚生を提供します。

Dunhill Advertising 社のウェブサイトwww.dunhilladvertising.comにアクセスし，応募用紙をダウンロードの上，必要な書類をご提出ください。締め切りは1月16日です。

語句 　☐ seek 〜を探す　☐ experienced 熟練した　☐ region 地域　☐ applicant 応募者
　　　☐ be required to *do* 〜する必要がある　☐ previous work 過去の制作物
　　　☐ along with 〜 〜とともに　☐ résumé 履歴書　☐ firm 会社
　　　☐ be expected to *do* 〜すると期待されている　☐ carry out 〜 〜を実行する
　　　☐ a number of 〜 複数の〜，たくさんの〜　☐ in addition to 〜 〜に加えて
　　　☐ associated with 〜 〜に関連した　☐ regarding 〜に関して　☐ fee 料金，手数料
　　　☐ prospective 有望な　☐ publication 出版物　☐ in recent years 近年
　　　☐ expand into 〜 〜に拡大する
　　　☐ competitive salary 水準以上の［他に引けをとらない］給与
　　　☐ benefits package 福利厚生　☐ company car 社用車
　　　☐ download 〜をダウンロードする　☐ application form 応募用紙

宛先：Ichiho Fukazawa <ifukazawa@redbird.com>
送信者：Fred Scaramouch <fscaramouch@dunhilladvertising.com>
件名：欠員
日付：1月17日

Fukazawa様

ご応募いただきありがとうございます。あなたの履歴書にとても感銘を受けました。ですが，広告に記載された他の文書をご送付いただくのをお忘れのようです。残念ながら，全ての必要文書がないとあなたのご応募について検討することができません。公式な応募締切日は昨日でした。ですが，あなたの履歴書はすでに頂いておりますので，今晩までに未提出文書をご提出いただければ結構です。

私の秘書が明日の午前中に面接の予定を立てます。もし本日中に弊社にご連絡いただければ，明朝秘書からお電話いたします。1月30日に面接を行う予定です。ご都合の良い時間を秘書にお伝えください。

敬具

Fred Scaramouch
Dunhill Advertising 社 管理部長

語句 　☐ vacant position 空きがある職　☐ be impressed with 〜 〜に感銘を受ける
　　　☐ cutoff date 締め切り日　☐ outstanding 未提出の　☐ provided 〜 もし〜なら

To: Ichiho Fukazawa
From: Fred Scaramouch
Thanks for coming in to discuss the position at Dunhill Advertising today. I was impressed with many of your ideas and excited to hear more about your experience in both radio and online advertising. You have been put on a shortlist for the position. My secretary will be in touch in the coming days to schedule another interview.
Sent at 5:20 P.M., January 30

宛先：Ichiho Fukazawa
送信者：Fred Scaramouch
本日は職務の件でDunhill Advertising社にお越しいただき，ありがとうございました。あなたのお考えの多くに感銘を受け，ラジオやネット広告でのご経験についてさらにいろいろと伺い，刺激を受けました。あなたは最終候補者リストに残っています。次回の面接の予定を立てるため私の秘書が数日中にご連絡します。
送信日時：1月30日午後5時20分

語句 □ put on ～ ～に載せる　□ shortlist 最終候補者リスト

50.
選択肢照合型問題

What is suggested about Dunhill Advertising?	Dunhill Advertising社について何が示されていますか。
(A) It has offices in numerous capital cities.	(A) 多くの首都に事務所を持つ。
(B) It is broadening its range of services.	(B) 業務の幅を広げつつある。
(C) It allows employees to work flexible hours.	(C) 従業員にフレックス制での勤務を許可している。
(D) It will soon hire a new managing director.	(D) 間もなく新しい管理部長を雇用する。

正解 (B)

解説 Dunhill Advertising社について示されていることが問われています。求人広告の❸に「近年はインターネット広告にも進出している」とあるので，ここから「業務の幅を広げつつある」と言い換えた(B)が正解となります。❸のexpand intoと正解選択肢のbroadenの言い換えに注目しましょう。今回採用しようとしているのは広告制作者なので，(D)は不正解です。また事務所所在地や勤務時間については触れられていません。

語句 □ numerous 多数の　□ capital city 首都　□ broaden ～を広げる　□ range 範囲，幅
□ flexible 柔軟な，融通の利く

51.

NOT問題

What is NOT a responsibility of the advertised position?	広告されている職の業務でないものは何ですか。
(A) Writing reports on sales performance	(A) 売上成績報告書の作成
(B) Negotiating advertising rates with publishers	(B) 出版社との広告費用の交渉
(C) Attracting new clients to the firm	(C) 会社の新規顧客の獲得
(D) Photographing clients' products	(D) 顧客の製品の撮影

正解 (A)

解説 NOT問題で，広告に記載されている職の業務でないものが問われています。広告の❷で業務内容が述べられており「出版社と料金面で合意に至ること」「仕事を依頼してくれそうな顧客に向けたプレゼンをすること」「印刷用の写真撮影をすること」がそれぞれ(B)，(C)，(D)に言い換えられているので，残った(A)が正解となります。

語句 □ negotiate ～を交渉する　□ rate 費用

52.

クロスリファレンス問題

What required item has Ms. Fukazawa forgotten to attach to her e-mail?	Fukazawaさんはどんな必要なものをメールに添付し忘れましたか。
(A) Her résumé	(A) 履歴書
(B) A letter of reference	(B) 照会状
(C) Her portfolio	(C) 作品集
(D) A copy of her driver's license	(D) 自動車免許証の写し

正解 (C)

解説 Fukazawaさんがメールに添付し忘れたものが問われています。まず広告の❶に「履歴書とともに過去の制作物を提出」とあるので，履歴書と過去の制作物を提出する必要があるとわかります。次にメールの❺でScaramouchさんがFukazawaさんに「履歴書には感銘を受けたが，必要な提出物を送付し忘れている」と伝えています。つまり，制作物を提出していないということがわかるので，ここからexamples of previous workをportfolioと言い換えた(C)が正解となります。ということで，この問題はクロスリファレンス問題でした。この問題はメールの「別の文書の提出忘れ」というくだりから広告に戻って解くこともできますが，広告を読んだときに「必要な提出物が2つある」ということを頭の隅に置いておくと効率よく文書を検索することができます。求人の業務内容はクロスリファレンスとして狙われるポイントの1つです。

語句 □ portfolio 作品集

53.

When did Ms. Fukazawa probably respond to Mr. Scaramouch's e-mail?	FukazawaさんはおそらくいつScaramouchさんのメールに返信しましたか。
(A) On January 16	(A) 1月16日
(B) On January 17	(B) 1月17日
(C) On January 18	(C) 1月18日
(D) On January 30	(D) 1月30日

正解 (B)

解説 FukazawaさんがScaramouchさんに返信した日が問われています。Scaramouchさんからのメールは❹にあるように1月17日付で送信され，その内容としては，❻に「応募に必要な提出物がないと応募は受け付けられない」「すでに締め切りは過ぎているが，今晩までに提出してほしい」，❼に「本日中に連絡してくれれば秘書が面接の予約を入れる」とあります。次にテキストメッセージを見ると，すでに1次面接が行われたことがわかります。ここから，FukazawaさんがScaramouchさんからのメールを受け取った1月17日中に提出物を送ったと推測できます。以上から(B)が正解となります。この問題はメールを見ながらテキストメッセージで話の展開を把握する，という少し変わったタイプのクロスリファレンス問題でした。

54.

What is the purpose of the text message?	テキストメッセージの目的は何ですか。
(A) To recommend that Ms. Fukazawa obtain some additional qualifications	(A) Fukazawaさんが，追加の資格を得るように推奨すること
(B) To advise Ms. Fukazawa of some changes to the position's requirements	(B) Fukazawaさんに職の要件の変更を忠告すること
(C) To inform Ms. Fukazawa that she has cleared the first round of interviews	(C) Fukazawaさんに1次面接を通過したことを知らせること
(D) To request that Ms. Fukazawa provide a full list of her previous works	(D) Fukazawaさんに過去の作品の全リストを提供するよう要請すること

正解 (C)

解説 テキストメッセージの目的が何か問われています。❽・❾から，これはScaramouchさんがFukazawaさんに宛てたメッセージで，1次面接に来てくれたお礼を述べた後，Fukazawaさんが最終選考に残っていて今後の予定について伝えている，ということがわかります。❿に「私の秘書が次回の面接のセッティングで後日連絡する」とあることからもFukazawaさんが1次面接をパスしたと確認できるので，(C)が正解となります。(D)にprovide a full list of her previous worksとありますが，Scaramouchさんが過去に制作した広告作品の提出を依頼しているのはメールの中でのことなので，不正解です。

語句 □ obtain ～を獲得する，得る　□ qualification 資格　□ requirement 必要要件
□ the first round of interviews 1次面接

答え合わせをし，自分の得意・苦手な文書［設問］タイプを確認し，あなたの今の "型" を確認しましょう。この結果をもとに，学習計画を立てます。学習計画の立て方は p.100 をご覧ください。

設問番号	正解	文書タイプ	設問タイプ	チェック
1	A	4　リスト	2　情報をもとに推測する問題	
2	D	4　リスト	9　情報分散型問題	
3	B	5　テキストメッセージ・チャット	8　意図問題	
4	C	5　テキストメッセージ・チャット	4　選択肢照合型問題	
5	D	3　フォーム	1　詳細を問う問題	
6	C	3　フォーム	1　詳細を問う問題	
7	B	2　メモ	3　目的・テーマを問う問題	
8	C	2　メモ	1　詳細を問う問題	
9	B	6　広告・宣伝／プレスリリース	4　選択肢照合型問題	
10	A	6　広告・宣伝／プレスリリース	5　NOT問題	
11	C	6　広告・宣伝／プレスリリース	1　詳細を問う問題	
12	D	6　広告・宣伝／プレスリリース	3　目的・テーマを問う問題	
13	A	6　広告・宣伝／プレスリリース	4　選択肢照合型問題	
14	D	6　広告・宣伝／プレスリリース	1　詳細を問う問題	
15	A	10　記事	3　目的・テーマを問う問題	
16	A	10　記事	4　選択肢照合型問題	
17	D	10　記事	6　文挿入位置問題	
18	A	7　ウェブページ	5　NOT問題	
19	B	7　ウェブページ	7　同義語問題	
20	B	7　ウェブページ	1　詳細を問う問題	
21	C	7　ウェブページ	9　情報分散型問題	
22	A	9　レビュー	4　選択肢照合型問題	
23	B	9　レビュー	1　詳細を問う問題	
24	A	9　レビュー	5　NOT問題	
25	B	9　レビュー	6　文挿入位置問題	
26	C	5　テキストメッセージ・チャット	3　目的・テーマを問う問題	
27	D	5　テキストメッセージ・チャット	2　情報をもとに推測する問題	
28	B	5　テキストメッセージ・チャット	1　詳細を問う問題	
29	B	5　テキストメッセージ・チャット	8　意図問題	
30	B	8　Eメール・手紙	3　目的・テーマを問う問題	
31	D	8　Eメール・手紙	4　選択肢照合型問題	
32	A	7　ウェブページ 8　Eメール・手紙	10　クロスリファレンス問題	
33	A	8　Eメール・手紙	1　詳細を問う問題	
34	B	7　ウェブページ	4　選択肢照合型問題	
35	A	8　Eメール・手紙	2　情報をもとに推測する問題	
36	D	8　Eメール・手紙	1　詳細を問う問題	

37	A	8 Eメール・手紙	4 選択肢照合型問題	
38	A	4 リスト	1 詳細を問う問題	
39	B	4 リスト 8 Eメール・手紙	10 クロスリファレンス問題	
40	A	6 広告・宣伝／プレスリリース	3 目的・テーマを問う問題	
41	D	6 広告・宣伝／プレスリリース	4 選択肢照合型問題	
42	B	1 簡単な案内・お知らせ 6 広告・宣伝／プレスリリース	10 クロスリファレンス問題	
43	A	1 簡単な案内・お知らせ	7 同義語問題	
44	C	1 簡単な案内・お知らせ 1 簡単な案内・お知らせ	10 クロスリファレンス問題	
45	C	6 広告・宣伝／プレスリリース	5 NOT問題	
46	A	6 広告・宣伝／プレスリリース	1 詳細を問う問題	
47	D	6 広告・宣伝／プレスリリース 8 Eメール・手紙	10 クロスリファレンス問題	
48	B	8 Eメール・手紙	1 詳細を問う問題	
49	B	4 リスト 6 広告・宣伝／プレスリリース	10 クロスリファレンス問題	
50	B	6 広告・宣伝／プレスリリース	4 選択肢照合型問題	
51	A	6 広告・宣伝／プレスリリース	5 NOT問題	
52	C	6 広告・宣伝／プレスリリース 8 Eメール・手紙	10 クロスリファレンス問題	
53	B	5 テキストメッセージ・チャット 8 Eメール・手紙	10 クロスリファレンス問題	
54	C	5 テキストメッセージ・チャット	3 目的・テーマを問う問題	

型診断

正答数・誤答数からあなたの型を診断しましょう。

	文書タイプ		設問タイプ	
	正答数	誤答数	正答数	誤答数
タイプ1				
タイプ2				
タイプ3				
タイプ4				
タイプ5				
タイプ6				
タイプ7				
タイプ8				
タイプ9				
タイプ10				

A キソガタメ型
診断テストで全てのタイプの正答率が4割以下だった方

B 弱点補強型
正答率が4割を超えるタイプがある一方, 弱点が特定のタイプに偏っている方

C ブラッシュアップ型
全てのタイプが正答率4割を超え, 突出して苦手なタイプがない方

D 満点志向型
診断テストを全問正解した方

トレーニング・カウンセリング

▌▌ 自分の型の診断

診断テストを解いたら，まず答え合わせをし，文書タイプ別・設問タイプ別に正答数を集計します。セルフチェックをした方は，結果とのずれがないかも確認しましょう。「想定外に苦手なタイプ」が見つかるかもしれません。なお，セルフチェック（p.8参照）に書いた内容が，本書の文書［設問］タイプとずれている場合があるかもしれません。セルフチェックで「長めの文書が苦手」と書いた場合などです。その場合は「長めの文書を自分でピックアップして解く」など，自分で対応を考え，試してみましょう。自分の課題を把握し，自分なりの解決策を試してみる，それで克服できなければ次の方法を考える，と試行錯誤することで，実力がアップします。

本書では，単純に得意・苦手なタイプを把握するだけではなく，4つのタイプに分けて現状を診断し，次のトレーニング計画につなげることを勧めます。

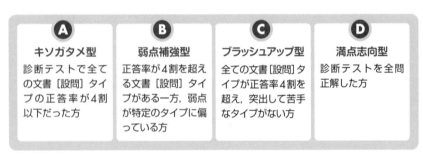

A キソガタメ型
診断テストで全ての文書［設問］タイプの正答率が4割以下だった方

B 弱点補強型
正答率が4割を超える文書［設問］タイプがある一方，弱点が特定のタイプに偏っている方

C ブラッシュアップ型
全ての文書［設問］タイプが正答率4割を超え，突出して苦手なタイプがない方

D 満点志向型
診断テストを全問正解した方

▌▌ 型に合わせたトレーニングメニュー

あなたの型に合わせて，お勧めのトレーニングメニューを紹介します。

A キソガタメ型メニュー

┌───┐
│ **学習順** 最初から順に学習し，簡単な題材や短い文書から少しずつ取り組む │
└───┘

全体的に苦手な文書［設問］タイプが多い場合，基礎をしっかり身に付けないまま苦手だと思うタイプだけを1つずつ解いていっても，結果に結び付かない可能性があります。本書の前から順に学習を進めましょう。

このメニューでは，1つの文をしっかり読んで理解することがテーマでもあります。Exercise や Practice で間違えた問題は，まず解説・訳・語句を読んでチェックし，語彙や文法を理解してから再度，文書を読むことをお勧めします。基礎からしっかり学習しましょう。

Ⓑ 弱点補強型メニュー

学習順　① 苦手な文書タイプ・設問タイプを学習する
　　　　　② それ以外のところに取り組む

自分の苦手な文書［設問］タイプを重点的に学習するメニューです。その後，残りの部分の学習を進め，得意なタイプは，より短い時間で解けるように意識するなど，さらに力を伸ばしていきましょう。

Ⓒ ブラッシュアップ型メニュー

学習順　① 得意なタイプの文書や設問を，負荷をかけて解く
　　　　　② それ以外のところに取り組む

得意なタイプの文書や設問を，負荷をかけて解いてみるメニューです。例えば，1問1分ペースで解ける文書や設問に対して，解答時間を45秒や30秒と短くし，解答の精度が落ちるような状況をわざと作って取り組んでみるなどです。このようにして得意な文書［設問］タイプ（強み）を徹底的に磨いてから，苦手克服に移ります。負荷をかけて強みを磨く過程で，解答時間を短縮する限界を知ることができるので，試験で残り時間わずかとなったときでも，焦らずタイムマネジメントできるようになります。

攻略法と自分の解き方が違う場合は，自信を持って解けるタイプの問題であれば，自分の解き方を優先して構いません。「なるほど，自分の解き方にこのやり方をアレンジしよう」と参考にしたり，「このやり方には賛同できないので自己流で解こう」と自分の解き方の再確認をしてみたりするとよいでしょう。

Ⓓ 満点志向型メニュー

学習順　① 解答時間を短くして負荷をかけ，精度の落ちる文書［設問］タイプをあ
　　　　　　ぶり出す
　　　　　② 間違いの選択肢がなぜ間違いかを確認する
　　　　　③ 同義語問題は英英辞典を使ってチェックする

リーディング・セクションで450点以上を取れる方（またはPart 7で54問中50問程度正解できる方）には，いわゆる「苦手な文書［設問］タイプ」はありません。ただし，「このタイプの問題に時間がかかる」「こういった問題でケアレスミスをする」「仮定法が苦手で正しく意味が取れていなかった！」など，自分の潜在的な苦手ポイントをクリアしてこなかったために，ある程度のところでスコアが停滞してしまう可能性があります。「自分の苦手ポイント」を克服し，満点獲得を目指しましょう。

また，間違いの選択肢がなぜ間違いなのかもきちんと確認しましょう。「本文に書かれていない」「この部分が引っかけになっている」など，出題者の意図を読むようにすることで，解答時に選択肢の取捨選択力がアップします。

「同義語問題」では，英英辞典を引いて各選択肢の同義語をチェックし，英語を英語で覚える感覚を身に付けましょう。この感覚はPart 5の語彙問題でも力を発揮します。

学習計画を立てる上での時間配分

学習計画を立てる上で，どのように時間をかければよいのか迷う方もいるでしょう。ここでは，1文書［設問］タイプのお勧めの学習の流れと，それぞれにかかる時間を紹介します。自分が1日に使える時間をもとに，あなただけの計画を立ててみてください。

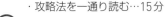

文書タイプ	・攻略法を一通り読む…10分 ・Exerciseに取り組む…30分 ・Exerciseの復習…30分
	復習のタスク…① 問題の解説を全て読む（10分） ② 音声を聞きながら読んでつまずいたところを確認する（10分） ③ 音声に合わせて読む。可能であれば音読する。（10分）
設問タイプ	・攻略法を一通り読む…15分 ・Practiceを解く…5〜10分（1分×設問数が目安） ・Practiceの復習…130分（65分×2セットが目安）
	復習のタスク…① 問題の解説を全て読む（20分） ② 音声を聞きながら読んでつまずいたところを確認する（15分） ③ 文法・語彙を確認する（15分） ④ 音声に合わせて読む。可能であれば音読する。（15分）

本書に毎日60分程度の学習時間を捻出できる方は，1タイプを2日間で終了させるペースでいくと，おおよそ1カ月で本書の学習を終えることができるでしょう。しかし，本書にどのくらいの時間をかけることができるかは，受験日までの日数や他のパートとの学習のバランスなどにより，人それぞれです。あなたの状況に応じて，学習量を調整してください。「全ての問題を音読するのではなく，間違えた問題・苦手だと感じた問題だけに限定する」など，メリハリをつける工夫が必要です。

Part 7 (読解問題) の攻略法

問題数	54問（No. 147〜200）
出題内容	1〜3つの文書の内容に関する設問が各2〜5問出題され，その答えとして最も適切なものを4つの選択肢から選ぶ。
目標解答時間	54分（1問あたり1分）

❚❚ 解く際の流れ

問題を解き始める前に，Part 7全体をパラパラ見て各文書のボリュームやタイプを確認し，全体像をつかんでおきます。こうすることで，時間が足りなくなってきたときに「この問題はスキップしよう」「この問題だけは解くようにしよう」などの戦略を立てることができます。

①文書を読んで内容を理解する

各文書の冒頭にはQuestions 147-148 refer to the following XX. という指示文があります。このXXの部分にe-mail「Eメール」，letter「手紙」，memo「メモ」など「文書タイプ」を表す情報がありますので，ここを必ずチェックしてから文書を読みましょう。文書は段落ごとに内容をつかむよう心掛けてください。本書の「文書タイプ別攻略法」では，文書タイプごとに読み方を解説していますので，ここで各文書の特徴をつかんでください。

②設問を読む

設問の主語と目的語に注目し，何が問われているかを「正確に」読むことを意識してください。うっかり主語を読み間違ったりすると正解にたどり着けないので注意が必要です。設問タイプごとのアプローチについては本書の「設問タイプ別攻略法」で詳しく解説していきます。

③文書から解答の根拠を検索し，確認する

設問で問われている内容を理解したら，それが文書のどこに書かれているか検索しましょう。文書の内容と一致しているか，きちんと確認した上で，選択肢をマークします。

なお，①と②に関しては，②→①の順で解いている方もいると思います。どちらで進めても構いませんが，①→②，②→①，どちらにもメリットとデメリットがあることを理解しておきましょう。

①→②の順に解いた場合

文書を読み終えた後に設問を読むので，文書の内容を全て理解した状態で効率的に問題を解くことができます。ただし，文書の内容がきちんと理解できていないと，設問を読んだ後にもう一度文書を読み直すことになり，時間を浪費する可能性があります。

②→①の順に解いた場合

設問を先に読んでいるため，文書を読みながら解答の根拠を見つけられます。一方で，設問を読んで，文書を読んで，また設問を読んで…と行ったり来たりすることになったり，文書の全体像が見えていないので，最初の段落で書かれていたことが最後の段落やもう1つの文書で否定・変更されていたりする場合に解答を誤る可能性があります。

▓ Part 7に必要な力

Part 7で高得点を狙うには，①速読力 ②記憶力（情報検索力）③解答力の3つの力を高めていく必要があります。本書では，①②を「文書タイプ別攻略法」で，③を「設問タイプ別攻略法」で高めていきます。

①速読力を身に付ける

Part 7の正答率を上げるには，ある程度のスピードで文書を読み，理解する必要があります。自分が1分間に読んで理解できる語数であるwpm（words per minute）を把握し，これを上げていきましょう。TOEIC L&Rテストのリーディング・セクションは，毎回多少の増減はありますが，文書が約3,000語，設問が約2,500語，合計約5,500語で構成されています。Part 7の目標解答時間である54分で，この約5,500語を読んだ上で解答までするには，最低でも130wpmが必要です。そのため，このwpmを意識することが非常に重要となってきます（130wpmの根拠とwpmの計算方法についてはp.108で詳しく説明します）。

速読力を身に付けるには，同じ題材を何度も繰り返し読んで，定型表現，頻出表現を身に付けることに尽きます。こうすることで，各文書タイプの典型的な展開パターンが頭に残っていきますので，自然と文書を読むスピードが上がります。読む量に比例して伸びていきますので，しっかり練習していきましょう。本書では，「文書タイプ別攻略法」のExerciseで同じ文書を3回読んだり，読んだ内容を理解できているか確認するための問題を解いたりしますので，しっかり取り組んでください。

また，文の読み方も確認していきましょう。主語，述語動詞，目的語，修飾語などの要素で切り分けながら読むと意味がつかみやすくなり，読むスピードが上がりま

す。このコツをつかむには，文の構成要素ごとに「/（スラッシュ）」を入れながら読む「スラッシュ・リーディング（p.107参照）」がお勧めです。

②記憶力（情報検索力）を身に付ける

ここで言う記憶力とは，一字一句正確に記憶する力，ということではありません。文書のストーリーや目的などの概要と，どんな内容がどこに書いてあるかを把握しておく，ということです。すなわち，内容を理解し，その概要を記憶する力であり，また解答に必要な情報を文書から的確に探し出す情報検索力であると言えます。

この力を養うためには，各文書タイプの典型的な構成を把握しておくことが重要です。本書ではPart 7によく出題される文書を10のタイプに分け，各文書タイプの構成例を解説しています。

【文書タイプ別攻略法】

- 1 簡単な案内・お知らせ
- 2 メモ
- 3 フォーム
- 4 リスト
- 5 テキストメッセージ・チャット
- 6 広告・宣伝／プレスリリース
- 7 ウェブページ
- 8 Eメール・手紙
- 9 レビュー
- 10 記事

それぞれの特徴をつかんで展開パターンをストックし，どんな文書が出題されてもすぐに対応できるようにトレーニングを積んでいきましょう。

また，情報検索力に関しては，書かれている情報を端的にまとめる力が重要になります。段落ごとの要旨や，表・リストなどの概要を記憶し，解答の際に「ここに書いてあったな」と素早く検索できる力を養っていきましょう。本書の「文書タイプ別攻略法」では，この「まとめる力」を高めるために「メモ」を取るExerciseがあります。こちらに取り組んで，力をつけていきましょう。

③解答力を身に付ける

文書を読む力が身に付いても，設問で何が問われているかを正しく理解できなければ正解の選択肢は選べません。本書ではPart 7の設問を以下の10のタイプに分け，タイプ別に問題の解き方を解説しています。

【設問タイプ別攻略法】

1　詳細を問う問題
2　情報をもとに推測する問題
3　目的・テーマを問う問題
4　選択肢照合型問題
5　NOT問題
6　文挿入位置問題
7　同義語問題
8　意図問題
9　情報分散型問題
10　クロスリファレンス問題

また，TOEIC L&Rテストでは，文書中の表現が選択肢では別の表現に言い換えられている（パラフレーズ）問題も多く，これが苦手な方も多いことでしょう。パラフレーズについても問題の解説などで触れていますので，しっかり確認して解答力を高めていきましょう。

✂ スラッシュ・リーディングの方法

p.105で触れた「スラッシュ・リーディング」とは，文の構成要素ごとにスラッシュを入れて区切る読み方のことです。読解のスピードアップにつながります。

例えば，以下のような文があったとします。

> The new office will have a wide range of new devices for examination which enable us to improve our quality assurance.

語句 □a wide range of ～ 多様な～ □device 装置 □examination 試験
□quality assurance 品質保証

これを名詞のカタマリや動詞のカタマリ，修飾語句（副詞や〈前置詞＋名詞〉のカタマリ）などの文の構成要素に分け，意味を取っていくと以下のようになります。

> The new office / will have / a wide range of new devices /
> 新しい事務所は / 持つだろう / 多様な新しい装置を /
>
> for examination / which enable / us / to improve /
> 試験向けの /（その試験は）可能としてくれる / 我々に / 改善することを /
>
> our quality assurance.
> 我々の品質保証を

日本語の語順に合わせて訳すと

「新しい事務所は，我々の品質保証の改善を可能とする試験のための，多様で新しい装置を持つでしょう」

という文になりますが，上のスラッシュを入れた区切りのまま，頭から訳していくのでも，同じように意味が把握できたのではないでしょうか。

スラッシュ・リーディングで英文を読む練習をすると，英語の語順のまま意味を理解することができ，日本語の語順に置き換える作業が省略されるので，英文を読むスピードが上がります。

Part 7を読む目安のスピード

p.104で触れたwpmとは「1分間に読める語数」のことで，以下のように計算します。

> wpmの計算式＝文書の語数÷かかった時間（秒）×60（秒）

例えば，280wordsの文書を136秒で読んだ場合，wpmは以下のように計算します。

280words÷136秒×60秒＝123.5≒**124wpm**

※小数点以下は四捨五入

Part 7の総語数は文書と設問で合計約5,500words程度です。これを100wpmで読んだとすると，5,500 words÷100 wpm＝55分かかる計算になります。リーディング・セクションの解答時間75分のうち，Part 5＆6の解答時間を20分と考えると，Part 7を100wpmの速さで読んだ場合，読んだだけで試験時間が終わってしまいます。「解く時間」を考慮に入れ，もう少しスピードを上げる必要があります。Part 7（54問）の解答に55分かけるとすると，目安のスピードは次のようになります。

wpmと1問当たりの解答時間

①wpm	②読む時間（分） ＝5,500words÷①	③余裕時間（分） ＝55分−②	④1問の解答時間（秒） ＝③÷54問×60秒
110	50分	5分	約5.6秒
120	約46分	約9分	約10秒
130	約42分	約13分	約14秒
140	約39分	約16分	約18秒
150	約37分	約18分	約20秒

これで見ていくと，1問当たり10秒以上確保できる130wpmくらいのスピードは欲しいところです。これくらいのスピードで読めると，内容がしっかり理解でき，設問も落ち着いて考える時間ができるので，全問解答することができます。

なお，本書付属音声（詳細はp.11参照）はスピードを，この130wpmに機械的に調整したものも一部，用意してあります。音声を聞いて，ぜひ130wpmのスピードを体感してみてください。決して速くはないと思います。この音声に合わせて文書を読み，意味を一度できちんと理解できているかどうか，確認してみてください。

■■「文書タイプ別攻略法Exercise」wpm記録表

p.111からの「文書タイプ別攻略法」では，1つの文書を3回読み，各回のwpmを記録するExerciseがあります。1回目から3回目までのwpmをこのページに記録して，伸びを確認しましょう。

wpmの計算方法：words ÷ 時間（秒）× 60（秒）

ページ	words	1回目		2回目		3回目	
		時間（秒）	wpm	時間（秒）	wpm	時間（秒）	wpm
例	80	60	80	45	107	30	160
p.114	79						
p.120	113						
p.126	76						
p.132	96						
p.138	122						
p.144	118						
p.150	113						
p.156	147						
p.162	98						
p.168	248						

「設問タイプ別攻略法」のPracticeにはwpmを記録するアクティビティはありませんが，同様の記録表をweb特典としてアップしています（詳細はp.11参照）。設問タイプ別攻略法でも継続してwpmを記録し，読む速さを常に意識するようにしましょう。

Chapter 1
文書タイプ別攻略法

毎日 コツコツと積み重ね、継続する。
これが とてつもない大きな成長につながる。
Keep going !

1 簡単な案内・お知らせ

「簡単な案内・お知らせ」は，絵的な要素の多い広告（advertisement）や短いお知らせ（notice）などのことです。Part 7の冒頭に来ることが多く，情報量は少ないものの，内容をしっかり把握しながら読まないと，思わぬ落とし穴にはまります。

POINT 1 イラストや会社名などから状況や背景を推測しよう。

このタイプの文書はイラストや装飾があり，取り組みやすそうな印象を与える一方で，文章が短く情報量が少ないため，状況や背景を推測する力が求められます。会社名や役職などをヒントに，どういう立場の人からのメッセージかを考えて読むと，イメージがわきやすくなります。

それでは，具体的に文書を見てみましょう。

例 Questions XX-XX refer to the following business card. ♪ 024

---

❶ **Simpson Taylor Residential**

└ 家の絵と社名（不動産屋さんの名刺かな？）

Roland Kelly
Sales Associate ── 名前と役職（営業マンだね）

❷ To arrange same-day inspections of properties for sale, please get in touch with me using the following contact information or you can simply walk in my office. Also, you can make an appointment online at www.simpsontaylorre.com.

└ 業務内容など（売却物件の査定には連絡か直接訪問／ウェブでもアポOK）

Mobile: 040-555-6464
Office: 804-555-6464
❸ E-mail: rk@simpsontaylorre.com
Address: 773 Maxwell Drive, Richmond, VA 23266
Office hours: Tuesday to Sunday, from 11:00 A.M. to 7:00 P.M.

└ 連絡先など（TEL2種類・メールアドレス・住所・営業時間）

❹ 10 years serving loyal clients in the Richmond Area!

└ 備考（設立10年・リッチモンド地区のお客さん向け）

●簡単な案内・お知らせの構成例（名刺）

❶タイトル（会社名・名前と役職）

❷メイン情報（業務内容など）
❸サブ情報（連絡先など）

❹備考など

POINT 2 注釈などの「問われやすい箇所」は丁寧にチェックしよう。

注釈，備考などで補足情報がある箇所はよくチェックしましょう。設問で問われる
可能性が高いです。

訳 設問XX-XXは次の名刺に関するものです。

Simpson Taylor Residential
Roland Kelly
営業担当者

即日の売却物件査定を手配するためには，以下の連絡先情報をご利用いただき私までご連絡ください。もしくは直接事務所へお越しいただいても結構です。また，www.simpsontaylorre.com からオンラインでのご予約も可能です。

携帯電話：040-555-6464
事務所電話：804-555-6464
メールアドレス：rk@simpsontaylorre.com
住所：郵便番号23266 Virginia州Richmond市Maxwell通り773番地
営業時間：火曜日から日曜日，午前11時から午後7時

Richmond地区で10年間，ご愛顧いただいているお客さまにサービスを提供しています！

語句 □ sales associate 営業担当者，店員 □ arrange 〜を手配する
□ same-day 同日の，即日の □ inspection 査定，調査
□ property（不動産）物件 □ get in touch with 〜 〜と連絡を取る
□ contact information 連絡先情報 □ make an appointment 予約する
□ VA（= Virginia）アメリカ・バージニア州
※アメリカでは50州をアルファベット大文字2文字で表す
□ office hours 営業時間 □ loyal client 忠実な顧客，常連客

攻略法まとめ 簡単な案内・お知らせ

• イラストや会社名などから状況や背景を推測しよう。
• 注釈などの「問われやすい箇所」は丁寧にチェックしよう。

Exercise　指示に従って，以下の文書を3回読みましょう。

1回目　① 次の文書をきちんと理解しながら読み，wpmを記録しましょう。

※wpmの算出方法と記録はp.109参照

Question 1 refers to the following advertisement.

❶ **Dine at Normandy!**

❷ Make your next dinner reservation at Normandy, the classiest French restaurant in the metropolitan area. Award-winning chef Michel Luyat will impress you with his perfect balance of sweet, sour, spicy, and bitter flavors.

❸ After experiencing our fine dining, leave us a review via our Web site. Doing this earns you a chance to win a $50 gift card! Visit www.normandy-restaurant.com for more information.

❹ *You'll need the code on your receipt to verify you as a customer.

（79words）

② 文書のポイントをメモし，わからなかった語句や文法をチェックしましょう。

	要素	内容
❶		
❷		
❸		
❹		

2回目 文書を読み，wpmを記録しましょう。

3回目 文書を読んでwpmを記録し，次の問題を解きましょう。

1. What is indicated about the online review of Normandy's?
(A) It offers a weekly newsletter to its reviewers.
(B) It is updated twice a day.
(C) It is not available to the public.
(D) It requires the submission of a code.

Question 1 refers to the following advertisement.

♪ 025

Dine at Normandy!

Make your next dinner reservation at Normandy,
the classiest French restaurant in the metropolitan area.
Award-winning chef Michel Luyat will impress you with
his perfect balance of sweet, sour, spicy, and bitter flavors.

After experiencing our fine dining, leave us a review via our
Web site. Doing this earns you a chance to win a $50 gift card!
Visit www.normandy-restaurant.com for more information.

*You'll need the code on your receipt to verify you as a customer.

訳 設問1は次の広告に関するものです。

❶ Normandyでお食事を！

❷ 次回のディナーのご予約は大都市圏で最高級のフレンチレストラン，Normandyへどうぞ。受賞歴のあるシェフMichel Luyatが，甘味，酸味，辛味，そして苦味が完璧に調和した味わいを，あなたの心に刻むでしょう。

❸ 素晴らしい食事をお楽しみいただきましたら，私どものウェブサイトからレビューをお願いします。レビューをしていただくと，50ドルのギフトカードが当たるチャンスが得られます。詳細はwww.normandy-restaurant.comでご確認ください。

❹ *お客さまであることを証明するために，レシートにあるコードが必要です。

語句 □ dine 食事をする　□ classy 高級な　□ metropolitan area 大都市圏
□ impress A with B AにBを印象づける　□ flavor 味わい，風味　□ via ～を経由して
□ earn ～を得る，獲得する　□ verify ～を証明する，検証する

┇┇ メモ例

	要素	内容
❶	タイトル	Normandyで食事を！ （レストランの広告かな？）
❷	メイン情報	ディナーの予約　フレンチレストラン　賞を取ったシェフ おいしい料理
❸	サブ情報	食事後のレビューのお願い　レビューで50ドルの金券が当たるかも サイトのアドレス　そこに詳細あり
❹	備考	レビューにはレシートのコードが必要

┇┇ 設問の解答・解説

1.

What is indicated about the online review of Normandy's? (A) It offers a weekly newsletter to its reviewers. (B) It is updated twice a day. (C) It is not available to the public. (D) It requires the submission of a code.	Normandyのオンラインレビューについて, 何が述べられていますか。 (A) レビューを書いた人に週刊ニュースレターを提供する。 (B) 1日2回更新される。 (C) 一般公開されていない。 (D) コードの提示を要求する。

正解 (D)

解説 Normandyのオンラインレビューについて, 何が述べられているかが問われています。❸の1文目に「ウェブサイトからレビューをお願いしたい」とあり, これ以降にオンラインレビューに関する記述があることをつかみましょう。❹に「レシートのコードが客の証明として必要」とあるので, これをrequire「～を必要とする」とthe submission of a code「コードの提示」を使って言い換えた(D)が正解です。(A)週刊ニュースレター, (B)更新回数, (C)一般公開の有無については, いずれも本文で述べられていません。

語句 □ to the public 一般に向けて　□ require ～を要求する　□ submission 提示, 提出

2 メモ

TOEIC L&Rテストで出題される「メモ（memo）」には，電話の伝言メモなどのいわゆる「メモ」のほか，同じ組織に属する人宛てのメール文書のような形式のものがあります。まず，前者の比較的文章量が少ない「メモ」から見ていきましょう。

POINT レイアウトなどから内容を推測し，解答に必要な情報を検索しよう。

メモはレイアウトやタイトルから内容を推測することができます。下の例を見てください。TELEPHONE MEMOという部分から「これは電話の伝言メモだな」と察しがつくでしょう。このようにメモの内容をまず推測し，その上で情報を整理しながら読んでいくことがポイントです。下の例では「誰が」「どのような情報を」「誰のために」メモしているのかなどを整理しながら読み，解答の際に，必要な情報を文書からすぐに検索できるようにしておきましょう。

例 **Questions XX-XX** refer to the following memo.　♪ 026

---

❶ TELEPHONE MEMO

└ メモの種類（電話メモ）

❷
To: Brad Thomas
From: Marilyn Hatton
Taken By: Arnold Daley
Time: Tuesday, 15 July, 10:40 A.M.

└ メモの宛先や日付など（誰から誰宛ての伝言か，誰がいつ受けたか）

❸
Ms. Hatton called to say she is not able to attend the Emery Exhibition next Wednesday. She would like someone to go in her place to represent our company. Please call her back to let her know who that will be. Then she'll contact that person with information about the event, where to sit, and who to talk to while there. You can reach her at 555-3128 extension 52.

└ メッセージ
・電話の目的（来週のイベント出席NG，他の人に頼みたい）
・今後の対応（電話がほしい，人選してもらいたい，連絡先）

● メモの構成例

❶メモの種類
❷メモの宛先や日付など
❸メッセージ

メモは短いものが多いので，冒頭からすべて頭にたたきこむつもりで読み進めても
よいですが，構成を大まかに把握しておくことで，情報の整理がしやすくなります。

訳 設問XX-XXは次のメモに関するものです。

電話メモ

Brad Thomas様へ
Marilyn Hatton様より
Arnold Daley受付
日時　7月15日（火）午前10時40分

Hattonさんから，来週水曜日のEmery Exhibitionに出席できない旨，電話がありました。当社の
代表として，誰か代わりに行ってほしいそうです。折り返し電話でそれが誰になるか伝えてくださ
い。その後，Hattonさんがその人にイベントの情報や座る席，そこで話すべき相手について連絡
するとのことです。Hattonさんには555-3128，内線52で連絡できます。

語句 □ attend ～に出席する　□ in *one's* place ～の代わりに　□ represent ～を代表する
　　　□ contact ～と連絡を取る　□ where to *do* どこに～すべきか
　　　□ who to *do* 誰に～すべきか
　　　　　※本来は目的格のwhomを用いるべきだが，現在ではwhoを用いるのが一般的
　　　□ reach ～と連絡を取る　□ extension 内線（電話番号）

攻略法まとめ メモ

・メモはレイアウトやタイトルから内容を推測しよう。

・概要を把握し，解答の際に必要な情報を検索しよう。

1回目 ① 次の文書をきちんと理解しながら読み，wpmを記録しましょう。

※ wpmの算出方法と記録はp.109参照

Question 1 refers to the following memo.

---

❶ **MEMO**

❷
To: All Mason Theater employees
From: Tomas Connell, Theater Manager
Date: February 14
Subject: Richard Haden's plays

Mason Theater will perform three plays by Richard Haden three months in a row, to celebrate the centenary of his birth.

A Tale of a Misfit   March 7 to March 28
   The journey of a lost man finding where he truly belongs.

Don't Sing a Lullaby   April 5 to April 27
❸   A sweeping tale of love and romance. Based on Haden's real-life experiences.

Because I Said So   May 3 to May 26
   The award-winning comedy about two fishermen.

Discount tickets for friends and family members of employees are available. Please check www.masontheater.com/employees for more information.

(113words)

②文書のポイントをメモし，わからなかった語句や文法をチェックしましょう。

	要素	内容
❶		
❷		
❸		

2回目 文書を読み，wpmを記録しましょう。

3回目 文書を読んでwpmを記録し，次の問題を解きましょう。

1. What is indicated about Richard Haden?

    (A) He was raised in the city of Mason.

    (B) His play received a prize.

    (C) His first occupation was fisherman.

    (D) He was a member of Mason Theater.

解答・解説

Question 1 refers to the following memo.

♪ 027

---

❶ **MEMO**

To: All Mason Theater employees
❷ From: Tomas Connell, Theater Manager
Date: February 14
Subject: Richard Haden's plays

Mason Theater will perform three plays by Richard Haden three months in a row, to celebrate the centenary of his birth.

A Tale of a Misfit   March 7 to March 28
    The journey of a lost man finding where he truly belongs.

Don't Sing a Lullaby   April 5 to April 27
    A sweeping tale of love and romance. Based on Haden's real-life
❸ experiences.

Because I Said So   May 3 to May 26
    The award-winning comedy about two fishermen.

Discount tickets for friends and family members of employees are available. Please check www.masontheater.com/employees for more information.

訳 設問1は次のメモに関するものです。

❶メモ

宛先：Mason劇場全従業員
❷ 差出人：Tomas Connell 劇場支配人
日付：2月14日
件名：Richard Haden氏の演劇

Mason劇場はRichard Haden氏の3つの演劇を3カ月連続で上演し，氏の生誕100周年をお祝いします。

『はみだし者の話』   3月7日〜3月28日
    さまよえる男が本当の居場所を見つける旅。
❸ 『子守歌を歌わないで』   4月5日〜4月27日
    愛とロマンスの大作。Haden氏の実体験に基づくもの。
『なぜなら私がそう言ったから』   5月3日〜5月26日
    2人の釣り人についての，賞を獲得したコメディー作品。

従業員のご友人やご家族への割引券を購入できます。詳しくはwww.masontheater.com/employeesを確認してください。

語句 □ in a row 連続で □ centenary 100周年記念 □ misfit はみだし者 □ truly 本当に
□ belong （いるべき場所に）いる □ sweeping 決定的な，圧倒的な
□ real-life 現実の □ award-winning 賞を獲得した □ comedy コメディー，喜劇
□ fisherman 釣り人，漁師 □ discount ticket 割引券
□ for more information 詳しくは

■■ メモ例

	要素	内容
❶	タイトル	メモ
❷	メモの宛先や日付など	全従業員へ支配人より，2月14日，Richard Haden の演劇
❸	メッセージ	・Richard Haden の生誕100周年記念の上演 ・3つの演目と上演日程，簡単な内容紹介 ・割引券の購入可能，詳細はウェブサイトへ

■■ 設問の解答・解説

1.

What is indicated about Richard Haden?	Richard Haden 氏について何が述べられていますか。
(A) He was raised in the city of Mason.	(A) Mason 市内で育った。
(B) His play received a prize.	(B) 彼の演劇は賞を獲得した。
(C) His first occupation was fisherman.	(C) 彼の最初の職業は漁師だった。
(D) He was a member of Mason Theater.	(D) Mason 劇場の会員だった。

正解 (B)

解説 Richard Haden 氏について述べられていることが問われています。❸冒頭の下線部から，3つの演目はHaden 氏が手掛けたことがわかり，❸後半の下線部から，演目の1つは賞を獲得したことがわかります。よって(B)が正解です。

語句 □ raise ～を育てる □ occupation 職業

3 フォーム

「フォーム」はアンケート，応募・申込用紙，調査記入用紙などを指します。指定の書式に書き込んだり，チェックボックスにチェックを入れたりするものなどです。どこに何が書かれているかを把握し，解答時に検索する読み方が基本です。

POINT 1 フォームの種類から，内容をある程度イメージしよう。

フォームの場合はまず，これが何のフォームなのかを見極めます。サービスを受けた後の「アンケート」なのか，何かの「申込書」なのか，などをレイアウトと項目を見てつかみます。

では，下の例でフォームの構成を具体的に見てみましょう。

例 **Questions XX-XX** refer to the following form. ♪ 028

Weinberg Industries
Parking Permit Request
❶ └─ フォームの種類を把握（駐車許可の申請書）

❷
- Name of employee making request: Pat O'Malley
- Phone: 235-555-0998
- Name of user: Stefanie Bateman
- Weinberg Industries employee? Yes ☐ No ☑
- If no, place of employment: MN Department of Revenue
- Permit request from: March 12 to March 16

└─ 記入項目（従業員氏名，電話番号，使用者氏名，社員か否か，Noの場合は勤務先，使用日）

❸
- Reason: Ms. Bateman is coming to Weinberg Industries to update the financial department on the new financial laws.
- Special requests: As Ms. Bateman uses a cane, it would be helpful if she could receive an appropriate parking space.

└─ 備考の有無チェック（「スペシャルなリクエスト」はいかにも怪しい！）

●フォームの構成例

❶フォームの種類
❷記入欄
❸備考など（自由記述欄）

POINT 2 「備考」などの自由記述欄に注目しよう。

フォームで何よりも注目したいのは「備考」などの自由記述欄です。ここは書き手の意見や要望が自由に記入されており，テスティングポイントになりやすいためです。ここの文章が長めの場合は，ほぼ必ずと言っていいほどここから出題されると思ってください。

訳 設問XX-XXは次のフォームに関するものです。

Weinberg Industries社 **駐車許可申請書**
申請従業員氏名：Pat O'Malley
電話番号：235-555-0998
使用者氏名：Stefanie Bateman
Weinberg Industries社の従業員ですか。 はい □ いいえ ☑
「いいえ」の場合，勤務先：Minnesota州税務局
駐車許可希望日：3月12日 〜 3月16日
理由：Bateman氏が新金融法に関する最新情報を財務部に説明するため，Weinberg Industries社に来社予定のため。
特別な要望：Bateman氏は杖を使用しているので，適切な駐車場を割り当てていただけると助かります。

語句 □ parking permit request 駐車許可申請 □ place of employment 勤務先
□ MN（= Minnesota）アメリカ・ミネソタ州 □ update 〜に最新情報を与える
□ financial 金融の，財政の □ cane 杖，ステッキ
□ it would be helpful if 〜 もし〜だと助かるでしょう
□ appropriate 適切な，ふさわしい

攻略法まとめ フォーム

・フォームの種類から内容をある程度イメージしよう。

・「備考」などの自由記述欄の内容をしっかり押さえよう。

Exercise 指示に従って，以下の文書を3回読みましょう。

1回目 ① 次の文書をきちんと理解しながら読み，wpmを記録しましょう。

※wpmの算出方法と記録はp.109参照

Question 1 refers to the following survey.

---

❶ Welcome to the postal service experience survey!

❷
- **Date:** May 11　　**Name:** Naomi Patel

- **How satisfied were you with your most recent visit to Landsdale Post Office?**

  Not at all satisfied　1　②　3　4　5　Very satisfied

- **Was there a problem during your visit?**　Yes ☑　No ☐

❸
- **If yes, what was the problem about?**

  The clerk miscounted the stamps I was buying, so the total wasn't right. I had to come back and ask for a refund.

(76words)

② 文書のポイントをメモし，わからなかった語句や文法をチェックしましょう。

	要素	内容
❶		
❷		
❸		

2回目 文書を読み，wpmを記録しましょう。

3回目 文書を読んでwpmを記録し，次の問題を解きましょう。

3

1. What is true about Ms. Patel?

   (A) She was charged incorrectly.

   (B) She received a complimentary stamp.

   (C) She has experience working in the post office.

   (D) She lives in the Landsdale area.

Question 1 refers to the following survey.　♪ 029

---

❶ # Welcome to the postal service experience survey!

❷
■ **Date:** May 11　　■ **Name:** Naomi Patel

■ **How satisfied were you with your most recent visit to Landsdale Post Office?**

Not at all satisfied　1　②　3　4　5　Very satisfied

■ **Was there a problem during your visit?**　Yes ☑　No ☐

❸
■ **If yes, what was the problem about?**

The clerk miscounted the stamps I was buying, so the total wasn't right. I had to come back and ask for a refund.

訳　設問1は次の調査票に関するものです。

---

❶ **郵便業務体験調査にようこそ！**

日付：5月11日　　　氏名：Naomi Patel

❷
直近のLandsdale郵便局訪問時の満足度はいかがでしたか？
全く満足していない　1　②　3　4　5　大いに満足

訪問時に問題はありましたか？　　　はい ☑　　　いいえ ☐

❸
「はい」の場合、どんな問題でしたか？
購入しようとした切手を局員が数え間違えたために、合計金額が正しくありませんでした。
戻ってきて払い戻しを受けなくてはいけませんでした。

語句　□ postal 郵便の，郵政に関する　□ satisfied 満足した
□ miscount ～を間違えて数える　□ stamp 切手　□ ask for ～ ～を求める
□ refund 払い戻し

🔳 メモ例

	要素	内容
❶	フォームの種類	postal service experience survey → 郵便局の利用に関する調査票
❷	記入日・記入者 質問①	5月11日，Naomi Patel 郵便局満足度 → やや不満
	質問②	訪問時の問題 → あった
❸	質問③ （自由記述）	問題は具体的に何？ → 購入した切手の枚数を局員が数え間違えた。戻って返金を頼む必要があった。

🔳 設問の解答・解説

1.

What is true about Ms. Patel?	Patelさんについて正しいことは何ですか。
(A) She was charged incorrectly.	(A) 間違った金額を請求された。
(B) She received a complimentary stamp.	(B) 無料の切手を受け取った。
(C) She has experience working in the post office.	(C) 郵便局での勤務経験がある。
(D) She lives in the Landsdale area.	(D) Landsdale地区に住んでいる。

正解 (A)

解説 Patelさんについて正しいことが問われています。❸の下線部に，郵便局で購入しようとした切手の数を局員が数え間違えたため，再び訪問して払い戻しを受けた，とあるので，それを言い換えた(A)が正解です。the total wasn't rightがwas charged incorrectlyと言い換えられています。Patelさんは切手を購入していますが，本文を見る限り無料で手に入れた切手はないので(B)は不正解です。

語句 □ charge 〜に請求する　□ complimentary 無料の

4 リスト

このタイプには請求書や予算詳細, スケジュール, 旅程表などがあります。情報量はそれほど多くないため, 出題されやすい箇所を事前に把握しておけば対処しやすいタイプの文書とも言えます。

POINT 指示文からリストの種類を把握し, どこに何が書かれているか押さえよう。

リストは, 設問の指示文にある invoice, schedule などの語から何のリストかをまず把握します。その上で, 細部を読む前に項目（商品名・数量・価格など）を確認し, どこに何が書かれているのかをつかみます。例を見てみましょう。

例 **Questions XX-XX** refer to the following receipt. ♪ 030

Thank you for choosing Akino's in Montreal
❶ www.akinos.com
└ 店名

❷ February 18 2:05 P.M.   Dine-in
Order #: 2568883   Staff: Angela
└ 購入日時, 担当スタッフなど

❸ 2 Black Tea $4.50
1 Coffee $2.25
1 Strawberry Shortcake $5.49
1 Raspberry Tart $5.49
1 Blueberry Pie $5.75
└ 購入した商品

❹ Subtotal $23.48
Food tax (1.75%) $0.41
TOTAL   **$23.89**
└ 小計, 税, 合計

❺ Credit card   Approved
**** **** **** 3328 $23.89
Authorization code   239875201746
└ カードの支払い情報

❻ *Present this receipt during your next visit and enjoy a cup of black tea for free! See an employee for details.
└ 次回このレシート持参でいいことがある！

●リストの構成例（レシート）

❶タイトル（店名）
リスト部分 ❷購入日時 ❸購入品 ❹料金 ❺支払い情報
❻備考など

備考や補足は出題されやすいので要チェック！

このように，リストの場合は情報が項目ごとに並んでいます。どこに何が書かれているか大枠をつかんでから設問を読み，必要な情報を検索すれば素早く解くことができます。

訳 設問XX-XXは次のレシートに関するものです。

お選びいただきありがとうございます
Akino's Montreal店
www.akinos.com

2月18日午後2時5分　　　　　　　店内でのご飲食
注文番号：2568883　　　　　　　　担当者：Angela

紅茶 2点　　　　　　　　　　　　4.50ドル
コーヒー 1点　　　　　　　　　　2.25ドル
イチゴショートケーキ 1点　　　　5.49ドル
ラズベリータルト 1点　　　　　　5.49ドル
ブルーベリーパイ 1点　　　　　　5.75ドル

小計　　　　　　　　　　　　　　23.48ドル
食品税（1.75%）　　　　　　　　 0.41ドル
合計　　　　　　　　　　　　 **23.89ドル**

クレジットカード　　　　　　　　認証済み
**** **** **** 3328　　　　　　23.89ドル
承認番号　　　　　　　　　　　　239875201746

---

*次回ご来店時にこのレシートをご提示いただければ，紅茶を1杯無料でお楽しみいただけます。詳細は従業員までお願いいたします。

語句 □ dine-in（持ち帰りではなく）店内で食事をする　□ subtotal 小計
□ approved 認証済みの，承認済みの　□ authorization code 承認番号
□ present ～を提示する　□ details 詳細

攻略法まとめ リスト

・指示文からリストの種類を把握し，どこに何が書かれているか押さえよう。
・大枠の情報を押さえ，細かい情報は設問を読んで検索できるようにしよう。

Exercise

指示に従って，以下の文書を3回読みましょう。

1回目 ① 次の文書をきちんと理解しながら読み，wpmを記録しましょう。

※wpmの算出方法と記録はp.109参照

Question 1 refers to the following invoice.

Westford Packaging Supplies, Inc. **Ordered By:** Bill Hodgkins
10883 Inverness Trail   Dennison Gifts and Souvenirs
1 Westford, MA 01886   23497 Mussel Beach Road
(351) 555-8024   Davenport, FL 33836
www.westfordpacksup.com   (863) 555-2794 ext. 97

2 Invoice No.: 009723497   **Order Date:** January 15

3

Item No.	Description	Quantity	Unit Price	Total Price
052305	Box 5"x5"x5"	100	$0.26	$26.00
132820	Box 12"x20"x20"	50	$2.58	$129.00
290543	Masking tape 2' x 110 yds	20	$3.51	$70.20
122412	WP bubble wrap 4" x 100'	10	$50.00	$500.00
			Subtotal	$725.20
			Shipping/Handling	$30.72
			GRAND TOTAL:	**$755.92**

4

5 Thank you for your business!   **Payment is due upon receipt.**

(96words)

② 文書のポイントをメモし，わからなかった語句や文法をチェックしましょう。

	要素	内容
❶		
❷		
❸		
❹		
❺		

2回目 文書を読み，wpmを記録しましょう。

3回目 文書を読んでwpmを記録し，次の問題を解きましょう。

1. What is suggested about Mr. Hodgkins?

    (A) He is a repeat customer.

    (B) His order was done over the phone.

    (C) His shipping fee was waived.

    (D) He is supposed to pay after receiving the invoice.

4

リスト

Question 1 refers to the following invoice.　　　🎵 031

---

① Westford Packaging Supplies, Inc.　**Ordered By:** Bill Hodgkins
10883 Inverness Trail　　　　　　　　Dennison Gifts and Souvenirs
Westford, MA 01886　　　　　　　　23497 Mussel Beach Road
(351) 555-8024　　　　　　　　　　Davenport, FL 33836
www.westfordpacksup.com　　　　　(863) 555-2794 ext. 97

② **Invoice No.:** 009723497　　　　**Order Date:** January 15

Item No.	Description	Quantity	Unit Price	Total Price
052305	Box 5"x5"x5"	100	$0.26	$26.00
③ 132820	Box 12"x20"x20"	50	$2.58	$129.00
290543	Masking tape 2' x 110 yds	20	$3.51	$70.20
122412	WP bubble wrap 4" x 100'	10	$50.00	$500.00
			Subtotal:	$725.20
④			Shipping/Handling:	$30.72
			GRAND TOTAL:	**$755.92**

⑤ Thank you for your business!　　　　**Payment is due upon receipt.**

訳　設問1は次の請求書に関するものです。

① Westford Packaging Supplies社　　　注文者：Bill Hodgkins様
Inverness Trail 10883番地　　　　　　　Dennison Gifts and Souvenirs社
郵便番号01886 Massachusetts州Westford市　Mussel Beach通り23497番地
(351) 555-8024　　　　　　　　　　　郵便番号33836 Florida州Davenport市
www.westfordpacksup.com　　　　　　　(863) 555-2794 内線番号97

② 請求書番号：009723497　　　　注文日：1月15日

商品番号	品目	数量	単価	計
052305	箱 5インチ×5インチ×5インチ	100	0.26 ドル	26.00 ドル
③ 132820	箱 12インチ×20インチ×20インチ	50	2.58 ドル	129.00 ドル
290543	マスキングテープ 2フィート×110ヤード	20	3.51 ドル	70.20 ドル
122412	WP気泡緩衝材 4インチ×100フィート	10	50.00 ドル	500.00 ドル
			小計：	725.20 ドル
④			送料/手数料：	30.72 ドル
			総額：	**755.92 ドル**

⑤ お取引ありがとうございます！　　　お受け取り次第，代金をお支払い願います。

語句　□ ordered by 〜　〜より注文された
　　　□ MA（= Massachusetts）アメリカ・マサチューセッツ州
　　　□ FL（= Florida）アメリカ・フロリダ州　□ ext.（= extension）内線（番号）
　　　□ description 品目，記載事項　□ quantity 量　□ unit price 単価
　　　□ ”（= inch）インチ（単位）　□ masking tape マスキングテープ
　　　□ '（= feet）フィート（単位）　□ yd（= yard）ヤード（単位）
　　　□ bubble wrap 気泡緩衝材　□ subtotal 小計　□ shipping 送料
　　　□ handling 手数料　□ grand total 総計

4
リスト

■■ メモ例

	要素	内容
❶	会社情報	左側：受注した会社情報 右側：発注した会社情報
❷	日付など	請求書番号，発注日
❸	発注内容	品名，数量，単価，合計
❹	合計	小計，送料・手数料，総計
❺	備考	請求書受け取り後に支払い

■■ 設問の解答・解説

1.

What is suggested about Mr. Hodgkins?
(A) He is a repeat customer.
(B) His order was done over the phone.
(C) His shipping fee was waived.
(D) He is supposed to pay after receiving the invoice.

Hodgkins さんについて何が示されていますか。
(A) リピート客である。
(B) 注文は電話で行われた。
(C) 送料は免除された。
(D) 請求書受領後に支払いを行う。

正解　(D)

解説　Hodgkins さんについて示されていることが問われています。❺に「お受け取り次第，代金をお支払い願います」とあるので，ここから(D)が正解だとわかります。ここでのdueは「支払われるべき」という意味で使われています。(A)は2回目以降の購入だという根拠がありません。(B)，(C)についても注文が電話で行われたという記載はなく，また送料は手数料込みで30.72ドルと明記されており免除されていないため，いずれも不正解です。

語句　□ repeat customer リピート客　□ over the phone 電話で
　　　□ waive（規則など）を適用するのを控える
　　　□ be supposed to *do* 〜することになっている

5 テキストメッセージ・チャット

テキストメッセージ・チャットには，スマートフォンなどの画面に2人のメッセージのやりとりが示されたものや，3人以上によるチャットなどがあります。口語表現も含まれ，「意図を問う問題」（p.276～）が出題されるのが特徴です。

POINT 会話のようなメッセージのやりとりを意識しよう。

このタイプの文書は，パソコンやタブレットの画面のレイアウトで示されていることが多く，指示文にも text message / text-message chain / online chat discussion などと書かれているので容易に判別できます。まずは例を見てみましょう。

例 **Questions XX-XX** refer to the following text-message chain. 　♪ 032

Pete Hamm　　　8:50 A.M.　── 発言者の名前と時刻。人数をチェックしよう（今回は2人）
Thanks for giving that presentation yesterday. The new recruits really seem to have enjoyed it.

Anessa Day　　　8:51 A.M.　　　└ 発言内容 ┘
Wow, I'm glad to hear that. They were a really friendly group. I'm sure they'll make great customer service representatives.

Pete Hamm　　　8:53 A.M.
I get that feeling, too. By the way, one of them asked if she could have the slides from the class yesterday. She wants to review them on her own.

Anessa Day　　　8:54 A.M.
I can do better than that.　── このタイプに特徴的な口語っぽい表現。前後から意味を把握！

Pete Hamm　　　8:56 A.M.
What do you mean?

Anessa Day　　　8:59 A.M.
I had James Nichol record the presentation on video. I was planning on giving you a copy so that you could use it in future.

└ 次の展開を示唆（プレゼン動画をシェアするのかな？）

●テキストメッセージ・チャットの構成例

❶発言者の名前と時刻 ❷発言内容
（以下，❶・❷の繰り返し）

文書は会話のようなメッセージのやりとりで展開されるため，リスニングセクションのPart 3（会話問題）を読むようなイメージで取り組むとよいでしょう。平易な表現で書かれていることが多く，他のタイプの文書よりも読み進めやすいのが特徴です。一方で，口語表現の中には，知らないと意味が取りにくいものもあります。なじみのない表現が出てきた場合は，前後の文脈から推測して読み進めましょう。

また，やりとりの最後では，今後の展開などが示され，その部分が問われる傾向があります。文書の結論をよくチェックするようにしましょう。

訳 設問XX-XXは次のテキストメッセージのやりとりに関するものです。

Pete Hamm 午前8時50分
昨日はプレゼンをありがとうございました。新入社員たちも本当に楽しんでいたようです。

Anessa Day 午前8時51分
ああ，それはうれしいですね。彼らは本当に友好的なグループでした。きっと素晴らしい顧客サービス担当者になると思います。

Pete Hamm 午前8時53分
私もそう感じています。ところで，彼らのうちの1人が昨日の講義のスライドをもらえないかと尋ねてきました。彼女は自分で復習をしたいようです。

Anessa Day 午前8時54分
もっといいことをしてあげられますよ。

Pete Hamm 午前8時56分
どういう意味ですか。

Anessa Day 午前8時59分
James Nicholさんにプレゼンをビデオに撮ってもらいました。今後使えるように，そのコピーをあなたに差し上げようと思っていたのです。

語句 □ recruit 新入社員 □ customer service 顧客サービス
□ representative 担当者，代表者 □ slide スライド □ class 講義，授業
□ review ～を復習する □ on *one's* own 自分で □ in future 今後，この先

攻略法まとめ テキストメッセージ・チャット

• Part 3のような会話のやりとりを意識しよう。
• 口語表現は前後の文脈から意味をくみ取ろう。

5

テキストメッセージ・チャット

1回目 ① 次の文書をきちんと理解しながら読み，wpmを記録しましょう。

※wpmの算出方法と記録はp.109参照

Question 1 refers to the following online chat discussion.

Jasper Simon   11:06 A.M.

1 There were some great points made in the feedback meeting with Mr. Miller this morning. Let's get the work done as soon as possible. Does everyone know what to do?

Alyssa Roberts   11:08 A.M.

2 Yes. I'll make changes to the presentation handouts.

Jasper Simon   11:09 A.M.

3 Great. I'll proofread it. Do you think it will be ready by tomorrow at 3 P.M.?

Alyssa Roberts   11:10 A.M.

4 Thank you, Jasper. I think I can make it by then.

Kevin Nakajima   11:11 A.M.

5 I will work on the prototype. It won't take us long to change the color and resize the logo.

Jasper Simon   11:12 A.M.

6 That's good to hear. I guess we can get everything ready by tomorrow evening.

(122words)

② 文書のポイントをメモし，わからなかった語句や文法をチェックしましょう。

	発言者	発言内容
❶		
❷		
❸		
❹		
❺		
❻		

2回目 文書を読み，wpmを記録しましょう。

3回目 文書を読んでwpmを記録し，次の問題を解きましょう。

1. What is indicated about Mr. Nakajima?

    (A) He will alter the model's appearance.

    (B) He will repair parts of a device.

    (C) He will print out some handouts.

    (D) He will brainstorm ideas for a new logo.

Question 1 refers to the following online chat discussion.

🎵 033

×

Jasper Simon　　　　11:06 A.M.

① There were some great points made in the feedback meeting with Mr. Miller this morning. Let's get the work done as soon as possible. Does everyone know what to do?

Alyssa Roberts　　　　11:08 A.M.

② Yes. I'll make changes to the presentation handouts.

Jasper Simon　　　　11:09 A.M.

③ Great. I'll proofread it. Do you think it will be ready by tomorrow at 3 P.M.?

Alyssa Roberts　　　　11:10 A.M.

④ Thank you, Jasper. I think I can make it by then.

Kevin Nakajima　　　　11:11 A.M.

⑤ I will work on the prototype. It won't take us long to change the color and resize the logo.

Jasper Simon　　　　11:12 A.M.

⑥ That's good to hear. I guess we can get everything ready by tomorrow evening.

訳　設問1は次のオンラインチャットの話し合いに関するものです。

Jasper Simon　　　　午前11時06分
① 今朝のMillerさんとのフィードバックミーティングで，素晴らしい指摘がいくつかあった。できるだけ早く終わらせよう。みんな，自分のやるべきことはわかっているかい？

Alyssa Roberts　　　　午前11時08分
② はい。私はプレゼンの資料を修正します。

Jasper Simon　　　　午前11時09分
③ 素晴らしい。私がそれを校正しよう。明日の午後3時までに準備できるかい？

Alyssa Roberts　　　　午前11時10分
④ ありがとうございます，Jasperさん。そのときまでにできると思います。

Kevin Nakajima　　　　午前11時11分
⑤ 私が試作品を担当します。色やロゴのサイズの変更にはそれほど時間はかからないでしょう。

Jasper Simon　　　　午前11時12分
⑥ それは良かった。明日の夕方までに全て準備できそうだね。

語句 □ feedback フィードバック □ get ～ done ～を終わらせる
□ make changes to ～ ～を変更する □ proofread ～を校正する
□ work on ～ ～に取り組む □ prototype 試作品 □ resize ～のサイズを変更する
□ That's good to hear. それは良かった。 □ guess ～と推測する

■■ メモ例

	発言者	発言内容
❶	Jasper Simon	今後のアクションをメンバーに確認
❷	Alyssa Roberts	資料を修正する
❸	Jasper Simon	それを校正する，明日の3時までにできる？
❹	Alyssa Roberts	できる
❺	Kevin Nakajima	試作品を担当する
❻	Jasper Simon	良かった，明日の夕方までに完了しそう

5

テキストメッセージ・チャット

■■ 設問の解答・解説

1.

What is indicated about Mr. Nakajima?
(A) He will alter the model's appearance.
(B) He will repair parts of a device.
(C) He will print out some handouts.
(D) He will brainstorm ideas for a new logo.

Nakajimaさんについて何が述べられていますか。
(A) 試作品の外観を変更する。
(B) 装置の部品を修理する。
(C) 資料を印刷する。
(D) 新しいロゴのアイデアを引き出す。

正解 (A)

解説 Nakajimaさんについて述べられていることが問われています。❺に「試作品を担当し，色やロゴのサイズを変える」とあるので，これを言い換えた(A)が正解です。文中のchangeがalterに，prototypeがmodelに，color, logoがappearanceにそれぞれ言い換えられている点に注意しましょう。

語句 □ alter ～を変える □ model 見本，ひな形 □ appearance 外観 □ device 装置
□ brainstorm ～をブレーンストーミングにかける

6 広告・宣伝／プレスリリース

文書タイプ別攻略法1「簡単な案内・お知らせ」で取り上げた「広告」は視覚的要素が多かったのに対し，ここで取り上げる「広告」は文章メインで情報量が多いのが特徴です。「プレスリリース」は報道機関に新商品や新規事業に関する情報や展望を発表するものです。それぞれの性質を知り，限られた時間で読み切れるようにしていきましょう。

POINT 1 広告・宣伝は「誰」が「何を広告・宣伝したいのか」に注意して読もう。

広告・宣伝の場合は，「誰」が「何を広告・宣伝したいのか」を把握します。まず，「化粧品販売会社」「不動産会社」などの「会社情報」を探しましょう。そして，「何を広告したいのか」に注目します。広告・宣伝なので，ライバル社にはない，差別化された内容（付加価値）が書かれていることが多いです。

では，広告の例を見ていきましょう。

例 **Questions XX-XX** refer to the following advertisement.　♪ 034

The International Gazette is hiring a journalist at our office in Bangkok!

❶ Are you interested in pursuing a career in journalism?
Do you love to travel?
This may be the job for you! Read on:

└─ 冒頭から何の広告か把握しよう（求人広告だな…）

❷ (A) The International Gazette is looking for candidates with at least 2 years' experience in journalism. Our top requirement is an excellent command of English. (B) The successful applicant will be assertive, adaptable, and a rapid learner, making him or her an asset to the team right away. After working for 2 years at our office in Bangkok, there will be an opportunity to transfer to the Singapore branch as a new home base for covering assignments all over Asia. (C) If you are interested, visit www.internationalgazette.com and complete an online application form. Also, be sure to attach the following documents: a résumé, university transcripts, recommendation letters, and a selection of previously written articles.

└─ (A) 応募要件を確認！
(B) 具体的な業務内容なども出てくるのでチェック！
(C) 応募者はどうする？を確認！（たいていは連絡先＋提出物情報あり）

●広告の構成例

❶タイトル&導入

❷広告内容

(A) 応募要件
(B) 具体的な業務内容
(C) 応募するには

POINT 2 プレスリリースは「何を知らせようとしているか」と「次の展望」に注意しよう。

プレスリリースについては次ページからのExerciseで具体的に取り上げますが，「新商品の発表」など，プレスリリース特有の「ミッション」があり，根本的な部分では広告と似た発想を持っています。その商品がなぜ生まれ，それにより消費者の生活はどうなるのかなど，特定のテーマに沿って文章が展開されますので，テーマを押さえ，次の展開を意識して読みましょう。

6

広告・宣伝／プレスリリース

訳 設問XX-XXは次の広告に関するものです。

**International Gazette社が
Bangkok事務所の記者を募集！**

報道のキャリアを積みたいですか？
旅行は好きですか？
そんなあなたにうってつけの仕事です！以下をお読みください。

International Gazette社は少なくとも2年の報道の経験を持つ人材を探しています。最重要要件は英語が堪能なことです。合格者は積極的で適応能力があり，素早く学習できて，すぐに組織にとって貴重な人材となる人です。Bangkok事務所で2年勤務した後は，新たにアジア全域の業務を担う本拠地となるSingapore支社への異動のチャンスがあります。興味がありましたら，www.internationalgazette.com にアクセスしてオンライン応募フォームにご記入ください。また，次の文書も必ず添付してください：履歴書，大学の成績証明書，推薦状，過去に書いた記事のえり抜き。

語句
□ journalist ジャーナリスト，報道記者　□ pursue ～を追求する
□ journalism ジャーナリズム，報道　□ candidate 候補者　□ requirement 要件
□ command of English 英語運用能力　□ successful applicant 合格者
□ assertive 積極的な　□ adaptable 順応性のある　□ asset 貴重な人材
□ transfer to ～ ～に異動する　□ home base 本拠地　□ assignment 業務，任務
□ attach ～を添付する　□ résumé 履歴書　□ transcript 成績証明書

攻略法まとめ 広告・宣伝／プレスリリース

• 広告・宣伝は，「誰」が「何を広告・宣伝したいのか」に注意して読もう。

• プレスリリースは「何を知らせようとしているか」と「次の展望」に注意しよう。

Exercise

指示に従って，以下の文書を3回読みましょう。

1回目 ① 次の文書をきちんと理解しながら読み，wpmを記録しましょう。

※wpmの算出方法と記録はp.109参照

Question 1 refers to the following press release.

❶ Up-and-coming juice maker SqueezFresh has just announced that they will begin exporting their products to Southeast Asia this fall. ❷ According to several surveys conducted by the company over the last few years, Mango Passion Juice is their most popular drink and has been selected as the product with which to test new markets overseas. Following this, SqueezFresh plans to try three more flavors there: Sour Apple, Cranberry Grape, and Pomegranate Blueberry. Going forward, construction of a SqueezFresh factory in Hanoi is slated to begin next July. Director Julie Ames will transfer to the new factory to hire and train local employees. ❸ SqueezFresh will post updates to their Web site regularly, so check there often for breaking news: www.squeezfresh.com.

(118words)

② 文書のポイントをメモし，わからなかった語句や文法をチェックしましょう。

	要素	内容
❶		
❷		
❸		

2回目 文書を読み，wpm を記録しましょう。

3回目 文書を読んで wpm を記録し，次の問題を解きましょう。

1. What is implied about SqueezFresh?

    (A) It offers flavors only available in Southeast Asia.

    (B) Its first store will be opened next July.

    (C) It will expand the employment in Hanoi.

    (D) Its headquarters will be renovated.

6

広告・宣伝／プレスリリース

Question 1 refers to the following press release.

🎵 035

❶ Up-and-coming juice maker SqueezFresh has just announced that they will begin exporting their products to Southeast Asia this fall. ❷ According to several surveys conducted by the company over the last few years, Mango Passion Juice is their most popular drink and has been selected as the product with which to test new markets overseas. Following this, SqueezFresh plans to try three more flavors there: Sour Apple, Cranberry Grape, and Pomegranate Blueberry. Going forward, construction of a SqueezFresh factory in Hanoi is slated to begin next July. Director Julie Ames will transfer to the new factory to hire and train local employees. ❸ SqueezFresh will post updates to their Web site regularly, so check there often for breaking news: www.squeezfresh.com.

訳 設問1は次のプレスリリースに関するものです。

❶ 新進気鋭のジュースメーカーSqueezFresh社はこの秋から東南アジアへの製品輸出を開始すると発表しました。❷ ここ数年会社が行ったいくつかの調査によると、マンゴーパッションジュースが一番人気で、これが海外の新市場で試す商品に選ばれました。これに続き、SqueezFresh社は現地でさらに3つの味を試す予定で、それがサワーアップル、クランベリーグレープ、そしてザクロブルーベリーです。今後は、HanoiでSqueezFresh社の工場建設が来年7月から始まる予定です。Julie Ames部長が新工場に異動し、現地で従業員の採用、教育に当たります。❸ SqueezFresh社は定期的にウェブサイトに最新情報を掲載しますので、www.squeezfresh.comにて最新ニュースをこまめにチェックしてください。

語句 □ up-and-coming 新進気鋭の、将来有望な　□ export 〜を輸出する
□ conduct 〜を実施する　□ representative 代表する物〔人〕
□ going forward 今後は、将来は　□ be slated to *do* 〜する予定である
□ breaking news 最新ニュース、ニュース速報

🔴 メモ例

	要素	内容
❶	導入	ジュースメーカーが東南アジアへの輸出を開始
❷	本題	・一番人気のジュースでまず勝負する ・その後3つの味を出す ・Hanoiで工場建設 ・Julie Ames部長が異動、現地で従業員を採用・教育
❸	まとめ	詳しくはウェブでチェック

:: 設問の解答・解説

1.

What is implied about SqueezFresh?	SqueezFresh社について何が示唆されていますか。
(A) It offers flavors only available in Southeast Asia.	(A) 東南アジアでしか手に入らない味がある。
(B) Its first store will be opened next July.	(B) 来年の7月に最初の店舗が開店する。
(C) It will expand the employment in Hanoi.	(C) Hanoiでの雇用を拡大する。
(D) Its headquarters will be renovated.	(D) 本社が改装される。

正解 (C)

解説 SqueezFresh社について示されていることが問われています。❷の下線部に「Hanoiでの工場建設が始まる」「部長が異動して現地従業員の採用と教育を行う」とあり，Hanoiでの雇用が拡大することが示唆されています。よって (C)が正解です。(A)の「東南アジアでしか手に入らない」という記載はありません。(B)の「来年の7月」はHanoiでの工場建設が始まる時期です。(D)は本社に関する記載がなく，いずれも不正解です。

語句 □ expand ～を拡大する □ employment 雇用 □ headquarters 本社

6

広告・宣伝／プレスリリース

7 ウェブページ

Part 7で出題される「ウェブページ」には，企業の広告や求人情報，各種団体のイベントの詳細など，さまざまな情報が示されています。ウェブページの構成をしっかり把握し，的確にリーディングできるようにしていきましょう。

POINT ウェブページ特有のURLやタブ（見出し），リンクなどに注意しよう。

ウェブページには，URL（ウェブサイトの住所に当たるもの）や，タブ（インデックスのような見出し）があるのが特徴です。特にタブは，本文の内容を把握するためのヒントになります。また，他のタブにある情報から，このウェブページに掲載されている内容を一覧することができます。ウェブページにはこのほか，他のページへのリンクなどがある場合もあります。これらも見逃さないようにしましょう。

本文については，ウェブページだから特にこうだ，ということはありません。広告・宣伝などと同様に読み進めていきましょう。

例 **Questions XX-XX** refer to the following Web page. ♪ 036

●ウェブページの構成例

❶URL
❷タブ（今開いているページが何かをチェック） ＊左側に，縦に並んでいる場合もあります。
❸本文

訳 設問XX-XXは次のウェブページに関するものです。

---

http://www.divingdepot.com/contact-us

Diving Depot社

ホーム　　　弊社について　　　製品　　　サービス　　　| **お問い合わせ** |

Diving Depot社は，プロの方，アマチュアの方を問わず，ダイビング用品を提供してきたハワイ随一のオンライン販売会社で，過去10年間，堅調に売り上げを伸ばしてきました。これは，製造業者と協力して最安値を実現するだけでなく―その価格でお客さまに直接お届けします―製品のブランドを知り尽くすことで，お客さまのニーズに合ったものをご提案できているからです。もしお送りした用具がうまく動作しない，またはぴったり合わない場合は，弊社の優秀なお客さま担当係にご連絡ください。すぐに問題を解決，あるいは返金いたします。

お電話ください：(888) 555-2347
オンラインチャット：www.divingdepot.com/online-chat
Eメール：customercare@divingdepot.com

語句 □ supplier 供給会社，販売会社　□ consistently 堅実に，堅調に　□ rise 上昇する
　　　　□ manufacturer 製造業者　□ pass on to ～ ～に渡す　□ directly 直接
　　　　□ inside out 徹底的に　□ gear 用具　□ properly きちんと，正しく
　　　　□ fabulous 素晴らしい　□ fix（問題など）を解決する　□ refund ～を払い戻す

7

ウェブページ

攻略法まとめ ウェブページ

• ウェブページ特有のURLやタブ（見出し），リンクなどに注意しよう。

• 本文自体は他の文書と同様に読み進めよう。

Exercise 指示に従って，以下の文書を3回読みましょう。

1回目 ① 次の文書をきちんと理解しながら読み，wpmを記録しましょう。

※wpmの算出方法と記録はp.109参照

Question 1 refers to the following Web page.

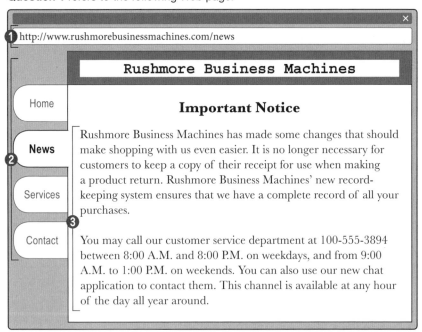

(113words)

② 文書のポイントをメモし，わからなかった語句や文法をチェックしましょう。

	要素	内容
❶		
❷		
❸		

2回目 文書を読み，wpmを記録しましょう。

3回目 文書を読んでwpmを記録し，次の問題を解きましょう。

1. What is indicated about the customer service department?

(A) It is currently training new staff members.
(B) It uses phone numbers to search for customer information.
(C) A customer can arrange same-day product replacement.
(D) A customer can send a message 24 hours a day.

7

ウェブページ

Question 1 refers to the following Web page.

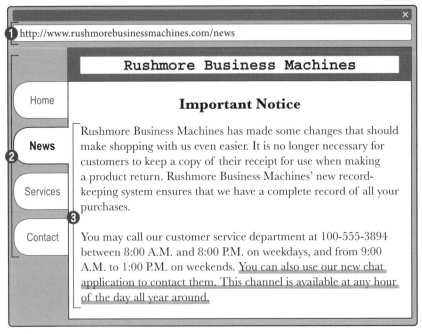

訳 設問1は次のウェブページに関するものです。

http://www.rushmorebusinessmachines.com/news

Rushmore Business Machines社

重要なお知らせ

ホーム
お知らせ
業務内容
お問い合わせ

Rushmore Business Machines社は，当店でのお買い物がさらに簡単になる変更を行いました。お客さまには返品する場合に備えてレシートを保管していただく必要はもうありません。Rushmore Business Machines社の最新の記録保管システムはお客さまのご購入品全てを完全に記録します。

お客さま相談室100-555-3894には平日の午前8時から午後8時まで，および週末の午前9時から午後1時の間にお電話いただけます。また新しいチャットアプリを使って担当者にご連絡いただくこともできます。こちらの通信回線は1年中どの時間帯でもご利用いただけます。

語句 □ even（比較級を強めて）ずっと □ no longer ~ もはや~ではない
□ application アプリ（ケーション） □ available 利用できる □ all year around 年中

┅┅ メモ例

	要素	内容
❶	URL	オンライン画面
❷	社名＆タブ	ある会社の情報ページ
❸	本文	重要なお知らせ ・システムが変わり，レシートの保管が不要に ・新システムは顧客の購買履歴を記録 連絡方法 ・連絡は電話もしくはアプリ（チャット）で ・チャットでの連絡は年中いつでも可

┅┅ 設問の解答・解説

1.

What is indicated about the customer service department? (A) It is currently training new staff members. (B) It uses phone numbers to search for customer information. (C) A customer can arrange same-day product replacement. (D) A customer can send a message 24 hours a day.	お客さま相談部門について何が述べられていますか。 (A) 現在，新しいスタッフを教育している。 (B) 顧客情報を検索するのに電話番号を使用している。 (C) 顧客は同日の商品交換を手配することができる。 (D) 顧客は24時間メッセージを送付することができる。

正解 (D)

解説 お客さま相談部門について述べられていることが問われています。❸の下線部に「新しいチャットアプリは1年中どの時間帯でも利用可能」とあるので，それを言い換えた(D)が正解となります。社員教育，顧客情報検索，同日の商品交換に関する記載は本文にないので，他の選択肢は不正解です。

語句 □ train ～を教育する　□ arrange ～を手配する　□ replacement 交換

8 Eメール・手紙

TOEIC L&Rテストで出題されるEメール・手紙は，ビジネスに関するものがほとんどですが，相手との関係性や話題によって表現が若干異なります。Eメール・手紙がPart 7に占める割合は高いので，読み方をマスターして得点源にしましょう。

POINT 1 やりとりしている人の関係を把握しよう。

まず，ヘッダーから差出人と受取人の関係を把握しましょう。Eメールの場合，メールアドレスの@以下が同じであれば社内の人とのやりとり，異なっていれば社外の人とのやりとりと見当がつきます。手紙の場合は，ヘッダーに差出人の肩書などがわかるキーワードが含まれています。初めてのやりとりか，これまでにも何度かやりとりしているかは，本文から確認していきましょう。Eメールの場合は，件名（Subject）にRe:とある場合，何度目かのやりとりであると推測できます。

例 **Questions XX-XX** refer to the following e-mail. ♪ 038

― 誰から誰に宛てているかチェック！

❶

To:	Stanford Marek<mareks@hks.org>
From:	Francisco Alameda<alamedaf@hks.org>
Date:	September 9
Subject:	Recognition for volunteers

❷ Stanford,

(A) I read an article about the value of volunteers, and one thing in particular struck me deeply. (B) While we rely heavily on monetary donations for our salaries and supplies, volunteers often match or exceed those monetary donations with the amount of time they give us. (C) Therefore, I'd like to recognize our volunteers with a special dinner. I'll bring it up at the board meeting next week. (D) Let me know if you have any thoughts about this.

❸ All the best,

Francisco Alameda

(A) メールの目的をチェック
(B) 何を伝えたいか（理由・背景）をチェック！
(C) 伝えたいことを受けて意見・要望・提案をチェック！
(D) まとめ

POINT 2 主張を整理し，伝えたいメッセージをつかもう。

差出人は「何を伝えたいのか」をはっきりさせながら読み進めましょう。問題であればなぜ起きたか，それをどう解決するかなどを意識して読み進めます。

●Eメールの構成例

❶ヘッダー
❷本文 ・メールの目的…(A) ・具体的な内容…(B)(C) ・まとめ…(D)
❸結び・署名

訳 設問XX-XXは次のEメールに関するものです。

宛先：Stanford Marek<mareks@hks.org>
送信者：Francisco Alameda<alamedaf@hks.org>
日付：9月9日
件名：ボランティアの人たちへのお礼

Stanfordさん

ボランティアの価値に関する記事を読み，1つ特に深く感動したことがあります。我々は給料や備品を寄付金に大きく依存していますが，ボランティアの人たちは自分たちの時間を割くことで，寄付金と同じくらい，またはそれを超えるものを提供してくれています。そこで，特別夕食会を開催してボランティアの人たちにお礼をしたいと思います。この件について来週の役員会で提案します。これに関して何か考えがあれば教えてください。

よろしく。

Francisco Alameda

語句 □ recognition for ～ ～に対する表彰，お礼 □ in particular 特に
□ strike（人）の心を打つ（strike-struck-struck） □ rely on ～ ～に頼る
□ monetary 金銭の □ match ～に匹敵する □ exceed ～を超える
□ amount 量，額 □ recognize ～を表彰する，評価する
□ bring ～ up ～を話題にする □ board meeting 役員会 □ thought 考え

攻略法まとめ Eメール・手紙

- 誰が誰に宛てたものか，差出人と受取人の関係を素早く把握しよう。
- 主張，伝えたいメッセージ（意見・要望・提案など）をつかもう。

8

Eメール・手紙

1回目 ① 次の文書をきちんと理解しながら読み，wpmを記録しましょう。

※wpmの算出方法と記録はp.109参照

Question 1 refers to the following letter.

Ms. Mira Daing
15 Shelford Road #0112
Singapore 288408

❶ Dear Ms. Daing,

❷ Thank you for your application for our journalist position. We at the
International Gazette are impressed by your enthusiasm for journalism
and travel as well as your dedication to completing projects thoroughly.
Unfortunately, applicants not meeting our top requirement cannot be considered
for the position. However, you seem extremely capable of benefitting our
company in other ways. We are likely to have an opening in the general affairs
department in the next two to three months, and we would be pleased if you
would consider applying again at that time. If this is something you may be
interested in, I will grant you an interview when that opportunity arises.
Thank you so much for taking the time to apply to our available position.

❸ All the best,

Gary Reid

Gary Reid
Human Resources Director
International Gazette

(147words)

② 文書のポイントをメモし，わからなかった語句や文法をチェックしましょう。

	要素	内容
❶		
❷		
❸		

2回目 文書を読み，wpmを記録しましょう。

3回目 文書を読んでwpmを記録し，次の問題を解きましょう。

1. What is true about Ms. Daing?

    (A) She is not qualified for the job.

    (B) She has experience working as a journalist.

    (C) She majored in journalism at university.

    (D) She is an avid reader of the newspaper.

8

Eメール・手紙

Question 1 refers to the following letter.　🎵 039

Ms. Mira Daing
15 Shelford Road #0112
Singapore 288408

❶ Dear Ms. Daing,

❷ Thank you for your application for our journalist position. We at the
International Gazette are impressed by your enthusiasm for journalism
and travel as well as your dedication to completing projects thoroughly.
Unfortunately, applicants not meeting our top requirement cannot be considered
for the position. However, you seem extremely capable of benefitting our
company in other ways. We are likely to have an opening in the general affairs
department in the next two to three months, and we would be pleased if you
would consider applying again at that time. If this is something you may be
interested in, I will grant you an interview when that opportunity arises.
Thank you so much for taking the time to apply to our available position.

❸ All the best,

Gary Reid

Gary Reid
Human Resources Director
International Gazette

訳　設問1は次の手紙に関するものです。

Mira Daing 様
Shelford Road 15番地0112号
郵便番号288408 シンガポール

❶ Daing 様

❷ このたびは弊社の記者職にご応募いただきありがとうございました。私どもInternational
Gazette社では貴殿のジャーナリズムと旅行に対する情熱，そしてプロジェクトを完遂させようと
打ち込む姿勢に感銘を受けました。残念ながら，弊社の最重要要件を満たしていない応募者は今回
の職の選考対象にはなりません。しかしながら，貴殿には別途，弊社に貢献していただける多大な
能力があると存じます。弊社では今後2，3カ月中には総務部に欠員が出る見込みですので，その
際に再度応募をご検討いただけますと幸いです。もしこの件にご興味がおありでしたら，その機会
が生じた際に面接をさせていただきます。このたびは弊社の求人にご応募いただく時間を割いてい
ただき，誠にありがとうございました。

❸ 敬具

Gary Reid（署名）
Gary Reid
人事部長
International Gazette社

語句 □ be impressed by ～ ～に感銘を受ける　□ enthusiasm 熱意，熱狂
　　　 □ dedication 献身，専念　□ thoroughly 徹底的に　□ extremely 極めて
　　　 □ be capable of *doing* ～する能力がある　□ benefit ～に利益を与える
　　　 □ be likely to *do* ～しそうである　□ general affairs 総務
　　　 □ grant *A B* A（人）にBを与える　□ arise 生じる

■■ メモ例

	要素	内容
❶	宛先	Daingさん（誰だろう？本文で確認）
❷	本文	・手紙の目的：求人の返答 ・内容①：要件を満たさず不採用 ・内容②：別の部署では採用の可能性あり ・内容③：興味があれば面接があるかもしれない
❸	結び・署名	Gary Reid（人事部長）

■■ 設問の解答・解説

1.

What is true about Ms. Daing?
(A) She is not qualified for the job.
(B) She has experience working as a journalist.
(C) She majored in journalism at university.
(D) She is an avid reader of the newspaper.

Daingさんについて正しいことは何ですか。
(A) その仕事の資格がない。
(B) 記者として働いた経験がある。
(C) 大学でジャーナリズムを専攻した。
(D) その新聞の熱心な読者である。

正解 (A)

解説 手紙の受取人であるDaingさんについて，正しいことが問われています。❷の下線部に「残念ながら最重要要件を満たしていない人は今回の選考で考慮されない」とあるので，ここからDaingさんは応募要件を満たしていないことがわかります。よって正解は(A)です。

語句 □ be qualified for ～ ～の資格がある　□ major in ～ ～を専攻する　□ avid 熱心な

9 レビュー

「レビュー」とは商品やサービスなどに対して，購入者や利用者自身が感想や評価を述べたものです。TOEIC L&Rテストではどのようなレビューが登場するか，見ていきましょう。

POINT 1 レビューの対象を把握し，レビューの観点をイメージしよう。

まず，「レビューの対象が何か」に注目します。「商品」であれば，機能や価格などについて，レストランやホテルなどの「サービス」であれば，部屋，従業員の態度，待ち時間などについて書かれているでしょう。このように，「レビューの対象」がわかると，書かれている観点がイメージしやすくなります。

POINT 2 レビュー本文の展開に注意し，レビュー対象の良い点と悪い点を見極めよう。

レビュー本文の展開は，①全部◎，②全部×，③一部は◎だが一部は×，の3タイプに分かれます。これは★の数などで示される「評価点」とある程度連動しますが，どのようなスタンスの評価かは，レビューの内容をよく確認しましょう。評価点としては高評価（ポジティブ）であっても，ネガティブな内容が書かれているレビューも当然あり，その部分が出題されることが少なくありません。

例 **Questions XX-XX** refer to the following review. 🎵 **040**

---

❶ Cassowaries of the World ── 何のレビューかをチェック
By Simon Geffrey （これだけじゃわからないな…）

Great book! ★★★★★
❷ By Elijah McMasters
Date: June 22, 9:13 P.M. ── 本のレビューらしい。評価点を中心にチェック
（今回は星5つ…べた褒めかな？）

This book on cassowaries covers the bird's history and connection to dinosaurs millions of years ago. The author is obviously very familiar with the bird's area **❸** of origin, as he uses many Australian words and expressions. One downside may be that he uses technical terms and includes details unimportant and uninteresting to amateurs. This is definitely a book for professionals!

└─ 具体的に良い点・悪い点をチェック。全体的に高評価（ポジティブ）だが，素人には向かない（ネガティブ）。

●レビューの構成例

❶レビューの対象
❷評価点・投稿者名など
❸レビュー本文 ・良い点（ポジティブ） ・悪い点（ネガティブ）

訳 設問XX-XXは次のレビューに関するものです。

世界のヒクイドリ
Simon Geffrey 著

素晴らしい本です！ ★★★★★
Elijah McMasters 投稿
日付：6月22日午後9時13分

ヒクイドリに関するこの本は，この鳥の歴史と何百万年も前の恐竜との関連について取り扱っています。著者は明らかにこの鳥の出生地に精通しています，というのも著者はオーストラリアの言葉や表現を多用しているからです。1つ欠点を挙げるとすれば，彼は専門用語を使って素人にはあまり重要ではなく興味もわかないような細かい点まで含めています。これは間違いなく専門家向けの本ですね！

語句 □ cassowary ヒクイドリ（ダチョウに似た飛べない鳥） □ cover（話題など）を取り扱う
□ connection 関係 □ dinosaur 恐竜 □ obviously 明らかに
□ be familiar with 〜 〜に精通している □ origin 起源
□ downside 欠点，否定的側面 □ technical term 専門用語 □ details 詳細
□ unimportant 重要でない □ uninteresting 面白くない
□ amateur 素人，専門外の人 □ definitely 間違いなく □ professional プロ，専門家

9

レビュー

攻略法まとめ レビュー

・レビューの対象をチェックし，何についてのレビューかをイメージしよう。

・レビュー本文から，レビュー対象の良い点・悪い点を捉えよう。

1回目 ① 次の文書をきちんと理解しながら読み，wpmを記録しましょう。

※wpmの算出方法と記録はp.109参照

Question 1 refers to the following review.

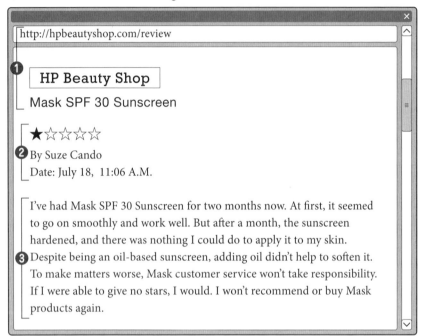

(98 words)

② 文書のポイントをメモし，わからなかった語句や文法をチェックしましょう。

	要素	内容
❶		
❷		
❸		

2回目　文書を読み，wpmを記録しましょう。

3回目　文書を読んでwpmを記録し，次の問題を解きましょう。

1. What does Ms. Cando suggest about HP Beauty Shop?

(A) It offers free shipping service.
(B) Its rating requires at least one star.
(C) It sells their products online.
(D) Its customer service operates 24 hours a day.

解答・解説

Question 1 refers to the following review.

🎵 041

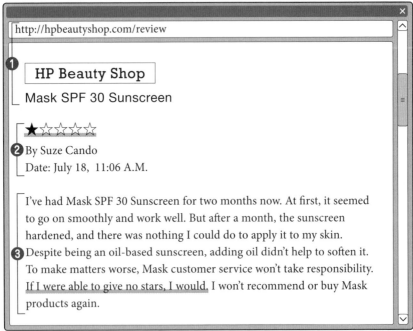

http://hpbeautyshop.com/review

① HP Beauty Shop

Mask SPF 30 Sunscreen

★☆☆☆☆
② By Suze Cando
Date: July 18, 11:06 A.M.

I've had Mask SPF 30 Sunscreen for two months now. At first, it seemed to go on smoothly and work well. But after a month, the sunscreen hardened, and there was nothing I could do to apply it to my skin. **③** Despite being an oil-based sunscreen, adding oil didn't help to soften it. To make matters worse, Mask customer service won't take responsibility. If I were able to give no stars, I would. I won't recommend or buy Mask products again.

訳 設問1は次のレビューに関するものです。

http://hpbeautyshop.com/review
❶ HP Beauty Shop
Mask SPF 30 サンスクリーン

★☆☆☆☆
❷ Suze Cando 投稿
日付：7月18日　午前11時06分

Mask SPF 30 サンスクリーンを購入して2カ月になります。最初のうちは滑らかにのびていい感じでした。しかし1カ月後に硬くなり，どうやっても肌に塗ることができなくなりました。**❸** オイルベースの日焼け止めなのに，オイルを加えても柔らかくなりませんでした。さらにひどいのはMask社のカスタマーサービスが責任を取ろうとしないことです。もし星を付けなくても良かったら，そうしたでしょう。Mask社の製品はお薦めしませんし，二度と買いません。

語句 □ sunscreen 日焼け止め　□ smoothly 滑らかに　□ harden 硬くなる
□ apply ～を塗る　□ skin 肌　□ despite ～にかかわらず
□ soften ～を柔らかくする　□ to make matters worse さらに悪いことに
□ take responsibility 責任を取る

▓▓ メモ例

	要素	内容
❶	レビュー対象	日焼け止め
❷	評価など	★1つ／投稿者の名前／投稿日時
❸	具体的な評価内容	・最初はいいが硬化してすぐ使えなくなった ・カスタマーサービスも対応が悪い ・本当は★1つも付けたくない／二度と買わない，薦めない （→全体的にはネガティブな文章だな…）

▓▓ 設問の解答・解説

1.

What does Ms. Cando suggest about HP Beauty Shop? (A) It offers free shipping service. (B) Its rating requires at least one star. (C) It sells their products online. (D) Its customer service operates 24 hours a day.	Candoさんは HP Beauty Shopについて何を示していますか。 (A) 送料無料のサービスを提供している。 (B) 評価には最低1つ星を付ける必要がある。 (C) 商品をオンラインで販売している。 (D) カスタマーサービスは24時間対応している。

正解 (B)

解説 HP Beauty ShopについてCandoさんが示していることが問われています。レビューを書いたCandoさんは，❷の下線部で商品に対し星1つの評価をしています。また，❸の下線部で仮定法を使い「もし星を付けなくても良かったなら付けなかったのに」と言っています。ここから「最低1つは星を付けなくてはいけなかった」ということが示唆されるので，(B)が正解です。その他の選択肢は本文中に明確な根拠がないので不正解です。

語句 □ free shipping 送料無料　□ rating 評価　□ operate 稼働［営業］する

10 記事

記事は，多くの人があまり得意ではないようで，「苦手だ！」という声をよく耳にします。これは，文章量が多くとっつきにくい話題が多いためです。記事の構成パターンをつかむことで少しでも苦手意識をなくしていきましょう。

POINT 1 段落ごとのキーメッセージを的確に捉えよう。

記事は文章量が多いので，各段落に主に何が書かれているか（キーメッセージ）を抜き出してみましょう。例えば「第1段落：ある会社が利益を上げた」→「第2段落：社長が社員のおかげと言っている」→「第3段落：その中でも最も素晴らしいのはXXさんだ」というように，各段落にはその段落に書かれている内容の中心となるキーメッセージがあります。記事の場合はこれを意識することで，より読みやすくなります。

POINT 2 固有名詞や登場人物を整理しながら読もう。

記事には固有名詞が使われていることが多いので，慣れるようにしましょう。あまりなじみのない英語圏以外の名前や都市名なども出てきますが，読み方に悩んで止まらないように注意！　冒頭の2文字だけ意識して読み進めるなど工夫しましょう。

特に長い記事の場合は，どこに何が書かれていたか，わからなくなりがちです。設問を見たときに正解の根拠が書かれている部分にすぐに戻れるよう，前述のキーメッセージと併せて固有名詞を意識して読み進めましょう。

例 **Questions XX-XX** refer to the following article. 🎵 **042**

---

❶ MARSHALL (May 15) — Friedman, Inc. announced today that CEO Alexander Popowitz is retiring from the company, and Jameson McCoy of Belmont Products will succeed him starting June 1. **❷** Popowitz has been Friedman's CEO for over 18 years, during which time the company has consistently grown ahead of its competitors. **❸** McCoy has been the vice president of Belmont Products for 7 years and has a superior track record of expanding the business overseas. **❹** Friedman, Inc. is already experiencing a rise in stock value with this news. Let's see what this change will bring to the company's future.

●記事の構成例

❶キーメッセージ ❷補足情報① ❸補足情報② ❹補足情報③	キーメッセージ：CEO退任と後任のアナウンスメント。都市と社名，新旧CEOの名前をチェック！ 補足情報①現CEOの功績 補足情報②新CEOの実績 補足情報③株価上昇，今後が期待される

訳 設問XX-XXは次の記事に関するものです。

MARSHALL（5月15日）— Friedman社は本日，CEOのAlexander Popowitz氏が会社から退き，Belmont Products社のJameson McCoy氏が6月1日付けで後任となることを発表した。Popowitz氏は18年間Friedman社のCEOを務め，その間同社は競合他社を制して持続的成長を果たしてきた。McCoy氏はBelmont Products社の副社長を7年間務め，海外への事業拡大に優れた実績を持っている。Friedman社はこのニュースによりすでに株価が上昇している。この変化がFriedman社の将来に何をもたらすかに注目したい。

語句 □ retire 引退する　□ succeed 〜の跡を継ぐ　□ consistently 絶えず，着実に
□ grow 成長する　□ ahead of 〜 〜より優位に，〜の前に
□ competitor 競合他社，競争相手　□ superior 優れた，上質の
□ track record 業績，成績　□ rise 上昇　□ stock value 株価

10
記事

攻略法まとめ 記事

・段落ごとのキーメッセージを的確に捉えよう。

・固有名詞や登場人物を整理しながら読もう。

Exercise 指示に従って，以下の文書を3回読みましょう。

1回目 ① 次の文書をきちんと理解しながら読み，wpmを記録しましょう。

※ wpm の算出方法と記録は p.109 参照

Question 1 refers to the following article.

---

❶ Edinburgh (3 January) — After 18 years, Edinburgh native Ailsa Wallace has returned to her roots. Three months ago, Wallace took over the gourmet seafood restaurant The Lennox upon the retirement of her father, Lennox Boyd, who opened the establishment 45 years ago. Wallace, who studied economics at the University of London, worked as head of marketing at the London Theatre for 13 years.

❷ As soon as she took charge of The Lennox, Wallace gave the interior a new coat of paint, including the murals of local sites that have brought fame to the establishment for decades. And besides adding a private outdoor patio for customers desiring a more natural setting, Wallace introduced an element of entertainment, connecting her past with her present. Every Sunday afternoon, local actors entertain patrons during a 1-hour improvisational theatre performance. The volunteer actors hope to not only benefit The Lennox but also promote the performances they put on through the Edinburgh Theatre Guild.

❸ Wallace's business and marketing finesse, along with her local connections, have proven beneficial thus far, as The Lennox's popularity is soaring. Thanks to this success, Wallace is currently developing plans to open a second location in London, to be called by the same name. The location and timeline are yet unknown. Since returning to Edinburgh, Wallace has stood by her promise to continue her family's commitment to the community. She serves on the board of directors for both the Edinburgh Partnership for Economic Development and the Polytechnic University of Edinburgh.

(248words)

② 文書のポイントをメモし，わからなかった語句や文法をチェックしましょう。

	要素	内容
❶	キーメッセージ	
	補足情報	
❷	キーメッセージ	
	補足情報	
❸	キーメッセージ	
	補足情報	

2回目 文書を読み，wpmを記録しましょう。

3回目 文書を読んでwpmを記録し，次の問題を解きましょう。

10
記事

1. What is true about Ms. Wallace?

    (A) She inherited a family business.

    (B) She was a famous actress in the local theatre guild.

    (C) She studied at the University of Edinburgh.

    (D) She used to play a musical instrument every Sunday.

Question 1 refers to the following article.

♪ 043

❶ Edinburgh (3 January) — After 18 years, Edinburgh native Ailsa Wallace has returned to her roots. Three months ago, <u>Wallace took over the gourmet seafood restaurant The Lennox upon the retirement of her father, Lennox Boyd, who opened the establishment 45 years ago.</u> Wallace, who studied economics at the University of London, worked as head of marketing at the London Theatre for 13 years.

❷ As soon as she took charge of The Lennox, Wallace gave the interior a new coat of paint, including the murals of local sites that have brought fame to the establishment for decades. And besides adding a private outdoor patio for customers desiring a more natural setting, Wallace introduced an element of entertainment, connecting her past with her present. Every Sunday afternoon, local actors entertain patrons during a 1-hour improvisational theatre performance. The volunteer actors hope to not only benefit The Lennox but also promote the performances they put on through the Edinburgh Theatre Guild.

❸ Wallace's business and marketing finesse, along with her local connections, have proven beneficial thus far, as The Lennox's popularity is soaring. Thanks to this success, Wallace is currently developing plans to open a second location in London, to be called by the same name. The location and timeline are yet unknown. Since returning to Edinburgh, Wallace has stood by her promise to continue her family's commitment to the community. She serves on the board of directors for both the Edinburgh Partnership for Economic Development and the Polytechnic University of Edinburgh.

訳 設問1は次の記事に関するものです。

❶ Edinburgh（1月3日）— 18年の時を経て，Edinburgh出身のAilsa Wallaceさんは故郷に戻ってきた。3カ月前，<u>Wallaceさんは高級シーフードレストランのThe Lennoxを，父親であり，45年前に創業したLennox Boyd氏の引退に伴い引き継いだ。</u>Wallaceさんは London大学で経済学を学び，London劇場のマーケティング部長を13年間務めた。

❷ The Lennoxを引き継ぐとすぐに，Wallaceさんは，長年レストランに名声をもたらしてきた地元の風景を描いた壁画を含めて，内装を塗り直した。また，より自然な雰囲気を求める客のために専用の野外テラスを作ったのに加えて，エンターテインメント要素も取り入れ，自身の過去と現在を結び付けた。毎週日曜日の午後に，地元の俳優たちが1時間の即興劇を上演し，常連客を楽しませている。そのボランティア俳優たちは，The Lennoxに寄与するだけではなく，Edinburgh Theatre Guildで上演する興行の宣伝にもなることを期待している。

❸ The Lennoxの人気は急上昇しており，地元の人脈にも支えられたWallaceさんの経営戦略が，これまでのところ効果を上げていることを証明している。この成功により，Wallaceさんは現在Londonに2番目の店舗をオープンさせる計画を策定しており，同じ店名になる見込みだ。場所や時期については未定である。Edinburghに戻ってから，Wallaceさんは一家で地域とのかかわりを持ち続けるという約束を守り，Edinburgh 経済開発協力機構とEdinburgh 職業能力開発総合大学校の役員を務めている。

語句 　□ native その土地に生まれた人　□ roots（人・事物の）ルーツ，ふるさと
　　　　□ gourmet（食事などが）高級な，美食家向けの　□ establishment 店，店舗
　　　　□ take charge of ~ ~を担当する，管理する　□ interior 内装　□ mural 壁画
　　　　□ fame 名声　□ for decades 数十年の間　□ besides ~に加えて
　　　　□ patio テラス，中庭　□ desire ~を要望する　□ setting 背景，環境
　　　　□ element 要素　□ entertain ~を楽しませる　□ patron お得意客，常連
　　　　□ improvisational 即興の　□ put on ~（芝居など）を上演する　□ guild 組合，同盟
　　　　□ finesse 策略，手際の良さ　□ along with ~ ~とともに　□ prove ~を証明する
　　　　□ beneficial 有益な　□ thus far これまでのところ　□ soar 急上昇する
　　　　□ stand by ~（約束など）を守る　□ commitment かかわり，関与，献身

██ メモ例

	要素	内容
❶	キーメッセージ	Wallace さんが父親のレストランを引き継ぐ
	補足情報	Wallace さんは故郷 Edinburgh に戻ってきた London 大学で経済学を学び，マーケティングの仕事に就いた
❷	キーメッセージ	Wallace さんがレストランで行った改革
	補足情報	内装一新，エンタメ要素を入れる 地元俳優とも WINWIN
❸	キーメッセージ	Wallace さん才能あり＋2店舗目オープンを計画
	補足情報	Wallace さんの信条：地域コミュニティーに貢献

10
記事

██ 設問の解答・解説

1.

What is true about Ms. Wallace?
(A) She inherited a family business.
(B) She was a famous actress in the local theatre guild.
(C) She studied at the University of Edinburgh.
(D) She used to play a musical instrument every Sunday.

Wallace さんについて正しいことは何ですか。
(A) 家業を継いだ。
(B) 地元の演劇協会の有名な女優だった。
(C) Edinburgh 大学で勉強した。
(D) 以前は毎週日曜日に楽器を演奏した。

正解 (A)

解説 Wallace さんについて正しいことが問われています。❶の下線部に「父親の経営していたレストランを引退時に引き継いだ」とあるので，これを言い換えた (A) が正解です。文中の take over が選択肢では inherit，restaurant が family business と言い換えられていることにも注目しましょう。なお，Wallace さんは女優ではなくレストラン経営者なので (B) は不正解です。また，Edinburgh 大学ではなく London 大学を出ているので (C) も不正解です。(D) については本文中に記載がありません。

語句 　□ inherit ~を引き継ぐ　□ actress 女優

濱﨑潤之輔＆大里秀介のパワーアップ対談②

自分の「解き方」を見つけよう

編集部（以下，編）：Part 7の解き方は，文書の前にまず設問を読んだり，設問は読まずに文書から読んだり，人によってさまざまだと思います。お二人のPart 7の解き方も，それぞれ異なっていますね。ご自身のPart 7の解き方について，まずはお聞かせください。

大里秀介（以下，大）：僕の場合は，Part 7の最後にあるトリプルパッセージ（3つの文書の問題）から解答しています。Part 5とPart 6を解いたら，Part 7は設問196〜200のセットから解き始めて，前に前に戻っていくというスタイルですね。

以前は前から順番に解いていましたが，トリプルパッセージのように分量が多い問題を最後に残すとしんどいと感じるようになったのが解き方を変えた理由です。試験時間残り5分の時点でトリプルパッセージが1題残っているのと，シングルパッセージが2題残っているのとでは，設問数自体は同じ5問でも，後者の方が僕は楽だったんです。ところで，濱﨑さんはPart 7の解答時間が比較的短いですよね。

濱﨑潤之輔（以下，濱）：多分，短いと思います。

大：僕は比較的長い方で，60分弱をPart 7に使います。Part 7は文書の中に必ず答えが書いてあるので，たとえ時間がかかっても，きちんと読んで正解を探したいんです。設問を先に読むか読まないかですが，985点くらいまでは設問を先に読んで，設問の答えを探しながら文書を読んでいました。でも，設問の答えがなかなか見つからないと，焦って読み方が荒くなって内容がきちんと頭に入らない…ということがよくありました。そこで，文書を最初から最後まで1回ちゃんと読んで，それから設問を読んで解くという方法に切り替えてみたんです。すると，文書の内容がしっかり頭に入るようになり，設問を読んだ時点で「この設問の答えはここにある」とわかるようになりました。結果的に速く解けるようになり，解答の精度も良くなりました。

編：なるほど。文書を1回全部読んでから解くには，情報の処理能力やリテンション（文書の内容を記憶する）力を高める必要がありそうですね。

大：はい。文書の内容をイメージして覚えておくというのは，結構大変なことだと思います。僕の場合は，自分がこうして問題を作成する立場になり，出題者の視点を持つようになったことで，解答者として文書を読んでいるときも，設問で問われそうな場所が何となくわかるようになってきて，それで文書の内容を覚えておくことに対する負荷は減りました。

編：「正解に関係する場所」が感覚的にわかるようになってきたんですね。

大：Part 7では記事やメール，手紙など，色々なタイプの文書が出ますが，そのタイプの中にもそれぞれよくある展開ってある

と思うんですよね。それを意識しながら読むといいですね。例えばメールで I am writing to inform you that...「〜ということをお知らせするために書いています」とあったら「ああ，何か知らせたいんだな，何かな？」という意識で読む，というように，ポイントを押さえてメリハリをつけて読むと，意外とボリュームのある文書でも内容をきちんと把握しながら読むことができます。

先日も「長文が苦手です」という相談があったのですが，一つ一つを丁寧に読むことと，段落を意識して読むことをアドバイスしました。Part 7の文書は段落で区切ると大体3つか4つになりますが，1つずつにはそんなにボリュームはありません。1つの文書はその1つずつの集合体と捉えれば，長文に対する苦手意識や抵抗感は減るのかなと思います。

後は，日頃からいかに英文を読んでいるかが重要です。あまり読みもしないのに，公開テストで点数を取ろうとする方が浅ましい（笑）。正直，「この本を買って，さらっとやって満点取っちゃいました」なんて絶対ウソですよね。やっぱり，苦手だと思ったら毎日読まないと。筋トレだってそうですよね。筋トレのやり方を教わったから筋肉がつくわけじゃなくて，ちょっとずつ体を動かしてこそ力がつくわけです。多分，長文読解も毎日読むからこそ，力がつくのだと思います。

編：続いて，濵﨑先生の解き方についてもお聞かせください。

濵：まず1問目の設問だけは読んで，文書が短めのシングルパッセージだったら最後まで全部読みます。文書を読んでいる途中で1問目の解答の根拠が出てきたら，すぐに解答をマークします。そうじゃない場合は，文書を全部読み終えてから1問目を解答します。次に2問目の設問を読みます。文書はすでに全部読んでその設問に対応する内容は覚えているので，すぐに選択肢を見て解答します。2問付き，3問付きの問題はこういう感じで解いています。

心掛けているのは，とにかく文書を何度も読み返さないことです。速いスピードで読んだとしても，途中で内容がわからなくなって戻ってもう1回読んでいたら，結局2倍の量，読むことになりますよね。だったら，スピードを落としてでも1回でしっかりと理解した方が速いじゃないですか。ですから，頭の中で音読しながら1回で英文を全部理解するつもりで読んでいます。

ダブルパッセージとトリプルパッセージは，2問目くらいまではシングルパッセージの解き方と同じです。3問目くらいから，1つ目の文書の中に根拠が出てこないなと思う設問が出てくるので，この時点で2つ目の文書に進み，2つ目の文書を最初から最後まで全部読んで，解きます。このやり方は，一度にたくさん読まなきゃいけないから初めは大変ですが，慣れれば4問付き，5問付

きの問題だったら，3問目，4問目からはパパッと解けるようになります。多分，3問目，4問目は5秒とか10秒以内で解いています。逆に1問目はおそらく1分では解けていなくて，2分とか2分半かかっています。それでも，総合的には速く解答できていますね。

編：ちなみにPart 7はトータルで何分くらいかけていらっしゃいますか。

濵：40分くらいじゃないですか。

編：速いですね！大里先生はPart 7は60分弱ということでしたが，速くてどれくらいですか。

大：50分くらいですね。

編：濵﨑先生は，これが正解って思ったら，もう他の選択肢は見ずに次の設問にいくんですよね。

濵：（A）が正解だったら，もう（B）以下は読みません。ラッキーと思って次にいきます。とにかくゴールしたいから。

編：大里先生はその設問の正解が（A）と思っても（B）以下は読まれますか。

大：そうですね。それをやらなかったためにうっかりミスをしたことが過去にあったので，念のために確認しています。解答スピードは落ちるかもしれませんが，それでも時間は余るので，やっています。

編：読者の皆さんも，今，自分が持っている力がフルに発揮できる解き方が見つかる

といいですね。

大：Part 7は時間内に終わらない人も多いと思います。それはおそらく英文を読むスピードが足りていないからなので，「文書タイプ別攻略法」ではwpmを記録するExerciseを入れました。自分がどのくらいのスピードで読んでいるか，しっかり認識するようにしましょう。

公式問題集を見るとPart 7全体の語数は選択肢も入れて平均5500 wordsあります。それを1分間に100 words（100 wpm）の速さで読んだら，文書と設問を読み切るだけで55分かかります。Part 5，6を20分で解いたとしたら，Part 7は読むだけで試験時間が終わってしまう計算です。しかし，1分間に120 words（120 wpm）読めば，1問につき10秒くらい考える時間が生まれます。130 words（130 wpm）くらいだと，もう少し余裕ができます。でも，1分間に130 wordsを読むのは結構つらいです。だからこそ，どれくらいの速さで読めているのか，しっかり認識してほしいです。その上で，一つ一つ丁寧に積み上げていきましょう。定型文は覚え，段落ごとに意味をつかみます。最初は難しくても，少しずつできるようになってきます。

Chapter 2
設問タイプ別攻略法

失敗は成功の糧！
その気持ちで Step by Step!

1 詳細を問う問題

「詳細を問う問題」はPart 7で最もスタンダードな問題で、54問中10～15問程度出題されます。文書から具体的な情報を見つける力が問われていますが、文書の内容をきちんと理解していれば、正解の根拠は見つけやすいのが特徴です。

POINT 1 「何が問われているか」をきちんと把握しよう。

「詳細を問う問題」は、具体的な情報を探したり、参照したりする力を問う問題です。具体的には、以下の点が問われます。

①「誰（Who）」か？

例：Who submitted the report last week?

「先週報告書を提出したのは誰ですか」

— Mr. Sasaki

「Sasakiさんです」

②「いつ（When）」か？

例：When did Mr. Sasaki submit the report?

「Sasakiさんはいつ報告書を提出しましたか」

— Last week

「先週です」

③「どこ（Where）」か？

例：Where did Mr. Sasaki submit the report?

「Sasakiさんはどこに報告書を提出しましたか」

— To the IT department

「IT部にです」

④「何（What）」か？

例：What did Mr. Sasaki submit last week?

「Sasakiさんは先週何を提出しましたか」

— A technical report

「技術報告書です」

⑤「なぜ（Why）」か？

例：Why did Mr. Sasaki submit the report last week?

「Sasakiさんは先週なぜ報告書を提出したのですか」
— His co-worker was on vacation.
「彼の同僚が休暇中だったからです」

⑥「どうやって（How）」か？
例：How did Mr. Sasaki submit the report last week?
「Sasakiさんは先週どのようにして報告書を提出しましたか」
— In person
「直接です」

「詳細を問う問題」は，**「何が問われているか」をきちんと把握すること**，そしてその**正解の根拠を文書から効率よく検索すること**が重要です。

POINT 2 文書を効率よく検索しよう。

「詳細を問う問題」ではPOINT 1で見たような細かな点が問われます。しかし，文書を読む際にこれら詳細を全て記憶しておくことは，脳にかなりの負荷をかけることになります。文書の内容の記憶は後で検索できる程度にとどめ，脳への負荷を軽くしましょう。そして，解答の際は，文書できちんと正解の根拠を確認します。こうすることで，脳の負担を軽くすると同時に，解答の精度を上げることができます。

例えば，設問にWhen did Mr. Sasaki submit the report?「Sasakiさんはいつ報告書を提出しましたか」とあったとしましょう。ここですぐに「ええと，先週だったかな？」と記憶を頼りに正解を選ぶのではなく，「確か先週だったと思うけど，書かれているところをチェックしよう…あ，あった。そうそう，先週だった」と，**必ず文書を確認してから正解を選ぶ**ようにします。

これは，文書中には正解に当たる「先週」以外にも，日時を表す表現が複数登場していると考えられるからです。これらを全て記憶しておくと，脳にかなりの負荷をかけてしまいます。「詳細を問う問題」で問われるような細かい情報は，全て記憶するのではなく，解答の際に「確かこの辺りに正解の根拠が書いてあったな」と検索できる程度の記憶にとどめ，脳への負荷を軽くすることが重要です。

「文書タイプ別攻略法」でメモを取るExerciseを行ったのは，この**「検索できる程度に記憶する」読み方をマスターする**ためでした。「設問タイプ別攻略法」でも，同じようなトレーニングを積んでいくと，コツがつかめてくるでしょう。

それでは例題を解いてみましょう。

To: All employees
From: Hilda Greyson
Date: May 18
Subject: New staff member

Dear All,

I am pleased to announce that we have finally filled the assistant engineer position. The successful applicant's name is Stephanie Walters. She has just finished a 12-month internship at Harper and Donaldson in New York.

Ms. Walters will be starting here on May 25. To welcome her to the company, I have arranged a lunch party in the cafeteria. I hope you will all attend. I have hired a caterer for the party. Just so we know how much food to order, please call Brian Chang in administration by May 20 if you will not be able to attend. His extension is 667.

Sincerely,

Hilda Greyson

1. What are employees invited to do on May 25?
   (A) Attend an award ceremony
   (B) Evaluate a design
   (C) Meet a new staff member
   (D) Apply for a position

まず，文書の概要を確認しましょう。ストーリーが大まかに把握できれば，細かな情報は後で検索できる程度の記憶で構いません。

Question 1 refers to the following memo.

〔メモ〕 ♪ 044

To: All employees ← 全従業員宛てのメモ（TOEICによくあるタイプだな）
From: Hilda Greyson
Date: May 18 ← 日付は設問にかかわるかもしれないのでチェック
Subject: New staff member ← 件名から内容をつかもう。「新しいスタッフ」についてだな

Dear All,

I am pleased to announce that we have finally filled the assistant
└ announce that ～「～ということを知らせる」＝文書の「目的」になることが多いので注意
engineer position. The successful applicant's name is Stephanie
┌ 件名にある「新しいスタッフ」の名前はWaltersさん
Walters. She has just finished a 12-month internship at Harper and

Donaldson in New York.

Ms. Walters will be starting here on May 25. To welcome her to the
└ Waltersさんの初出勤は5月25日
company, I have arranged a lunch party in the cafeteria. I hope you
ランチパーティーが開かれる ┘
will all attend. I have hired a caterer for the party. Just so we know how
└ 参加してほしいようだ
much food to order, please call Brian Chang in administration by May

20 if you will not be able to attend. His extension is 667.
└ ランチパーティーへの出欠を知らせる期日（明後日だな）

Sincerely,

Hilda Greyson

要素		内容
ヘッダー		・全従業員宛てのメモ，5/18付け ・新しいスタッフについて
第1段落	導入	・新入社員（アシスタントエンジニア）が入る ・新入社員の名前と経歴
第2段落	本題	・新入社員の仕事開始日は5/25 ・歓迎会が行われる，従業員は参加を促されている ・ケータリングの関係で，参加可否を連絡してほしい ・担当者の名前と連絡先

次に，設問を確認しましょう。従業員は5月25日に何をするよう勧められているか
が問われています。「5月25日（May 25）」を文書から検索すると，第2段落1文目
に見つかります。この日は新入社員のWaltersさんが働き始める日で，従業員は彼
女の歓迎ランチパーティーに出席を求められていることがわかります。従って，正
解は (C) です。

その他の選択肢については，いずれもこの文書に関連情報がありません。唯一 (D)
が職に関連する内容ですが，空いていたポジションにはすでに，Waltersさんが採
用されているので違います。正解の選択肢がわかったら，このようにその他の選択
肢についても不正解の理由をきちんと確認すると，解答の精度が上がります。

正解と訳 設問1は次のメモに関するものです。

宛先：全従業員
差出人：Hilda Greyson
日付：5月18日
件名：新しいスタッフ

各位，

アシスタントエンジニア職をついに補充したことを喜んでお知らせいたします。合格者の名前は
Stephanie Waltersさんです。彼女はNew YorkのHarper and Donaldson社での12カ月のイン
ターン期間を終了したばかりです。

Waltersさんは，こちらで5月25日から勤務します。彼女をわが社に歓迎するために，社員食堂に
てランチパーティーを企画しました。皆さん全員に参加してもらいたいと思います。パーティーの
ためにケータリング業者に依頼しました。ついては注文する料理の量を把握したいので，もし参加
できない場合は5月20日までに総務部のBrian Changに連絡してください。彼の内線は667で
す。

よろしくお願いします。
Hilda Greyson

1. 従業員は5月25日に何をするよう勧められていますか。
   (A) 表彰式に参加する
   (B) デザインを評価する
   (C) 新しいスタッフを迎える
   (D) 職に応募する

正解 (C)

語句 □ position 職, 役職　□ successful applicant 合格者　□ internship 実習期間
　　□ cafeteria 社員食堂　□ caterer ケータリング [仕出し] 業者
　　□ administration 総務部門, 管理部門　□ extension 内線 (番号)
　　□ award ceremony 表彰式　□ evaluate ～を評価する
　　□ apply for ～　～に応募する

攻略法まとめ 詳細を問う問題

• 「誰が」「いつ」「どこで」など, 何が問われているかを把握しよう。

• 文書を短時間でピンポイントに検索できるよう, どこに何が書いてあるかを押さえた
  読み方をしよう。

次の文書を読み，各設問に対して最も適切な答えを(A)(B)(C)(D)の中から1つ選びなさい。

Questions 1-2 refer to the following e-mail.

To:	Mel Davis <mdavis@foremanplumbing.com>
From:	Greg Smith <gsmith@printone.com>
Date:	June 7
Subject:	RE: Request for estimate

This is an automated reply. I regret that I am not able to respond to your e-mail immediately. I will be out of the office from June 3 to June 14 for my annual vacation. I intend to reply to all e-mail inquiries as soon as I return. If you have an urgent matter, I recommend that you contact my personal assistant Rod Weaver at 555-9321. He will put you in touch with the appropriate staff member.

Sincerely,

Greg Smith
Customer Service
Print One

1. Why is Mr. Smith unavailable on June 7?

   (A) He is on vacation.
   (B) He is visiting a client.
   (C) He has a doctor's appointment.
   (D) He is attending a conference.

2. What should Ms. Davis do in case of an emergency?

   (A) Send a text message
   (B) Call Mr. Smith's mobile phone
   (C) Check an employee directory
   (D) Contact Mr. Smith's secretary

Questions 3-5 refer to the following invitation.

September 9

Ms. Hilary King
RHB Company
742 Hillbridge Crescent
Beaumont, New York 71655

Dear Ms. King,

I am writing to invite you to a banquet at the Columbus Hotel in Beaumont.
It will be held on October 15 from 6:00 P.M. The event will include a speech
by the president of the Beaumont Tourism Association, Ms. Keiko Yamada.
Ms. Yamada has been our president for some 14 years, and during that time,
she has made an amazing contribution to the growth of Beaumont as a tourist
destination. The campaign she led this year with the cooperation of several
local tour companies, restaurants, and accommodation providers has produced
excellent results. Your highway bus services were integral to our success.

This invitation is for you and one other employee at RHB Company. There is
a charge of $50 per person to cover expenses. However, those who reply by
September 20 will receive a 15 percent discount.

Sincerely,

Kate Dawson — Beaumont Tourism Association

---

3. What did Ms. Yamada do this year?

(A) She hired many local people.
(B) She founded the Beaumont Tourism Association.
(C) She coordinated a campaign.
(D) She stayed at the Columbus Hotel.

4. Where does Ms. King work?

(A) At a tourism association
(B) At a transportation company
(C) At a restaurant
(D) At an accommodation provider

5. How can Ms. King get a discount?

(A) By choosing a diet meal option
(B) By becoming a member of the association
(C) By replying to the invitation before a deadline
(D) By filling out an evaluation form

Questions 1-2 refer to the following e-mail.

Eメール・手紙　♪ 045

To:	Mel Davis <mdavis@foremanplumbing.com>
From:	Greg Smith <gsmith@printone.com>
Date:	June 7
Subject:	RE: Request for estimate

❶This is an automated reply. **❷**I regret that I am not able to respond to your e-mail immediately. I will be out of the office from June 3 to June 14 for my annual vacation. I intend to reply to all e-mail inquiries as soon as I return. **❸**If you have an urgent matter, I recommend that you contact my personal assistant Rod Weaver at 555-9321. He will put you in touch with the appropriate staff member.

Sincerely,

Greg Smith
Customer Service
Print One

訳　設問1-2は次のEメールに関するものです。

宛先：Mel Davis <mdavis@foremanplumbing.com>
送信者：Greg Smith <gsmith@printone.com>
日付：6月7日
件名：RE：見積依頼

これは自動返信メールです。申し訳ありませんが，頂いたメールにすぐにご返信できません。6月3日から6月14日まで年次休暇のため不在となります。戻りましたらすぐに全てのメールでのお問い合わせに返信いたします。緊急のご用件がありましたら，私の個人秘書であるRod Weaver宛てに555-9321までご連絡いただくことをお勧めします。彼が適切な職員に取り次いでくれます。

敬具

Greg Smith
お客さまサービス担当
Print One社

語句 □ request 依頼　□ automated reply 自動返信　□ I regret that ～ 残念ながら～
□ immediately 直ちに　□ be out of the office 会社にいない，不在である
□ urgent matter 緊急の用件　□ put *A* in touch with *B* AをBに取り次ぐ，紹介する
□ appropriate 適切な，適任の

1.

詳細を問う問題

Why is Mr. Smith unavailable on June 7?
(A) He is on vacation.
(B) He is visiting a client.
(C) He has a doctor's appointment.
(D) He is attending a conference.

Smithさんはなぜ6月7日に対応することができないのですか。
(A) 休暇中である。
(B) 顧客を訪問している。
(C) 医者の予約がある。
(D) 会議に出席している。

正解 (A)

解説 Smithさんが6月7日にEメールに対応できない理由が問われています。❶に「これは自動返信メールです」とあり，続いて❷に「頂いたメールにすぐには返信できない」「6月3日から14日まで休暇を取る」とあるので，6月7日の時点で受け取ったメールに対応できないのはSmithさんが休暇中だから，ということがわかります。以上から(A)が正解です。

語句 □ on vacation 休暇（中）で

2.

詳細を問う問題

What should Ms. Davis do in case of an emergency?
(A) Send a text message
(B) Call Mr. Smith's mobile phone
(C) Check an employee directory
(D) Contact Mr. Smith's secretary

Davisさんは緊急の場合に何をすべきですか。
(A) テキストメッセージを送る
(B) Smithさんの携帯電話にかける
(C) 従業員名簿を調べる
(D) Smithさんの秘書に連絡する

正解 (D)

解説 Davisさんは緊急時に何をすべきか問われています。❸に「緊急の用件があれば自分の個人秘書であるRod Weaverに連絡を」とあるので，Davisさんは緊急の場合Weaverさんに連絡すればよいということになります。以上から，本文中のpersonal assistantをsecretaryと言い換えた(D)が正解となります。

語句 □ in case of ～ もし～の場合には
□ text message（携帯電話などの）テキスト［ショート］メッセージ
□ directory 住所録，名簿

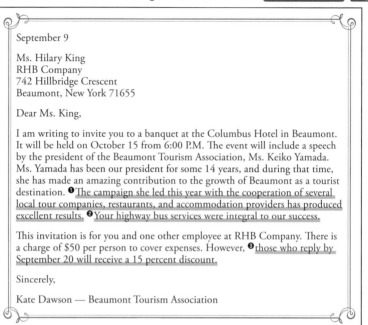

September 9

Ms. Hilary King
RHB Company
742 Hillbridge Crescent
Beaumont, New York 71655

Dear Ms. King,

I am writing to invite you to a banquet at the Columbus Hotel in Beaumont. It will be held on October 15 from 6:00 P.M. The event will include a speech by the president of the Beaumont Tourism Association, Ms. Keiko Yamada. Ms. Yamada has been our president for some 14 years, and during that time, she has made an amazing contribution to the growth of Beaumont as a tourist destination. ❶The campaign she led this year with the cooperation of several local tour companies, restaurants, and accommodation providers has produced excellent results. ❷Your highway bus services were integral to our success.

This invitation is for you and one other employee at RHB Company. There is a charge of $50 per person to cover expenses. However, ❸those who reply by September 20 will receive a 15 percent discount.

Sincerely,

Kate Dawson — Beaumont Tourism Association

訳 設問3-5は次の招待状に関するものです。

9月9日
Hilary King 様
RHB社
Hillbridge Crescent 742番地
郵便番号71655 New York州Beaumont市

King 様
Beaumont市のColumbusホテルでの祝宴にご招待させていただきたく，これを書いています。開催日時は10月15日午後6時からです。このイベントではBeaumont観光協会会長であるKeiko Yamada氏のスピーチがございます。Yamada氏は約14年間にわたって当協会の会長を務め，その間Beaumont市が観光目的地として発展するのに多大な貢献をしてきました。今年，彼女が指揮を取って地元の旅行会社やレストラン，宿泊施設業者と協働で進めたキャンペーンは素晴らしい結果を生んでいます。貴社の高速バスサービスは，私どもの成功に欠かせないものでした。

この招待状は，貴殿ともう1名のRHB社社員の方のためのものです。1名様につき50ドルの会費がかかりますが，9月20日までにご返答いただいた方は15パーセントの割引になります。
敬具
Kate Dawson — Beaumont観光協会

語句 □ banquet 宴会，夕食会　□ tourism association 観光協会
□ accommodation provider 宿泊施設の運営業者　□ cover expenses 費用を賄う

3.

What did Ms. Yamada do this year?	Yamadaさんは今年何をしましたか。
(A) She hired many local people.	(A) たくさんの地元の人を雇用した。
(B) She founded the Beaumont Tourism Association.	(B) Beaumont観光協会を設立した。
(C) She coordinated a campaign.	(C) キャンペーンを取り仕切った。
(D) She stayed at the Columbus Hotel.	(D) Columbusホテルに滞在した。

正解 (C)

解説 今年Yamadaさんが行ったことが問われています。❶に「今年地元の業者との協働キャンペーンを指揮し，成功した」とあるので，彼女が今年行ったのは地元業者と協働したキャンペーンを指揮することだとわかります。正解はそれをcoordinated a campaignと言い換えた(C)です。

語句 □ found ～を設立する　□ coordinate ～を組織［調整］する

4.

Where does Ms. King work?	Kingさんはどこで働いていますか。
(A) At a tourism association	(A) 観光協会
(B) At a transportation company	(B) 運輸会社
(C) At a restaurant	(C) レストラン
(D) At an accommodation provider	(D) 宿泊施設業者

正解 (B)

解説 Kingさんがどこで働いているか問われています。❷に「貴社の高速バスサービス」という記載があるので，ここからKingさんは高速バスサービスを提供する会社に勤めていることがわかります。これをa transportation companyと表現した(B)が正解です。

5.

How can Ms. King get a discount?	Kingさんはどうすれば割引してもらえますか。
(A) By choosing a diet meal option	
(B) By becoming a member of the association	(A) ダイエット食を選ぶことで
(C) By replying to the invitation before a deadline	(B) 協会のメンバーになることで
(D) By filling out an evaluation form	(C) 締め切り前に招待に返答することで
	(D) 評価表に記入することで

正解 (C)

解説 Kingさんはどうすれば割引を受けられるか問われています。❸に「9月20日までに返答した人は15パーセント割引」という記載があるので，一定の期日までに返答すれば割引を受けられることがわかります。ここからその期日をdeadlineと表した(C)が正解となります。

語句 □ diet meal ダイエット食　□ option 選択（肢）　□ evaluation form 評価表

2 情報をもとに推測する問題

このタイプは本文中に正解の根拠がはっきりとは書かれていません。そのため，正解の根拠になると思われる複数の情報から，正解を推測する必要があります。54問中5〜10問程度出題され，正解を導く情報を見極めて「正しく推測する」力が問われる問題です。

POINT 1 質問にmost likelyがあったら注意しよう。

このタイプの問題は，**質問にmost likely「おそらく」という表現が入っている**場合が多いです。というのも，正解と断定できる決定的な表現が本文中になく，情報・状況からして確からしい選択肢が正解となるからです。この**「断定はできないが確からしい」**というのがこのタイプの設問を解く際のポイントになります。

POINT 2 手掛かりとなる情報から正解を推測しよう。

「情報をもとに推測する」と言うと，何だか難しく感じられますが，これは前回学習した「詳細を問う問題」のように，文書の1カ所に正解の根拠がずばり書かれているわけではない，という意味です。従って，**文書全体から手掛かりとなる表現などを探し，推測して問題を解く**必要があります。

例えば，質問がWhere does Mr. Tomas most likely work?「Tomasさんはおそらくどこで働いていますか」だったとしましょう。本文中にTomasさんの職場や職業について，はっきり書かれていなかったとしても，Tomasさんの職場の説明としてstudent「学生」, class「授業」, textbook「教科書」, teach XX「XXを教えている」などの表現が登場していたら，Tomasさんはschool「学校」などのeducational institution「教育機関」で働いている，と推測できます。このような考え方で解くのが「情報をもとに推測する問題」です。

それでは，例題を見てみましょう。

例 題 Question 1 refers to the following text message.

From: Rick Krasinski, Wednesday, 6 November, 2:30 P.M.

Gail, I'm at Evens Paper Company and we're loading all of their old furniture into the truck to take to the recycling center. Mark has had to leave suddenly to deal with a problem at Clarkson Engineering. We helped them relocate to their new office this morning and they can't find a couple of pieces of furniture. Anyway, unless someone comes to give me a hand, I won't be able to load everything into the truck in time. Is there someone you could send?

---

1. Where does Mr. Krasinski most likely work?
   (A) At a moving company
   (B) At a furniture store
   (C) At a recycling center
   (D) At a travel agency

まず，設問を見てみましょう。

1. Where does Mr. Krasinski <u>most likely</u> work?

(A) At a moving company
(B) At a furniture store
(C) At a recycling center
(D) At a travel agency

質問に most likely が含まれていますね。Krasinski さんが「おそらくどこで」働いているかが問われています。従って，間接的な手掛かりから正解を導く必要がありそうです。

では，文書の流れを追っていきましょう。

Question 1 refers to the following text message.

テキストメッセージ・チャット　♪ 047

From: Rick Krasinski, Wednesday, 6 November, 2:30 P.M.
└ 送信者は Krasinski さん

Gail, I'm at Evens Paper Company and we're loading all of their old
　　　Krasinski さんを含む人たちが積み込み作業をしている ┘

furniture into the truck to take to the recycling center. Mark has had to

leave suddenly to deal with a problem at Clarkson Engineering. We

helped them relocate to their new office this morning and they can't find
└ Krasinski さんたちは今朝，別の会社の移転を手伝った

a couple of pieces of furniture. Anyway, unless someone comes to give

me a hand, I won't be able to load everything into the truck in time. Is

there someone you could send?

■■文書の概要

要素	内容
ヘッダー	・送信者は Krasinski さん
本文	・Krasinski さんを含む人たちが積み込み作業中 ・古い家具をトラックに積んでリサイクルセンターに行くところ ・Mark が Clarkson Engineering 社の対応のため離脱 　（今朝，移転を手伝ったがいくつか家具が見つからないようだ） ・Mark の埋め合わせに誰か人をよこしてほしい

「古い家具をリサイクルセンターに運んでいる」

「他の会社の移転を手伝ったところ，家具の何点かが見つからない」

これらの情報から，文書中にはっきりと書かれてはいませんが，Krasinski さんは「引っ越しの手伝い」を職業としていることがわかります。よって (A) At a moving company「引っ越し会社」が正解です。文書には (C) の recycling center「リサイクルセンター」も登場しますが，それは荷物を運ぼうとしている場所で，そこで働いているわけではありません。引っ掛からないようにしましょう。

正解と訳 設問1は次のテキストメッセージに関するものです。

送信者：Rick Krasinski　11月6日（水）午後2時30分

Gail，僕は Evens Paper Company 社にいて，彼らの古い家具を全てリサイクルセンターに運ぶため，トラックに積み込んでいるところだ。Mark が急に Clarkson Engineering 社の問題に対応するために行かなくてはならなくなってしまった。僕らは今朝その会社の新しいオフィスへの移転を手伝ったんだが，家具が何点か見つからないらしい。ともかく，誰か手伝いに来てくれないと，時間内に全部をトラックに積み込めないだろう。誰かよこしてくれないか。

1. Krasinski さんはおそらくどこで働いていますか。
   (A) 引っ越し会社
   (B) 家具店
   (C) リサイクルセンター
   (D) 旅行代理店

正解 (A)

. . . .

語句 □ load ～を積み込む　□ deal with ～ ～に対応する　□ relocate 移転する
□ unless もし～でなければ　□ give ～ a hand ～に手を貸す，～を手伝う
□ in time 時間内に，間に合って　□ travel agency 旅行代理店

攻略法まとめ 情報をもとに推測する問題

- 質問に most likely が含まれていたらこのタイプだと思おう。
- 文書の中から手掛かりになりそうな表現を見つけよう。

次の文書を読み，各設問に対して最も適切な答えを(A)(B)(C)(D)の中から1つ選びなさい。

Questions 1-2 refer to the following invoice.

Deal Direct
E-mail Invoice

Mr. Kym Daw
Cranston College of Art
12 Valley Road
Seven Hills, IL 60056

Order number: 74732
Estimated delivery date: September 13

Product Information:

Item #	Description	Quantity	Price per Unit	Price
A7472	Hippo Art Pencils	10	$12.00	$120.00
CP838	Painting Canvas (out of stock)	4	$65.50	$262.00
BB583	Bronson Oil Painting Brushes (1 set)	10	$30.00	$300.00
HO232	Huttenmeister Oils	5	$36.25	$181.25
			TOTAL	$863.25

Thank you for shopping at Deal Direct. We offer same-day shipping on all items we have in stock. Items marked as *out of stock* will be sent as soon as they arrive from our supplier. Thanks to our partnership with FSC, we have been able to eliminate the inclusion of any fees on all our shipments.

---

1. What kind of business most likely is FSC?

   (A) An equipment manufacturer
   (B) A shipping company
   (C) An online store
   (D) An art school

2. What item will be shipped separately?

   (A) A7472
   (B) CP838
   (C) BB583
   (D) HO232

Questions **3-5** refer to the following schedule.

Workshop: Developing Leadership Skills

Date: June 21   **Admission:** $35 for members / $50 for non-members

9:00	Self-Introductions	by Nigel Reedus
9:15	Workshop 1 Motivating Teams	by Seth Colbert
10:15	Workshop 2 Providing Effective Feedback	by Valerie Day
12:00	**Lunchtime** (Lunch is not included. Please visit one of the nearby eateries. A list of recommended places will be sent at a later date.)	
1:00	Workshop 3 Improving Office Morale	by Jack Eastern
2:30	Workshop 4 Delegating Responsibility	by Freda Holmes
5:00	Closing Words	by Nigel Reedus

If you are coming by car, we recommend that you park at FT Parking. It is right beside the venue, and they are offering discount rates for ticket holders. Please show the attendant your ticket at the exit.

---

3. For whom is the workshop most likely intended?

(A) Office managers
(B) Job applicants
(C) Freelance writers
(D) Professional athletes

4. According to the schedule, what will be provided later?

(A) Printed admission tickets
(B) A list of affordable parking locations
(C) The room numbers for the different workshops
(D) Information about convenient restaurants

5. How can people get discount parking?

(A) By registering for tickets online
(B) By using a suggested parking garage
(C) By using a shuttle bus service
(D) By reserving a space in advance

情報をもとに推測する問題

Questions 1-2 refer to the following invoice.

リスト　♪ 048

Deal Direct
E-mail Invoice

Mr. Kym Daw
Cranston College of Art
12 Valley Road
Seven Hills, IL 60056

Order number: 74732
Estimated delivery date: September 13

Product Information:

Item #	Description	Quantity	Price per Unit	Price
A7472	Hippo Art Pencils	10	$12.00	$120.00
❶ CP838	❷Painting Canvas (out of stock)	4	$65.50	$262.00
BB583	Bronson Oil Painting Brushes (1 set)	10	$30.00	$300.00
HO232	Huttenmeister Oils	5	$36.25	$181.25
			TOTAL	$863.25

Thank you for shopping at Deal Direct. We offer same-day shipping on all items we have in stock. ❸Items marked as *out of stock* will be sent as soon as they arrive from our supplier. ❹Thanks to our partnership with FSC, we have been able to eliminate the inclusion of any fees on all our shipments.

訳　設問1-2は次の請求書に関するものです。

Deal Direct
電子メール請求書

Kym Daw 様
Cranston 美術大学
Valley 通り12番地
郵便番号60056 Illinois州Seven Hills市

注文番号：74732
配送予定日：9月13日

製品情報

製品番号	品目	数量	単価	価格
A7472	Hippoデッサン用鉛筆	10	12.00 ドル	120.00 ドル
CP838	絵画キャンバス（在庫切れ）	4	65.50 ドル	262.00 ドル
BB583	Bronson油絵用絵筆（1セット）	10	30.00 ドル	300.00 ドル
HO232	Huttenmeisterオイル	5	36.25 ドル	181.25 ドル
			合計	863.25 ドル

Deal Directでお買い上げいただきありがとうございます。私どもは在庫のある商品は全て即日発送します。「在庫切れ」の記載があるものは、納入業者から入荷次第発送します。FSC社との提携により、全ての配送にかかる料金を一切除外させていただいております。

語句 □ IL（＝Illinois）アメリカ・イリノイ州 □ description 品目，（商品の）銘柄
□ out of stock 在庫切れで □ thanks to ～ ～のおかげで □ partnership 提携
□ eliminate ～を除外する □ inclusion 含むこと

1.

What kind of business most likely is FSC?	FSC社はおそらくどのような業種の会社ですか。
(A) An equipment manufacturer	
(B) A shipping company	(A) 機器メーカー
(C) An online store	(B) 運送会社
(D) An art school	(C) インターネットショップ
	(D) 美術学校

正解 (B)

解説 FSC社がどのような業種か問われています。請求書の一番下を見ると、❹に「FSC社と提携しているので、送料は発生しない」とあります。ここからFSC社は商品の発送に関係している会社であることが推測できるので、これをshipping companyと表した(B)が正解となります。

語句 □ equipment 装置，設備

2.

What item will be shipped separately?	どの品物が別に発送されますか。
(A) A7472	(A) A7472
(B) CP838	(B) CP838
(C) BB583	(C) BB583
(D) HO232	(D) HO232

正解 (B)

解説 選択肢の製品のうちどれが別送されるか問われています。❸に「out of stock（在庫切れ）と記載されたものは入荷次第発送する」とあります。請求書の品目を確認すると、❷のPainting Canvasにその記載があるので、この商品の製品番号❶より(B)が正解です。

語句 □ separately 別々に

Workshop: ❶Developing Leadership Skills

Date: June 21　　**Admission:** $35 for members / $50 for non-members

9:00	Self-Introductions	by Nigel Reedus
9:15	❷Workshop 1 Motivating Teams	by Seth Colbert
10:15	❸Workshop 2 Providing Effective Feedback	by Valerie Day
12:00	**Lunchtime** (❹Lunch is not included. Please visit one of the nearby eateries. A list of recommended places will be sent at a later date.)	
1:00	❺Workshop 3 Improving Office Morale	by Jack Eastern
2:30	❻Workshop 4 Delegating Responsibility	by Freda Holmes
5:00	Closing Words	by Nigel Reedus

❼If you are coming by car, we recommend that you park at FT Parking. It is right beside the venue, and they are offering discount rates for ticket holders. Please show the attendant your ticket at the exit.

訳　設問3-5は次の予定表に関するものです。

	研修：リーダーシップスキルの養成	
日付：6月21日　　参加費用：会員35ドル／非会員50ドル		
9：00	自己紹介	担当　Nigel Reedus
9：15	研修1　チームへの動機付け	担当　Seth Colbert
10：15	研修2　効果的なフィードバックの提供	担当　Valerie Day
12：00	**昼食** （昼食は研修費用に含まれません。近隣の飲食店をご利用ください。後日，推奨店のリストをお送りします。）	
1：00	研修3　社内の士気の向上	担当　Jack Eastern
2：30	研修4　責任の委譲	担当　Freda Holmes
5：00	閉会の辞	担当　Nigel Reedus

お車でお越しの場合は，FTパーキングでの駐車をお勧めします。その駐車場は会場のすぐ隣にあり，チケット保有者に割引価格を提供しています。係員に出口でチケットをお見せください。

語句　□ workshop 研修，ワークショップ　□ develop ～を開発する，発達させる
□ admission 入場料，参加費用　□ self-introduction 自己紹介
□ motivate ～に動機を与える　□ effective 効果的な　□ eatery 食堂
□ at a later date 後日　□ morale やる気，士気　□ delegate ～を委任する
□ right ちょうど，すぐ　□ attendant 係員

3.

情報をもとに推測する問題

For whom is the workshop most likely intended?	研修はおそらく誰を対象としていますか。
(A) Office managers	(A) 会社の管理職
(B) Job applicants	(B) 求職者
(C) Freelance writers	(C) フリーライター
(D) Professional athletes	(D) プロの運動選手

正解 (A)

解説 この研修は誰向けのものか問われています。❶の研修全体のタイトルと各研修のテーマ❷，❸，❺，❻を見ると，「リーダーシップスキルの養成」「チームへの動機付け」「効果的なフィードバックの提供」「社内の士気の向上」「責任の委譲」といった，会社で部下を管理する上司が身に付けるべきスキルが並んでいます。ここから正解は(A)だとわかります。

語句 □ freelance フリーランスの，自由契約の　□ athlete 運動選手

4.

詳細を問う問題

According to the schedule, what will be provided later?	予定表によると，後で何が提供されますか。
(A) Printed admission tickets	(A) 印刷された参加チケット
(B) A list of affordable parking locations	(B) 手頃な駐車場所のリスト
(C) The room numbers for the different workshops	(C) さまざまな研修の部屋番号
(D) Information about convenient restaurants	(D) 便利なレストランに関する情報

正解 (D)

解説 予定表に後で何が提供されると書いてあるか問われています。❹に「昼食は研修費用に含まれていないので，近隣の飲食店のリストを後日送付する」とあるので，それを言い換えた(D)が正解です。文書に登場するeateries（単数形はeatery）はrestaurant(s)と言い換え可能なので，押さえておきましょう。

語句 □ admission ticket 入場チケット　□ affordable 手頃な　□ convenient 便利な

5.

詳細を問う問題

How can people get discount parking?	どうすれば駐車料金の割引を受けられますか。
(A) By registering for tickets online	(A) インターネットでチケットを申し込むことで
(B) By using a suggested parking garage	(B) 勧められた駐車場を利用することで
(C) By using a shuttle bus service	(C) シャトルバスを利用することで
(D) By reserving a space in advance	(D) 事前にスペースを予約することで

正解 (B)

解説 どうすれば駐車料金の割引を受けられるか問われています。❼で「勧めているFTパーキングは会場に近く，チケット保有者に割引価格を提供している」と述べているので，このFTパーキングを使えば割引になるとわかります。「勧められた駐車場を利用する」という(B)が正解です。

語句 □ register for ～ ～を申し込む　□ suggested 勧められた　□ parking garage 駐車場　□ shuttle bus シャトルバス（近距離の往復バス）　□ reserve ～を予約する　□ in advance 前もって，事前に

3 目的・テーマを問う問題

「目的・テーマを問う問題」は毎回5問程度出題されます。文書が書かれた理由や背景をつかむことは，文書を正しく読み取る上でも重要なタスクなので，常に意識して文書を読む習慣をつけておきましょう。

POINT 1 目的・テーマを問う問題の典型的な形を押さえよう。

「目的・テーマを問う問題」は以下のような形をしていることが多いです。

· What is the purpose of the notice?
「お知らせの目的は何ですか」（目的・テーマ）
· Why was the e-mail sent?
「なぜEメールは送られましたか」（理由≒目的）

質問文がこのような形をしていたら「目的・テーマ」が問われていると考えましょう。

POINT 2 目的・テーマは冒頭にくることが多いので注意しよう。

文書の目的は冒頭にくることが多いです。その方が相手にきちんと文書の内容を理解してもらえるからです。文書の第1段落，特に冒頭の2, 3行は「目的・テーマが出てくるぞ」と注意して読みましょう。

POINT 3 目的やテーマを誘導する表現に注目し，ストックを作っておこう。

目的やテーマはこれらを誘導する表現に着目すると，見抜きやすくなります。例えば以下のような表現です。

· I am writing to let you know that 〜 「〜についてお知らせします」
· We are happy to notify you of 〜 「〜のことを喜んでお伝えします」
· We regret to inform you that 〜 「残念ながら〜についてお知らせします」

このような「何かを知らせる」系の動詞の後には，目的やテーマを示す内容が続くことが多いです。こうした表現をストックしておくと，正解を探しやすくなります。

それでは，例題を見てみましょう。

例 題 **Question 1** refers to the following article.

Marsden — The McGillicutty Bridge on Cusack Lane will be closed to traffic from March 14 to March 21 so that maintenance work can be carried out. Motorists are advised that they will need to take an alternative route to reach the addresses in that area. The city council recommends that you use Mulholland Street until the work is complete. An update on the work will be published as the completion date approaches.

1. What is the purpose of the article?

    (A) To explain a council regulation

    (B) To announce the opening of a new road

    (C) To inform motorists of a detour

    (D) To recommend a sightseeing area

3

目的・テーマを問う問題

どうでしょうか。今回は4つの文から成る短い文書です。

Question 1 refers to the following article.

記事 ♪ 050

Marsden — The McGillicutty Bridge on Cusack Lane will be closed to
　　　　　　　└ まずは冒頭に注意。橋が通行止めになる，という情報
traffic from March 14 to March 21 so that maintenance work can be

carried out. Motorists are advised that they will need to take an alternative
　　　　　　　└ be advised that ...「何かを知らせる」表現だ
route to reach the addresses in that area. The city council recommends that

you use Mulholland Street until the work is complete. An update on the

work will be published as the completion date approaches.

■■文書の概要

	要素	内容
本文	導入（1文目）	道路工事のため一定期間橋が通行止めに（背景）
	本題（2～4文目）	車を運転する人は迂回しなければならない（主題） 推奨ルートを提示，最新情報は改めて（補足）

鍵は2文目のMotorists are advised that ～.「自動車を運転する人は～を通知され
ている」です。通行止めという状況を受けて留意すべきことを伝えるのが，この記
事の目的です。

設問を見てみましょう。

1. What is the purpose of the article?
   (A) To explain a council regulation
   (B) To announce the opening of a new road
   (C) To inform motorists of a detour　　detour = take an alternative route
   (D) To recommend a sightseeing area

(C)のdetourが2文目のtake an alternative route「迂回する」を言い換えているこ
とに気付けば正解できる問題でした。

今回は短い文書でしたが，長めの文書でもどこが背景でどこが本題（目的・テーマ）
か，見極めていきましょう。

正解と訳 設問1は次の記事に関するものです。

Marsden市 — Cusack通りにあるMcGillicutty橋は補修工事が行われるため，3月14日から3月21日まで通行止めになる。自動車を運転する人は，その地域にある場所へ行くには別のルートを通らなければならなくなると通知されている。市議会では工事終了までMulholland通りを利用することを推奨している。工事の最新情報は完了日が近づいてきたら公表される。

1. 記事の目的は何ですか。
   (A) 市議会の規則を説明すること
   (B) 新道路の開通を発表すること
   (C) 自動車運転者に迂回を知らせること
   (D) 観光名所を推奨すること

正解 (C)

語句 □ lane 通り □ be closed to traffic 通行止めになる
   □ maintenance work 補修工事 □ carry out ～ ～を実行する
   □ motorist 自動車を運転する人 □ be advised that ～ ～だと通知される
   □ alternative 代わりの，別の □ city council 市議会 □ update 最新情報
   □ publish ～を発表 [公表] する □ completion date 完了日 □ approach 近づく
   □ regulation 規則 □ inform A of B AにBを知らせる □ detour 迂回 (路)
   □ sightseeing 観光

攻略法まとめ 目的・テーマを問う問題

• まずは文書の冒頭に注目しよう。

• 目的やテーマを誘導する表現に注目し，そのストックを作ろう。

次の文書を読み，各設問に対して最も適切な答えを(A)(B)(C)(D)の中から1つ選びなさい。

Questions 1-2 refer to the following memo.

From: Pete Rosenthal
To: All assembly line workers
Subject: Hydration
Date: August 10

Dear All,

This summer is one of the hottest on record, so it is more important than ever to drink enough water. You may have already noticed the refrigerators that have been installed in each section of the factory. These are to be used exclusively for beverages. At the end of every hour, a chime will be played to remind employees to take a drink. At this time, production will be halted for a period of three minutes.

Sincerely,

Pete Rosenthal

1. What is the purpose of the memo?

(A) To remind employees of a deadline
(B) To explain a new company policy
(C) To announce the opening of a new section
(D) To find employees willing to work overtime

2. Where do the recipients of the memo most likely work?

(A) At a manufacturing plant
(B) At a college
(C) At a fitness center
(D) At a music store

Questions **3-5** refer to the following information.

Woodhill Tourism Center Newsletter
Look what's happening this month in Woodhill!

March 6	Annual Woodhill Fun Run — Starts and finishes at Hadfield Community Center. Entry is $35 for adults.
March 7	A Night at the Woodhill Historical Museum — Come and enjoy a tour of the museum with a local expert.
March 13 through 16	The Woodhill Arts and Crafts Festival — A popular event with plenty of entertainment. Mayor, Rod Judy will announce the winners of the annual art competition on the final day of the festival.

If you require any further information about local events, please call our helpline at 555-6764. We will do our best to answer your call in a timely manner. However, we kindly ask you to keep in mind that all our office staff are volunteers. Please enjoy your stay in our town.

3. What is the purpose of the information?

(A) To explain where volunteers are needed
(B) To describe the efforts of a business association
(C) To promote some local events
(D) To announce a recycling procedure

4. When will the winners of the art competition be announced?

(A) On March 13
(B) On March 14
(C) On March 16
(D) On March 17

5. What is implied about the staff at the Woodhill Tourism Center?

(A) They are the owners of local businesses.
(B) They publish reviews of events.
(C) They are city council members.
(D) They are not working for money.

Questions 1-2 refer to the following memo.

〔メモ〕 ♪ 051

From: Pete Rosenthal
To: ❶All assembly line workers
Subject: Hydration
Date: August 10

Dear All,

This summer is one of the hottest on record, so ❷it is more important than ever to drink enough water. ❸You may have already noticed the refrigerators that have been installed in each section of the factory. These are to be used exclusively for beverages. ❹At the end of every hour, a chime will be played to remind employees to take a drink. ❺At this time, production will be halted for a period of three minutes.

Sincerely,

Pete Rosenthal

訳 設問1-2は次のメモに関するものです。

差出人：Pete Rosenthal
宛先：組立ライン全作業員
件名：水分補給
日付：8月10日

皆さま

この夏は記録的な暑さになっているため，十分な水分を取ることがこれまで以上に重要です。工場の各セクションに設置された冷蔵庫にもうすでにお気付きかもしれません。これらは飲み物専用としてご利用ください。毎時間の終わりに，従業員に飲み物を飲むようお知らせするチャイムが鳴ります。この時，製造は3分間停止されます。

よろしくお願いします。

Pete Rosenthal

語句 □ assembly line（生産などの）組立ライン □ hydration 水分補給
□ on record 記録上 □ than ever これまで以上に □ refrigerator 冷蔵庫

□ exclusively 独占的に □ beverage 飲み物 □ chime チャイム
□ halt ～を止める □ a period of ～ ～の間

1.

目的・テーマを問う問題

What is the purpose of the memo?	メモの目的は何ですか。
(A) To remind employees of a deadline	(A) 従業員に納期について念を押すこと
(B) To explain a new company policy	(B) 新しい会社の方針を説明すること
(C) To announce the opening of a new section	(C) 新しい部門の開業を発表すること
(D) To find employees willing to work overtime	(D) 残業をいとわない従業員を探すこと

正解 (B)

解説 メモの目的が問われています。❷で「(暑いので)水分補給が重要」と背景を述べ，❸，❹で工場内に冷蔵庫を設置し，定期的に水分を取るようにする施策について述べています。以上からメモはこの会社の新たな方針について説明していると判断できるので，正解は(B)です。

語句 □ deadline 納期，期限 □ policy 方針，指針
□ be willing to *do* ～しようという気持ちがある □ work overtime 残業する

2.

情報をもとに推測する問題

Where do the recipients of the memo most likely work?	メモの受取人たちはおそらくどこで働いていますか。
(A) At a manufacturing plant	(A) 製造工場
(B) At a college	(B) 大学
(C) At a fitness center	(C) フィットネスセンター
(D) At a music store	(D) 楽器店

正解 (A)

解説 このメモの受取人たちがどこで働いているか問われています。❶，❸，❺に「組立作業をする従業員」「工場の各セクションに」「製造が一時止まる」とあることから，彼らは何かを製造する工場で働いている人たちだと推測できます。それをmanufacturing plantと表した(A)が正解です。

語句 □ recipient 受取人，受信者 □ manufacturing plant 製造工場

Questions 3-5 refer to the following information. 簡単な案内・お知らせ ♪ 052

Woodhill Tourism Center Newsletter
❶Look what's happening this month in Woodhill!

March 6	Annual Woodhill Fun Run — Starts and finishes at Hadfield Community Center. Entry is $35 for adults.
March 7	A Night at the Woodhill Historical Museum — Come and enjoy a tour of the museum with a local expert.
❷March 13 through 16	The Woodhill Arts and Crafts Festival — A popular event with plenty of entertainment. ❸Mayor, Rod Judy will announce the winners of the annual art competition on the final day of the festival.

If you require any further information about local events, please call our helpline at 555-6764. We will do our best to answer your call in a timely manner. ❹However, we kindly ask you to keep in mind that all our office staff are volunteers. ❺Please enjoy your stay in our town.

訳 設問3-5は次の案内に関するものです。

	Woodhill観光センター・ニュースレター 今月Woodhill市で起きることに注目！
3月6日	毎年恒例Woodhill市民マラソン ─ スタートとゴール地点はHadfieldコミュニティーセンター。参加は大人35ドルです。
3月7日	Woodhill歴史博物館での夕べ ─ 地元の専門家と回る博物館の見学ツアーをお楽しみください。
3月13日～16日	Woodhill美術工芸祭り ─ お楽しみがいっぱいの人気イベントです。Rod Judy市長が祭りの最終日に今年の美術コンテスト入賞者を発表します。

地域イベントに関してより詳しい情報が必要な場合は，電話相談555-6764にご連絡ください。お電話に適時にお答えするよう最善を尽くします。しかしながら，当センターのスタッフは全員ボランティアだということをどうか心に留めておいてください。それではこの街での滞在をお楽しみください。

語句 □ annual 毎年の □ fun run 市民マラソン □ entry 参加 □ expert 専門家
□ arts and crafts 美術工芸 □ plenty of ～たくさんの～ □ mayor 市長
□ art competition 美術コンテスト □ further information さらなる情報
□ helpline 電話相談 □ in a timely manner 適時に
□ kindly どうか（～してください） □ keep in mind 覚えておく

3.

What is the purpose of the information?
(A) To explain where volunteers are needed
(B) To describe the efforts of a business association
(C) To promote some local events
(D) To announce a recycling procedure

案内の目的は何ですか。
(A) どこでボランティアが必要か説明すること
(B) ビジネス団体の努力について述べること
(C) 地域のイベントを宣伝すること
(D) リサイクルの手順を伝えること

正解 (C)

解説 案内の目的が何か問われています。文書の冒頭❶に「Woodhill市で起きることに注目！」とあり，複数のイベントの日程と内容が表にまとめられています。さらに問い合わせ先を示した後，最後の❺で「お楽しみください」と締めくくっていることから，Woodhill市で行われるイベントを宣伝していることがわかります。以上から(C)が正解です。

語句 □ describe ～を描写する，述べる　□ business association ビジネス団体
　　　□ promote ～を宣伝［促進］する　□ procedure 手順

4.

When will the winners of the art competition be announced?
(A) On March 13
(B) On March 14
(C) On March 16
(D) On March 17

美術コンテストの入賞者はいつ発表されますか。
(A) 3月13日
(B) 3月14日
(C) 3月16日
(D) 3月17日

正解 (C)

解説 美術コンテストの入賞者がいつ発表されるか問われています。質問のキーワードであるart competitionを探すと，❸に「市長が祭りの最終日に美術コンテストの入賞者を発表する」とあります。❷の日程を見ると祭りの最終日は3月16日なので，(C)が正解です。

5.

What is implied about the staff at the Woodhill Tourism Center?
(A) They are the owners of local businesses.
(B) They publish reviews of events.
(C) They are city council members.
(D) They are not working for money.

Woodhill観光センターのスタッフに関して何が示唆されていますか。
(A) 地元企業のオーナーである。
(B) イベントの総括を発行している。
(C) 市議会議員である。
(D) お金のために働いているのではない。

正解 (D)

解説 Woodhill観光センターのスタッフに関して示唆されていることが問われています。❹で「当センターのスタッフは全員ボランティアだ」と述べていることから，スタッフはお金のために働いていないことが示唆されています。よって(D)が正解です。

4 選択肢照合型問題

これまで取り上げてきた設問タイプは，直接的にせよ間接的にせよ「正解の根拠と一致する選択肢を1つ探す」というアプローチで解いてきました。しかし，今回取り上げる「選択肢照合型問題」はこのアプローチでは解けないので注意が必要です。

POINT 1 質問文の形から，問題のタイプを見抜こう。

選択肢照合型問題は，質問文の形から見抜くことができます。質問文が以下のような形をしていたら，**他の設問タイプとは問題の解き方を変える必要がある**ので，注意しましょう。

(1) What is indicated [mentioned/stated] about XX?

　「XXについて何が述べられていますか」

(2) What is suggested [implied] about YY?

　「YYについて何が示されて [示唆されて] いますか」

(3) What is true about ZZ?

　「ZZについて正しいことは何ですか」

(1) は本文に直接的に書かれていることが多いですが，(2), (3) はやや間接的な表現になっていることがあります。例えば，メール本文に「私はTorontoでのトークショーを楽しんだ」という記述があれば，私は「Torontoであるイベントに参加した」ということが推測できます。また，記事の本文に「ある新聞によると，△△社が将来業績を回復できるか懐疑的だ」とあれば「△△社は経営難だ」ということが推測できます。

POINT 2 本文を適切に検索し，各選択肢と照合しよう。

このタイプの問題は，正解がピンポイントで答えられる問題ではない（つまり，選択肢がないと正解を導くことができない）ので，**各選択肢を文書と照合して解いていく**必要があります。4つの選択肢のうち「本文と合致する」選択肢1つが正解で，他の3つの選択肢は「本文に記載がない」もしくは「本文の内容と異なる」のいずれかになります。

例えば，質問文がWhat is indicated about XX?「XXについて何が述べられていますか」だったとします。その場合，XXについて書かれている箇所を文書の中から見つけて各選択肢の情報が正しいかどうかを確認することになるのですが，このときいかに文書の内容を把握しながら読んでいるかが物を言います。何がどこに書かれているかをしっかり押さえておけば，確認すべき箇所を素早く見つけて本文と選択肢を照合することができるからです。

また選択肢の情報が本文に書かれていないな，と思ったものの確信が持てない場合はいったん保留にし，その他の選択肢を先に確認しましょう。全ての選択肢を読むことで，正解がはっきりとわかる場合もあります。

このように**文書を適切に検索し，各選択肢と照合するためには，文書の内容をきちんと理解していることが何よりも大切**です。本文を読んでも内容がなかなか頭に入ってこない人は少しずつ読む量を増やし，情報を整理しながら英文を読むことに慣れていきましょう。

それでは，例題を見てみましょう。

例題 **Question 1** refers to the following excerpt from an instruction manual.

1.4 Intended use
The Vullox 23C is designed to handle daily loads of up to 8 kilograms. The expected service life of the unit is around 10 years. The terms of the warranty for this model are explained on the last page of this manual. Any malfunctions that occur during the period described there are fully covered, and Vullox will provide repairs or a replacement free of charge. Please be advised, however, that the warranty for this dryer only covers home use.

Customers needing a dryer to handle heavier and more frequent loads should consider the Vullox B12A model. With regular service, it can handle multiple loads of up to 20 kilograms daily for many years. The warranty covers all types of use.

---

1. What is implied about the Vullox 23C?

   (A) It requires regular servicing.
   (B) It weighs 8 kilograms.
   (C) It is covered by a 10-year warranty.
   (D) It is not intended for commercial applications.

文書は乾燥機の取扱説明書（instruction manual）の抜粋です。

まず，各段落に書かれている情報を整理してみましょう。

Question 1 refers to the following excerpt from an instruction manual.

1.4 Intended use

The Vullox 23C is designed to handle daily loads of up to 8 kilograms. The expected service life of the unit is around 10 years. The terms of the warranty for this model are explained on the last page of this manual. Any malfunctions that occur during the period described there are fully covered, and Vullox will provide repairs or a replacement free of charge. Please be advised, however, that the warranty for this dryer only covers home use.

Customers needing a dryer to handle heavier and more frequent loads should consider the Vullox B12A model. With regular service, it can handle multiple loads of up to 20 kilograms daily for many years. The warranty covers all types of use.

■■文書の概要

要素	内容
第1段落	Vullox 23C について ・製品の特徴，保証，保証範囲
第2段落	Vullox B12A model について ・大量かつ頻繁な使用に対応，製品の特徴，保証範囲

次に，質問文を確認しましょう。

What is implied about the Vullox 23C?

「Vullox 23C について何が示唆されていますか」

about以下に注目すると，about the Vullox 23C とあるので，Vullox 23C について書かれた第1段落と各選択肢を照合していきましょう。

(A) It requires regular servicing. 「定期点検が必要である」

第1段落に regular servicing「定期点検」に関する記述はなさそうです。その場合は，次の選択肢をすぐ確認するようにしましょう。

(B) It weighs 8 kilograms. 「重さは8キロである」

乾燥機が扱える容量については up to 8 kilograms「8キロまで」とありますが，乾

燥機自体の重さに関する記述はなさそうです。このとき，8 kilogramsという数字だけに気を取られて正解だと早合点しないよう気を付けましょう。

(C) It is covered by a <u>10-year warranty</u>. 「10年保証が付いている」

第1段落の2文目，The expected service life of the unit is around <u>10 years</u>. に 10 years とありますが，これは耐用年数です。warranty「保証」に関しては年数の記述はありません。

(D) It is not intended for commercial applications. 「商業用途向けではない」

第1段落の最後にhome useとあります。保証は家庭での使用に限られると書かれていることから，Vullox 23Cは商業用ではないと考えられます。よって，(D) が正解です。

このタイプの問題は，各選択肢が文書と合致しているかをそれぞれ確認する必要があり，時間がかかります。苦手なうちは後回しにするか，(A) から順に照合していき，途中で正解だと確信できる選択肢があったら以降の選択肢は確認せず次の設問に進むなどして，解答時間を短縮しましょう。ただし，選択肢全てを確認しない場合，解答の精度はどうしても落ちてしまうので注意が必要です。

正解と訳 設問1は次の取扱説明書からの抜粋に関するものです。

1.4 使用用途
Vullox 23Cは毎日の洗濯物を最大8キロまで扱えるように設計されています。この製品の想定耐用年数は約10年です。この機種の保証条件については，このマニュアルの最終ページに説明があります。そこに記載された期間中に発生した全ての故障について完全に保証し，Vullox社は無償で修理または交換します。ただし，この乾燥機の保証はご家庭での使用に限るということをご了承ください。

より大量の，また頻繁な使用に対応した乾燥機をお求めのお客さまは，Vullox B12Aモデルをご検討ください。この機種は，定期点検をすることで長期間，最大20キロまでの洗濯物を1日に何度も扱うことができます。全ての使用用途に保証が付いています。

1. Vullox 23Cについて何が示唆されていますか。
  (A) 定期点検が必要である。
  (B) 重さは8キロである。
  (C) 10年保証が付いている。
  (D) 商業用途向けではない。

正解 (D)

語句 □ intended use 使用用途　□ be designed to *do* ～するよう設計されている
　　　□ handle ～を取り扱う　□ daily 毎日の，日々の　□ load（1回分の）洗濯量
　　　□ up to ～ 最大～まで　□ expected 予想された　□ service life 耐用年数
　　　□ unit 製品　□ around 約　□ terms 条件，条項　□ warranty 保証（書）

□ malfunction 故障　□ describe 〜を記載する
□ cover （損失など）を補填する，〜に適用される　□ replacement 交換品
□ free of charge 無料で　□ Please be advised (that) 〜 〜をご了承ください
□ dryer 乾燥機　□ frequent 頻繁な　□ consider 〜を検討する
□ regular service 定期点検　□ multiple 多数の，多様な
□ commercial application 商業用に応用すること

攻略法まとめ　選択肢照合型問題

・問題のタイプを見抜き，解答のアプローチを決めよう。

・段落ごとに要旨をまとめながら読み，選択肢を文書と効率よく照合しよう。

・時間をかけすぎないように注意しよう。

4

選択肢照合型問題

次の文書を読み，各設問に対して最も適切な答えを(A)(B)(C)(D)の中から1つ選びなさい。

Questions 1-4 refer to the following e-mail.

To:	Clarence Freeman <cfreeman@sapphirelandscaping.com>
From:	Morgan Salinger <msalinger@candcadvertising.com>
Date:	May 17
Subject:	Draft of the advertisement

Dear Mr. Freeman,

Following our discussion the other day, I had my team design an advertisement for Sapphire Landscaping. Please check the following draft of the advertisement and let us know what you think.

Sapphire Landscaping Company (SLC)

Bradford's Most Trusted Name in Landscaping and Garden Maintenance

When creating outdoor spaces, Sapphire Landscaping Company strives to satisfy the design requirements of its clients while keeping in mind other important factors such as long-term maintenance costs. Having been in the business for more than 40 years, we know that these considerations can be just as important as visual appeal.

SLC can create flower gardens, water features, low-maintenance courtyards, rooftop nature spaces, as well as many other outdoor environments. Visit our Web site at www.sapphirelc.com to view our full list of services and see photographs of our past projects.

To arrange a consultation, call us at the number below now. We can offer a quotation within 24 hours and it won't cost you anything.

PHONE: 555-9349

If you and your business partner find this acceptable, we would like to discuss strategies such as when and in which publications to place it. Of course, the financial considerations will need to be taken into account. We will provide detailed information about cost along with each suggested plan before our next meeting.

Sincerely,

Morgan Salinger

1. What is the purpose of the e-mail?

(A) To announce the completion of a campaign

(B) To request clarification of an order

(C) To promote a business' new service

(D) To follow up on a client's request

2. How are potential customers directed to contact SLC?

(A) In person

(B) By e-mail

(C) Over the phone

(D) Through online chat

3. What is indicated about SLC?

(A) It has recently expanded its service area.

(B) It offers free price estimates.

(C) It is currently offering discounts.

(D) It has received an award.

4. What is true about Mr. Freeman?

(A) He has a business associate.

(B) He founded SLC.

(C) He suggested an advertising strategy.

(D) He will appear in an online advertisement.

4

選択肢照合型問題

Questions 5-8 refer to the following article.

Boston, May 7— Despite the fact that Doreen Harper's first three books each sold more than 50,000 copies, she has received little attention from the press or the voters at literary awards. That changed last night, when her new book was named Historical Book of the Year by the New England Literary Society.

The book was nominated for the award after Steve Daly at the *Boston Tribune* wrote in his weekly review of new books that *Founding Fathers* was one of the most thorough yet exciting books he had read in many years. Sales skyrocketed across the country, putting her on the bestseller list in most major cities.

Apparently, Ms. Harper had very low expectations of winning. She chose not to attend the ceremony in favor of taking a research trip to France for her next book. Her editor, Gwen Chu, accepted the rather large trophy on her behalf. She said that she would pass on the trophy when Ms. Harper arrives back in New England in June. Until then, it will be proudly displayed in the lobby of Sacamano Publishing.

5. What is the purpose of the article?

  (A) To announce the establishment of a new literary award

  (B) To examine a recent trend in publishing

  (C) To discuss the history of a large city

  (D) To report on an author's recent success

6. Who most likely is Steve Daly?

  (A) A novelist

  (B) A literary agent

  (C) A critic

  (D) A bookstore owner

7. What is indicated about Ms. Harper?

  (A) She helped judge a contest.

  (B) She is currently abroad.

  (C) She has been attending book signings.

  (D) She will give a speech at a ceremony.

8. What will be exhibited at Sacamano Publishing?

  (A) Some historical documents

  (B) A book

  (C) An award

  (D) Some photographs

4

選択肢照合型問題

Questions 1-4 refer to the following e-mail.

Ｅメール・手紙　♪ 054

To:	❶Clarence Freeman <cfreeman@sapphirelandscaping.com>
From:	Morgan Salinger <msalinger@candcadvertising.com>
Date:	May 17
Subject:	Draft of the advertisement

Dear Mr. Freeman,

❷Following our discussion the other day, I had my team design an advertisement for Sapphire Landscaping. ❸Please check the following draft of the advertisement and let us know what you think.

Sapphire Landscaping Company (SLC)

Bradford's Most Trusted Name in Landscaping and Garden Maintenance

When creating outdoor spaces, Sapphire Landscaping Company strives to satisfy the design requirements of its clients while keeping in mind other important factors such as long-term maintenance costs. Having been in the business for more than 40 years, we know that these considerations can be just as important as visual appeal.

SLC can create flower gardens, water features, low-maintenance courtyards, rooftop nature spaces, as well as many other outdoor environments. Visit our Web site at www.sapphirelc.com to view our full list of services and see photographs of our past projects.

❹To arrange a consultation, call us at the number below now. ❺We can offer a quotation within 24 hours and it won't cost you anything.

PHONE: 555-9349

---

❻If you and your business partner find this acceptable, we would like to discuss strategies such as when and in which publications to place it. Of course, the financial considerations will need to be taken into account. We will provide detailed information about cost along with each suggested plan before our next meeting.

Sincerely,

Morgan Salinger

訳 設問1-4は次のEメールに関するものです。

宛先：Clarence Freeman <cfreeman@sapphirelandscaping.com>
送信者：Morgan Salinger <msalinger@candcadvertising.com>
日付：5月17日
件名：広告案

Freeman様

先日の打ち合わせの後，私のチームにSapphire Landscaping社の広告をデザインさせました。以下の広告原稿案をご確認いただき，お考えをお聞かせいただければと存じます。

Sapphire Landscaping社 (SLC)
Bradford市で最も信頼されている造園と庭園メンテナンスの会社

野外スペースを造成する際，Sapphire Landscaping社は，長い目で見たメンテナンス費用などの重要な要件を考慮しつつ，お客さまのデザインのご要望を満たすよう努力します。40年以上この仕事に携わり，このような配慮が見た目の良さと同等に重要だと理解しています。

SLC社は，他の多くの野外環境同様に，花の庭園や水を使ったもの，あまり手入れのいらない中庭や屋上緑地を創ることができます。当社ウェブサイトwww.sapphirelc.comにアクセスして，サービスの全リストや過去のプロジェクトの写真をご覧ください。

ご相談のご予約は，今すぐ下の番号にお電話ください。24時間以内にお見積もりをご提供でき，お客さまには一切費用はかかりません。

電話番号：555-9349

Freeman様ならびに共同事業者の方がこちらでよろしければ，いつどの出版物に掲載するかというような戦略についてご相談したいと思います。当然ながら，費用面についての検討も必要になります。次回の打ち合わせの前に，ご提案する各プランと併せて費用に関する詳しい情報をお送りします。

敬具

Morgan Salinger

語句 □ draft 草案，下書き　□ landscaping 造園　□ outdoor space 屋外スペース
□ strive to *do* 〜しようと努力する　□ satisfy 〜を満足させる
□ requirement 要件　□ keep in mind 覚えておく　□ factor 要素，要因
□ long-term 長期間の　□ consideration 考慮，検討
□ visual appeal 視覚的な魅力　□ feature 呼び物，特徴
□ low-maintenance 維持に手間がかからない　□ courtyard 中庭
□ rooftop 屋上，屋根　□ consultation 相談　□ quotation 見積もり（額）
□ acceptable 受け入れられる　□ strategy 戦略　□ publication 出版物
□ place 〜を載せる　□ take into account 考慮する　□ detailed 詳細な

1.

What is the purpose of the e-mail?	Eメールの目的は何ですか。
(A) To announce the completion of a campaign	(A) キャンペーンの終了を伝えること
(B) To request clarification of an order	(B) 注文について明確な説明を求めること
(C) To promote a business' new service	(C) 会社の新サービスを促進すること
(D) To follow up on a client's request	(D) 顧客の要望に対処すること

正解 (D)

解説 Eメールの目的が問われています。まず❶のアドレスから，受信者であるFreemanさんはSapphire Landscaping社の人だとわかります。❷，❸で送信者であるSalingerさんが「打ち合わせの後，広告の原稿案を作成したので考えを聞かせてほしい」と書いていることから，FreemanさんはSalingerさんの顧客であり，Salingerさんは依頼された仕事の進捗について連絡していることがわかるので，それをfollow up onと表した(D)が正解です。follow up onは仕事の進捗を確かめたり，先方の返事を待っているときにやんわりと催促したりする場合など，ビジネスシーンでよく使われる表現です。

語句 □ clarification 説明，明確化　□ promote ～を促進する
□ follow up on ～ ～に（引き続き）対処する

2.

How are potential customers directed to contact SLC?	見込み顧客はどのようにSLC社に連絡するよう指示されていますか。
(A) In person	(A) 直接訪ねて
(B) By e-mail	(B) Eメールで
(C) Over the phone	(C) 電話で
(D) Through online chat	(D) オンラインチャットで

正解 (C)

解説 見込み顧客がSLC社に連絡するにはどうすればよいか問われています。❹に「ご相談のご予約は下の番号までお電話を」とあることから，(C)が正解です。

語句 □ be directed to *do* ～するように指示される

3.

What is indicated about SLC?
(A) It has recently expanded its service area.
(B) It offers free price estimates.
(C) It is currently offering discounts.
(D) It has received an award.

SLC社について何が述べられています
か。
(A) 最近, そのサービス範囲を拡大した。
(B) 無料の見積もりを提供している。
(C) 現在値引きを実施している。
(D) 賞を受賞した。

正解 (B)

解説 SLC社について述べられていることが問われています。SLC社の広告案の❺に「24時間以内に見積もりを提供し，それには費用はかからない」とあるので，これを言い換えた(B)が正解です。(A)サービス範囲の拡大，(C)現在割引中，(D)受賞についてはいずれも記載がないため，不正解です。

語句 □ expand 〜を拡大する　□ price estimate 見積もり（書）

4.

What is true about Mr. Freeman?
(A) He has a business associate.
(B) He founded SLC.
(C) He suggested an advertising strategy.
(D) He will appear in an online advertisement.

Freemanさんについて何が正しいです
か。
(A) 共同経営者がいる。
(B) SLC社を設立した。
(C) 広告戦略を提案した。
(D) インターネット広告に出演する。

正解 (A)

解説 Freemanさんについて正しいことは何か問われています。❻でSalingerさんが「Freeman様ならびに共同事業者の方がこの案でよろしければ」と書いていることから，Freemanさんには一緒に事業を行う人がいるとわかるので，business partnerをbusiness associateと言い換えた(A)が正解です。Freemanさんは SLC社の人ですが，(B)設立したかどうかは述べられていませんし，(C)広告戦略を提案するのはSalingerさんであり，(D)インターネット広告についての言及はないので，ここではいずれも不正解となります。

語句 □ business associate 共同経営者　□ found 〜を設立［創立］する　□ strategy 戦略

Questions 5-8 refer to the following article.

Boston, May 7— ❶Despite the fact that Doreen Harper's first three books each sold more than 50,000 copies, she has received little attention from the press or the voters at literary awards. That changed last night, when her new book was named Historical Book of the Year by the New England Literary Society.

❷The book was nominated for the award after Steve Daly at the *Boston Tribune* wrote in his weekly review of new books that *Founding Fathers* was one of the most thorough yet exciting books he had read in many years. Sales skyrocketed across the country, putting her on the bestseller list in most major cities.

Apparently, Ms. Harper had very low expectations of winning. ❸She chose not to attend the ceremony in favor of taking a research trip to France for her next book. ❹Her editor, Gwen Chu, accepted the rather large trophy on her behalf. ❺She said that she would pass on the trophy when Ms. Harper arrives back in New England in June. ❻Until then, it will be proudly displayed in the lobby of Sacamano Publishing.

訳 設問5-8は次の記事に関するものです。

Boston市，5月7日—Doreen Harper氏の最初の3冊の本はそれぞれ50,000部以上売れたという事実にもかかわらず，Harper氏はマスコミや文学賞の選考者からはほとんど注目されてこなかった。昨晩それが変わり，New England文学協会は彼女の新刊を年間最優秀歴史書に選んだ。

『Boston Tribune』紙のSteve Daly氏が新刊本の週刊レビューで，『Founding Fathers』は長年読んできた中で最も緻密で，それでいてわくわくする本の1冊だと述べると，同書はこの賞にノミネートされた。売り上げは全国で急上昇し，主要都市のほとんどで彼女はベストセラーリストに名を連ねるようになった。

どうやらHarper氏は受賞するとはほぼ思っていなかったようだ。彼女は式典に参加するよりも次作のためにフランスに取材旅行に行くことを選んだ。彼女の編集者であるGwen Chu氏が彼女の代理でかなり大きなトロフィーを受け取った。Chu氏は，Harper氏が6月にNew Englandに戻ってきたときにトロフィーを手渡すと語った。それまでトロフィーは堂々とSacamano Publishing社のロビーに展示されることになる。

語句
□ despite the fact that ~ ～という事実にもかかわらず　□ copy （本などの）部，冊
□ attention 注目　□ the press 報道機関　□ literary 文学の
□ name ～を指名する　□ historical 歴史的な　□ society 協会，団体
□ nominate ～を推薦する　□ thorough 徹底的な，緻密な
□ yet それでいて，その上　□ skyrocket 急上昇する　□ across the country 国中で
□ bestseller ベストセラー（最も売れ行きの良い本）
□ apparently どうやら，見たところ　□ ceremony 式典
□ in favor of ~ ～の方を選んで　□ editor 編集者　□ rather かなり
□ trophy トロフィー　□ on *one's* behalf ～の代理で　□ pass on ~ ～を渡す
□ proudly 堂々と，誇らしげに

4

選択肢照合型問題

5.

What is the purpose of the article?	記事の目的は何ですか。
(A) To announce the establishment of a new literary award	(A) 新しい文学賞の設立を発表すること
(B) To examine a recent trend in publishing	(B) 出版業界の最近の傾向を調査すること
(C) To discuss the history of a large city	(C) ある大都市の歴史について話すこと
(D) To report on an author's recent success	(D) ある著者の最近の成功について伝えること

正解 (D)

解説 記事の目的が問われています。最初の段落❶で「最初の3冊の本はそれぞれ50,000部以上売れたものの，メディアには注目されなかった。それが，昨晩ある賞を受賞して変わった」と作家Harper氏のサクセスストーリーを要約しています。続く段落でも受賞に関する内容が述べられているので，正解は(D)です。

語句 □ establishment 設立　□ examine ～を調査する　□ trend 傾向

6.

Who most likely is Steve Daly?	Steve Dalyさんとはおそらく誰ですか。
(A) A novelist	(A) 小説家
(B) A literary agent	(B) 著作権代理人
(C) A critic	(C) 批評家
(D) A bookstore owner	(D) 書店のオーナー

正解 (C)

解説 Steve Dalyさんは誰か問われています。第2段落の❷に「Steve Daly氏が新刊本の週刊レビューの中で，『Founding Fathers』を…と述べた」とあります。ここからDalyさんは本の書評を書いていることがわかるので，(C)の「批評家」が正解です。

語句 □ novelist 小説家　□ literary agent 著作権代理人　□ critic 批評家

7.

選択肢照合型問題

What is indicated about Ms. Harper?
(A) She helped judge a contest.
(B) She is currently abroad.
(C) She has been attending book signings.
(D) She will give a speech at a ceremony.

Harperさんについて何が述べられていますか。
(A) コンテストの審査を手伝った。
(B) 現在海外にいる。
(C) 本のサイン会に出席していた。
(D) 式典でスピーチをする予定だ。

正解 (B)

解説 Harperさんについて述べられていることが問われています。第3段落の❸で「彼女は式典に参加せず，次作のためにフランスに取材旅行に出かけている」と述べています。ここから現在海外にいるとわかるので，これを言い換えた(B)が正解です。

語句 □ judge ～を審査する　□ abroad 海外に　□ signing サイン会

8.

詳細を問う問題

What will be exhibited at Sacamano
Publishing?
(A) Some historical documents
(B) A book
(C) An award
(D) Some photographs

Sacamano Publishing社で何が展示されますか。
(A) 歴史的な文書
(B) 書籍
(C) 賞
(D) 写真

正解 (C)

解説 Sacamano Publishing社で展示されるものが問われています。第3段落の❹～❻で「Harper氏の代わりにトロフィーを受け取った編集者のChu氏は6月にHarper氏にトロフィーを渡す。トロフィーはそれまでSacamano Publishing社のロビーに展示されることになる」とあるので，トロフィーを「賞」と言い換えた(C)が正解となります。

5 NOT問題

NOT問題は「本文に書かれていないもの」が正解となるタイプの問題です。その点でやや注意が必要な問題ですが、攻略法は前回取り上げた「選択肢照合型問題」と似ています。

POINT 1 NOT問題は「選択肢照合型問題」の一種と考えよう。

NOT問題とは、以下のような形をしています。

What is NOT mentioned about AA?
「AAについて述べられていないことは何ですか」

このように、質問文中に大文字のNOTが入っていることに注意しましょう。選択肢を全て照合する必要があるので**「選択肢照合型問題」の一種**と言えます。選択肢のうち3つが本文と合致しており、合致しない残った1つが正解となるので、この問題も解答に時間がかかります。

なお、以下のような小文字のnotが含まれる問題は「詳細を問う問題」なので区別する必要があります。

Why has not Mr. Kato received the letter yet?
「Katoさんはなぜまだ手紙を受け取っていないのですか」

ここで問われている「手紙を受け取っていない理由」は、「悪天候で配達遅延が生じている」などのように理由が1カ所に明記され、ここを根拠に正解を導くことのできる「詳細を問う問題」です。全ての選択肢を本文と照合しなくても解ける問題なので、NOT問題とは解法が異なります。注意しましょう。

POINT 2 ケアレスミスに注意しよう。

NOT問題は**特にケアレスミスに注意が必要**です。例えばこんなケースがあります。

(1) NOT問題であることを忘れて(A)を選んでしまった！
最初の選択肢の(A)が本文と合致しており、そのままそれを正解に選んでしまったという例ですね。気を付けましょう。

(2) 選択肢を照合している間にNOT問題であることを忘れてしまった！

(A), (B) が本文と合致したので正解候補から消去したが，残った (C), (D) で正解を絞り切れないでいた。やっとのことで，(C) が本文と合致しているのを見つけたが，うれしさのあまり，合致した (C) にマークしてしまった，という例ですね。

このようなミスをしやすいのがNOT問題です。そのことを意識して解くようにしましょう。

では，例題を見てみましょう。

例題 **Question 1** refers to the following advertisement.

Avalon Apartments at 123 Georgina Street, Darlinghurst is located in one of Sydney's most desirable neighborhoods. It offers spectacular views of the harbor and the city and is extremely convenient with a train station and bus stop within walking distance. At present, Dalton Realty has two three-bedroom apartments for sale in this highly sought-after address. Inspection is by appointment only. Please call senior sales associate Reg Summer to arrange a guided tour. PHONE: 555-9393

Tommy Sato — Manager
45 Sullivan Road, Dolby NSW 2053
Open 9:00 A.M. to 5:00 P.M., Monday through Friday

---

1. What is NOT mentioned about Avalon Apartments?

(A) Its location
(B) The availability of parking
(C) Its access to public transportation
(D) Its scenic views

文書はAvalon Apartmentsという住居の広告で，「物件の概要・売買に関する情報」がまとめられていることが確認できましたか。

■■文書の概要

要素		内容
本文	1文目	・Avalon Apartments の所在地
	2文目	・Avalon Apartments のセールスポイント
	3文目	・Dalton Realty の所有物件
	4〜5文目	・見学は予約のみ，予約方法
フッター		広告主の情報（名前，所在地，営業時間）

続いて，質問文を確認しましょう。

What is NOT mentioned about Avalon Apartments?

「Avalon Apartmentsについて述べられていないことは何ですか」

NOT問題なので「選択肢のうち3つは物件についての説明と合致しているな」という意識で，文書と選択肢の合致箇所を検索していきます。各選択肢の情報を文書中で検索すると，以下のようになります。

Question 1 refers to the following advertisement.

広告・宣伝／プレスリリース　♪ 056

Avalon Apartments (A) at 123 Georgina Street, Darlinghurst is located in one of Sydney's most desirable neighborhoods. (D) It offers spectacular views of the harbor and the city and is (C) extremely convenient with a train station and bus stop within walking distance. At present, Dalton Realty has two three-bedroom apartments for sale in this highly sought-after address. Inspection is by appointment only. Please call senior sales associate Reg Summer to arrange a guided tour. PHONE: 555-9393

Tommy Sato — Manager
45 Sullivan Road, Dolby NSW 2053
Open 9:00 A.M. to 5:00 P.M., Monday through Friday

(A) Its location　「所在地」→ある
(B) The availability of parking　「駐車場があること」→なさそう

(C) Its access to public transportation 「公共交通機関へのアクセス」→ある
(D) Its scenic views 「眺めの良い景色」→ある

よって，正解は (B) です。

正解と訳 設問1は次の広告に関するものです。

Darlinghurst市Georgina通り123番地にあるAvalon ApartmentsはSydneyで最も望ましい地区の1つに位置しています。そこからは港湾と都市の壮観な景色が見え，駅やバス停まで歩いて行けてとても便利です。現在Dalton Realty社はこの大人気の場所にある，寝室が3つの販売用物件を2戸ご用意しています。見学はご予約のみとさせていただきます。上級販売担当者のReg Summerまでお電話いただき，案内付きの見学を手配してください。電話番号：555-9393

Tommy Sato — 部長
郵便番号2053 New South Wales州Dolby市Sullivan通り45番地
営業時間　午前9時～午後5時，月曜日から金曜日まで

1. Avalon Apartmentsについて述べられていないことは何ですか。
(A) 所在地
(B) 駐車場があること
(C) 公共交通機関へのアクセス
(D) 眺めの良い景色

正解 (B)

語句 □ desirable 望ましい　□ spectacular 壮観な　□ harbor 港湾
□ extremely 非常に　□ within walking distance 徒歩圏内に　□ at present 現在
□ three-bedroom 寝室が3つの　□ for sale 売り出し中の
□ sought-after 引く手あまたの，需要の多い　□ address 所在地，住所
□ inspection 見学，内覧　□ guided tour 案内付きの見学
□ NSW（＝ New South Wales）オーストラリア・ニューサウスウェールズ州
□ availability 利用できること，（入手の）可能性　□ scenic 眺めの良い

攻略法まとめ NOT問題

・NOT問題は「選択肢照合型問題」の一種と考えよう。
・解答中にNOT問題であることを忘れるケアレスミスに注意しよう。

Questions 1-3 refer to the following e-mail.

To:	GP_all@gladdenph.com
From:	Gina Tesch <gtesch@gladdenph.com>
Date:	August 12
Subject:	Parking lot

Dear All,

On Tuesday, August 27, construction work will begin on the parking lot. We are providing 20 additional parking spaces to accommodate our growing workforce. Unfortunately, the parking lot will be closed during construction. Staff will be provided parking passes for a local parking garage. They can only be used at Kenneth Parking at 23 Dolby Street. Please speak to your immediate supervisor if you need one. The passes will only be valid from 8:00 A.M. to 6:00 P.M. If you are parked there outside those hours, you will be charged an additional fee. Please retain any receipts for such charges and submit them to administration. Your reimbursement will be made by bank transfer along with your monthly salary. The work is scheduled to finish on October 16.

Sincerely,

Gina Tesch
Administration
Gladden Pharmaceuticals

1. What is the purpose of the e-mail?
   (A) To announce a temporary situation at a company
   (B) To thank employees for assisting with a project
   (C) To warn people of upcoming traffic delays
   (D) To provide information about a price increase

2. Where can employees obtain a permit?
   (A) From administration
   (B) From a parking garage
   (C) From a section manager
   (D) From a Web site

3. What is NOT implied about Gladden Pharmaceuticals?
   (A) It compensates employees for expenses by bank transfer.
   (B) It has hired additional employees.
   (C) It has an agreement with another local business.
   (D) It will be closed during some construction work.

Basin City, September 23 — A recent survey of commuters has revealed that people choose not to ride bicycles into town for a number of reasons. The most commonly cited reason is that there are limited places to park bicycles in town. That was unexpected as there are no restrictions that stop cyclists from leaving their bicycles on the street. It turns out that few people do so as there is no security and no protection from our very unpredictable weather. Other reasons were the lack of dedicated bicycle lanes and the convenience of trains and buses.

The mayor of Basin City has promised to spend more on infrastructure for people who choose to walk, run, or ride bicycles to work. Ms. Biggers is not the only one voicing support for carbon-free travel options. The dean of Gladstone University, which is located on the north shore of the Durant River, has said that the university will build a footbridge over the river to improve accessibility for students. It is highly likely that many workers in the central business district will also make use of the crossing. If you would like to learn more about that structure, you can view its plans in the city planning department at City Hall.

4. What is one purpose of the article?

(A) To announce the outcome of a study

(B) To encourage people to vote in an election

(C) To examine the activities of an environmental group

(D) To comment on a new rule

5. Who most likely is Ms. Biggers?

(A) A university administrator

(B) A cycling enthusiast

(C) A local businessperson

(D) A politician

6. What is NOT suggested about Basin City?

(A) Its population has been growing.

(B) It allows people to leave bicycles on the street.

(C) It has an effective public transportation system.

(D) Its weather conditions change suddenly.

7. According to the article, how can people learn more about the planned bridge?

(A) By visiting City Hall

(B) By calling Gladstone University

(C) By reading a newspaper article

(D) By viewing a construction company's Web site

5
NOT問題

Questions 1-3 refer to the following e-mail.

To:	GP_all@gladdenph.com
From:	Gina Tesch <gtesch@gladdenph.com>
Date:	August 12
Subject:	Parking lot

Dear All,

❶On Tuesday, August 27, construction work will begin on the parking lot. ❷We are providing 20 additional parking spaces to accommodate our growing workforce. Unfortunately, ❸the parking lot will be closed during construction. ❹Staff will be provided parking passes for a local parking garage. ❺They can only be used at Kenneth Parking at 23 Dolby Street. ❻Please speak to your immediate supervisor if you need one. ❼The passes will only be valid from 8:00 A.M. to 6:00 P.M. If you are parked there outside those hours, you will be charged an additional fee. ❽Please retain any receipts for such charges and submit them to administration. Your reimbursement will be made by bank transfer along with your monthly salary. The work is scheduled to finish on October 16.

Sincerely,

Gina Tesch
Administration
Gladden Pharmaceuticals

訳 設問1-3は次のEメールに関するものです。

宛先：GP_all@gladdenph.com
送信者：Gina Tesch <gtesch@gladdenph.com>
日付：8月12日
件名：駐車場

各位

8月27日火曜日に，駐車場の工事が始まります。当社は増加している従業員に対応するため，追加で20台分の駐車スペースを配備する予定です。残念ながら，工事期間中は駐車場が閉鎖されます。従業員には地元の駐車場の駐車許可証が配布されます。そのカードはDolby通り23番地のKennethパーキングでのみ使用できます。カードが必要な場合は直属の上司に申し出てください。許可証は午前8時から午後6時までの間のみ有効です。もし時間外に駐車すると，追加料金が課せられます。そのような料金の領収書は全て保管し，管理部に提出してください。払い戻しは銀行振込により，月給と合わせて支払われます。工事は10月16日に終了する予定です。

敬具

Gina Tesch
管理部
Gladden Pharmaceuticals社

語句 ☐ parking lot 駐車場　☐ construction work 建設工事　☐ additional 追加の
　　　☐ accommodate 〜を収容する　☐ workforce 総従業員
　　　☐ parking pass 駐車許可証　☐ immediate supervisor 直属の上司
　　　☐ valid 有効な　☐ retain 〜を保持する　☐ administration 管理部門
　　　☐ reimbursement 払い戻し，返金　☐ bank transfer 銀行振込
　　　☐ pharmaceuticals 薬品，薬剤

1.

What is the purpose of the e-mail?	Eメールの目的は何ですか。
(A) To announce a temporary situation at a company	(A) 会社の一時的な状況を知らせること
(B) To thank employees for assisting with a project	(B) プロジェクトを補佐した従業員に感謝すること
(C) To warn people of upcoming traffic delays	(C) 人々に来るべき交通の遅れについて警告すること
(D) To provide information about a price increase	(D) 値上げに関する情報を提供すること

正解 (A)

解説 Eメールの目的について問われています。❶，❸で「駐車場の工事が近く始まる」「工事期間中は駐車場が閉鎖される」と一時的に会社の駐車場が使用できないことを伝えているので，これをa temporary situationと言い換えた(A)が正解となります。

語句 □ temporary 一時的な　□ warn *A* of *B* AにBのことを警告する
　　　□ upcoming 来るべき　□ price increase 値上げ

2.

Where can employees obtain a permit?	従業員はどこで許可証を得ることができますか。
(A) From administration	
(B) From a parking garage	(A) 管理部から
(C) From a section manager	(B) 駐車場から
(D) From a Web site	(C) 部門長から
	(D) ウェブサイトから

正解 (C)

解説 従業員はどこで許可証をもらえるか問われています。❻に「カードが必要な場合は直属の上司に申し出るように」とあるので，直属の上司をsection managerと言い換えた(C)が正解となります。immediate supervisorは「直属の上司」を意味するので，それぞれの「所属長」に当たります。(A)管理部は従業員が追加料金の領収書を提出して精算してもらう部門であり，ここでは不正解です。

語句 □ permit 許可証

3.

What is NOT implied about Gladden Pharmaceuticals?

(A) It compensates employees for expenses by bank transfer.
(B) It has hired additional employees.
(C) It has an agreement with another local business.
(D) It will be closed during some construction work.

Gladden Pharmaceuticals社について示唆されていないことは何ですか。

(A) 従業員に銀行振込で経費を支払う。
(B) 追加の従業員を雇用した。
(C) 他の地元の会社と契約している。
(D) 建設工事の間閉鎖される。

正解 (D)

解説 Gladden Pharmaceuticals社について示唆されていないことは何かというNOT問題です。(A)については❽に追加料金発生時の返金に関する記載が、(B)については❷に従業員が増えたという記載が、(C)については❹、❺、❼に工事期間中はKennethパーキングで駐車できるよう対応している記載がそれぞれあります。よって、残った(D)が正解です。closed during some construction workは一見正しい記述のように見えるかもしれませんが、主語のItは質問文中のGladden Pharmaceuticals社を指しています。閉鎖されるのは会社の駐車場であって、会社自体ではありません。文中に出てきた表現につられて誤答選択肢に引っ掛からないようにしましょう。

語句 □ compensate *A* for *B* AにBを補償する　□ agreement 合意

Basin City, September 23 — ❶A recent survey of commuters has revealed that people choose not to ride bicycles into town for a number of reasons. The most commonly cited reason is that there are limited places to park bicycles in town. That was unexpected as ❷there are no restrictions that stop cyclists from leaving their bicycles on the street. ❸It turns out that few people do so as there is no security and no protection from our very unpredictable weather. ❹Other reasons were the lack of dedicated bicycle lanes and the convenience of trains and buses.

❺The mayor of Basin City has promised to spend more on infrastructure for people who choose to walk, run, or ride bicycles to work. Ms. Biggers is not the only one voicing support for carbon-free travel options. ❻The dean of Gladstone University, which is located on the north shore of the Durant River, has said that the university will build a footbridge over the river to improve accessibility for students. It is highly likely that many workers in the central business district will also make use of the crossing. ❼If you would like to learn more about that structure, you can view its plans in the city planning department at City Hall.

訳 設問4-7は次の記事に関するものです。

Basin City, 9月23日 — 通勤者に関する最近の調査結果から，人々は複数の理由により街には自転車を乗り入れないことを選んでいるとわかった。最も頻繁に引き合いに出された理由は，街には駐輪場所が限られているということだ。自転車利用者に路上駐輪をやめさせる規制はないので，それは予想外だった。安全ではないということと，この地域の予測できない天候からの保護がないという理由で，ほとんどの人が路上駐輪をしないと判明している。その他の理由としては，自転車専用レーンが不足していることと，電車やバスの利便性だった。

Basin City市長は，歩いて・走って・自転車に乗って通勤することを選択した人々のために，インフラにもっとお金をかけることを約束した。脱炭素の移動方法に支援を表明しているのはBiggers氏だけではない。Durant川北岸にあるGladstone大学の学部長は，学生の通いやすさを改善するため大学は川に歩道橋を建設すると言った。中央ビジネス街の多くのビジネスマンもまたその歩道橋を利用することは大いにあり得る。もしこの橋についてもっと知りたければ市役所の都市計画課で計画を閲覧することができる。

語句
- commuter 通勤者　reveal ～を明らかにする
- a number of ～ いくつかの～；たくさんの～（文脈によって区別する）
- commonly cited 頻繁に引き合いに出される　unexpected 予期しない
- restriction 規制，制限　stop ～ from doing ～が…するのをやめさせる
- turn out わかる，判明する　protection 保護　unpredictable 予測できない
- lack 不足　dedicated 専用の　convenience 利便性　mayor 市長
- promise to do ～することを約束する
- infrastructure インフラストラクチャー，社会基盤　voice ～を声明する
- carbon-free 炭素を含まない　dean 学部長　footbridge 歩道橋
- accessibility アクセス［接近］しやすさ　likely ありそうな
- make use of ～ ～を利用する　crossing 横断橋［歩道］
- structure 建造物，構造　city planning 都市計画　city hall 市役所

5
NOT 問題

4.

What is one purpose of the article?	記事の目的の1つは何ですか。
(A) To announce the outcome of a study	(A) 調査結果を伝えること
(B) To encourage people to vote in an election	(B) 人々に選挙での投票を奨励すること
(C) To examine the activities of an environmental group	(C) 環境団体の活動を調査すること
(D) To comment on a new rule	(D) 新しい規則に関して意見を述べること

正解 (A)

解説 記事の目的の1つが問われています。❶に「通勤者に関する最近の調査結果から，複数の理由により人々が自転車に乗っていないとわかった」とあり，第1段落全体を通してこの調査に関することが述べられています。第2段落では炭素排出量削減に向けた市と大学の取り組みについて述べられていますが，(B) (C) (D)に当たる内容は出てきません。よって，調査結果をthe outcome of a studyと表した(A)が正解となります。

語句 □ outcome 結果 □ study 調査，研究 □ vote 投票する □ election 選挙
□ examine ～を調査する

5.

Who most likely is Ms. Biggers?	Biggers氏とはおそらく誰ですか。
(A) A university administrator	(A) 大学幹部
(B) A cycling enthusiast	(B) 自転車愛好家
(C) A local businessperson	(C) 地元の実業家
(D) A politician	(D) 政治家

正解 (D)

解説 Biggers氏が誰か問われています。第2段落の❺に「Basin City市長は，歩いて・走って・自転車に乗って通勤することを選択した人々のためにインフラをもっと整備する」とあり，その直後にBiggers氏が登場し，「Biggers氏だけが脱炭素の移動方法に支援を表明しているわけではない」と述べています。つまり「歩いて・走って・自転車に乗っての通勤を奨励するBasin City市長」＝「脱酸素の移動方法支援の声明を出したBiggers氏」であることがわかります。よって，mayorをpoliticianと表した(D)が正解です。

語句 □ enthusiast 熱心な人 □ politician 政治家

6.

What is NOT suggested about Basin City?

(A) Its population has been growing.
(B) It allows people to leave bicycles on the street.
(C) It has an effective public transportation system.
(D) Its weather conditions change suddenly.

Basin Cityについて示されていないことは何ですか。

(A) 人口が増えてきている。
(B) 人々が路上に駐輪するのを容認している。
(C) 効率的な公共交通機関がある。
(D) 天候状況が急に変わる。

正解 (A)

解説 Basin Cityについて示されていないことが問われているNOT問題です。選択肢と本文を読むと，(B)は❷の「自転車利用者に路上駐輪をやめさせる規制はない」に，(C)は❹の「電車やバスの利便性」に，(D)は❸の「予測できない天候」にそれぞれ記載があります。一方，(A)の「人口が増えている」という記載は本文にはないので，これが正解となります。

語句 □ population 人口

7.

According to the article, how can people learn more about the planned bridge?

(A) By visiting City Hall
(B) By calling Gladstone University
(C) By reading a newspaper article
(D) By viewing a construction company's Web site

記事によると，人々はどのように計画された橋について詳しく知ることができますか。

(A) 市役所を訪ねることで
(B) Gladstone大学に電話をすることで
(C) 新聞記事を読むことで
(D) 建築会社のウェブサイトにアクセスすることで

正解 (A)

解説 人々は建設予定の橋についてどのように情報を得ればよいか問われています。❻でGladstone大学の学部長が，大学は川に橋を建設する予定だということを表明し，❼で「この橋に関してもっと知りたいなら市役所の都市計画課で閲覧可能」と述べているので，ここから(A)が正解だとわかります。

語句 □ view（ウェブサイトなど）を見る

6 文挿入位置問題

文挿入位置問題は，設問に示された文が文書のどこに入るかを問う問題です。シングルパッセージで毎回2問出題されます。一見難しそうですが，慣れると解きやすいタイプの問題でもありますので，解き方をマスターしていきましょう。

POINT 1 まずは文書を最後まで読み，文書の全体像を把握しよう。

文挿入位置問題の設問は，以下のような形をしています。文の挿入箇所の候補は文書中に—[1]—のように示されています。

In which of the positions marked [1], [2], [3], and [4] does the following sentence best belong?
"In addition, Mr. Osato loves TOEIC L&R Test very much."
(A) [1]
(B) [2]
(C) [3]
(D) [4]

文書を読んでいると—[1]—といった挿入箇所が目に入るので，つい気になってしまいますが，途中で正解を選ぼうとしてはいけません。文書の全体像が見えていない中途半端な状態では，文脈を正しく把握できないからです。**文挿入位置問題は，必ず文書を最後まで読んでから解く**ようにしましょう。

POINT 2 挿入文に着目し，まず，その中にヒントがないか探そう。

文書を最後まで読んだら，**挿入する文を確認し，文書との関連をチェック**しましょう。その際，以下のような表現がヒントになります。

接続副詞
【順接】so (that)「そのため」，therefore「それゆえ」，consequently「その結果」，hence「従って」
【逆接】however「しかしながら」，nevertheless / nonetheless「それにもかかわらず」，still「それでもなお」，yet「だが」

挿入文がTherefore, you should take an umbrella in case it rains.「従って，雨が降る場合に備えて傘を持っていった方がいいですよ」だったとしましょう。文頭に

Therefore「それゆえ」という接続副詞があります。thereforeは結果を示す際の表現なので，この前にはその根拠を示す情報（「今日は雨が降るかもしれない」など）があるはずです。

【追加・補足】furthermore「さらに」，in addition「加えて」，moreover「その上」，besides「加えて」

レストランの感想を述べている文書で，挿入文が <u>In addition</u>, the service was excellent!「加えて，サービスが素晴らしかったです！」だとします。in additionは追加を表す表現なので，この挿入文の前にFood was great.「料理が素晴らしかったです」などの情報があれば，レストランの「料理」に加えて「サービス」の素晴らしさについて述べることになり，自然な流れになります。

【順番】first「第一に」，second「第二に」，then「それから」，meanwhile「その間」など

挿入文が <u>Third</u>, it is very important to take exercise.「第三に，運動することがとても重要です」となっていた場合，挿入文が入る位置より前にFirst, ... , Second, ... などの情報が示されているはずです。これらをヒントに挿入位置を検討します。

▉▉接続詞
【順接】and「そして」，so「そのため」　　【逆接】but「しかし」など
接続詞の前後の内容が順接（または逆接）の関係になっていることに注意しましょう。

▉▉副詞
also / as well「〜もまた」，alike「同じように」など
これらの表現が含まれていれば，その前に類似・同等の内容が述べられています。

▉▉指示代名詞
this「これは」，these「これらは」，that「あれは」など
これらの代名詞が指す具体的な内容は，これらの語より前で示されていることがほとんどです。

POINT 3　どこに当てはめるか，挿入箇所の前後をチェックしよう。

挿入文を確認したら，次は**挿入箇所の前後をチェック**します。順接・逆接，原因・結果，追加・補足，類似・同等などの情報をヒントに，**そこに入れた場合，文脈が自然な流れになるか検討して正解を判断**します。次の例で考えてみましょう。

【挿入文】

Therefore, you should postpone the meeting.

「従って，会議を延期した方がよいでしょう」

文頭にTherefore「従って」とあるので，「会議を延期するべき理由」が直前にくると考えられます。文書を見てみましょう。

【文書】

My understanding is you are going to organize the annual regional sales meeting in Chicago. － [1] － . I heard a storm is approaching around there. － [2] － . Otherwise, you should set up a conference call instead.

「私の理解するところでは，あなたはChicagoで年次地区営業会議を開く予定ですね。－ [1] － その周辺は嵐が近づいていると聞きました。－ [2] － そうでなければ，代わりに電話会議を開催すべきです」

文書を確認したら，挿入文を当てはめて流れをチェックしてみます。

まず [1] です。

> My understanding is you are going to organize the annual regional sales meeting in Chicago.
> 「私の理解するところでは，あなたはChicagoで年次地区営業会議を開く予定ですね」
>
> Therefore, you should postpone the meeting.
> 「従って，会議を延期した方がよいでしょう」
>
> I heard a storm is approaching around there.
> 「その周辺は嵐が近づいていると聞きました」

会議の延期を勧める理由が「Chicagoで営業会議を開く予定であること」では，文意に合いませんね。

次に [2] に入れてみます。

I heard a storm is approaching around there.
「その周辺は嵐が近づいていると聞きました」

Therefore, you should postpone the meeting.
「従って，会議を延期した方がよいでしょう」

Otherwise, you should set up a conference call instead.
「そうでなければ，代わりに電話会議を開催すべきです」

どうでしょうか。会議の延期を勧める理由が「嵐が近づいているから」となり，文意が通りそうです。また，その後のOtherwise「そうでなければ」の指す内容も「会議を延期するのでなければ」という意味になり，こちらも文意が通ります。

このように**挿入文の前後を検証する方法**を本書では「**ハンバーガー方式**」と呼んでいます。挿入文を前後の文ではさんで文脈をしっかり確認できるので，大抵の問題は正解が見えてくるはずです。それでは，例題を見てみましょう。

例題 **Question 1** refers to the following article.

---

23 March — Work has started on the expansion of Brisbane City's Central Station. —[1]— . The work will take 18 months and cost just over $70 million to complete.

According to city planners, this is necessary to accommodate the city's growing population. —[2]— . The work should be completed in time for the Rohnson International Tennis Tournament, which the city will host next year. —[3]— .

It is a massive construction project, and planners warned that it would cause some problems. —[4]— . Indeed, traffic jams have become a common occurrence around the station and many trains have been arriving late because of work on the lines.

---

1. In which of the positions marked [1], [2], [3], and [4] does the following sentence best belong?

   "Already, many commuters have been complaining of delays caused by the work."

   (A) [1]
   (B) [2]
   (C) [3]
   (D) [4]

Question 1 refers to the following article.

記事　♪ 059

---

23 March — Work has started on the expansion of Brisbane City's Central Station. —[1]— . The work will take 18 months and cost just over $70 million to complete.

According to city planners, this is necessary to accommodate the city's growing population. —[2]— . The work should be completed in time for the Rohnson International Tennis Tournament, which the city will host next year. —[3]— .

It is a massive construction project, and planners warned that it would cause some problems. —[4]— . Indeed, traffic jams have become a common occurrence around the station and many trains have been arriving late because of work on the lines.

---

1. In which of the positions marked [1], [2], [3], and [4] does the following sentence best belong?

"Already, many commuters have been complaining of delays caused by
　└ 副詞はヒントになりやすい　　　　　　　　　　　└ 迷惑な内容がきそうだ
the work."

(A) [1]
(B) [2]
(C) [3]
(D) [4]

■■文書の概要

要素	内容
第1段落	・expansion ＝ 拡張工事について ・工事にかかる時間と費用（18カ月，約7,000万ドル）
第2段落	・市の人口が増えたので必要 ・テニスの国際試合までに完了する予定
第3段落	・問題が発生する可能性あり ・実際に，交通渋滞や列車遅延が発生している

挿入文は「すでに工事が原因の遅れに対して文句が出ている」という内容です。こ
こから「遅れの原因になっている工事」について，この前で触れられていると考え
られます。問題が発生していることは第3段落に書かれていました。そこで，[4]に
挿入文を入れてハンバーガー方式で確認してみます。

「大規模建設工事は問題を引き起こすかもしれない」

「すでに通勤者が文句を言っている」
「確かに，交通渋滞が頻繁に起きている」

となり，文意が通ります。従って，正解は (D) です。

正解と訳 設問1は次の記事に関するものです。

3月23日ー Brisbane City中央駅の拡張工事が開始された。―[1]― 工事の完了までには18カ月を要し，費用は7,000万ドル強かかる見通しだ。

都市設計担当者によると，これは増大する市の人口に対応するために必要だということである。―[2]― 工事は，来年市が主催するRohnson国際テニストーナメントまでには完了する予定だ。―[3]―

これは大規模な建設計画なので，担当者はいくつか問題が出てくるだろうと警告していた。―[4]― 確かに，駅周辺では交通渋滞が頻繁に発生し，多くの列車が線路上での作業のために遅延している。

1. 以下の文は[1]，[2]，[3]，[4]のどの位置に入るのが最も適していますか。
「すでに多くの通勤者が工事で生じる遅延について不平を言っている」
(A) [1]
(B) [2]
(C) [3]
(D) [4]

正解 (D)

語句 □ expansion 拡張，拡大 □ accommodate 〜を収容する，受け入れる
□ in time for 〜 〜に間に合って □ host 〜を主催する
□ massive 大規模な，巨大な □ cause 〜を引き起こす，〜の原因となる
□ indeed 確かに，本当に □ traffic jam 交通渋滞
□ common occurrence よくあること □ commuter 通勤者
□ complain of 〜 〜について不平を言う

6

文挿入位置問題

攻略法まとめ 文挿入位置問題

• まずは一通り文書全体を読んで意味をつかもう。

• 問われている文に着目し，その中にヒントがないか探そう。

• どこに当てはめるか，挿入箇所の前後をチェックしよう。

次の文書を読み，各設問に対して最も適切な答えを(A)(B)(C)(D)の
中から1つ選びなさい。

Questions 1-3 refer to the following e-mail.

To:	All Grafton Hotel Employees
From:	Trish Belmont
Date:	October 14
Subject:	Maintenance

Dear All,

It is impossible for the maintenance staff to check every section of the hotel every day. —[1]— . Even small imperfections can have a negative effect on reviews. —[2]— . We rely on employees in every department to help us identify problem areas.

Recently, management provided each staff member with a mobile phone. —[3]— . You will find that every department's phone number has been preprogrammed into the device. I urge you to use it to contact us the moment you find something that needs our attention. —[4]— . To help us prioritize work, please let us know when guests are likely to use the area in question. Otherwise, we will resolve all issues in the order that they occur.

Sincerely,

Trish Belmont
Director of Maintenance

1. What is the purpose of the e-mail?

   (A) To thank employees for helping with a cleanup
   (B) To encourage employees to report problems
   (C) To announce the launch of a publicity campaign
   (D) To warn staff members about the rules of mobile phone use

2. What is mentioned about the employees' mobile phones?

   (A) They include a list of phone numbers.
   (B) They should be exchanged for new ones.
   (C) They must be charged at the start of each day.
   (D) They have been malfunctioning.

3. In which of the positions marked [1], [2], [3], and [4] does the following sentence best belong?

   "However, letting a burned-out light bulb go unchecked for even a few hours makes the hotel seem run-down in the eyes of our guests."

   (A) [1]
   (B) [2]
   (C) [3]
   (D) [4]

6

文挿入位置問題

Bronson Appoints New CEO

By Helen Rasmussen, December 3

TOKYO— In Japan and the USA, the Bronson Corporation has been a household name for many years. —[1]— . Its line of hair care products has always been popular, but when the company started offering skincare products as well as deodorants, sales almost doubled. —[2]— . Nevertheless, due to increased competition, Bronson has gone from number one to number three in its two main markets, the USA and Japan. Company founder and CEO, Junichiro Tanaka, recently retired giving control of the company to an outsider by the name of Takanori Shimizu. —[3]— . Mr. Shimizu has previously held executive positions at TRJ Inc., Duraplay, and Rutsu Appliances — a diverse list of companies to say the least. All three of these companies were in a much better position at the end of his leadership. As a result, there is a lot of expectation that he will reverse Bronson Corporation's fortunes. While Bronson's sales declined under its previous management, there is a lot of respect for the former CEO. —[4]— . At his retirement ceremony at Tokyo's prestigious Belvedere Hotel, he was presented with a lifetime achievement award by the board of directors and the company's shareholders.

4. What type of business most likely is Bronson Corporation?

(A) A consultancy firm for international businesses

(B) A chain of appliance stores

(C) A manufacturer of consumer goods

(D) A promoter of sports events

5. According to the article, what is Mr. Shimizu best known for?

(A) Hiring experts from diverse fields

(B) Making companies more profitable

(C) Coming up with clever product designs

(D) Promoting products in foreign markets

6. What is mentioned about Mr. Tanaka's contribution to Bronson Corporation?

(A) It will be covered in a magazine article.

(B) It has been criticized by company shareholders.

(C) It inspired the directors of other companies.

(D) It was recognized despite decreased sales.

7. In which of the positions marked [1], [2], [3], and [4] does the following sentence best belong?

"This was somewhat of a shock to many people familiar with the company because such decisions have traditionally been made internally."

(A) [1]

(B) [2]

(C) [3]

(D) [4]

6

文挿入位置問題

Questions 1-3 refer to the following e-mail.

Eメール・手紙 ♪ 060

To:	All Grafton Hotel Employees
From:	Trish Belmont
Date:	October 14
Subject:	Maintenance

Dear All,

❶It is impossible for the maintenance staff to check every section of the hotel every day. —[1]— . ❷Even small imperfections can have a negative effect on reviews. —[2]— . We rely on employees in every department to help us identify problem areas.

Recently, management provided each staff member with a mobile phone. —[3]— . ❸You will find that every department's phone number has been preprogrammed into the device. ❹I urge you to use it to contact us the moment you find something that needs our attention. —[4]— . To help us prioritize work, please let us know when guests are likely to use the area in question. Otherwise, we will resolve all issues in the order that they occur.

Sincerely,

Trish Belmont
Director of Maintenance

訳 設問1-3は次のEメールに関するものです。

宛先：Graftonホテル全従業員
送信者：Trish Belmont
日付：10月14日
件名：メンテナンス

各位

メンテナンススタッフが毎日ホテルの全ての区域を確認するのは不可能です。—[1]— 小さな不備であっても，お客さまのレビューに悪い影響を及ぼすことがあります。—[2]— 私たちは各部署の従業員の皆さんが問題箇所の特定に協力してくれることを期待しています。

最近，経営幹部は各従業員に携帯電話を支給しました。—[3]— その機器には全部署の電話番号があらかじめ設定されているのがわかると思います。皆さんには，私たちの対応が必要な案件を見つけた場合はすぐにそれを使って私たちにご連絡いただきたいと思います。—[4]— 私たちが作業の優先順位をつける際の参考になるように，問題の箇所をお客さまがいつお使いになりそうかをお知らせください。そうでなければ，私たちは全ての案件に発生順に対応することになります。

よろしくお願いします。

Trish Belmont
メンテナンス部長

語句 □ imperfection 不備，不完全なこと □ negative effect 悪影響
□ rely on ～ ～に［を］頼る □ identify （問題など）を特定する
□ management 経営陣 □ mobile phone 携帯電話
□ preprogram ～にプログラムをあらかじめ組み入れる □ device 機器
□ urge ～ to *do* ～に…するよう促す □ the moment (that) ～ ～の瞬間
□ prioritize ～に優先順位をつける □ be likely to *do* ～しそうだ
□ otherwise そうでなければ □ order 順番 □ occur 発生する，起こる

1.

目的・テーマを問う問題

What is the purpose of the e-mail? | Eメールの目的は何ですか。
(A) To thank employees for helping with a cleanup | (A) 清掃に協力してくれた従業員に感謝すること
(B) To encourage employees to report problems | (B) 従業員に問題を報告するよう仕向けること
(C) To announce the launch of a publicity campaign | (C) 広報キャンペーンの開始を知らせること
(D) To warn staff members about the rules of mobile phone use | (D) 従業員に携帯電話の使用に関するルールについて警告すること

正解 (B)

解説 Eメールの目的が問われています。第1段落の❶で「メンテナンススタッフだけでホテル全体をチェックするのは難しい」と背景を述べ，第2段落の❹で「メンテナンス部の対応が必要な案件を見つけたらすぐに連絡を」と依頼しています。それを「問題を報告するよう仕向ける」と言い換えた(B)が正解です。メールの目的は一般的に冒頭の1文に示されることが多いですが，この文書のように「背景を説明してから本題へ移る」パターンもあるので注意しましょう。

語句 □ cleanup 清掃 □ encourage ～ to *do* ～に…するよう促す，仕向ける
□ launch 開始，着手 □ publicity 宣伝，広告

2.

What is mentioned about the employees' mobile phones?

(A) They include a list of phone numbers.
(B) They should be exchanged for new ones.
(C) They must be charged at the start of each day.
(D) They have been malfunctioning.

従業員の携帯電話について何が述べられていますか。

(A) 電話番号リストが入っている。
(B) 新しいものに交換されるべきである。
(C) 一日の始めに充電しなければならない。
(D) 故障を起こしている。

正解 (A)

解説 従業員の携帯電話について述べられていることを問う問題です。❸に「その機器には全部署の電話番号があらかじめ設定されている」とあるので，それを「電話番号リストが入っている」と言い換えた(A)が正解です。ここでは，❸の文に出てくるdeviceがmobile phoneを言い換えたものだと気付くことが解答のポイントです。

語句 □ exchange 〜を交換する □ malfunction（機械などが）故障を起こす

3.

In which of the positions marked [1], [2], [3], and [4] does the following sentence best belong?

"However, letting a burned-out light bulb go unchecked for even a few hours makes the hotel seem run-down in the eyes of our guests."

(A) [1]
(B) [2]
(C) [3]
(D) [4]

以下の文は[1]，[2]，[3]，[4]のどの位置に入るのが最も適していますか。

「しかし，切れた電球をたとえ数時間でも点検しないでいると，お客さまの目にはホテルが荒廃しているように見えてしまいます」

(A) [1]
(B) [2]
(C) [3]
(D) [4]

正解 (A)

解説 文挿入位置問題です。挿入する文は「しかし，切れた電球を放置するとお客さまの目にはネガティブに映る」という内容で，前の文に対して逆接で続いています。この文の当てはまる箇所を探すと，❶に「メンテナンス部がホテル全体を調べるのは困難」，そして❷に「小さな不備であってもお客さまのレビューに悪い影響を与える」とあります。この間に入れると，「メンテナンス部は全てを調べられない」→「しかし，切れた電球を放置しただけでお客さまに荒れた印象を与える（逆接）」→「小さな不備でもレビューに悪影響を及ぼす（前の文の補足）」と論理的につながり，(A)が正解だとわかります。「切れた電球を放置する」のは「小さな不備」の例の1つなので(B)にも入りそうですが，挿入文には逆接を表すhoweverが入っているためうまくつながりません。

語句 □ light bulb 電球 □ unchecked 点検されていない □ run-down 荒廃した

Questions 4-7 refer to the following article.

記事　♪ 061

Bronson Appoints New CEO

By Helen Rasmussen, December 3

TOKYO— In Japan and the USA, the Bronson Corporation has been a household name for many years. —[1]— . **①**Its line of hair care products has always been popular, but when the company started offering skincare products as well as deodorants, sales almost doubled. —[2]— . Nevertheless, due to increased competition, Bronson has gone from number one to number three in its two main markets, the USA and Japan. **②**Company founder and CEO, Junichiro Tanaka, recently retired giving control of the company to an outsider by the name of Takanori Shimizu. —[3]— . Mr. Shimizu has previously held executive positions at TRJ Inc., Duraplay, and Rutsu Appliances — a diverse list of companies to say the least. **③**All three of these companies were in a much better position at the end of his leadership. **④**As a result, there is a lot of expectation that he will reverse Bronson Corporation's fortunes. **⑤**While Bronson's sales declined under its previous management, there is a lot of respect for the former CEO. —[4]— . **⑥**At his retirement ceremony at Tokyo's prestigious Belvedere Hotel, he was presented with a lifetime achievement award by the board of directors and the company's shareholders.

6

文挿入位置問題

訳 設問4-7は次の記事に関するものです。

Bronson社，新CEOを任命

文責 Helen Rasmussen，12月3日

TOKYO —日本とアメリカでは，Bronson社は何年にもわたっておなじみの名前となっている。—[1]— そのヘアケア製品は常に人気商品だったが，同社がデオドラント用品やスキンケア製品の提供を始めると，売り上げはほぼ倍増した。—[2]— それにもかかわらず，競争激化により Bronson社は2つの主要な市場であるアメリカと日本で1位から3位へと後退してしまった。創業者でありCEOである Junichiro Tanaka氏は最近勇退し，会社の経営を外部の人間である Takanori Shimizu 氏に譲った。—[3]— Shimizu氏は以前，TRJ社，Duraplay 社，Rutsu Appliances社といった，控えめに言っても多様な企業で経営役員の職を担っていた。これらの3社全てがShimizu氏による経営の終盤には，業界でずっと良い位置につけていた。その結果，彼がBronson社の気運を転換させるという期待は大きい。Bronson社の売り上げは前経営陣の下で下落したが，前CEOに対する尊敬の念は強い。—[4]— Tokyoの一流ホテルであるBelvedereホテルで行われたTanaka氏の勇退セレモニーでは，取締役会と株主から特別功労賞が贈呈された。

語句 □ household name よく知られた名前　□ hair care 髪の手入れ
　　　□ skincare 肌の手入れ　□ deodorant デオドラント，（体臭の）消臭剤

4.

情報をもとに推測する問題

What type of business most likely is Bronson Corporation? (A) A consultancy firm for international businesses (B) A chain of appliance stores (C) A manufacturer of consumer goods (D) A promoter of sports events	Bronson社はおそらくどんな業種ですか。 (A) 国際的な事業のコンサルタント会社 (B) 家庭用電器店のチェーン (C) 消費財の製造会社 (D) スポーツイベントの興行会社

正解 (C)

解説 Bronson社は何の会社か問われています。❶から「ヘアケア製品，デオドラント用品，スキンケア製品を扱っている」ことがわかるので，「消費財の製造会社」という表現に言い換えた(C)が正解となります。

語句 □ consultancy firm コンサルタント会社　□ appliance 家庭用（電気）器具
□ consumer goods 消費財　□ promoter 興行者

5.

詳細を問う問題

According to the article, what is Mr. Shimizu best known for? (A) Hiring experts from diverse fields (B) Making companies more profitable (C) Coming up with clever product designs (D) Promoting products in foreign markets	記事によると，Shimizu氏は何で最も有名ですか。 (A) 多様な分野から専門家を雇うこと (B) 会社の収益を上げること (C) 巧みな製品デザインを考案すること (D) 海外市場で製品の販売を促進すること

正解 (B)

解説 記事からShimizu氏が何で知られているか問われています。❸，❹に「以前在任した会社全てでShimizu氏による経営の末，業績がかなり改善された」「その結果を受けて，Bronson社の気運をShimizu氏が転換させる（＝業績が回復する）と大いに期待されている」とあることから，Shimizu氏は「会社の収益を上げる」ことで知られているとわかります。(A) (C) (D)の内容はいずれも本文では述べられておらず，不正解です。

語句 □ expert 専門家　□ profitable 利益になる，もうかる
□ come up with 〜 〜を考案する　□ clever 巧みな

6.

What is mentioned about Mr. Tanaka's
contribution to Bronson Corporation?

(A) It will be covered in a magazine article.

(B) It has been criticized by company
shareholders.

(C) It inspired the directors of other
companies.

(D) It was recognized despite decreased
sales.

Bronson社に対するTanaka氏の貢献
について何が述べられていますか。

(A) 雑誌記事で報道されることになる。

(B) 会社の株主に批判されてきた。

(C) 他社の役員を奮起させた。

(D) 売り上げの減少にもかかわらず認め
られた。

正解 (D)

解説 前社長であるTanaka氏の会社に対する貢献について述べられていることが問われています。
❺，**❻**に「前社長の下で売り上げは下落したものの，尊敬されている」「Tokyoの一流ホテル
で行われた勇退セレモニーでは特別功労賞が贈呈された」とあるので，これまでの功績が認め
られていることがわかります。正解は(D)で，recognizeは「(功績など)を認める，高く評価
する」という意味です。

語句 □ contribution 貢献　□ criticize 〜を批判する　□ inspire 〜を奮起させる

7.

In which of the positions marked [1], [2], [3],
and [4] does the following sentence best
belong?

"This was somewhat of a shock to many
people familiar with the company because
such decisions have traditionally been made
internally."

(A) [1]

(B) [2]

(C) [3]

(D) [4]

以下の文は[1]，[2]，[3]，[4]のどの位置
に入るのが最も適していますか。

「そのような決定は伝統的に内輪で行わ
れてきたので，このことはこの会社に関
係の深い多くの人にとっては幾分驚き
であった」

(A) [1]

(B) [2]

(C) [3]

(D) [4]

正解 (C)

解説 文挿入位置問題です。挿入する文は「そのような決定は伝統的に内輪で行われてきたので，こ
のことは会社に関係の深い人々にとっては幾分驚きだった」という意味なので，この文の直前
で何らかの決定がなされたと推測できます。その観点から探すと，**❷**の「創業者でありCEO
のTanaka氏は最近勇退し，会社の経営を外部の人間に譲った」という社長交代人事がその決
定だと考えられます。また，今回の人事について，内部ではなく外部から社長を迎えたという
内容も文脈に合っています。以上から，(C)が正解です。

語句 □ somewhat of 〜　幾分〜　□ be familiar with 〜　〜と親しい，近い関係の
　　　□ internally 内部で

7 同義語問題

同義語問題はその名の通り，「文書中のある語（句）と同じ意味の語（句）を選ぶ問題」です。毎回1〜2問程度，出題されます。確実に正解するためにいくつかコツがありますので，以下のポイントをしっかり押さえましょう。

POINT 1 まずは，語彙問題のつもりで解こう。

同義語問題の設問は，以下のような形をしています。

In the e-mail, the word "equal" in paragraph 1, line 2, is closest in meaning to
(A) calculate
(B) divide
(C) match
(D) excel

このタイプの問題は，**問われている語（句）と同じ意味の語（句）を選択肢から選ぶので，基本的には語彙問題**と考えられます。

POINT 2 迷った場合は文脈を確認しよう。

問われている語が多くの意味を持つ語だと，選択肢の中に複数の同義語がある場合があります。**語彙力だけで正解を絞れないなと思ったら，必ず文脈を確認**しましょう。前後2〜3行の内容をつかめれば，そこから推測して解くことができます。例えば，次の文のcoveringに最も意味が近い語を選ぶ問題が出たとします。

I have just returned from covering the game. A lot of spectators turned out for the final.
(A) protecting (C) reporting
(B) hiding (D) including

「試合をcoverすることから戻ったところだ。大勢の観客が決勝戦に繰り出した」
(A) 保護すること (C) 報道すること
(B) 隠すこと (D) 含むこと

coverは多義語で，選択肢の語全ての意味を持っています。最初の1文だけで察しがつく人もいるかもしれませんが，次の文を読むと「観客（spectators）が決勝戦（final）を見に来た」とあります。それを念頭に置いて文脈になじむ語を選択肢から探すと「試合を報道すること（reporting）から戻った」と考えるのが最も自然な

文脈だとわかります。

問われている語自体の意味がわからない場合も同様に，その部分を空所と考えて，選択肢から文脈に合う語を選ぶという解き方がよいでしょう。

POINT 3 Part 5の語彙問題やPart 7のパラフレーズで語彙力を養おう。

同義語問題は，**Part 5の語彙問題で語彙を増やしたり，Part 7で問題文と選択肢の語の言い換え（パラフレーズ）をストックしたりしていく**と，「この語とこの語は同じ意味で使われるな」と，正解を絞り込むことができるようになってきます。

それでは，例題を解いてみましょう。

例題 Question 1 refers to the following e-mail.

To:	Dawn McKenzie <dmckenzie@nicholhomeservices.com>
From:	Hal Botham <hbotham@darkstars.com>
Date:	November 19
Subject:	Thanks

Dear Ms. McKenzie,

I am writing to express my gratitude for the gardening work you carried out at my home on November 5 and 12. I got home from my trip to the UK to find that my garden was looking even better than it did when I left. I am pretty sure that your service actually exceeded the promises made on your Web site. I really only expected you to mow the lawn and water the plants, so you can imagine how surprised I was to find that you had also cleaned the footpath and removed leaves from the pond. I will be writing a glowing review on your Web site and recommending you to all of my friends.

Sincerely,
Hal Botham

1. The word "glowing" in paragraph 1, line 7, is closest in meaning to
   (A) bright
   (B) positive
   (C) attractive
   (D) revealing

To:	Dawn McKenzie <dmckenzie@nicholhomeservices.com>
From:	Hal Botham <hbotham@darkstars.com>
Date:	November 19
Subject:	Thanks

Dear Ms. McKenzie,

┌─ メールはガーデニング業者へのお礼。素晴らしかったとべた褒めしている

I am writing to express my gratitude for the gardening work you carried out at my home on November 5 and 12. I got home from my trip to the UK to find that my garden was looking even better than it did when I left. I am pretty sure that your service actually exceeded the promises made on your Web site. I really only expected you to mow the lawn and water the plants, so you can imagine how surprised I was to find that you had also cleaned the footpath and removed leaves from the pond. I will be writing a glowing review on your Web site and recommending you to all of my friends.

└─ 「(glowing) なレビューを書いて友達に薦める」とあるので，glowingは好意的で肯定的な意味

Sincerely,

Hal Botham

1. The word "glowing" in paragraph 1, line 7, is closest in meaning to

(A) bright

(B) positive　→ 称賛するような好意的かつ肯定的な意味を示すのはこれ！

(C) attractive

(D) revealing

"glowing" という語の意味がわからなくても，「友達に薦める」という文脈から好意的かつ肯定的な語が入ることが推測できます。従って正解は (B) です。

正解と訳 設問1は次のEメールに関するものです。

宛先：Dawn McKenzie <dmckenzie@nicholhomeservices.com>
送信者：Hal Botham <hbotham@darkstars.com>
日付：11月19日
件名：お礼

McKenzieさんへ

11月5日と12日にわが家でやっていただいた庭仕事についてお礼を言いたくてこれを書いています。イギリス旅行から戻ると、私の庭は家を出る前よりもきれいになっていました。あなた方のサービスは、ウェブサイトで約束していることを実際に超えていると確信しています。私は本当に単に芝を刈って植物に水をやってもらうだけのつもりだったので、あなたが庭の小道を掃除したり、池に落ちた葉を取り除いてくれたりしたことに気付いたときの私の驚きようは想像に難くないでしょう。あなた方のウェブサイトに称賛に満ちたレビューを書いて、私の友人全員に薦めたいと思います。

敬具

Hal Botham

1. 第1段落・7行目にある"glowing"に最も意味が近いのは
(A) 明るい
(B) 前向きな
(C) 魅力的な
(D) 暴露的な

正解 (B)

語句 □ gratitude 感謝　□ even（比較級を強調して）ずっと　□ pretty かなり，とても
□ exceed ～を超える　□ mow（芝など）を刈る　□ water ～に水をやる
□ footpath 小道　□ pond 池

攻略法まとめ 同義語問題

・語彙問題（空所補充問題）のつもりで取り組もう。

・迷った場合は文脈をフル活用しよう。

・Part 5の語彙問題，Part 7のパラフレーズ（言い換え）などで語彙力を高めよう。

次の文書を読み，各設問に対して最も適切な答えを(A)(B)(C)(D)の中から1つ選びなさい。

Questions 1-5 refer to the following e-mail and article.

To:	Billy Rand <brand@randeventmanagement.com>
From:	Yurika Kawano <ykawano@kawanopromotions.com>
Date:	6 April
Subject:	Thanks

Dear Billy,

I am writing to thank you for taking the time to meet with me this afternoon. I enjoyed catching up after so long. It was interesting to hear that all our old classmates from university are doing so well. I hope you will attend the class reunion in Hull in September.

Regarding our discussions, Kawano Promotions would like to team up with Rand Event Management to arrange a national tour of the Broadway musical, *Raindancer*. We need to arrange a meeting between the relevant people from both of our companies to discuss issues such as the schedule and the budget.

I am hoping that we can start the tour in London around 10 October. The theater company has indicated that it will be available by then.

Sincerely,

Yurika Kawano

Raindancer Lives up to Expectations

By Breeze Dawson, staff writer

October 19

The UK premiere of *Raindancer* took place at Manchester's Lumiere Theater last night. The promoters claim that tickets sold out in hours, and that is understandable considering the excellent reviews the musical received in the United States. It certainly lived up to expectations. The full cast and crew from the New York performance is here, so there were none of the problems that most productions experience on their opening nights.

The two leads, Margaret Harris and Peter Patel, were both wonderful in their roles. In the UK, we have only ever seen him in daytime television dramas and the occasional movie, so it was surprising to find that Patel's singing voice was quite good. The supporting cast were all excellent, too. A spokesperson for the production company mentioned that some of them will leave during the tour to be replaced with local performers. After Manchester, *Raindancer* will tour other major cities including Liverpool, Edinburgh, Dublin, and London.

1. What is suggested about Mr. Rand and Ms. Kawano?

(A) They studied together in university.
(B) They have worked together before.
(C) They established a company together.
(D) They will meet again on April 7.

2. What is one purpose of the e-mail?

(A) To request tickets for a performance
(B) To recommend a production to a friend
(C) To suggest a partnership
(D) To invite a colleague to attend an event

3. In the e-mail, the word "issues" in paragraph 2, line 4, is closest in meaning to

(A) editions
(B) topics
(C) distributions
(D) results

4. Where did the writer of the article see the musical?

(A) In Hull
(B) In Manchester
(C) In London
(D) In New York

5. What is implied about Mr. Patel?

(A) He has not performed on stage before.
(B) He is not known for his singing.
(C) He will leave the production mid-tour.
(D) He is originally from the UK.

7

同義語問題

※通常，ダブルパッセージ，トリプルパッセージにはクロスリファレンス問題が出題されますが，本書では「設問タイプ別攻略法 10 クロスリファレンス問題」までこのタイプの問題はあえて出題していません。

Questions 6-10 refer to the following e-mail, notice, and article.

To:	Rod Butler <rbutler@rainydayco.com>
From:	Glenda Yates <gyates@ftassociates.com>
Date:	July 7
Subject:	Access

Dear Mr. Butler,

I received a call from a company called Freeman-Star Productions this afternoon. It's the production company responsible for the television program *How They Do It*. They want to make a video about the process of mass-producing umbrellas and asked me to introduce one of our clients. I told the caller that I would raise the topic with the management of Rainy Day Co. To produce the video, they would need access to the entire assembly line. Unfortunately, they are not offering any money, but they say they will mention the company name and show the logo in the video, so you should get some good exposure.

I've asked them to wait until this Wednesday for a reply.

Sincerely,

Glenda Yates
Business Advisor
FT Associates

Notice
Attention All Employees

Management has agreed to allow Freeman-Star Productions to film the assembly line from August 18 to August 21. It is highly likely that your faces will appear in the final program and it will be necessary for Freeman-Star Productions to have signed authorization from each employee. Of course, if you would prefer not to appear on video, you will not be required to do so. To help the film crew know who not to film, please put a green strap on your identification badge while they are here. Employees who do not mind being filmed should use the usual black strap.

Entertainment
A New Home for *How They Do It*

The popular television show *How They Do It* has moved from its original broadcaster to the online streaming service Vidster. KMG Television still has the rights to the first seven seasons of the program and will likely continue to show reruns on their free-to-air channel. However, according to the contract Freeman-Star Productions has signed with Vidster, seasons eight to twelve will only be available to people with paid subscriptions to Vidster. Subscriptions can cost as much as $23 a month, so this may come as a shock to some fans of the show.

The first episode of season eight will be available tonight. Vidster subscribers will get an exclusive look inside the production facility of Rainy Day Co., where Rainy Day brand umbrellas and parasols are made. Rainy Day Co. has been drawing a lot of attention since Mary Cortez, the star of the popular drama *Milford's Way*, was spotted using one of their umbrellas last month.

7 同義語問題

6. Where does Ms. Yates most likely work?

(A) At a consultancy firm
(B) At a manufacturing company
(C) At a department store
(D) At a production company

7. What is a benefit of the offer from Freeman-Star Productions?

(A) A financial payment
(B) Equipment upgrades
(C) Assistance with product design
(D) Some free publicity

8. What is the purpose of the notice?

(A) To request volunteers to give a tour of the facility
(B) To inform employees of a visit to the factory
(C) To announce a new company policy

(D) To thank staff members for complying with a request

9. In the notice, the word "mind" in paragraph 1, line 8, is closest in meaning to

(A) attend to
(B) perform
(C) object to
(D) agree upon

10. What is suggested about future episodes of *How They Do It*?

(A) They will profile the employees of Rainy Day Co.
(B) It will be possible for the audience to request filming locations.
(C) It will be necessary to pay money to view them.
(D) They will be narrated by famous personalities.

Questions 1-5 refer to the following e-mail and article.　Eメール・手紙　♪ 063

To:	Billy Rand <brand@randeventmanagement.com>
From:	Yurika Kawano <ykawano@kawanopromotions.com>
Date:	6 April
Subject:	Thanks

Dear Billy,

I am writing to thank you for taking the time to meet with me this afternoon. I enjoyed catching up after so long. ❶It was interesting to hear that all our old classmates from university are doing so well. I hope you will attend the class reunion in Hull in September.

❷Regarding our discussions, Kawano Promotions would like to team up with Rand Event Management to arrange a national tour of the Broadway musical, *Raindancer*. ❸We need to arrange a meeting between the relevant people from both of our companies to discuss issues such as the schedule and the budget.

I am hoping that we can start the tour in London around 10 October. The theater company has indicated that it will be available by then.

Sincerely,

Yurika Kawano

記事　♪ 064

Raindancer Lives up to Expectations

By Breeze Dawson, staff writer

October 19

❹The UK premiere of *Raindancer* took place at Manchester's Lumiere Theater last night. The promoters claim that tickets sold out in hours, and that is understandable considering the excellent reviews the musical received in the United States. It certainly lived up to expectations. The full cast and crew from the New York performance is here, so there were none of the problems that most productions experience on their opening nights.

The two leads, Margaret Harris and Peter Patel, were both wonderful in their roles. ❺In the UK, we have only ever seen him in daytime television dramas and the occasional movie, so it was surprising to find that Patel's singing voice was quite good. The supporting cast were all excellent, too. A spokesperson for the production company mentioned that some of them will leave during the tour to be replaced with local performers. After Manchester, *Raindancer* will tour other major cities including Liverpool, Edinburgh, Dublin, and London.

訳 設問1-5は次のEメールと記事に関するものです。

宛先：Billy Rand <brand@randeventmanagement.com>
送信者：Yurika Kawano <ykawano@kawanopromotions.com>
日付：4月6日
件名：お礼

Billyへ

今日の午後私と会う時間を取ってくれてありがとう。久しぶりにいろいろ話せて楽しかったです。大学のクラスメートたちが皆元気にやっていることを聞けてよかったです。9月にHullで行われる同窓会にあなたも出席してくれるといいなと思います。

話していたことですが, Kawano Promotions社はRand Event Management社と連携してブロードウェーミュージカル『Raindancer』の全国ツアーを企画したいと思います。我々両社の関係者間で打ち合わせを行い，スケジュールや予算といった課題について検討する必要があります。

10月10日ごろLondonでツアーを開始できればと考えています。劇団はそのころには可能だとのことでした。

敬具

Yurika Kawano

語句 □catch up（久しぶりに会って）近況などを聞く　□after so long 久しぶりに
□class reunion 同窓会　□regarding ～に関して
□team up with ～ ～とチームと組む，協働する　□relevant 関連した
□issue 課題　□indicate ～を示す，表明する

『Raindancer』が期待に応える

文責Breeze Dawson，専属ライター

10月19日

『Raindancer』のイギリスでの初演が昨夜, Manchesterの Lumiere劇場で上演された。興行会社はチケットが数時間で売り切れたと言っているが,このミュージカルがアメリカで大評判を博したことを考えれば納得できる。それはまさしく期待に応えるものだった。New York公演の全出演者とスタッフが来ており，多くの興行が初演の夜に遭遇する問題は何一つ起こらなかった。

主演の2人であるMargaret HarrisとPeter Patelは，双方ともに見事に役を演じた。イギリスではPatel氏のことを昼間のテレビドラマか時折の映画でしか見たことがなかったので,彼の歌声がとてもいいというのは驚きだった。また助演者も皆,本当に素晴らしかった。制作会社の広報担当者は出演者の何人かはツアーの途中で離れ,地元の俳優が代役を務めると話した。『Raindancer』はManchesterの後, Liverpool, Edinburgh, Dublin, そしてLondonを含むその他の主要都市を回ることになる。

語句 □live up to expectations 期待に応える　□staff writer 専属ライター
□premiere 初演，プレミア　□take place 開催される　□claim ～と主張する
□understandable 当然の　□certainly 確かに　□full cast 全出演者
□crew（一緒に仕事をする）一団　□lead 主役　□role 役
□daytime 昼間の，日中の　□occasional 時々の

1.

選択肢照合型問題

What is suggested about Mr. Rand and Ms. Kawano?	Rand さんと Kawano さんについて何が示されていますか。
(A) They studied together in university.	(A) 大学で一緒に勉強した。
(B) They have worked together before.	(B) かつて一緒に働いたことがある。
(C) They established a company together.	(C) 一緒に会社を設立した。
(D) They will meet again on April 7.	(D) 4月7日に再び会う。

正解 (A)

解説 Rand さんと Kawano さんについて示されていることが問われています。メールの❶で Kawano さんが Rand さんに対し、「大学の旧友たちについて話が聞けてよかった。9月にある大学の同窓会に出席してほしい」と書いていることから、2人は同じ大学に通っていたとわかります。これを言い換えた(A)が正解です。

語句 □ establish 〜を設立する

2.

目的・テーマを問う問題

What is one purpose of the e-mail?	E メールの目的の1つは何ですか。
(A) To request tickets for a performance	(A) ある公演のチケットを求めること
(B) To recommend a production to a friend	(B) 友人にある作品を推奨すること
(C) To suggest a partnership	(C) 業務提携を提案すること
(D) To invite a colleague to attend an event	(D) 同僚をあるイベントに招待すること

正解 (C)

解説 E メールの目的の1つが問われています。❷、❸で「Kawano Promotions 社は Rand Event Management 社と連携してミュージカルの全国ツアーを企画したい」「両社の担当者で打ち合わせを」と仕事上での連携を申し出ているので、ここからそれを言い換えた(C)が正解となります。

語句 □ partnership 協力、提携

3.

同義語問題

In the e-mail, the word "issues" in paragraph 2, line 4, is closest in meaning to	E メールの第2段落・4行目にある "issues" に最も意味が近いのは
(A) editions	(A) 版
(B) topics	(B) 話題
(C) distributions	(C) 配布
(D) results	(D) 結果

正解 (B)

解説 同義語問題です。問われている文を見ると、issues は「スケジュールや予算といった課題について」と、打ち合わせるべき「問題、課題」という意味で使われています。この語に最も近いのは「話題」を意味する(B)で、これが正解です。なお、issue には「(雑誌などの) ○月号」という意味もあるので覚えておきましょう。

語句 □ edition (雑誌・書籍の) 版　□ topic 話題　□ distribution 配布

4.

Where did the writer of the article see the musical?	記事の書き手はどこでミュージカルを見ましたか。
(A) In Hull	(A) Hullで
(B) In Manchester	(B) Manchesterで
(C) In London	(C) Londonで
(D) In New York	(D) New Yorkで

正解 (B)

解説 記事の書き手がどこでミュージカルを見たか問われています。記事の❹に「『Raindancer』のイギリス初演がManchesterの劇場で昨夜上演された」とあり、記事にはこの初演に関する感想が述べられていることから、正解は(B)だとわかります。(A)は同窓会の開催地、(C)は今後上演される場所、(D)はすでに上演された場所なので、いずれも不正解です。

5.

What is implied about Mr. Patel?	Patel氏について何が示唆されていますか。
(A) He has not performed on stage before.	(A) 以前舞台で演じたことがない。
(B) He is not known for his singing.	(B) 歌唱については知られていない。
(C) He will leave the production mid-tour.	(C) ツアーの中盤で興行から離れる。
(D) He is originally from the UK.	(D) もともとイギリス出身である。

正解 (B)

解説 Patel氏について示唆されていることが問われています。記事の❺で「イギリスではPatel氏のことをドラマか映画でしか見たことがなかったので、彼の歌声が素晴らしいのは驚きだった」とあります。ここからそれを言い換えた(B)が正解となります。Patel氏はすでにNew York公演に出演しているので(A)は誤り、(C)についてもPatel氏自身が途中でツアーを抜けるとは書かれていません。またPatel氏がどこの出身かについては言及がないので(D)も不正解です。

語句 □ originally もともと、生まれは

Questions 6-10 refer to the following e-mail, notice, and article.

Eメール・手紙　♪ 065

To:	Rod Butler <rbutler@rainydayco.com>
From:	Glenda Yates <gyates@ftassociates.com>
Date:	July 7
Subject:	Access

Dear Mr. Butler,

I received a call from a company called Freeman-Star Productions this afternoon. It's the production company responsible for the television program *How They Do It.* ❶They want to make a video about the process of mass-producing umbrellas and asked me to introduce one of our clients. I told the caller that I would raise the topic with the management of Rainy Day Co. To produce the video, they would need access to the entire assembly line. ❷Unfortunately, they are not offering any money, but they say they will mention the company name and show the logo in the video, so you should get some good exposure.

I've asked them to wait until this Wednesday for a reply.

Sincerely,

Glenda Yates
❸Business Advisor
FT Associates

簡単な案内・お知らせ　♪ 066

Notice
Attention All Employees

❹Management has agreed to allow Freeman-Star Productions to film the assembly line from August 18 to August 21. It is highly likely that your faces will appear in the final program and it will be necessary for Freeman-Star Productions to have signed authorization from each employee. Of course, if you would prefer not to appear on video, you will not be required to do so. To help the film crew know who not to film, please put a green strap on your identification badge while they are here. ❺Employees who do not mind being filmed should use the usual black strap.

訳 設問6-10は次のEメール，お知らせ，記事に関するものです。

宛先：Rod Butler <rbutler@rainydayco.com>
送信者：Glenda Yates <gyates@ftassociates.com>
日付：7月7日
件名：立ち入り

Butler様

今日の午後Freeman-Star Productionsという会社から電話がありました。『How They Do It』というテレビ番組の制作会社です。先方は量産型の傘の製造工程をビデオ撮影したいと希望しており，弊社の顧客を紹介してほしいとのことでした。電話をかけてきた人にはRainy Day社の経営者にこの件を提起するとお伝えしました。ビデオ制作に当たっては，組立ライン全体への立ち入りが必要になるでしょう。残念ながら謝礼金はありませんが，先方はビデオの中で社名を出し，ロゴも見せると言っているので，良い露出効果が得られると思います。

先方には今週水曜日まで回答を待ってもらうようお願いしました。

敬具

Glenda Yates
経営アドバイザー
FT Associates社

語句 ☐ mass-producing 量産の　☐ caller 電話をかける人，訪問者
☐ raise（話題）を提起する　☐ entire 全体の　☐ assembly line 組立ライン
☐ logo（組織などを示す）ロゴ，意匠文字　☐ exposure 露出

ご連絡
従業員の皆さまへ

経営陣はFreeman-Star Productions社に対し，8月18日から21日まで当社組立ラインの撮影を許可することで合意しました。最終的な番組の中で皆さんの顔が映る可能性が高く，Freeman-Star Productions社は従業員一人一人から署名入り承諾書を取る必要があります。もちろん，もしビデオに映りたくなければ，無理に映る必要はありません。撮影スタッフが誰を撮影してはいけないか判別できるように，撮影スタッフがここにいる間は身分証明バッジに緑色のストラップを付けてください。撮影されても構わない人は通常の黒色ストラップを使ってください。

語句 ☐ film ～を撮影する　☐ signed authorization 署名入りの承諾書
☐ strap ストラップ，細長いひも　☐ identification badge 身分証，社員証

Entertainment
A New Home for *How They Do It*

The popular television show *How They Do It* has moved from its original broadcaster to the online streaming service Vidster. KMG Television still has the rights to the first seven seasons of the program and will likely continue to show reruns on their free-to-air channel. ❻However, according to the contract Freeman-Star Productions has signed with Vidster, seasons eight to twelve will only be available to people with paid subscriptions to Vidster. Subscriptions can cost as much as $23 a month, so this may come as a shock to some fans of the show.

The first episode of season eight will be available tonight. Vidster subscribers will get an exclusive look inside the production facility of Rainy Day Co., where Rainy Day brand umbrellas and parasols are made. Rainy Day Co. has been drawing a lot of attention since Mary Cortez, the star of the popular drama *Milford's Way*, was spotted using one of their umbrellas last month.

エンターテインメント
『How They Do It』の新天地

人気テレビ番組『How They Do It』は元の放送局からオンラインストリーミングサービスのVidster社に移った。KMGテレビ局にはまだこの番組の最初の7シーズン分の放映権があり，無料チャンネルで再放送を続けると思われる。しかしFreeman-Star Productions社がVidster社と合意した契約によると，シーズン8から12についてはVidster社の有料定額サービス加入者しか見ることができなくなる。定額サービスは月に最大23ドルかかり，この番組の一部のファンにとっては衝撃かもしれない。

シーズン8の第1回は今夜見られる。Vidster社の定額サービス加入者はRainy Day社の製造工場の内部を独占見学でき，そこではRainy Dayブランドの傘や日傘が製造されている。Rainy Day社は人気ドラマ『Milford's Way』のスターであるMary Cortezが先月そのブランドの傘を使っているのを目撃されたことから多くの注目を集めている。

語句
- □ broadcaster 放送局
- □ online streaming service オンラインストリーミングサービス　□ rerun 再放送
- □ free-to-air 無料放送の　□ paid subscription 有料定期購読［視聴，使用］
- □ as much as ~ ~ほど，~と同じくらい　□ episode （テレビ番組の）1話分
- □ exclusive 独占的な　□ draw attention 注目を引く　□ star 人気者，スター
- □ spot ~ *doing* ~（人）が…しているのを見つける

6.

Where does Ms. Yates most likely work?

(A) At a consultancy firm
(B) At a manufacturing company
(C) At a department store
(D) At a production company

Yatesさんはおそらくどこで働いていますか。

(A) コンサルタント会社
(B) 製造会社
(C) デパート
(D) 制作会社

正解 (A)

解説 Yatesさんがどこで働いているか問われています。Yatesさんが書いたEメールの❶に「テレビ局から傘の製造工程を収録したいので，わが社の顧客を紹介してほしいと依頼された」とあります。また❸の「経営アドバイザー」という肩書からも，この会社がコンサルタント業務を行っていることがわかるので，(A)が正解です。

語句 □ consultancy firm コンサルタント会社　□ manufacturing company 製造会社

7.

What is a benefit of the offer from Freeman-Star Productions?

(A) A financial payment
(B) Equipment upgrades
(C) Assistance with product design
(D) Some free publicity

Freeman-Star Productions社のオファーの利点は何ですか。

(A) 金銭の支払い
(B) 備品のアップグレード
(C) 製品デザインでの協力
(D) 無料の宣伝

正解 (D)

解説 Freeman-Star Productions社のオファーの利点は何か問われています。Eメールの❷に「残念ながら謝礼金は出ないが，ビデオに社名やロゴが出るので，良い露出効果が得られる」とあり，ビデオに出ることは会社の宣伝になると期待されるので，それを言い換えた(D)が正解となります。「お金は支払われない」とあるので(A)は不正解，(B)(C)については，そのような記載はありません。

語句 □ benefit 利点，有益なこと　□ financial payment 金銭の支払い
□ equipment 備品，設備　□ upgrade アップグレード，改良
□ publicity 広報，宣伝活動

7

同義語問題

8.

What is the purpose of the notice?	お知らせの目的は何ですか。
(A) To request volunteers to give a tour of the facility	(A) 施設の見学を案内する有志を募ること
(B) To inform employees of a visit to the factory	(B) 従業員に工場への訪問があることを知らせること
(C) To announce a new company policy	(C) 新しい会社の方針を伝えること
(D) To thank staff members for complying with a request	(D) 要請に従ってくれたことをスタッフに感謝すること

正解 (B)

解説 お知らせの目的が問われています。❹に「経営陣はFreeman-Star Productions社に対し,8月18日から21日まで当社組立ラインの撮影を許可することで合意した」とあるので,工場で撮影が行われることを伝えているとわかります。それを「工場への訪問がある」と言い換えた(B)が正解です。

語句 □ comply with ~ ~に従う,応じる

9.

In the notice, the word "mind" in paragraph 1, line 8, is closest in meaning to	お知らせの第1段落・8行目にある "mind"に最も意味が近いのは
(A) attend to	(A) ~に応対する
(B) perform	(B) ~を演じる
(C) object to	(C) ~に反対する
(D) agree upon	(D) ~に同意する

正解 (C)

解説 同義語問題です。問われているmindを含む❺のEmployees who do not mind being filmedの部分は「撮影されても構わない従業員」という意味です。mindには「~を気にする,嫌だと思う」という意味があり,近い意味になる(C)が正解です。not mindで「気にしない」という意味で使われていることから(D)を選ばないように注意しましょう。

語句 □ attend to ~ ~に応対する　□ object to ~ ~に反対する
□ agree upon ~ ~について同意する

10.

What is suggested about future episodes of
How They Do It?
(A) They will profile the employees of Rainy
Day Co.
(B) It will be possible for the audience to
request filming locations.
(C) It will be necessary to pay money to view
them.
(D) They will be narrated by famous
personalities.

『How They Do It』の今後の放送回につ
いて何が示されていますか。
(A) Rainy Day社の従業員を紹介する。
(B) 視聴者が撮影場所のリクエストをす
ることが可能となる。
(C) 視聴するのにお金がかかるようにな
る。
(D) 有名人がナレーションをする。

正解 (C)

解説 『How They Do It』の今後の放送回について示されていることが問われています。記事を見
ると❻に「Freeman-Star Productions社がVidster社と合意した契約によると，シーズン8
から12についてはVidster社の有料定額サービス加入者しか見ることができなくなる」とある
ので，今後の放送回を見るためには有料定額サービスに加入する必要があることがわかりま
す。よって正解は(C)となります。

語句 □ profile（人物など）の紹介をする　□ narrate ～のナレーターを務める
□ personality 著名人

7

同義語問題

8 意図問題

意図問題はテキストメッセージやチャット形式の文書で毎回2問出題されます。書き手の発言の意図を問う設問で，会話の文脈を理解する必要があり，比較的難度が高いので苦手とする人も多い問題です。

POINT 1 問われている表現自体からヒントを得た上で，文脈を把握しよう。

意図問題とは，テキストメッセージ形式やチャット形式の文書中の，ある発言について書き手の意図を問う問題です。例えば，以下のような形をしています。

At 11:25 A.M., what does Mr. Smith mean when he writes, "I have no words"?

「午前11時25分に，Smithさんが"I have no words"と書いているのは何を意図していますか」

この例で問われている I have no words. という表現自体は「言葉がない」という意味です。しかし，これがポジティブな意味かネガティブな意味かは，文脈がないと判断できません。**意図問題では，この文脈理解が問われて**います。

このことを日本語の例題で考えてみましょう。

「午後3時45分に，Osato さんが「いけるよね？」と書いているのは何を意図していますか」
(A) 花を生けるかどうかを確認している。
(B) あるスポーツをたしなむかどうかを質問している。
(C) パーティーに参加するように念押ししている。
(D) ジャケットにズボンが似合っているかを尋ねている。

会話から「いけるよね？」だけを切り取ってしまうと，4つの選択肢のどの意味で使われているか判断できませんね。では，会話全体を見てみましょう。

Tanaka さん　　　午後3時35分
今週のゴルフコンペなんですが，忙しくて出られないんですよ。
Osato さん　　　午後3時38分
そうか。クライアントは楽しみにしているのに。
Tanaka さん　　　午後3時42分
誰か代わりがいないと盛り上がらないですよね。

> Osato さん　　　午後3時45分
> そうだ，後輩のSuzuki君はどうかな。彼はそこそこ**いけるよね**？
> Tanaka さん　　　午後3時47分
> そうですね。ウエアや用具は持っていませんが，先日プレーしました。
> Osato さん　　　午後3時49分
> じゃあ，私がウエアを貸すことにしよう。Tanaka さん，彼にゴルフセットを貸してあげられるかい？

どうですか。これなら (B) が正解だとわかりますね。

このように**前後の文脈を読むことで，発言の意図を推し量ることができる**ようになります。設問で問われている表現自体にどのような意味があるのかを考え，その上で，その表現の前後の文脈をつかむことが，意図問題を解く際には重要です。

POINT 2　口語表現で意味がわからない場合は，前後の文脈を活用しよう。

意図問題では，しばしば直訳では意味をつかみにくい口語表現も出題されます。例えば It's a piece of cake. という表現は，直訳すると「それはケーキ1切れだ」となりますが，これは口語表現で「（ペロリと食べられるくらい）とても簡単だ」という意味になります。

しかし，意図問題はこの口語表現の知識がなくても，**前後の文脈をヒントに解答できる**場合も多いです。「設問タイプ別攻略法 6」で紹介した「ハンバーガー方式（p.245参照）」で確認してみましょう。

> Are you able to submit the report by the end of the week?
> 「週末までに報告書を提出できるかい？」
>
> It's a piece of cake!
>
> OK. I look forward to reading it!
> 「わかった。読むのを楽しみにしているよ！」

「週末までに報告書を提出できるか」という質問に It's a piece of cake. と応じ，これに対して「読むのを楽しみにしている」というポジティブな反応があることから，It's a piece of cake. は「期日までに報告書を提出できる」ということを意図した発言であることがわかります。

それでは，例題を見てみましょう。

Todd Marx   10:50 A.M.
I'm afraid the company barbecue at Fairfield Park will have to be canceled. The weather forecast says that a storm is coming.

Andie Orley   10:51 A.M.
That's too bad. I know everyone is looking forward to it. Couldn't we reschedule it for Saturday?

Todd Marx   10:53 A.M.
That's a good idea. You'd better check with Mr. Davies before you make any announcements, though.

Andie Orley   10:54 A.M.
I'll call him now. Is he in his office?

1. At 10:53 A.M., what does Mr. Marx mean when he writes, "That's a good idea"?

(A) He thinks that they should check the weather forecast.
(B) He would like to call Mr. Davies himself.
(C) He believes that Fairfield Park is an appropriate venue.
(D) He agrees with changing the date of an event.

どうですか。まず，文書の流れを確認してみましょう。

Question 1 refers to the following text-message chain.

テキストメッセージ・チャット　♪ 068

> **Todd Marx**　　10:50 A.M.
> I'm afraid the company barbecue at Fairfield Park will have to be canceled. The weather forecast says that a storm is coming.
> └ 嵐になりそうなのでバーベキューは中止だな
>
> **Andie Orley**　　10:51 A.M.
> That's too bad. I know everyone is looking forward to it. Couldn't we reschedule it for Saturday?
> └ みんな楽しみにしているから土曜日に変更しては？
>
> **Todd Marx**　　10:53 A.M.
> That's a good idea. You'd better check with Mr. Davies before you make any
> └ それはいい考えだ
> announcements, though.
>
> **Andie Orley**　　10:54 A.M.
> I'll call him now. Is he in his office?

8

意図問題

1. At 10:53 A.M., what does Mr. Marx mean when he writes, "That's a good idea"?

　(A) He thinks that they should check the weather forecast.
　(B) He would like to call Mr. Davies himself.
　(C) He believes that Fairfield Park is an appropriate venue.
　(D) He agrees with changing the date of an event.

ハンバーガー方式で前後の文脈を確認してみましょう。

> Couldn't we reschedule it for Saturday?
> 「土曜日に日程変更できないかしら？」
>
> That's a good idea.
>
> You'd better check with Mr. Davies before you make any announcements, though.
> 「でも，発表する前にDaviesさんに確認取った方がいいよ」

上記から，意図を問われている発言では直前の提案に賛同していることがわかります。よって正解は (D) となります。

意図問題は毎回2問しか出題されませんが，**Part 3・Part 4の意図問題を解くこと**

も練習になります。スクリプトを読んで解いてみましょう。それはもちろんPart 3・Part 4自体の対策としても効果がありますよ。

正解と訳 設問1は次のテキストメッセージのやりとりに関するものです。

Todd Marx　　午前10時50分
残念だが，Fairfield公園での会社のバーベキューを中止せざるを得なくなりそうだ。天気予報によると嵐になるらしい。

Andie Orley　　午前10時51分
それは残念だわ。みんな楽しみにしているのに。土曜日に変更できないかしら。

Todd Marx　　午前10時53分
それはいい考えだ。ただそれを発表する前にDaviesさんに確認した方がいいよ。

Andie Orley　　午前10時54分
今電話してみます。彼はオフィスにいるかな？

1. 午前10時53分に，Marxさんが "That's a good idea" と書いているのは何を意図していますか。
   (A) 彼らは天気予報を確認するべきだと考えている。
   (B) Daviesさんに自ら電話したいと思っている。
   (C) Fairfield公園は適切な場所だと考えている。
   (D) イベントの日程変更に賛成している。

正解 (D)

語句 □ appropriate 適切な　□ venue（開催）場所

攻略法まとめ　意図問題

- 問われている表現からヒントを得よう。
- 口語表現で意味がわからない場合は前後の文脈から推測しよう。
- Part 3，Part 4の意図問題も参考にしよう。

Practice

次の文書を読み，各設問に対して最も適切な答えを(A)(B)(C)(D)の
中から1つ選びなさい。

Questions 1-2 refer to the following text-message chain.

Randy Fring   2:30 P.M.
I'm still in Scranton, but we've finished earlier than expected. The clients at Durant Banking Group have agreed with our original office designs, so I won't need to make any changes.

Greta Cheng   2:31 P.M.
That's great. We can submit the plans to the council tomorrow. With luck, we'll get building approval by the end of the month.

Randy Fring   2:33 P.M.
Right. So, as you know, my flight is tomorrow, but I was thinking of coming back to Chicago today instead. There will be a $100 charge to change the reservation, but I'd like to attend the architect's meeting tomorrow morning.

Greta Cheng   2:33 P.M.
That's fine. I can approve the expense. Just make sure you get a receipt from the airline and hand it in with all the others when you get back.

Randy Fring   2:34 P.M.
Will do.

8

意図問題

1. Where do the writers most likely work?

    (A) At a financial institution
    (B) At a construction company
    (C) At an advertising agency
    (D) At an airline company

2. At 2:34 P.M., what does Mr. Fring mean when he writes, "Will do"?

    (A) He will approve a request.
    (B) He will submit a receipt.
    (C) He will return from his trip tonight.
    (D) He will visit the bank today.

Questions 3-6 refer to the following online chat discussion.

Steve Cole   3:30 P.M.

I just had a call from the clients at GHT Automotive Group. They're not happy with our plans for the employee appreciation banquet and they want us to make some changes.

Richard Roylance   3:31 P.M.

What exactly don't they like?

Steve Cole   3:31 P.M.

The venue and the entertainment. They say that it's too far from their office. As for the entertainment, they'd prefer to let some of their own employees perform.

Lisa Paulson   3:33 P.M.

They're in Springwood. I don't know of any venues near there that are big enough.

Steve Cole   3:35 P.M.

I know. I might have to explain that to them. They might consider a shuttle bus. Would one of you get a cost estimate from some of the local bus companies?

Richard Roylance   3:37 P.M.

I'll do that. Give me a couple of hours.

Lisa Paulson   3:38 P.M.

I'll call Vince Silk and let him know we won't need him. I hope there's no cancellation charge.

Richard Roylance   3:39 P.M.

There shouldn't be. The event isn't for another three months.

Steve Cole   3:45 P.M.

The clients have requested a meeting tomorrow afternoon to discuss the details. Unfortunately, I'll be out of town. Richard, would you mind going instead of me?

Richard Roylance   3:49 P.M.

Not at all.

3. Who most likely are the writers?

(A) Event planners
(B) Hotel employees
(C) Bus drivers
(D) Advertising agents

4. What does Mr. Cole ask for?

(A) A price quotation
(B) Meeting notes
(C) Some suggestions
(D) A product review

5. At 3:39 P.M., what does Mr. Roylance most likely mean when he writes, "There shouldn't be"?

(A) He believes a product is very reliable.
(B) He does not think any other venues are available.
(C) He hopes a plan will go smoothly.
(D) He does not expect to pay a cancellation fee.

6. What will Mr. Roylance probably do tomorrow?

(A) Cancel an event
(B) Take a flight
(C) Negotiate a price
(D) Visit a client

8

意図問題

Questions 1-2 refer to the following text-message chain.

テキストメッセージ・チャット　♪ 069

Randy Fring　　2:30 P.M.
I'm still in Scranton, but we've finished earlier than expected. ❶The clients at Durant Banking Group have agreed with our original office designs, so I won't need to make any changes.

Greta Cheng　　2:31 P.M.
That's great. ❷We can submit the plans to the council tomorrow. With luck, we'll get building approval by the end of the month.

Randy Fring　　2:33 P.M.
Right. So, as you know, my flight is tomorrow, but I was thinking of coming back to Chicago today instead. There will be a $100 charge to change the reservation, but I'd like to attend the architect's meeting tomorrow morning.

Greta Cheng　　2:33 P.M.
That's fine. I can approve the expense. ❸Just make sure you get a receipt from the airline and hand it in with all the others when you get back.

Randy Fring　　2:34 P.M.
Will do.

訳　設問1-2は次のテキストメッセージのやりとりに関するものです。

Randy Fring　　　　午後2時30分
今まだScrantonにいるんですが, 思ったより早く終わりました。Durant Banking Groupのクライアントは当社が出した最初のオフィス設計案に同意してくれたので, もう変更する必要はないでしょう。

Greta Cheng　　　　午後2時31分
良かったわ。明日には審査委員会に計画を提出できるわね。運が良ければ今月末までには建設許可がもらえるわよ。

Randy Fring　　　　午後2時33分
そうですね。それで, ご存じのとおり私のフライトは明日なのですが, Chicagoに今日戻ろうかと考えていたんです。予約を変更するのに100ドルかかるのですが, 明日の朝の建築家との打ち合わせに参加したいので。

Greta Cheng　　　　午後2時33分
いいわよ。その出費は認めます。航空会社の領収書を忘れずにもらって, 戻って来たら他のものと一緒に提出してください。

Randy Fring　　　　午後2時34分
わかりました。

語句 □ than expected 予想していたよりも □ council 審議会
　　□ with luck 運が良ければ □ instead 代わりに □ architect 建築家
　　□ make sure 確かめる，確認する □ airline 航空会社 □ hand ~ in ~を提出する
　　□ Will do. 了解しました（Eメールやチャットで用いるくだけた返答）

1.

情報をもとに推測する問題

Where do the writers most likely work?

(A) At a financial institution
(B) At a construction company
(C) At an advertising agency
(D) At an airline company

書き手たちはおそらくどこで働いていますか。

(A) 金融機関
(B) 建設会社
(C) 広告代理店
(D) 航空会社

正解 (B)

解説 書き手の2人がどこで働いているか問われています。やりとりの❶，❷に「クライアントは当社が出した設計案に同意した」「今月末までに建設許可がもらえる」とあることから，2人は建物を設計，建設する会社に勤めていると推測できます。以上から(B)が正解となります。

語句 □ financial institution 金融機関

2.

意図問題

At 2:34 P.M., what does Mr. Fring mean when he writes, "Will do"?

(A) He will approve a request.
(B) He will submit a receipt.
(C) He will return from his trip tonight.
(D) He will visit the bank today.

午後2時34分に，Fringさんが"Will do"と書いているのは何を意図していますか。

(A) 要求を承認する。
(B) 領収書を提出する。
(C) 今夜出張から戻る。
(D) 今日銀行を訪問する。

正解 (B)

解説 意図問題です。問われている表現はやりとりの最後にある発言で，直前の内容に対して「了解した」と答えるものです。そこで直前のメッセージを見ると，❸に「（予約変更手数料について）航空会社の領収書をもらって，戻って来たら他のものと一緒に提出するように」とあるので，指示の内容は領収書の提出に関することだとわかります。よって，この表現を言い換えた(B)が正解です。

Questions 3-6 refer to the following online chat discussion.

×

Steve Cole　　　　3:30 P.M.
❶I just had a call from the clients at GHT Automotive Group. ❷They're not happy with our plans for the employee appreciation banquet and they want us to make some changes.

Richard Roylance　　　　3:31 P.M.
What exactly don't they like?

Steve Cole　　　　3:31 P.M.
The venue and the entertainment. They say that it's too far from their office. As for the entertainment, they'd prefer to let some of their own employees perform.

Lisa Paulson　　　　3:33 P.M.
They're in Springwood. I don't know of any venues near there that are big enough.

Steve Cole　　　　3:35 P.M.
I know. I might have to explain that to them. They might consider a shuttle bus. ❸Would one of you get a cost estimate from some of the local bus companies?

Richard Roylance　　　　3:37 P.M.
I'll do that. Give me a couple of hours.

Lisa Paulson　　　　3:38 P.M.
I'll call Vince Silk and let him know we won't need him. ❹I hope there's no cancellation charge.

Richard Roylance　　　　3:39 P.M.
There shouldn't be. ❺The event isn't for another three months.

Steve Cole　　　　3:45 P.M.
❻The clients have requested a meeting tomorrow afternoon to discuss the details. ❼Unfortunately, I'll be out of town. Richard, would you mind going instead of me?

Richard Roylance　　　　3:49 P.M.
❽Not at all.

訳 設問3-6は次のオンラインチャットの話し合いに関するものです。

Steve Cole　　　　午後3時30分
ついさっきGHT Automotive Groupのクライアントから電話があった。我々が出した従業員慰労夕食会の企画が気に入らないので，いくつか変更してほしいそうだ。

Richard Roylance　午後3時31分
具体的に何が気に入らないんですか。

Steve Cole　　　　午後3時31分
会場と余興だ。会場は先方の会社から遠すぎると言っている。余興に関しては，自社の社員の何人かにやらせる方がいいみたいだ。

Lisa Paulson　　　午後3時33分
会社はSpringwoodにあるのですよね。私はその近くで十分な広さのある会場は1つも知りません。

Steve Cole　　　　午後3時35分
そうなんだ。そのことを彼らに説明しなければいけないかもしれない。シャトルバスなら検討してくれるかもしれないな。君たちのうちのどちらかが地元のバス会社数社から費用の見積もりを取ってくれないか。

Richard Roylance　午後3時37分
私がやります。2，3時間ください。

Lisa Paulson　　　午後3時38分
私はVince Silkさんに電話して彼に依頼する必要がなくなったことを伝えるわ。キャンセル料がかからないといいけど。

Richard Roylance　午後3時39分
かからないはずだよ。イベントは3カ月先だしね。

Steve Cole　　　　午後3時45分
クライアントは詳細について話し合うため，明日の午後に打ち合わせを希望している。あいにく，私は市外に出ているんだ。Richard，私の代わりに行ってもらえるかい？

Richard Roylance　午後3時49分
もちろんです。

語句 □ automotive 自動車の　□ employee appreciation banquet 従業員慰労の夕食会
□ exactly 正確に言って　□ venue 会場，開催地
□ far from ～ ～から遠く［離れて］　□ prefer to *do* ～する方を好む
□ cost estimate 費用の見積もり　□ cancellation charge キャンセル料金
□ details 詳細　□ be out of town 市外に出かけている
□ instead of ～ ～の代わりに

3.

Who most likely are the writers?	書き手たちはおそらく誰ですか。
(A) Event planners	(A) イベント企画者
(B) Hotel employees	(B) ホテル従業員
(C) Bus drivers	(C) バス運転手
(D) Advertising agents	(D) 広告代理業者

正解 (A)

解説 チャットの話し合いをしている人たちは誰か問われています。冒頭の❶, ❷に「クライアントから電話があり, 夕食会の企画が気に入らず変更を希望している」とあるので, 彼らはクライアントのためにイベントを企画する会社で働いていることがわかります。ここから正解は(A)になります。

語句 □ event planner イベント企画者　□ advertising agent 広告代理業者

4.

What does Mr. Cole ask for?	Coleさんは何を依頼していますか。
(A) A price quotation	(A) 価格の見積もり
(B) Meeting notes	(B) 会議の議事録
(C) Some suggestions	(C) 提案
(D) A product review	(D) 製品のレビュー

正解 (A)

解説 Coleさんが依頼していることが問われています。❸に「君たちのうちのどちらかが地元のバス会社から見積もりを取ってくれないか」とあり, チャットの相手のどちらかに見積もりを取るよう依頼していることがわかります。ここから見積もりをprice quotationと言い換えた(A)が正解です。

語句 □ meeting notes 会議の議事録

5.

At 3:39 P.M., what does Mr. Roylance most likely mean when he writes, "There shouldn't be"?
(A) He believes a product is very reliable.
(B) He does not think any other venues are available.
(C) He hopes a plan will go smoothly.
(D) He does not expect to pay a cancellation fee.

午後3時39分に，Roylanceさんが "There shouldn't be" と書いているのはおそらく何を意図していますか。
(A) 製品がとても信頼できると思っている。
(B) 他の開催場所はどこも使えないと思っている。
(C) 企画がうまくいくよう願っている。
(D) キャンセル料を払うとは思っていない。

正解 (D)

解説 意図問題です。問われている表現は「(〜は) あるはずがない」という意味です。「何」があるはずがないか，前後のやりとりを見てみましょう。❹「キャンセル料がかからないといいけど」→「あるはずがない (＝キャンセル料はかかるはずがない)」→❺「(その理由は) イベントは3カ月先だから」とあることから，「キャンセル料は発生しないだろう」という意図で書いていることがわかります。よって，(D)が正解となります。

語句 □ reliable 信頼できる　□ go smoothly うまくいく

6.

What will Mr. Roylance probably do tomorrow?
(A) Cancel an event
(B) Take a flight
(C) Negotiate a price
(D) Visit a client

Roylanceさんは明日おそらく何をしますか。
(A) イベントをキャンセルする
(B) 飛行機に乗る
(C) 価格を交渉する
(D) クライアントを訪ねる

正解 (D)

解説 Roylanceさんが明日何をするか問われています。チャットの後半でColeさんはRoylanceさんに対し，❻，❼で「明日の打ち合わせに自分は参加できないので，代わりに行ってくれないか」と依頼し，Roylanceさんが❽で「もちろんです」と書いていることから，Roylanceさんは明日クライアントのところに打ち合わせに行くとわかります。よって正解は(D)です。

語句 □ negotiate 〜を交渉する

9 情報分散型問題

情報分散型問題は，正解の根拠が複数箇所に分散しているタイプの問題です。1回のテストで3〜4問程度出題されます。

POINT 1 1つの情報だけでは正解が絞り切れない場合は，このタイプだと考えよう。

このタイプの問題は，<u>正解の根拠となる情報が1カ所にまとまっていないという点が特徴</u>です。例えば，会社の野外ピクニック候補日を問う設問があったとしましょう。文書を読み進めていくと「候補日は今週土曜日か来週日曜日」という情報が現れます。ここだけでは「今週土曜日」と「来週日曜日」のどちらが正解かわかりません。この先に，さらに正解を絞る根拠があると考えて文書を読み進めていく必要があります。

POINT 2 分散した情報からわかることを整理して，正解を導こう。

文書を読み進めていく中で「来週の日曜日は土砂降りで気温が下がる予報なので避けた方がよい」と書いてあったとすると，おそらく来週日曜日は候補から外れ，この時点で残った「今週土曜日」が正解になります。

このように，情報分散型問題は
・ピクニック候補日は今週土曜日か来週日曜日
・来週日曜は悪天候になりそうなので避けたい
という**複数の情報をまとめることで，正解を導き出す**ことができます。

POINT 3 段落ごとに読んで要約する習慣をつけよう。

情報分散型問題を解く際にありがちなのが，正解が見つからず，文書を最初から何度も読み直してしまうことです。これではいくら時間があっても足りません。「文書タイプ別攻略法」で文書の要点をメモするExerciseを行いましたが，文書を読む際には常に頭の中でメモを取るような感じで，**段落ごとに書かれている内容を要約する習慣**をつけましょう。こうすることで，必要な情報が書かれている箇所を特定し，文書を読み直すにしても効率よく読み直したり，検索したりできるようになります。

それでは，例題を見てみましょう。

例題 **Question 1** refers to the following e-mail.

To:	Max Roper <mroper@syndex.com>
From:	Yvette Lauper <ylauper@dreamscapefp.com>
Date:	March 12
Subject:	Photo shoot

Dear Mr. Roper,

We would like to hire your services for our upcoming advertising campaign. Dreamscape Fun Park is planning on shooting a television commercial. Shooting will take place over three days from April 23 to 25. We would like you to take some still photographs of the park and the models and actors we have hired.

We will only need you here on the final day of shooting but we would like you to arrive in Miami the night before as we hope to start work very early in the morning. Of course, we will pay for your accommodation and transportation as well as your usual fees for photography. Please let me know as soon as possible whether or not you are available.

Sincerely,

Yvette Lauper
Dreamscape Fun Park

9

情報分散型問題

1. When is Mr. Roper asked to arrive in Miami?

   (A) On April 22
   (B) On April 23
   (C) On April 24
   (D) On April 25

まずは文書の流れを追っていきましょう。

Question 1 refers to the following e-mail.

〔Eメール・手紙〕 ♪ 071

To:	Max Roper <mroper@syndex.com>
From:	Yvette Lauper <ylauper@dreamscapefp.com>
Date:	March 12
Subject:	Photo shoot

└─ 写真撮影の件で，社外の人に連絡するメール

Dear Mr. Roper,

┌─ 写真撮影の依頼。4月23日～4月25日に行われるので写真を撮ってほしい

We would like to hire your services for our upcoming advertising campaign. Dreamscape Fun Park is planning on shooting a television commercial. Shooting will take place over three days from April 23 to 25. We would like you to take some still photographs of the park and the models and actors we have hired.

┌─ 最終日にだけいてくれればよいが，朝早いので前日の夜にMiami入りしてほしい

We will only need you here on the final day of shooting but we would like you to arrive in Miami the night before as we hope to start work very early in the morning. Of course, we will pay for your accommodation and transportation as well as your usual fees for photography. Please let me know as soon as possible whether or not you are available.

└─ 必要経費は払う。引き受けられるかどうか，早急に回答がほしい

Sincerely,

Yvette Lauper
Dreamscape Fun Park

---

1. When is Mr. Roper asked to arrive in Miami?

   (A) On April 22
   (B) On April 23
   (C) On April 24
   (D) On April 25

第1段落に撮影日が4月23日から4月25日とあるので，Roperさんは23日か前日の22日の到着を依頼されていると思うかもしれません。しかし，第2段落冒頭にWe will only need you here on the final day of shooting but we would like you to arrive in Miami the night beforeとあり，ここからRoperさんは最終日の前夜，つまり24日に来るように依頼されていることがわかります。このように，1カ所の情報だけでは正解を絞り切れないのが情報分散型問題の特徴です。

正解と訳 設問1は次のEメールに関するものです。

宛先：Max Roper <mroper@syndex.com>
送信者：Yvette Lauper <ylauper@dreamscapefp.com>
日付：3月12日
件名：写真撮影

Roperさん

来る広告キャンペーンの際に御社のサービスを利用したいと考えております。現在, Dreamscape遊園地はテレビCMの撮影を予定しています。撮影は4月23日から25日までの3日間にわたって行われます。Roperさんには園内と弊社が採用したモデルと俳優のスチール写真を撮影してもらいたいと思います。

こちらには撮影の最終日にいらしていただければよいのですが, 撮影を早朝から始めたいので, 前日の夜にはMiamiに到着してくださるようお願いします。もちろん, 宿泊費と交通費は通常の撮影料金と同様にお支払いします。お引き受けいただけるかどうか, できるだけ早くお知らせください。

敬具

Yvette Lauper
Dreamscape遊園地

1. RoperさんはMiamiにいつ到着するように依頼されていますか。
  (A) 4月22日
  (B) 4月23日
  (C) 4月24日
  (D) 4月25日

正解 (C)

語句 □ shoot 撮影；～を撮影する □ still （写真が）スチールの, 静止した
  □ pay for accommodation and transportation 宿泊料金と交通費を払う
  □ whether or not ～ ～か否か

9

情報分散型問題

攻略法まとめ 情報分散型問題

• 1つの情報だけでは正解が絞れない場合は, このタイプと考えよう。

• 分散した情報からわかることを整理して, 正解を導こう。

• 段落ごとの要約を行おう。

次の文書を読み，各設問に対して最も適切な答えを(A)(B)(C)(D)の中から1つ選びなさい。

Questions 1-5 refer to the following article, e-mail, and notice.

On May 12, the city of Thornton will be opening its first sports stadium. To be known as the Travis Drysdale Stadium, it is being built to host a variety of sports events such as track and field, football, and hockey. The stadium, which is named after one of the city's past sporting heroes, will have seats for 50,000 people.

Many Thornton residents have complained that the seating capacity may be too small considering the city's recent population growth. However, city mayor Sarah Steele points out that it is larger than the stadium in Centennial, which has far more residents. Until now, fans of local sports teams such as the Thornton Ducks have had to drive all the way to Centennial or Howard Valley to attend games. City planners predict that the new stadium will draw crowds of at least 20,000, even for minor matches.

According to Thornton city planner Rich Hill, the revenue from ticket sales to football games, concerts, and other events is expected to cover the cost of construction in just 20 years.

To:	Rebecca Jolie <rjolie@thorntonducks.com>
From:	Tim Gleeson <tgleeson@tdstadium.com>
Date:	August 12
Subject:	Ticket sales

Dear Ms. Jolie,

As I am sure you are aware, ticket sales for last night's football game were quite disappointing. We need to do something to bring more people to the games. Otherwise, holding games in Thornton will not be financially viable. I would like to schedule a get-together for representatives of the Thornton Ducks football team, Travis Drysdale Stadium Management, and a marketing expert from Hanson Promotions.

Please share any ideas you have for increasing ticket sales with us and let me know when you will be available this week.

Sincerely,

Tim Gleeson
Travis Drysdale Stadium Management

> ### The Thornton Ducks Football Team — Outreach Program
>
> The Thornton Ducks Community Outreach Program is offering free sports workshops for young football players in the Thornton region. Workshops will be held at our home ground, Travis Drysdale Stadium.
>
> Thornton Ducks' team members are also available to come to your school or club to help inspire players with motivational talks or skills training sessions.
>
> If you would like to take part, visit the team's Web site at www.thorntonducks.com.

---

1. Who is Travis Drysdale?

(A) A retired athlete
(B) A local politician
(C) A city planner
(D) A marketing expert

2. What is true about Centennial?

(A) It is easy to get there from Thornton.
(B) It has a larger population than Thornton.
(C) It has a successful football team.
(D) It recently built a new stadium.

3. What is the purpose of the e-mail?

(A) To organize a workshop
(B) To welcome a new employee
(C) To congratulate a team manager
(D) To arrange a meeting

4. What is Ms. Jolie asked to do?

(A) Choose a colleague to accompany her on a trip
(B) Detail her thoughts about promotional activities
(C) Give a talk on managing a successful sports team
(D) Explain the history of the Thornton Ducks Football Team

5. What is NOT indicated about the Thornton Ducks Football Team?

(A) It is based at Travis Drysdale Stadium.
(B) Its players will help train young footballers.
(C) Its founder was given an award.
(D) It has its own Web site.

9

情報分散型問題

Questions 6-10 refer to the following e-mail, advertisement, and product review.

To:	Hank Jeffries <hjeffries@jeffriesmechanical.com>
From:	Diane Smith <dsmith@jeffriesmechanical.com>
Date:	December 7
Subject:	Health and Safety

Hank,

We had a staff meeting yesterday, and a couple of the mechanics mentioned that they would like more heavy-duty gloves. The current ones don't seem to be providing enough protection. After checking online, I have found a brand that is very highly rated. They cost $27 a pair, which seems quite reasonable. Would you mind if I purchased a pair for each of our employees?

For your reference, I have placed a link for the gloves in question below. If I order them tomorrow, they should arrive here by December 9 or 10.

www.nilewaysos.com/workwear/gloves/9993949

Sincerely,

Diane Smith

Revtough Gloves
The Best You Can Get!

All Revtough gloves are manufactured in our factory in Kentucky. They are extremely heavy-duty yet soft enough to allow work requiring a sensitive touch. The Revtough E980 model is specially designed for use by people in the car repair industry. The back of the glove has a magnetic knuckle protector, where you can temporarily store nuts, bolts, and screws while reaching into tight spaces. The fingertips are covered with an ultrathin synthetic leather called Sheerguard, which offers excellent protection with maximum flexibility.

Functional yet attractive, reasonably priced yet high quality — these gloves are a must for people in construction, engineering, and mechanical repair.

Customer Reviews

Peter Fleming 1:23 P.M., Friday, May 4

★★★★★ (Excellent)

My employer purchased these gloves for everyone in the garage. We all love them. We can reach into the narrow spaces around the engine to replace parts without cutting or scratching our hands. Also, working with oil and grease all day, my hands used to be stained even after careful washing. Now, they stay clean all day. At just $27 a pair, these gloves are an amazing bargain.

---

6. What is the purpose of the e-mail?

(A) To suggest changes to a product design
(B) To request permission to make a purchase
(C) To thank a colleague for recommending an item
(D) To remind an employee of an appointment

7. When did the employees at Jeffries Mechanical have a meeting?

(A) On December 6
(B) On December 7
(C) On December 9
(D) On December 10

8. What is stated about the Revtough E980 gloves?

(A) They are covered by a five-year warranty.
(B) They are designed for professional drivers.
(C) They are to be disposed of after use.
(D) They are manufactured for auto mechanics.

9. Where does the writer of the review most likely work?

(A) At a fresh food market
(B) At an auto repair shop
(C) At a landscaping firm
(D) At a shipping company

10. What does Mr. Fleming praise about the gloves?

(A) The design
(B) The value for money
(C) The washability
(D) The size

9
情報分散型問題

Questions 1-5 refer to the following article, e-mail, and notice.

記事　♪ 072

❶On May 12, the city of Thornton will be opening its first sports stadium. ❷To be known as the Travis Drysdale Stadium, it is being built to host a variety of sports events such as track and field, football, and hockey. ❸The stadium, which is named after one of the city's past sporting heroes, will have seats for 50,000 people.

❹Many Thornton residents have complained that the seating capacity may be too small considering the city's recent population growth. ❺However, city mayor Sarah Steele points out that it is larger than the stadium in Centennial, which has far more residents. Until now, fans of local sports teams such as the Thornton Ducks have had to drive all the way to Centennial or Howard Valley to attend games. City planners predict that the new stadium will draw crowds of at least 20,000, even for minor matches.

According to Thornton city planner Rich Hill, the revenue from ticket sales to football games, concerts, and other events is expected to cover the cost of construction in just 20 years.

Eメール・手紙　♪ 073

To:	Rebecca Jolie <rjolie@thorntonducks.com>
From:	Tim Gleeson <tgleeson@tdstadium.com>
Date:	August 12
Subject:	Ticket sales

Dear Ms. Jolie,

As I am sure you are aware, ticket sales for last night's football game were quite disappointing. We need to do something to bring more people to the games. Otherwise, holding games in Thornton will not be financially viable. ❻I would like to schedule a get-together for representatives of the Thornton Ducks football team, Travis Drysdale Stadium Management, and a marketing expert from Hanson Promotions.

❼Please share any ideas you have for increasing ticket sales with us and let me know when you will be available this week.

Sincerely,

Tim Gleeson
Travis Drysdale Stadium Management

訳 設問1-5は次の記事，Eメール，お知らせに関するものです。

5月12日，Thornton市は初のスポーツスタジアムを開業する。Travis Drysdaleスタジアムとして知られることになるこの施設は，陸上競技，フットボール，ホッケーといったさまざまなスポーツ競技を開催するべく目下建設中だ。スタジアムはかつての市のスポーツの英雄にちなんで名付けられ，5万人を収容する予定だ。

Thorntonの多くの住民が，最近の市の人口増加を考慮すると収容人数が少なすぎるのではと言っている。しかしSarah Steele市長は，このスタジアムははるかに住民が多いCentennialのスタジアムより大きい，と指摘

している。これまでThornton Ducksなど地元のスポーツチームのファンたちは試合を見るためはるばるCentennialやHoward Valleyまで車を運転しなければならなかった。都市計画担当者は，新スタジアムはあまり重要ではない試合でも，少なくとも2万人の観客を集めると予測している。

Thornton 都市計画担当者 Rich Hill 氏によると，フットボールの試合やコンサート，その他のイベントのチケット売り上げの収入により，20年ほどで建設費用をまかなえると見込んでいる。

語句 □ a variety of ～ さまざまな～ □ track and field 陸上競技
□ resident 住民，居住者 □ capacity 収容能力 □ growth 増加，成長
□ far （比較級の前において比較を強調）ずっと □ all the way to ～ はるばる～まで
□ city planner 都市設計者 □ predict ～を予測する □ crowd 観客，群衆
□ at least 少なくとも □ revenue 収入，歳入
□ be expected to *do* ～すると期待されている

宛先：Rebecca Jolie <rjolie@thorntonducks.com>
送信者：Tim Gleeson <tgleeson@tdstadium.com>
日付：8月12日
件名：チケットの売り上げ

Jolie様，

ご存じかと思いますが，昨晩のフットボール試合のチケット売り上げはとても残念なものでした。もっと集客を伸ばすために何か手を打つ必要があります。さもないと，Thornton市内での試合開催は財政的に成り立ちません。Thornton DucksフットボールチームおよびTravis Drysdaleスタジアム運営団体の代表者とHanson Promotions社のマーケティング専門家との間で会合を持ちたいと思います。

チケット売り上げを増大させるアイデアがあればぜひお教えください。また今週ご都合のつく日もお知らせください。

敬具

Tim Gleeson
Travis Drysdaleスタジアム運営団体

語句 □ otherwise さもなければ □ viable 実行可能である □ representative 代表者
□ expert 専門家

The Thornton Ducks Football Team — **Outreach Program**

❽The Thornton Ducks Community Outreach Program is offering free sports workshops for young football players in the Thornton region. ❾Workshops will be held at our home ground, Travis Drysdale Stadium.

Thornton Ducks' team members are also available to come to your school or club to help inspire players with motivational talks or skills training sessions.

❿If you would like to take part, visit the team's Web site at www. thorntonducks.com.

Thornton Ducksフットボールチーム— 社会奉仕プログラム

Thornton Ducks社会奉仕プログラムはThornton地区の若いフットボール選手に無料のスポーツ講習会を提供します。講習会はホームグラウンドのTravis Drysdaleスタジアムで行われます。

Thornton Ducksの選手たちがあなたの学校やクラブに赴き，やる気を引き出すトークや技術講習会で選手を鼓舞するのを手伝うこともできます。

参加ご希望の方はチームのウェブサイトwww.thorntonducks.comをご覧ください。

- - - - - - - -

語句 □ outreach（地域社会への）奉仕活動　□ inspire ～を鼓舞する
□ motivational 動機となる　□ take part 参加する

1.

Who is Travis Drysdale?	Travis Drysdaleさんとは誰ですか。
(A) A retired athlete	(A) 引退したスポーツ選手
(B) A local politician	(B) 地元の政治家
(C) A city planner	(C) 都市計画担当者
(D) A marketing expert	(D) マーケティングの専門家

正解 (A)

解説 Travis Drysdaleさんは誰か問われています。記事の❶，❷から「新設されるスタジアムが Travis Drysdaleスタジアムという名称であること」，❸から「スタジアム名はかつての市のスポーツの英雄にちなんでいること」がわかるので，Travis Drysdaleさんは引退したスポーツ選手だと判断できます。よって正解は(A)です。

2.

What is true about Centennial?	Centennial について正しいことは何ですか。
(A) It is easy to get there from Thornton.	(A) Thorntonからそこに行くのは簡単である。
(B) It has a larger population than Thornton.	(B) Thorntonより人口が多い。
(C) It has a successful football team.	(C) 成功しているフットボールチームがある。
(D) It recently built a new stadium.	(D) 最近新しいスタジアムを建設した。

正解 (B)

解説 Centennialについて何が正しいか問われています。記事を見ると❹，❺に「Thorntonの住民は収容人数が少ないのではと言っている」が，「市長によると，Thorntonより住民の多い Centennialのスタジアムより大きい」とあるので，CentennialはThorntonよりも人口が多いことがわかります。よって正解は(B)です。❺の後の文にCentennialはThorntonから車ではるばる行かなければいけないとあるので，(A)は不正解です。

3.

What is the purpose of the e-mail?	Eメールの目的は何ですか。
(A) To organize a workshop	(A) 講習会を企画すること
(B) To welcome a new employee	(B) 新入社員を迎えること
(C) To congratulate a team manager	(C) チームマネージャーを祝福すること
(D) To arrange a meeting	(D) 会合を設定すること

正解 (D)

解説 Eメールの目的は何か問われています。❻に「チーム・スタジアムそれぞれの代表とマーケティング専門家との間で会合を持ちたい」とあるので，(D)が正解だとわかります。

語句 □ organize（イベントなど）を企画する　□ congratulate ～を祝う

4.

What is Ms. Jolie asked to do?	Jolieさんは何をするよう依頼されていますか。
(A) Choose a colleague to accompany her on a trip	(A) 出張に帯同する同僚を選ぶ
(B) Detail her thoughts about promotional activities	(B) 販促活動に関する考えについて詳しく述べる
(C) Give a talk on managing a successful sports team	(C) 成功するスポーツチームの運営について講演する
(D) Explain the history of the Thornton Ducks Football Team	(D) Thornton Ducksフットボールチームの歴史を説明する

正解 (B)

解説 Jolieさんが依頼されていることは何か問われています。Eメールの❼でJolieさんはGleesonさんから「チケット売り上げを増大させるアイデアがあれば共有してほしい」と頼まれており，集客増につながる販促案を求められていることがわかります。以上からこれを言い換えた(B)が正解となります。

語句 □ detail ～について詳しく述べる　□ promotional activity 販促活動

5.

What is NOT indicated about the Thornton Ducks Football Team?
(A) It is based at Travis Drysdale Stadium.
(B) Its players will help train young footballers.
(C) Its founder was given an award.
(D) It has its own Web site.

Thornton Ducksフットボールチームに関して述べられていないことは何ですか。
(A) Travis Drysdaleスタジアムが本拠地である。
(B) その選手たちは若いフットボール選手の訓練を手伝う。
(C) その設立者は賞を贈られた。
(D) 自身のウェブサイトがある。

正解 (C)

解説 NOT問題で，Thornton Ducksフットボールチームに関して述べられていないことは何か問われています。お知らせを見ると，(A)は❾の「研修はホームグラウンドのTravis Drysdaleスタジアムで行う」という記載と，(B)は❽の「若いフットボール選手に向けた無料講習会を提供」という記載と，(D)は❿の「チームのウェブサイトにアクセスを」という記載とそれぞれ一致しており，残った(C)については記載がないので，これが正解となります。

語句 □ base 〜に拠点を置く　□ footballer フットボール選手　□ founder 設立者

9

情報分散型問題

Questions 6-10 refer to the following e-mail, advertisement, and product review.

Eメール・手紙　♪ 075

To:	Hank Jeffries <hjeffries@jeffriesmechanical.com>
From:	Diane Smith <dsmith@jeffriesmechanical.com>
❶Date:	December 7
Subject:	Health and Safety

Hank,

❷We had a staff meeting yesterday, and a couple of the mechanics mentioned that they would like more heavy-duty gloves. The current ones don't seem to be providing enough protection. After checking online, I have found a brand that is very highly rated. They cost $27 a pair, which seems quite reasonable. ❸Would you mind if I purchased a pair for each of our employees?

For your reference, I have placed a link for the gloves in question below. If I order them tomorrow, they should arrive here by December 9 or 10.

www.nilewaysos.com/workwear/gloves/9993949

Sincerely,

Diane Smith

広告・宣伝／プレスリリース　♪ 076

Revtough Gloves
The Best You Can Get!

All Revtough gloves are manufactured in our factory in Kentucky. They are extremely heavy-duty yet soft enough to allow work requiring a sensitive touch. ❹The Revtough E980 model is specially designed for use by people in the car repair industry. The back of the glove has a magnetic knuckle protector, where you can temporarily store nuts, bolts, and screws while reaching into tight spaces. The fingertips are covered with an ultrathin synthetic leather called Sheerguard, which offers excellent protection with maximum flexibility.

Functional yet attractive, reasonably priced yet high quality — these gloves are a must for people in construction, engineering, and mechanical repair.

宛先：Hank Jeffries <hjeffries@jeffriesmechanical.com>
送信者：Diane Smith <dsmith@jeffriesmechanical.com>
日付：12月7日
件名：安全衛生

Hankへ

昨日スタッフミーティングをしましたが，整備士の何人かがもっと丈夫な手袋が欲しいと言っていました。現在のものは保護する機能が十分ではないようです。インターネットで調べて，とても高評価なものを見つけました。1組27ドルで，かなりお値打ちだと思います。各従業員に1組ずつ購入してもいいですか。

ご参考までに，その手袋のリンクを下に貼っておきます。明日発注すれば，12月9日か10日に届くと思います。

www.nilewaysos.com/workwear/gloves/9993949

敬具

Diane Smith

語句 □ health and safety 安全衛生　□ a couple of ～ 数人の～，いくつかの～
□ mechanic 整備士　□ heavy-duty 丈夫な　□ protection 保護，防御
□ highly rated 高く評価されている　□ reference 参考，参照
□ link （インターネットの）リンク　□ in question 問題の，当の

9
情報分散型問題

Revtough社製手袋
最高のものをあなたに！

Revtough社の手袋は全てKentucky州の弊社工場で製造されています。極めて丈夫でありながら，繊細なタッチを要求される作業ができる柔らかさがあります。Revtough E980モデルは特に自動車修理業で働く人向けにデザインされています。手袋の甲にはマグネットのナックルプロテクターが付いていて，狭いところに手を伸ばす際にそこに一時的にナットやボルト，ねじなどを保持しておくことができます。指先はSheerguardと呼ばれる極薄の合成皮革で覆われており，最上級の柔らかさとともに優れた防御性を提供します。

機能的でありながら魅力的，お手頃価格でありながら高品質のこの手袋は，建設，エンジニアリング，機械修理業界で働く人には必携です！

語句 □ sensitive 繊細な　□ automotive 自動車の
□ magnetic マグネットの，磁気を帯びた　□ knuckle ナックル，指の関節部分
□ temporarily 一時的に　□ nut ナット　□ bolt ボルト　□ screw ねじ
□ tight 窮屈な，狭い　□ fingertip 指先　□ ultrathin 極薄の
□ synthetic leather 合成皮革　□ maximum 最大限の　□ functional 機能的な
□ yet それでいて　□ reasonably priced 手頃な値段の

Customer Reviews

Peter Fleming 1:23 P.M., Friday, May 4

★★★★★ (Excellent)

❺My employer purchased these gloves for everyone in the garage. We all love them. ❻We can reach into the narrow spaces around the engine to replace parts without cutting or scratching our hands. ❼Also, working with oil and grease all day, my hands used to be stained even after careful washing. Now, they stay clean all day. ❽At just $27 a pair, these gloves are an amazing bargain.

お客さまのレビュー
Peter Fleming 午後1時23分，5月4日（金）
★★★★★（秀逸！）

雇い主がこの手袋を自動車修理工場で働く全員に購入してくれました。皆とても気に入っています。手を切ったり引っかいたりすることなく，エンジン周辺の狭いところに手を伸ばして部品交換することができます。また，一日中オイルやグリースを使っていると，以前は入念に手洗いしてもしみが残っていました。それが今では一日中きれいなままです。1組たった27ドルとは，この手袋は驚くべきお買い得品です。

語句 □ garage 自動車修理工場 □ reach into ～ ～に手を突っ込む □ narrow 狭い □ scratch ～を引っかく □ grease グリース □ stain ～にしみを付ける □ amazing 驚くべき □ bargain お買い得品

6.

What is the purpose of the e-mail?
(A) To suggest changes to a product design
(B) To request permission to make a purchase
(C) To thank a colleague for recommending an item
(D) To remind an employee of an appointment

Eメールの目的は何ですか。
(A) 製品デザインの変更を提案すること
(B) 購入する許可を求めること
(C) 商品を推奨した同僚にお礼を言うこと
(D) 従業員に面会の予定を思い出させること

正解 (B)

解説 Eメールの目的が問われています。冒頭で，まず従業員が丈夫な手袋を求めていることを伝え，続けて手袋に関する紹介をした後に❸で「各従業員に1組ずつ購入してもよいか」と尋ねているので，それを言い換えた(B)が正解となります。

語句 □ permission 許可

7.

When did the employees at Jeffries Mechanical have a meeting?
(A) On December 6
(B) On December 7
(C) On December 9
(D) On December 10

Jeffries Mechanical社の従業員はいつ打ち合わせを行いましたか。
(A) 12月6日
(B) 12月7日
(C) 12月9日
(D) 12月10日

正解 (A)

解説 Jeffries Mechanical社の従業員が打ち合わせを行った日にちが問われています。❶から「12月7日付のEメール」であること，❷に「昨日スタッフミーティングをした」とあることから，12月7日の前日，つまり12月6日に打ち合わせを行ったことがわかります。以上から(A)が正解となります。Eメールではメールアドレスの@以下にメールの送受信者の所属（この問題ではJeffries Mechanical社）が示されているので，必ず目を通すようにしましょう。

8.

What is stated about the Revtough E980 gloves? (A) They are covered by a five-year warranty. (B) They are designed for professional drivers. (C) They are to be disposed of after use. (D) They are manufactured for auto mechanics.	Revtough E980の手袋について述べられていることは何ですか。 (A) 5年間の保証がついている。 (B) 職業運転手向けにデザインされている。 (C) 使い捨てである。 (D) 自動車修理工向けに製造されている。

正解 (D)

解説 Revtough E980の手袋について述べられていることが問われています。広告の❺に「Revtough E980モデルは特に自動車修理業界で働く人向けにデザインされている」とあるので，自動車修理業界で働く人をauto mechanicsと表した(D)が正解となります。

語句 □ warranty 保証（書）　□ dispose of ～ ～を捨てる

9.

Where does the writer of the review most likely work? (A) At a fresh food market (B) At an auto repair shop (C) At a landscaping firm (D) At a shipping company	レビューの書き手はおそらくどこで働いていますか。 (A) 生鮮食品市場 (B) 自動車修理店 (C) 造園会社 (D) 運送会社

正解 (B)

解説 レビューの書き手が働いている場所が問われています。レビューを見ると，❺「自動車修理工場で働く」，❻「エンジン周辺の狭いところに手を伸ばして部品交換をする」，❼「オイルやグリースを使う」，など「自動車修理」に関連するフレーズがたくさん出てきます。よって，正解は(B)と判断できます。

語句 □ auto repair shop 自動車修理店　□ landscaping 造園

10.

詳細を問う問題

What does Mr. Fleming praise about the gloves?

(A) The design
(B) The value for money
(C) The washability
(D) The size

Flemingさんは手袋の何を称賛していますか。

(A) デザイン
(B) 金額に見合った価値
(C) 洗濯のきくこと
(D) サイズ

正解 (B)

解説 Flemingさんは手袋に関して何を称賛しているか問われています。レビューの❽で「たった1組27ドルとは，この手袋は驚くべきお買い得品だ」と述べているので，値段が安いのに高品質だと評価していることがわかります。よって正解は(B)です。

語句 □ praise 褒める　□ washability 洗濯のきくこと

10 クロスリファレンス問題

クロスリファレンス問題は情報分散型問題の1つで，正解の根拠が複数の文書にまたがっているタイプの問題です（cross-reference；相互参照）。「両文書参照型問題」「複数文書参照型問題」とも呼ばれています。

POINT 1 正解の根拠が複数の文書にまたがっている点に注意しよう。

情報分散型問題では正解の根拠が1つの文書の中で分散していることを確認しましたが，クロスリファレンス問題ではこれが**複数の文書に分散**しています。

例えば，1つ目の文書に「会社の野外ピクニック候補日は今週土曜日か来週日曜日」とあり，2つ目の文書に「今週土曜日は悪天候」とあることから，正解を「来週日曜日」と判断するような問題です。このように，クロスリファレンス問題では**それぞれの文書の情報を関連づけて正解を導く**必要があります。

POINT 2 各文書を読み進めながら，関連する情報を押さえよう。

クロスリファレンス問題は見た目で判別ができません。文書を読み進めていく中で，**各文書間で関連する情報を逃さず押さえていく**ことが重要です。

例えば，以下のように情報をリンクさせていきます。

1つ目の文書：予定表
・ABC社のピクニックは3月6日でJohnが幹事です。

2つ目の文書：メール
・雨なので3月のJohnの企画は1カ月延期しましょう。

問題：ABC社のイベントはいつですか。　→　正解：4月6日

この問題は1つ目の文書と2つ目の文書の両方を読まないと正解を導けません。
問題「ABC社のイベント日程」
　・1つ目の文書「Johnが幹事を務めるピクニック，3月6日予定」
　・2つ目の文書「Johnの企画（＝ピクニック）を1カ月延期→4月6日予定」
と情報をリンクさせることで，ABC社のイベントが当初の予定から1カ月延期，つまり4月6日に行われる，とわかりますね。

関連する情報がわかるようになれば，このタイプの問題はすぐ解けるようになります。文書間の関連情報に気付けるように，例題，練習問題で訓練していきましょう。特に登場人物や地名が文書間にまたがって登場していたり，代名詞が指すものが前の文書に書かれているような箇所があったりしたら，「おや，何かあるかも」と注意を払っておくことがコツです。

POINT **3** マルチプルパッセージは文書タイプによって読み方を変えよう。

これまでも繰り返し述べてきましたが，Part 7のどんな文書にも共通して言えることは「全文をしっかり読み，情報を頭に入れることが重要」ということです。従って，クロスリファレンス問題の含まれるマルチプルパッセージ（ダブルパッセージ，トリプルパッセージ）も，まずはしっかり全文を読むようにしましょう。

一方で，問題によっては300語以上の長い記事の後に，また長めのEメールを読むというパターンもあります。長い文書を常に全力で読んでいては疲れてしまいますね。このような場合は，記事をしっかり読んだ後にもう一度さっと読み直し，各段落の内容を自分なりに整理しておきます。こうすることで，解答の際に必要な情報をスムーズに検索できるようになります。記憶しておく情報量も圧縮できるので，脳にかかる負荷を軽くすることができて効率的です。また，フォームなどの図表に近い文書は「読む」のではなく，項目を「見て」おき，解答の際に検索重視で取り組む，という方法が有効です。**文書のタイプやボリュームによって，読み方を変える**工夫をしてみましょう。

POINT **4** マルチプルパッセージから先に解答してみよう。

クロスリファレンス問題を解くということは，176番〜200番のマルチプルパッセージに解答するということです。実際の試験で前から順番に解いていった場合，45分間のリスニング・セクションとPart 5・6，そしてPart 7のシングルパッセージまでを終えてマルチプルパッセージに着手するころには，心身ともにかなり疲れていることでしょう。

そこで，1つ提案です。頭が疲れていないうちにダブルパッセージ，トリプルパッセージに取り掛かってみてはどうでしょうか。つまり，Part 6まで解答を終えたらPart 7のシングルパッセージを後回しにして，ダブルパッセージ（176番〜）から取り組むのです。イレギュラーな順番で解答するのでマークの際には注意が必要ですが，文章量の多い**ダブルパッセージ，トリプルパッセージこそ，じっくり腰を据えて取り組むべき**なのは確かです。相性や慣れもあるので，実際の試験でいきなり

10

クロスリファレンス問題

試すことは避けた方がよいですが，家で模試を解く際などに試してみるとよいでしょう。自分にとって，**最も効率よく解答できる手順**を模索してみてください。

以上のPOINTを踏まえ，例題を解いてみましょう。

例題 **Question 1** refers to the following e-mail and weather forecast.

To:	Todd Mathers <tmathers@mathersphotography.com>
From:	Sally Winchester <swinchester@xanadu.com>
Date:	September 20
Subject:	Photo shoot

Dear Mr. Mathers,

I am writing about the upcoming photo shoot for our article on Grant Gold. It will be a full-day shoot and you may charge us at your usual rates. As he is known for surfing and kayaking, it is important that we get a lot of outdoor shots in good weather.

Thanks,

Sally Winchester

The Week Ahead

Thursday	Friday	Saturday	Sunday
September 22	September 23	September 24	September 25
Rainy	Cloudy but no rain	Cloudy in the morning with afternoon showers	Sunny

1. When will Mr. Mathers' services most likely be required by Ms. Winchester?

   (A) On September 22
   (B) On September 23
   (C) On September 24
   (D) On September 25

できましたか。まずは文書の展開を押さえていきましょう。

Question 1 refers to the following e-mail and weather forecast.

Eメール・手紙　🎵 078

To:	Todd Mathers <tmathers@mathersphotography.com>
From:	Sally Winchester <swinchester@xanadu.com>
Date:	September 20
Subject:	Photo shoot

└ 用件は冒頭の整理，写真撮影について

Dear Mr. Mathers,

I am writing about the upcoming photo shoot for our article on Grant Gold.

└ Goldさんの記事の撮影

It will be a full-day shoot and you may charge us at your usual rates. As he is

└ 終日の撮影になる

known for surfing and kayaking, it is important that we get a lot of outdoor

└ 晴れの日に写真を撮りたい

shots in good weather.

Thanks,

Sally Winchester

リスト　🎵 079

The Week Ahead

└ 天気予報 → 前の文書では「晴れ」希望だった

Thursday	Friday	Saturday	Sunday
September 22	September 23	September 24	September 25
Rainy	Cloudy but no rain	Cloudy in the morning with afternoon showers	Sunny

└ …とすれば実施日はここかな？

10

クロスリファレンス問題

1. When will Mr. Mathers' services most likely be required by Ms. Winchester?

(A) On September 22
(B) On September 23
(C) On September 24
(D) On September 25

Eメールのit is important that we get a lot of outdoor shots <u>in good weather.</u> から，Mathersさんの行うservices（＝写真撮影の仕事）には「天気の良い日」が求められていることがわかります。天気予報で天気が良いのはSunnyとあるSeptember 25なので，正解は(D)です。

Eメールで「実施日は晴れの日が良い」という情報を把握してから2つ目の文書の天気予報を見ると，自然と晴れの日に目が行きますね。その情報に留意していないと，全ての日の予報を同じように読む必要があり消耗します。情報を把握し，関連情報を意識しながら読み進めることで，軽重をつけて文書を読めるようになります。

正解と訳 設問1は次のEメールと天気予報に関するものです。

宛先：Todd Mathers <tmathers@mathersphotography.com>
送信者：Sally Winchester <swinchester@xanadu.com>
日付：9月20日
件名：写真撮影

Mathersさん

Grant Gold氏に関する記事のための写真撮影についてのご連絡です。それは終日の撮影となりますので，通常料金をご請求ください。Gold氏はサーフィンやカヤックで知られているので，良い天候の中，野外での写真をたくさん撮影することが重要です。

よろしくお願いします。

Sally Winchester

語句 □ photo shoot 写真撮影　□ kayaking カヤックに乗ること

週間天気

木曜日	金曜日	土曜日	日曜日
9月22日	9月23日	9月24日	9月25日
雨	曇りだが 雨は降らない	午前中は曇り， 午後はにわか雨	晴れ

1. Mathersさんの作業はおそらくいつWinchesterさんに必要とされますか。
 (A) 9月22日
 (B) 9月23日
 (C) 9月24日
 (D) 9月25日

正解 (D)

攻略法まとめ クロスリファレンス問題

• 複数の文書に正解の根拠が分散していることに注意しよう。

• 各文書間で関連する情報を押さえよう。

• 全文をしっかり読むことを基本に，文書タイプやボリュームによって読み方を変えよう。

• マルチプルパッセージを先に解くなど，自分に合った解答のしかたを工夫しよう。

次の文書を読み，各設問に対して最も適切な答えを(A)(B)(C)(D)の中から1つ選びなさい。

Questions 1-5 refer to the following schedule and e-mail.

The JDC Skills Workshops
At Brighton Convention Center

Workshop	Facilitator	Time
Improving Communication Skills	Sandra Pellegrino	9:00 A.M. to 10:20 A.M.
Help Desk Training	Ford Alexander	10:30 A.M. to 11:50 A.M.
Replying to Questions by Chat, Telephone, and E-mail	Harriett Moore	12:00 NOON to 1:00 P.M.
Break for Lunch (Provided) Participants will enjoy the excellent buffet at Dino's in the Flanders City Hotel right across the street from Brighton Convention Center.		1:00 P.M. to 2:00 P.M.
How to Turn Down Impossible Requests from Clients	We Ying Wu	2:00 P.M. to 3:20 P.M.
Improving Response Times	Ralph Banff	3:30 P.M. to 4:50 P.M.

NOTE
All workshops will be held in Conference Room C at the Brighton Convention Center. The location is subject to change, so please check the directory when you enter the building on the day.
Admission is $140 per person.
To reserve a seat, call our reservations line at 555-3478.

From:	Scott Launders <slaunders@gersontrading.com>
To:	Mia Styles <mstyles@gersontrading.com>
Date:	November 23
Subject:	JDC Workshops

Dear Ms. Styles,

Joe Kline tells me that you are considering attending the workshops by JDC this year. I went last year and really think that it is a good idea. Gerson Trading will cover your admission, accommodation, and transportation, so it won't cost you anything. While I was there, I even found time to attend a classical concert and play a game of golf.

The workshops are given by professionals in a variety of industries. They all have excellent credentials and the information was really relevant to our business. I especially enjoyed the talk on using different tools to communicate with customers. It's being given by the same presenter again this year, so I am sure you will get a lot out of it.

Last time, they handed out discount coupons to everyone who attended. I still have mine, so let me know if you decide to go. You can use the coupon to get 20 percent off and save the company a bit of money.

Regards,

Scott Launders

1. For whom are the workshops probably intended?

(A) Customer service representatives
(B) Software programmers
(C) Financial advisors
(D) Factory managers

2. What will participants do after the third workshop?

(A) Head to a local restaurant
(B) Fill out a survey
(C) Watch a video
(D) Attend a ceremony

3. What is the purpose of the e-mail?

(A) To encourage a colleague to register for a workshop
(B) To give an employee some feedback about a report
(C) To promote a networking event to a client
(D) To explain the procedure for making a purchase request

4. What is implied about Ms. Moore?

(A) She will accompany Ms. Styles on a trip.
(B) She has spoken at the JDC Skills Workshops before.
(C) She was recently hired at Gerson Trading.
(D) She played a game of golf with Mr. Launders.

5. In the e-mail, the word "cover" in paragraph 1, line 3, is closest in meaning to

(A) protect
(B) describe
(C) pay for
(D) respond to

10

クロスリファレンス問題

To:	All Safe and Sound Employees
From:	Fred Larkin
Subject:	Introduction
Date:	3 March

I would like to thank Dan Cobb for filling in as the acting warehouse supervisor since February. You will have a new supervisor from 6 March. Her name is Clarice Marsden. Her start has been a little delayed as she is currently taking the test for the ChemS Certificate. I have arranged a catered lunch in the conference room on her first day to welcome her to the company. Please join us there from 12:30.

Sincerely,

Fred Larkin

Business This Week

8 July—With the purchase of Veritaccred, Mercury Evaluation and Accreditation (MEA) has expanded the list of qualifications it provides. Veritaccred's ChemS Certificate is one of the most respected qualifications for people working in chemical storage facilities. Although more than 1,000 people obtain it each year, the only testing location in the country is in Manchester. Now that it is owned by MEA, people will be able to take the test at any of their 90 locations. The press release from MEA includes a quote from company president Don Birch saying, "We hope to expand the scope of ChemS to require knowledge of shipping and handling procedures." This will put it in direct competition with the Transafe Certificate, which is a requirement for all commercial drivers hauling dangerous goods on public roads.

At present, it costs £120 to sit for the ChemS examination. With the cost of producing the exam estimated to be only £7,000, MEA stands to make a healthy profit.

ChemS Certification Course by Foreman Education

Saul Ubudu 3:41 P.M., Monday, 7 September

★★★★★ (Excellent)

I took the course this August because I wanted to add some qualifications to my résumé. The teachers at Foreman Education were very knowledgeable and were able to answer our questions easily. The course cost £300 and took one month to complete. I paid £100 to take the exam and passed on the first try. A total of £400 is not cheap, but I am now qualified for a lot of excellent jobs in my area, so I recommend the course.

6. What kind of business most likely is Safe and Sound?

(A) A testing center
(B) A storage facility
(C) A recording studio
(D) A conference center

7. What is the purpose of the article?

(A) To comment on the importance of hiring properly qualified applicants
(B) To recommend that readers take a professional course
(C) To report on the business activities of an organization
(D) To announce the arrival of a new technology

8. What is suggested about Ms. Marsden?

(A) She has been to Manchester.
(B) She was trained by Mr. Cobb.
(C) She attended a course at Foreman Education.
(D) She will visit Safe and Sound on March 3.

9. According to the article, what is one of Mr. Birch's goals for ChemS?

(A) To get more test-takers
(B) To lower its production cost
(C) To make the test easier to pass
(D) To broaden its requirements

10. What is implied about the ChemS Certificate?

(A) Its popularity has been declining.
(B) Its fee has been reduced.
(C) It can be obtained online.
(D) It is a requirement of Foreman Education.

10

クロスリファレンス問題

Questions 1-5 refer to the following schedule and e-mail. 　リスト　♪ 080

The JDC Skills Workshops
At Brighton Convention Center

Workshop	Facilitator	Time
❶Improving Communication Skills	Sandra Pellegrino	9:00 A.M. to 10:20 A.M.
❷Help Desk Training	Ford Alexander	10:30 A.M. to 11:50 A.M.
❸Replying to Questions by Chat, Telephone, and E-mail	❹Harriett Moore	12:00 NOON to 1:00 P.M.
❺Break for Lunch (Provided) Participants will enjoy the excellent buffet at Dino's in the Flanders City Hotel right across the street from Brighton Convention Center.		1:00 P.M. to 2:00 P.M.
❻How to Turn Down Impossible Requests from Clients	We Ying Wu	2:00 P.M. to 3:20 P.M.
Improving Response Times	Ralph Banff	3:30 P.M. to 4:50 P.M.

NOTE
All workshops will be held in Conference Room C at the Brighton Convention Center. The location is subject to change, so please check the directory when you enter the building on the day.
Admission is $140 per person.
To reserve a seat, call our reservations line at 555-3478.

　Eメール・手紙　♪ 081

From:	Scott Launders <slaunders@gersontrading.com>
To:	Mia Styles <mstyles@gersontrading.com>
Date:	November 23
Subject:	JDC Workshops

Dear Ms. Styles,

❼Joe Kline tells me that you are considering attending the workshops by JDC this year. ❽I went last year and really think that it is a good idea. ❾Gerson Trading will cover your admission, accommodation, and transportation, so it won't cost you anything. While I was there, I even found time to attend a classical concert and play a game of golf.

The workshops are given by professionals in a variety of industries. They all have excellent credentials and the information was really relevant to our business. ❿I especially enjoyed the talk on using different tools to communicate with customers. ⓫It's being given by the same presenter again this year, so I am sure you will get a lot out of it.

Last time, they handed out discount coupons to everyone who attended. I still have mine, so let me know if you decide to go. You can use the coupon to get 20 percent off and save the company a bit of money.

Regards,

Scott Launders

訳 設問1-5は次の予定表とEメールに関するものです。

研修	進行役	時間
JDC技術研修 於　Brightonコンベンションセンター		
コミュニケーションスキルの向上	Sandra Pellegrino	午前9:00〜10:20
ヘルプデスクの養成	Ford Alexander	午前10:30〜11:50
チャット，電話，Eメールによる質問への回答	Harriett Moore	正午12:00〜午後1:00
昼食休憩（支給されます） 参加者にはBrightonコンベンションセンターのすぐ向かいにあるFlanders CityホテルのDino'sで素晴らしいビュッフェをお楽しみいただきます。		午後1:00〜2:00
お客さまからの理不尽な要求の断り方	We Ying Wu	午後2:00〜3:20
応答時間の改善	Ralph Banff	午後3:30〜4:50

備考
全ての研修はBrightonコンベンションセンターの会議室Cで行われます。場所は変更になる可能性がありますので，当日建物に入りましたら案内板をご確認ください。
参加費は1名様140ドルです。
ご予約は，予約専用電話555-3478までお電話ください。

語句 □ facilitator 進行役　□ help desk ヘルプデスク（コンピューターに関するお客さま相談窓口）　□ buffet ビュッフェ，立食式の食事　□ turn down 〜 〜を断る　□ be subject to change 変更することがある　□ directory 案内板　□ admission 参加費　□ line 電話（回線）

送信者：Scott Launders <slaunders@gersontrading.com>
宛先：Mia Styles <mstyles@gersontrading.com>
日付：11月23日
件名：JDC研修

Stylesさん

Joe Klineさんから聞いたのですが，あなたは今年JDCの研修への参加を検討しているそうですね。私は昨年行きましたが，本当に良い考えだと思います。Gerson Trading社が参加費，宿泊費及び交通費を負担してくれるので，一切費用はかかりません。私が行ったときは，クラシックコンサートを鑑賞したり，ゴルフをしたりする時間さえありました。
研修ではさまざまな業界のプロが指導してくれます。彼らは皆，素晴らしい資格を持っていて，情報も我々の事業にとても関連したものでした。特に顧客とさまざまなツールを使ってコミュニケーションをとる講演が面白かったです。今年もまた同じ講演者になるようですが，あなたもそこで得るものが多いと思います。

前回，参加者全員に割引クーポンが配布されました。私はまだ持っているので，もし行くことにしたら教えてください。クーポンを使えば20パーセント引きになり，会社の負担を少し減らすことができます。

敬具

Scott Launders

1.

情報をもとに推測する問題

For whom are the workshops probably intended?	研修はおそらく誰に向けたものですか。
(A) Customer service representatives	(A) 顧客サービス担当者
(B) Software programmers	(B) ソフトウエアプログラマー
(C) Financial advisors	(C) 金融アドバイザー
(D) Factory managers	(D) 工場経営者

正解 (A)

解説 研修が誰に向けたものか問われています。予定表を見ると，❶「コミュニケーションスキルの向上」，❷「ヘルプデスクの養成」，❻「顧客からの無理な要求の断り方」といった，顧客対応に関連するカリキュラムであることがわかります。よって，(A) が正解です。

語句 □ customer service 顧客サービス □ financial advisor 金融アドバイザー

2.

詳細を問う問題

What will participants do after the third workshop?	参加者は3番目の研修の後に何をしますか。
(A) Head to a local restaurant	(A) 地元のレストランに向かう
(B) Fill out a survey	(B) 調査用紙に記入する
(C) Watch a video	(C) ビデオを視聴する
(D) Attend a ceremony	(D) 式典に参加する

正解 (A)

解説 研修参加者は3番目の研修が終わったら何をするか問われています。予定表を見ると，3番目の研修の後は❺の昼食休憩となり，「参加者には Flanders City ホテル内の Dino's でビュッフェをお楽しみいただく」とあるので，レストランに移動することがわかります。ここから，正解は (A) です。

語句 □ head to ～ ～に向かう □ fill out ～ ～に記入する

3.

目的・テーマを問う問題

What is the purpose of the e-mail?	E メールの目的は何ですか。
(A) To encourage a colleague to register for a workshop	(A) 同僚に研修に登録するよう勧めること
(B) To give an employee some feedback about a report	(B) 従業員に報告書についてフィードバックすること
(C) To promote a networking event to a client	(C) 顧客に交流イベントを宣伝すること
(D) To explain the procedure for making a purchase request	(D) 購入要請をする場合の手順を説明すること

正解 (A)

解説 Eメールの目的は何か問われています。❼，❽に「あなたは今年，JDC研修への参加を検討していると聞いた」「私は昨年行ったが，(研修に行くのは)本当に良い考えだと思う」とあるので，同僚に研修への参加を勧めていることがわかります。以上から，正解は(A)となります。

語句 □ encourage ~ to *do* ~に…するよう奨励する
□ feedback フィードバック (意見や評価を伝えること) □ promote ~を主催する
□ networking event 交流会 □ procedure 手順 □ purchase request 購入の要請

4.

What is implied about Ms. Moore?	Mooreさんについて何が示唆されていますか。
(A) She will accompany Ms. Styles on a trip.	(A) 出張でStylesさんに同行する。
(B) She has spoken at the JDC Skills Workshops before.	(B) 以前JDC技術研修で講演したことがある。
(C) She was recently hired at Gerson Trading.	(C) 最近Gerson Trading社に雇用された。
(D) She played a game of golf with Mr. Launders.	(D) Laundersさんとゴルフをした。

正解 (B)

解説 Mooreさんについて何が示唆されているか問われています。予定表を見るとMooreさんは❸，❹より今年「チャット，電話，Eメールによる質問への回答」に関する講義の担当者とわかります。次にEメールを見ると❿，⓫に「昨年は特に顧客とさまざまな手段を使ってコミュニケーションをとる講演がためになった」「今年も同じ講演者になるようだ」とあるので，Mooreさんは昨年も同じ講演を担当したと推測できます。以上から正解は(B)となります。

語句 □ accompany ~に同行する

5.

In the e-mail, the word "cover" in paragraph 1, line 3, is closest in meaning to	Eメールの第1段落・3行目にある"cover"に最も意味が近いのは
(A) protect	(A) ~を保護する
(B) describe	(B) ~を説明する
(C) pay for	(C) ~の費用を支払う
(D) respond to	(D) ~に返答する

正解 (C)

解説 同義語問題です。問われている語を含む❾の文は「会社が参加費，宿泊費及び交通費を負担してくれる」という意味で，coverは「(費用)を負担する」，つまり「(費用)を支払う」という意味で使われています。よって正解は(C)です。なじみのある単語でも，自分の知らない意外な意味を持つものはたくさんあります。辞書や類語辞典を使って語彙力をつけましょう。

語句 □ protect ~を保護する □ describe ~について説明する

Questions 6-10 refer to the following e-mail, article, and online review.

Eメール・手紙　♪ 082

To:	All Safe and Sound Employees
From:	Fred Larkin
Subject:	Introduction
Date:	3 March

❶I would like to thank Dan Cobb for filling in as the acting warehouse supervisor since February. ❷You will have a new supervisor from 6 March. Her name is Clarice Marsden. ❸Her start has been a little delayed as she is currently taking the test for the ChemS Certificate. I have arranged a catered lunch in the conference room on her first day to welcome her to the company. Please join us there from 12:30.

Sincerely,

Fred Larkin

記事　♪ 083

Business This Week

8 July—❹With the purchase of Veritaccred, Mercury Evaluation and Accreditation (MEA) has expanded the list of qualifications it provides. Veritaccred's ChemS Certificate is one of the most respected qualifications for people working in chemical storage facilities. Although more than 1,000 people obtain it each year, ❺the only testing location in the country is in Manchester. Now that it is owned by MEA, people will be able to take the test at any of their 90 locations. The press release from MEA includes a quote from company president Don Birch saying, "❻We hope to expand the scope of ChemS to require knowledge of shipping and handling procedures." This will put it in direct competition with the Transafe Certificate, which is a requirement for all commercial drivers hauling dangerous goods on public roads.

❼At present, it costs £120 to sit for the ChemS examination. With the cost of producing the exam estimated to be only £7,000, MEA stands to make a healthy profit.

訳 設問6-10は次のEメール，記事，オンラインレビューに関するものです。

宛先：Safe and Sound社全従業員
送信者：Fred Larkin
件名：ご紹介
日付：3月3日

2月から倉庫管理者代行を務めてくれたDan Cobbさんに感謝します。3月6日からは新しい管理者が来ます。彼女の名前はClarice Marsdenさんです。彼女は現在ChemS検定を受験中のため，勤務の開始が若干遅れています。彼女をわが社に歓迎するために出勤初日に会議室で仕出しの昼食を用意しています。そこに12時30分に集まってください。

敬具

Fred Larkin

語句 ☐ fill in（人の）代理をする　☐ acting 代理の　☐ certificate 合格証書，証明証
☐ catered lunch 仕出しの昼食

今週のビジネス

7月8日—Veritaccred 社 の 買 収 に よ り Mercury Evaluation and Accreditation社（以下，MEA）は認定する資格のリストを拡張した。VeritaccredのChemS検定は化学薬品保管施設で働く人には最も尊重される資格の1つだ。毎年1,000人以上がその資格を得ているが，国内の受験地はManchesterにしかない。それが今ではMEAが所有することとなったため，90ある試験場所のどこででも受験することが可能になるだろう。MEAのプレスリリースにはDon Birch社長の「ChemSの出題範囲を運搬取扱手続きに関する知識を必要とするところまで拡げられたらと思っています」という発言が引用されている。これにより，全ての職業ドライバーが公道で危険物を運搬する際に必要な資格であるTransafe検定と直接競合することになるだろう。

現在，ChemSを受験するには120ポンドかかる。試験の制作にかかる費用はわずか7,000ポンドと見積もられており，MEAはかなりの収益を上げる可能性がある。

語句 ☐ qualification 資格　☐ chemical storage facility 化学薬品保管施設
☐ obtain ～を得る，獲得する　☐ now that ～ 今や～なので　☐ quote 引用文
☐ scope 範囲　☐ shipping and handling procedure 運搬取扱手続き
☐ direct competition 直接競争　☐ haul ～を車で運ぶ，運搬する
☐ public road 公道　☐ at present 現在のところ　☐ sit for ～（試験）を受ける
☐ stand to *do* ～する可能性がある　☐ healthy profit かなりの利益

ChemS Certification Course by Foreman Education

Saul Ubudu 3:41 P.M., Monday, 7 September

★★★★★ (Excellent)

I took the course this August because I wanted to add some qualifications to my résumé. The teachers at Foreman Education were very knowledgeable and were able to answer our questions easily. The course cost £300 and took one month to complete. ❽I paid £100 to take the exam and passed on the first try. A total of £400 is not cheap, but I am now qualified for a lot of excellent jobs in my area, so I recommend the course.

Foreman Education社のChemS検定講座
Saul Ubudu 午後3時41分，9月7日（月）
★★★★★（素晴らしい）

履歴書に資格をいくつか加えたかったため，8月に受講しました。Foreman Education社の講師はとても知識があり，受講者の質問にも容易に回答してくれました。受講費用は300ポンドで，修了まで1カ月でした。試験を受けるのに100ポンド支払い，一発合格しました。合計400ポンドは安くはないですが，今や私は地元でたくさんの素晴らしい仕事をする資格が得られました。なので，この講座をお勧めします。

語句 □ résumé 履歴書 □ on the first try 最初の挑戦で
□ be qualified for ～ ～の資格がある

6.
情報をもとに推測する問題

What kind of business most likely is Safe and Sound?
(A) A testing center
(B) A storage facility
(C) A recording studio
(D) A conference center

Safe and Sound社の事業内容はおそらく何ですか。
(A) 試験センター
(B) 保管施設
(C) 録音スタジオ
(D) 会議場

正解 (B)

解説 Safe and Sound社の事業内容が問われています。従業員宛てに送信されたEメールの冒頭❶に「倉庫管理者代行を務めてくれたDan Cobbさんに…」とあるので，この会社には物品を倉庫に保管する業務があるということがわかります。ここから正解は「保管」を表す語が入っている(B)が正解だと推測できます。

語句 □ testing center 試験センター

7.

What is the purpose of the article?
(A) To comment on the importance of hiring properly qualified applicants
(B) To recommend that readers take a professional course
(C) To report on the business activities of an organization
(D) To announce the arrival of a new technology

記事の目的は何ですか。
(A) 適切な有資格者を採用することの重要性について述べること
(B) 読み手に専門的な講座を受けることを推奨すること
(C) ある組織の事業活動について報道すること
(D) 新しい技術の到来について知らせること

正解 (C)

解説 記事の目的は何か問われています。❹に「MEAは認定する資格のリストを拡張した」とあり，その後もMEAの今後の展開について述べられていることから，この組織の事業活動について知らせる記事だと判断できます。よって(C)が正解です。組織・団体の一連の取り組みなどを(C)のような表現で正解とする場合がありますので，押さえておきましょう。

語句 □ properly 正しく，適切に　□ business activity 事業活動

8.

10

クロスリファレンス問題

What is suggested about Ms. Marsden?
(A) She has been to Manchester.
(B) She was trained by Mr. Cobb.
(C) She attended a course at Foreman Education.
(D) She will visit Safe and Sound on March 3.

Marsdenさんについて何が示されていますか。
(A) Manchesterに行ったことがある。
(B) Cobbさんから教育を受けた。
(C) Foreman Education社の講座を受けた。
(D) 3月3日にSafe and Sound社を訪れる。

正解 (A)

解説 Marsdenさんについて示されていることが問われています。Eメールを見ると❶，❷からMarsdenさんは6月6日からSafe and Sound社に倉庫管理者として入社する人だとわかります。また，CobbさんはMarsdenさんが来るまで管理者代行を務めた人なので，この時点で(B)(D)は誤答だとわかります。また，(C)のForeman Education社はレビューに登場しますが，Marsdenさんとは直接かかわりがありません。❸から彼女がChemS検定を受験していること，また記事の❺にChemS検定の受験地はManchesterにしかないとあることから，正解は(A)であることが確認できます。

語句 □ train ～を教育［指導］する

9.

According to the article, what is one of Mr. Birch's goals for ChemS?	記事によると，ChemS検定に対する Birch氏の目標の1つは何ですか。
(A) To get more test-takers	(A) より多くの受験者を獲得すること
(B) To lower its production cost	(B) 制作費用を下げること
(C) To make the test easier to pass	(C) 試験をもっと受かりやすいものにすること
(D) To broaden its requirements	(D) 要件を拡大すること

正解 (D)

解説 記事からChemS検定に対するBirch氏の目標の1つが問われています。❻にBirch氏の発言の引用として「ChemSの出題範囲を運搬取扱手続きに関する知識を必要とするところまで拡げたい」とあります。つまり，試験に合格するための要件を拡大しようと考えていると判断できることから，(D)が正解となります。

語句 □ test-taker 受験者　□ lower ～を下げる　□ production cost 制作費用
　　　□ broaden ～を拡大する　□ requirement 要件

10.

What is implied about the ChemS Certificate?	ChemS検定について何が示唆されていますか。
(A) Its popularity has been declining.	(A) 人気が下がってきている。
(B) Its fee has been reduced.	(B) 料金が安くなった。
(C) It can be obtained online.	(C) インターネットで取得できる。
(D) It is a requirement of Foreman Education.	(D) Foreman Education社の必要条件である。

正解 (B)

解説 ChemS検定について示唆されていることが問われています。記事は7月に書かれたものですが，❼で「現在，ChemSの受験には120ポンドかかる」とあります。一方，レビューの日付は9月で，❽に「(ChemSの)試験を受けるのに100ポンド支払った」とあることから，ChemSの受験料は記事が書かれた後に値下げされたと推測できます。よって，(B)が正解となります。

語句 □ popularity 人気　□ decline 減少する

900点の壁とは？

編集部 (以下，編)：本書は対象読者を「800点〜」としているので，読者の中には「900点の壁」を意識している方もいるのではと思います。そこで，今回はお二人の経験をもとに900点の壁についてお聞きしたく思います。

濵﨑潤之輔 (以下，濵)：900点を取るころ，大里さんはリスニング・セクションは満点に近い感じでしたか。

大里秀介 (以下，大)：僕は，リスニングが460点で，リーディングが440点でした。

濵：じゃあリスニングで9割以上はもう取れていたんですね。でも，まあ，リーディングもそんなに差がないですね。900点を突破するには，リスニングが450点だとしたら，リーディングも450点じゃないといけませんが，多くの人はリスニングの方がリーディングよりも高いスコアを取っていると思います。900点の壁を越えるカギを握るのは，足を引っ張るリーディングのスコアをいかに伸ばしていくか，ですね。ちなみに僕はそのころ，リーディングではPart 7よりもPart 5ができないという意識の方が強かった気がします。

大：Part 7に関して，まず読者の皆さんにお聞きしたいのは「Part 7の問題，日本語で読んで解くだけの読解力はありますか」ということです。Part 7の英文約5500 wordsを読むに当たって，毎日，日本語でもそれくらいの文書を読んでいますかと聞

きたいですね。日本語でさえ読んでいない人が，英語で読もうとしたって無理な話です。以前，セミナーでダブルパッセージ1題を和訳したものを読解問題として解いてもらったのですが，全問正解したのは20人中たった2，3人でした。日本語で読んで解けなかったら，英語では解けませんよ。つまり言いたいのは，900点の壁を越えるためには，Part 7は言語によらず，そもそもの「読解力」を磨いてください，ということです。そこが大前提。一方，Part 5の語彙や文法は知識という点では英語特有の問題です。ですので，濵﨑さん，最後の壁はおそらくPart 5ということになりますかね。

濵：最後はPart 5ですね。

大：Part 5を放置しておくと，文法力・語彙力に起因する問題がPart 7にも残ってきます。これは僕の経験ですが，「ホテルで宿泊した人にアンケートを取りました」というシチュエーションで，A flat TV would be nice.と文書に書いてあったんです。「フラットテレビが良かった」って書いてあると思ったら大間違い。実はwould be niceは「あれば良かったのに」という意味だったんですよね。つまり，ホテルの部屋にはフラットテレビは「ない」んです。でも，wouldの使い方を知らなくて正確に意味が取れなかったわけです。このときに，文法力や語彙力を鍛えていかないと900点は取れないんだな，と僕は気付きました。Part 5ができないということは，つまりPart 7

にも支障が出てくるということなんです。

編： Part 7のことだけ考えているのではなくて，Part 5，6を含めて詰めの甘いところを詰めていこうということですね。

大： 間違った理由は，語彙に由来しているかもしれないし，文法に由来しているかもしれない。そう思って，復習した方が良いのかもしれません。

編： なるほど深いですね。Part 7はPart 7だけでは成らず！同じシリーズの「壁越えトレーニング Part 5-6」も買った方が良いですね（笑）。濵﨑先生もPart 5が最後に残ったとおっしゃっていましたね。

濵： Part 5が最後に残るというのは，知識の問題です。結局，単語や語彙に対する知識が足りないから，コンプリートできなかったということなんです。Part 7って基本的には「ここにこう書いてあるので正解はこれです」という問題じゃないですか。だから解説を理解するのが容易でしたし，復習にはそんなに困らなかったんですよね。なのに，Part 5は「うわっ，これ知らなかった！」となって打ちのめされた部分が大きかったですね。

編： その気持ち，よくわかります…。では，最後に，ここまで学習を進めてきた読者に応援のメッセージをお願いします。

濵： 「これだけやれば絶対にTOEIC L&Rテストに出題される全ての範囲を網羅できる」ということはありません。ですが，信頼できる参考書や問題集を使うことにより，「有意義な知識」だけを培っていくことは可能です。本書とPart 5-6の2冊を余すところなく学習すれば，必ずや本番の試験で手応えを感じることができると思います。

大： 「まとまった英文を読んで理解する」というのは英語学習の基本の1つです。本書で文書や設問のタイプ別に攻略法を学び，ある程度の速さで文書を読んで設問を解く力を身に付けることは，全てのパートに効果があります。Part 7はボリュームがあり，最難関パートの1つでもありますので，毎日少しずつでも「読む」ということを心掛けてください。それにより必ず力はついてきます。この本を信じてぜひやり切ってください！

Final Test

※解答用紙は Web サイトよりダウンロードしてください。詳細
　は p.11 をご覧ください。

※自動採点サービスに対応しています。詳細は p.7 をご覧ください。

※指示文（Directions）は旺文社作成のものです。

Directions: In this part you will read a variety of selected texts. Examples include magazine and newspaper articles, e-mails, and instant messages. There will be several questions that follow each text or group of texts. Choose the answer that is the best for each question and mark (A), (B), (C), or (D) on the answer sheet.

Questions 147-148 refer to the following notice.

Help Wanted

Pollex Industries is seeking a full-time technician with experience in the repair and servicing of devices used in the manufacturing industry. We specialize in the production of automobile parts. However, applicants with experience in other kinds of manufacturing are also encouraged to apply. While relevant training will be provided, it is important that the applicants be electricians certified with the state licensing board. Working hours are Monday through Friday from 9:00 A.M. to 5:00 P.M. From time to time, the successful applicant may be required to work on Saturdays and Sundays. Apply by sending an e-mail with a résumé and cover letter attached to hr@pollexindustries.com.

147. What is the purpose of the notice?

(A) To promote a repair service
(B) To advertise automobile supplies
(C) To recruit a professional mechanic
(D) To introduce training courses

148. What is a requirement for the position?

(A) Possession of an electrician's certificate
(B) Experience in leading a team of workers
(C) Availability to work at night
(D) Willingness to travel internationally

Questions 149-150 refer to the following text-message chain.

Takanori Ueyama   8:50 A.M.
I'm having a party at my home on Saturday. Do you think you can come?

Andie Wilde   8:51 A.M.
Thanks for the invite. I have to check with my family before I answer.

Takanori Ueyama   8:53 A.M.
No problem. Let me know whenever you can.

Andie Wilde   9:00 A.M.
It looks like I'm free.

Takanori Ueyama   9:01 A.M.
Great news! I live at 34 Maxwell Drive in Hansford.

Andie Wilde   9:06 A.M.
OK. What time is the party?

Takanori Ueyama   9:09 A.M.
We're starting at around 4:00 P.M. You can leave your car on the street in front of my house, if you like.

Andie Wilde   9:10 A.M.
OK. I'll see you on Saturday.

---

149. At 9:00 A.M., what does Ms. Wilde mean when she writes, "It looks like I'm free"?

(A) She has checked her work schedule.
(B) She does not have any family commitments.
(C) She is willing to help Mr. Ueyama.
(D) She does not have to pay an admission fee.

150. What does Mr. Ueyama suggest that Ms. Wilde do?

(A) Bring a friend to his party
(B) Check his address on a map
(C) Park her car near his home
(D) Contact a colleague

Giordano Event Management Presents

the Convention for Unexplored Programming Opportunities

There is a huge separation between people in the programming industry and those in other fields. This means that there are hundreds, if not thousands, of important time-saving applications that never get made. Programmers are simply unaware of the necessity of them and potential users have no access to people with programming knowledge with whom to discuss their ideas.

The Convention for Unexplored Programming Opportunities seeks to bridge that divide. Giordano Event Management has sent its staff to survey people in hundreds of companies in dozens of industries to learn what kind of software they need. We have come up with more than a hundred potential products that are presently unavailable to consumers despite their high demand. At the convention, we will be discussing these needs in a series of presentations. Industry representatives will also be on hand to discuss their members' needs with programmers.

This is an event you cannot afford to miss.

Date: August 18 and August 19
Time: 9:00 A.M. to 5:00 P.M. (Both days)
Location: Parton Convention Center, Dallas, Texas
Price: $750
Reservations can be made on the Web site at www.giordanoem.com.

151. What is indicated about the event?

(A) It is held at the same location every year.
(B) It will supply refreshments to participants.
(C) It will introduce programmers to new markets.
(D) It has been promoted in industry publications.

152. What will be available to participants?

(A) Access to the raw data collected from surveys
(B) A chance to download applications
(C) Information about job opportunities at programming companies
(D) Opportunities to speak with people from a variety of industries

Questions 153-154 refer to the following notice.

NOTICE:

This is a shared area for all users of the Clement Camping Grounds.

The bathroom and kitchen facilities have been provided by the National Parks and Wildlife Department to promote the use of the park in a way that does not harm the natural environment.

It is the responsibility of all users to keep the area clean and to use the facilities carefully to ensure that others can enjoy the same convenience.

The National Parks and Wildlife Department is able to maintain this service due to funding from the general public. If you are able to contribute funds, please visit our Web site and click the donate button at the bottom of the page. Every little bit counts.

If you would like to report any damage or misuse of the facilities, please call the Clement National Park Rangers Office at 555-8342.

---

153. For whom is the notice most likely intended?

(A) Park rangers
(B) Campers
(C) Cleaning staff
(D) Business owners

154. What are readers of the notice encouraged to do?

(A) Take a tour
(B) Read a manual
(C) Donate money
(D) Carry out repairs

GO ON TO THE NEXT PAGE

Questions 155-157 refer to the following instructions.

You are required to leave a note with your contact number when the recipient is not home to receive a parcel. Parcels should only be left unattended if the sender has stipulated that course of action in their instructions. You can check these instructions by inputting the tracking number into the tablet computer you have been provided. If you are instructed to leave a parcel unattended, please take a photograph of the parcel at the delivery address as proof of delivery. Failure to follow these instructions may result in damage or loss of parcels, for which Dalton Logistics could be held responsible. Our insurance only covers us when you have complied with the above instructions.

If for any reason you believe that there is a high risk that a parcel will be damaged or lost due to unforeseen circumstances, do not leave it unattended. Leave a note for the recipient explaining the situation. Depending on the time of day, you may return later or suggest that the recipient come to our distribution center to pick up the parcel. Each district follows slightly different procedures. In such cases, you should discuss the situation with your district manager.

155. For whom are the instructions
most likely intended?

  (A) Insurance company
      employees
  (B) Online store owners
  (C) Delivery staff
  (D) Recipients of parcel
      deliveries

156. What is implied about Dalton
Logistics?

  (A) It provides ongoing training
      for its employees.
  (B) It encourages employees to
      purchase tablet computers.
  (C) It offers discounts to repeat
      customers.
  (D) It pays compensation for
      certain damages.

157. According to the instructions,
why might a staff member
contact a district manager?

  (A) To get an update on the
      location of a parcel
  (B) To ask for assistance
      finding an address
  (C) To notify colleagues about
      traffic conditions
  (D) To request information
      about local policies

GO ON TO THE NEXT PAGE

Hampton—In just two months, Hampton will be getting a new youth center, which will provide young people with a much-needed place to train for a variety of athletic events. With the announcement that Hampton will host the National Youth Athletics Meet in two years' time, city leaders have decided to invest in youth sports to ensure proper representation by local athletes. The center, to be known as the Joel Whittaker Memorial Youth Center, will have its grand opening on September 21. The date was chosen to coincide with the Hampton City to Bay Fun Run, and the new youth center will be used as the starting point.

The former mayor for whom the center was named will be in attendance to open the center and fire the starting pistol. If you would like to take part in the run, you can learn more about it by visiting the Web page at www.hamptonfr.org. As yet, the youth center does not have a Web site of its own. However, you can see the plans at Hampton City Hall and talk about opportunities for local youth groups by setting up an appointment with Fran Sanders, the city's director of youth welfare. Contact her office at 555-9392.

158. According to the article, what will soon be available in Hampton?

(A) An office to coordinate volunteer activities
(B) A college course for mature students
(C) A new performing arts center
(D) A public sports facility

159. What event will be held in September?

(A) An athletic event
(B) A riverside cleanup
(C) A cultural festival
(D) A local election

160. Who most likely is Joel Whittaker?

(A) An athlete
(B) A newspaper journalist
(C) An event organizer
(D) A politician

GO ON TO THE NEXT PAGE

The freshest ingredients to your door daily

Nutriplus provides daily deliveries of perfectly measured ingredients for our ultra-healthy menus for less than you would spend at the supermarket. —[1]—. What's more, all of our meals are designed by renowned chef and qualified nutritionist, Renee Strahovski. Every day, our delivery drivers drop off a refrigerated container at our customers' front doors. Inside is an easy-to-follow recipe and all the ingredients you need to make it. There are even online videos you can watch to learn from our expert chefs. —[2]—. Visit our Web site, input your dining preferences, and get your first meal for free. It's that easy. We are extending our reach every month. To find out whether or not your address is covered, call one of our friendly customer service representatives at 555-8348. —[3]—. They are waiting to take your call.

With Nutriplus, you will reduce your cooking time, spend less money, and enjoy the healthiest meals. —[4]—. You can't go wrong.

www.nutriplus.com

161. What is indicated about Ms. Strahovski?

(A) She helps customers choose a plan.

(B) She represents a supermarket chain.

(C) She has published a book on nutrition.

(D) She creates recipes for Nutriplus.

162. What is NOT mentioned about Nutriplus?

(A) It will negotiate on price.

(B) It provides home delivery.

(C) It is broadening its service area.

(D) It offers instructional videos.

163. In which of the positions marked [1], [2], [3], and [4] does the following sentence best belong?

"This means there is no waste, little trash, and only minimal cleaning required."

(A) [1]

(B) [2]

(C) [3]

(D) [4]

GO ON TO THE NEXT PAGE

To:	Dolly Holland <dholland@sybiotech.com>
From:	Greg Simon <gsimon@sybiotech.com>
Subject:	Welcome back
Date:	September 16

Dear Ms. Holland,

I am pleased to welcome you back from your holiday. The fact that Sybiotech allows us to take these extended holidays after 10 years of service is one of my favorite aspects of the job. I am looking forward to taking advantage of the arrangement again myself next year.

I'd like to inform you that Mr. Patel retired in your absence and he has been replaced by me. One of my first decisions as section supervisor was to make some changes to improve efficiency. I regret that I was unable to consult with you before rearranging your schedule, but I trust you will find the new situation advantageous.

In previous years, you have spent Mondays and Fridays at the factory in Maine and the rest of the week at the head office. When you return to work, you will be required to spend Mondays and Tuesdays in Maine. You can spend the night at a hotel there. The reduced number of trips will help us save on transportation costs.

I look forward to discussing the arrangements with you in detail when you get back on Monday morning.

Sincerely,

Greg Simon

164. What is suggested about Ms. Holland?

(A) She has recently acquired a new qualification.
(B) She was hired before Mr. Simon.
(C) She has been with Sybiotech for over a decade.
(D) She has been asked to run a training workshop.

165. Why did Ms. Holland receive the e-mail?

(A) Her work schedule has been changed.
(B) She will be given a promotion.
(C) Her office will be relocated.
(D) She is planning to retire.

166. Who most likely is Mr. Patel?

(A) A company president
(B) A former supervisor
(C) A human resources officer
(D) A maintenance worker

167. What is the reason that Mr. Simon made the change?

(A) To reduce air pressure
(B) To cut down on expenditures
(C) To better understand clients' needs
(D) To accommodate additional employees

GO ON TO THE NEXT PAGE

Questions 168-171 refer to the following online chat discussion.

Sam Cole   3:30 P.M.:
Who saw the advertisement for Carleton Window Dressings last night?

Rhod Harps   3:31 P.M.:
I did. The prices they were offering on drapes were even lower than what we pay our supplier.

Leanne Milton   3:31 P.M.:
Right. I don't know how they are doing it. It's going to be almost impossible for us to compete.

Sam Cole   3:33 P.M.:
That's what I thought. I've asked our supplier to come in and discuss the issue tomorrow afternoon. As we're all partners in the business, I think we should all try to attend.

Rhod Harps   3:35 P.M.:
I have an appointment at Haddonfield Public Hospital from 2:00 P.M.

Aina Rashid   3:35 P.M.:
I'll be out until 3:30 P.M. I have to show some samples to an interior decorator in Cork.

Rhod Harps   3:37 P.M.:
I'll be back at around 4:00 P.M., I suppose.

Sam Cole   3:45 P.M.:
That's when we will have to ask him to come, then.

Leanne Milton   3:46 P.M.:
I have a dinner reservation at 7:00 P.M. tomorrow night. Do you think I should reschedule?

Sam Cole   3:49 P.M.:
It should be fine. We'll be done by 5:00 P.M.

---

168. Where do the writers work?

    (A) At a fashion house
    (B) At a catering company
    (C) At a curtain store
    (D) At a medical facility

169. What will the writers most likely discuss with the supplier?

    (A) Improving production times
    (B) New design ideas
    (C) Changing delivery routes
    (D) A price reduction

170. What time will the meeting most likely take place?

    (A) At 2:00 P.M.
    (B) At 3:30 P.M.
    (C) At 4:00 P.M.
    (D) At 4:30 P.M.

171. At 3:49 P.M., what does Mr. Cole mean when he writes, "We'll be done by 5:00 P.M."?

    (A) Employees will not need to work overtime.
    (B) Ms. Milton does not need to change her plans.
    (C) They can avoid rush hour traffic.
    (D) A meeting will be shorter than planned.

GO ON TO THE NEXT PAGE

To: All office staff
From: Todd Nugent
Subject: Annual Somersby Riverbank Cleanup Day
Date: Wednesday, August 21

In order to improve our profile in the community and attract more local clients, I would like as many employees as possible to take part in the Annual Somersby Riverbank Cleanup Day this year. It will be held on Sunday, September 15 and it starts at 7:00 A.M. It is generally over by noon and everyone who contributes is invited to enjoy a barbecue lunch provided by the city council. — [1] —. I have attended as a volunteer for the last five years and noticed that many local businesses were sending teams. They were all wearing specially printed T-shirts which showed what business they worked for. They seem to attend every year, so they must be experiencing some benefits. — [2] —.

I'll be ordering T-shirts, so please let me know whether or not you will be able to attend. I also need to know whether you'd like a small, medium, or large. — [3] —. I have come up with a design for the T-shirts. Please take a look at it and give me your input. I've posted it on the notice board in the break room. You'll find a signup sheet there also. — [4] —. I hope you will be able to take part, but you should not feel overly pressured, as this will not be taken into account for your upcoming employee evaluation.

172. What is the purpose of the memo?

(A) To encourage attendance at an event

(B) To announce the end of a campaign

(C) To thank people for contributing funds

(D) To recommend a local business

173. What does Mr. Nugent claim to have done?

(A) Taken part in a fun run

(B) Contacted an advertising agency

(C) Volunteered in the community

(D) Completed an employee evaluation

174. What information does Mr. Nugent require from participants?

(A) Their T-shirt size

(B) Their home address

(C) Their telephone number

(D) Their cleaning schedule

175. In which of the positions marked [1], [2], [3], and [4] does the following sentence best belong?

"Just write your name in the space provided and I will take care of the registration process."

(A) [1]

(B) [2]

(C) [3]

(D) [4]

GO ON TO THE NEXT PAGE

MEMO

To: All Baxter Pools Staff
From: Steven Baxter
Subject: NPS
Date: Monday, April 3

I am sure many of you have already heard that we are in the process of purchasing Nolte Pool Services (NPS). NPS was advertised for sale last month and we have been negotiating with its owners. We expect to sign an agreement the day after tomorrow.

Through this arrangement, we should be able to save money by sharing some expenses such as bookkeeping, customer service, and advertising. Unfortunately, we do not have sufficient room in our current building to accommodate the staff and equipment of NPS. Therefore, we are planning an addition to the building, which should be completed at the end of July. At present, NPS is a little short-staffed but rather than hiring someone new on a temporary basis, I will be asking some of our staff to help out there for a few days a week. We need someone with a hazardous chemical handling certificate. If you are suitably qualified and willing to spend a couple of days at Hazlehurst every week until the construction is complete, please send me an e-mail at sb@baxterpools.com.

Roster for Baxter Pools Employees to Work at NPS (Hazlehurst)
The relocation is scheduled for September 9. Staff members whose names appear on the roster for that day are required to help with the office relocation.

Sunday	Monday	Tuesday	Wednesday	Thursday	Friday	Saturday
27	28 Trevor Lowry	29	30 Trevor Lowry	31 Valerie Singh	1 (September)	2
3	4 Trevor Lowry	5	6 Trevor Lowry	7 Valerie Singh	8	9 Peter Sanchez Bruce Tilley

176. What is one purpose of the memo?

(A) To announce the acquisition of another company

(B) To request assistance in arranging an industry event

(C) To suggest a change in company policy

(D) To recommend swimming exercise

177. When will the agreement with the owners of NPS probably be finalized?

(A) On April 3

(B) On April 4

(C) On April 5

(D) On April 6

178. Which of the following expenses is NOT mentioned in the memo?

(A) Marketing

(B) Accounting

(C) Insurance

(D) Customer service

179. What is suggested about Trevor Lowry?

(A) He will assist with the office relocation.

(B) He is certified to handle unsafe substances.

(C) He has worked at NPS in the past.

(D) He is a member of senior management.

180. What is implied about the construction work?

(A) It will be paid for by NPS.

(B) It cost more than originally planned.

(C) It does not provide enough room.

(D) It is behind schedule.

GO ON TO THE NEXT PAGE ➤

Brighton Technology District (BTD)

The Brighton Technology District is an area of reclaimed land by Lake Hawke. It has been designated for use by businesses in the technology sector. There are many advantages to locating a business here. The most compelling of these is the extremely low rent. Thanks to a generous subsidy from the local government, rent in the BTD is around half that of comparable offices elsewhere.

Another significant benefit is free electricity from the BTD Solar Power System. Businesses can also take advantage of agreements with the Brighton University of Technology, which is a private institution also located in the BTD. These agreements include access to their excellent internship program and assistance with research and development. The relationship also means that businesses in the BTD tend to recruit many of the university's top students.

There are some conditions which must be met in order to qualify as a tenant in the BTD. One is that businesses must generate their principal income from computer programming. Another is that businesses must employ at least one graduate of the Brighton University of Technology.

So far, the BTD has helped several of the nation's top technology companies get started. These include Geovech, Biowave, and Dolphware, all of which have had huge success both here and abroad. For more information about the BTD or if you would like to apply to be a tenant, please contact the BTD Administrator's Office at 637-555-3923.

Parking Permit for Tenants
in the Brighton Technology District

Vehicle Registration: 733YTU

Vehicle Owner: Todd Masterson

Employer: Velocidyne

Valid for 12 months from: 12 June

This pass must be affixed to the front windshield of your vehicle. Vehicles displaying valid parking permits are entitled to park in any parking space within the BTD.

181. What is a benefit of having a company in the BTD?

(A) Central location
(B) Subsidized rent
(C) Discount solar panels
(D) Excellent views

182. What is implied about the Brighton University of Technology?

(A) Its advertisements have appeared on television.
(B) Its students may park anywhere in the BTD.
(C) It has recently expanded its campus.
(D) It receives free electricity.

183. How does the Brighton University of Technology assist businesses in the BTD?

(A) By offering its rooms for use
(B) By helping with research projects
(C) By arranging visits by industry experts
(D) By providing free staff training

184. What is probably true about Velocidyne?

(A) It is in the software industry.
(B) It has been in business for less than 12 months.
(C) It occupies offices previously used by Dolphware.
(D) It only hires graduates of the Brighton University of Technology.

185. What is suggested about Mr. Masterson?

(A) He has not been assigned a specific parking space.
(B) He usually relies on public transportation.
(C) He received a parking permit with his rental agreement.
(D) He previously worked at Geovech.

GO ON TO THE NEXT PAGE

The Byron Bay Coffee Festival

Byron Bay (10 August)—The Byron Bay Farmers' Association, led by Gloria Waters, has managed to convince the city council to host Byron Bay's first-ever coffee festival. Coffee is one of the region's main industries and even though it exports coffee to North America and Europe, it is relatively unknown here in Australia. "Depending on the success of this year's festival, this may become an annual event" explained Terry Davis, one of the event organizers.

The festival will be held from 10 November to 14 November, during which time there will be a street parade as well as other events such as contests, farm tours, and cooking workshops. The council hopes to attract tourists to the area to boost the local economy. Gloria Waters explained that her members were more interested in gaining exposure so that they can sell more of their product domestically.

One business with a vested interest in the festival's success is the Steele Coffee Processing Plant. The company's owner Helena Barkworth is a major sponsor of the event. Her company is Byron Bay's only processing plant and it has recently expanded its operations in anticipation of increased demand.

To:	Terry Davis <tdavis@byronbaycc.org>
From:	Norma Harris <nharris@novacrane.com>
Date:	November 16
Subject:	Byron Bay Coffee Festival

Dear Mr. Davis,

I am writing with regard to the Byron Bay Coffee Festival. I thought it was a wonderful event and you and the other organizers should be commended. I particularly enjoyed visiting the coffee processing plant. The guide who showed us around was very knowledgeable and entertaining. Unfortunately, there was little activity at the plant as the harvesting is mostly finished by November. I suggest holding the festival in mid-October next year so that we can see the plant when it is at peak production.

Norma Harris

The Second Annual Byron Bay Coffee Festival
15 to 18 October

Event	Location	Date and Time
Cooking with Coffee — Expert chef Tina Day leads a free practical workshop.	Day School of Cooking	10:00 – 11:30 A.M. 15 and 17 October
Street Parade — Colorful floats sponsored by the various local growers and cafés pass along Main Street.	Main Street	4:00 – 5:00 P.M. 17 October
Best of the Fest — Festivalgoers can try the different blends of coffee that have been entered for the annual brewing contest.	Main Tent at Caulfield Park	10:00 A.M. – 7:00 P.M. 15 to 18 October
Coffees of Byron — A documentary film on the Byron Bay coffee industry	Byron Bay Community Hall	7:00 – 9:00 P.M 15 to 18 October

More information about special offers and events by local businesses is available from the Web site at www.byroncoffeefest.org.

186. What is the purpose of the article?

(A) To announce an event
(B) To discuss an economic trend
(C) To introduce a local club
(D) To profile a local politician

187. What does Ms. Waters mention that her members want to do?

(A) Attract investors to their business
(B) Launch a new Web site
(C) Find new production methods
(D) Raise the profile of a local product

188. What is indicated about Ms. Harris?

(A) She is not a resident of Byron Bay.
(B) She visited Ms. Barkworth's business.
(C) She took a tour of local growers.
(D) She was a judge in the brewing contest.

189. What is implied about Mr. Davis?

(A) He took Ms. Harris' advice.
(B) He will attend the cooking event.
(C) He left the organizing committee.
(D) He is collecting data on local tourism.

190. Where will the coffee tasting be held?

(A) At the Day School of Cooking
(B) On Main Street
(C) At Caulfield Park
(D) At Byron Bay Community Hall

GO ON TO THE NEXT PAGE

www.sweetridecarrental.com/springspecials

Sweetride Car Rental

Welcome back, Martin Mullholland

You have reached this page by clicking a link in our members' e-mail for spring. Below, you will find spring special offers available only to our customers who have agreed to receive periodic e-mails.

People renting vehicles for seven days or more during March, April, or May can select one of the following four options.
(1) A 10 percent discount on your total rental rate
(2) A free vehicle upgrade
(3) A free GPS system
(4) A free tank of fuel

Please let the reservation staff know which option you choose when you make your reservation.

Customer Survey

Thank you for renting a quality vehicle from Sweetride Car Rental. Please take a couple of minutes to fill out this survey to let us know about your rental experience.

Name: Martin Mullholland   **Booking Reference:** H83923NM

What was the purpose for renting this vehicle? (Business) / Pleasure

Do you intend to rent a vehicle from Sweetride again? Yes / (No)

Comment:

I forgot about the spring special and filled the tank just before I returned the car. As a result, I was unable to take advantage of the offer I chose. I asked the person operating the returns counter to change my selection to the 10 percent discount, but I was informed that that would not be possible. I think that Sweetride should be more understanding in this regard and not use this as an opportunity to make additional profit.

To:	Martin Mullholland <mmullholland@betatrading.com>
From:	Veronica Holden <vholden@sweetridecr.com>
Date:	June 27
Subject:	Spring specials

Dear Mr. Mullholland,

Regarding your desire to change your spring special selection, I am happy to inform you that we can accommodate your request. I regret that the clerk at the counter was not able to resolve the issue for you immediately. Yours was a rare case and the clerk had not been trained on how to deal with it.

If you check your next credit card statement, you will see that you have been refunded the appropriate amount.

Sincerely,

Veronica Holden
Customer Service, Sweetride Car Rental

191. What is implied about Mr. Mullholland?

(A) He rented a car during winter.
(B) He is an employee of Sweetride Car Rental.
(C) He subscribed to a mailing list.
(D) He updated the company Web site.

192. Which spring special option did Mr. Mullholland choose when he made the reservation?

(A) Option 1
(B) Option 2
(C) Option 3
(D) Option 4

193. What information is NOT required in the survey?

(A) The customer's name
(B) The vehicle preference

(C) The reservation code
(D) The renter's purpose

194. What is suggested about Ms. Holden?

(A) She read Mr. Mullholland's survey response.
(B) She is the president of Sweetride Car Rental.
(C) She is in charge of training new employees.
(D) She works at a credit card company.

195. In the e-mail, the phrase "deal with" in paragraph 1, line 4, is closest in meaning to

(A) advise
(B) concern
(C) record
(D) process

GO ON TO THE NEXT PAGE

Questions 196-200 refer to the following order confirmation, text message, and review.

Fennville Bookstore Online Order Confirmation

Thank you for shopping at Fennville Bookstore. We do not provide paper receipts. Please print out and keep this document for your records.

Customer: Ms. Paula Tran   **Date:** 11 June
Ship to: Clarkson Brothers   **Order number:** Y634623
Address: 234 Nautical Way, Miami, QLD
Contact telephone: 555-3489

Item	Quantity	Price
Sailing Solo Around the World	1	$39.00
Power Boat Maintenance for Beginners	1	$78.00
Buying and Selling Boats for Profit	1	$48.50
Fishing Around Fraser Island	1	$45.00
Frank Key's History of Water Skiing	1	$11.00
Shipping and handling		$0.00
Total:		$221.50

Orders may be shipped separately in order to meet weight requirements or if certain titles are out of stock. Shipping is free for members of our customer rewards program. Membership in the program is exclusive to customers who have spent more than $200 and completed a registration form at one of our physical stores.

If you require a return or a replacement, please quote the order number when making your request.

To: Paula Tran
From: Steve Prince
Date: 20 June

Paula, I see that you've purchased some books for the waiting room. I think it is a great idea as it can often take a long time to retrieve clients' boats for them. This is especially true when we have been asked to keep them in the long-term warehouse. It is nice to keep people occupied so that they do not feel like they've been waiting for a long time. Nevertheless, I would like to ask you to return the one about taking care of speedboats. It is unlikely to be of interest to our clients and it is over the maximum spending limit of $50.

Reviews of *Buying and Selling Boats for Profit*

Reviewed by: Roger Wang   **Date:** 12 August

I ordered this book from a seller in the United States as I was preparing to sell my boat. Unfortunately, I think that much of the advice is only applicable to selling boats in the United States. The rules and regulations in Australia are very different, so I don't really think it was worth the $20 I paid. There was, however, some good advice about buying boats that I wish I had read before I made my purchase.

196. What is most likely true about Ms. Tran?

(A) She bought the books as a present.

(B) She has visited a Fennville Bookstore in person.

(C) She got approval for the purchase in advance.

(D) She receives a corporate discount from Fennville Bookstore.

197. According to the order confirmation, when are customers required to provide their order number?

(A) When sending back an item

(B) When confirming a delivery date

(C) When checking on the warranty status

(D) When canceling a subscription

198. Where do Ms. Tran and Mr. Prince most likely work?

(A) At a bookstore

(B) At a travel agency

(C) At a boat storage facility

(D) At a fishing tour company

199. Which item is Ms. Tran asked to return?

(A) Sailing Solo Around the World

(B) Power Boat Maintenance for Beginners

(C) Fishing Around Fraser Island

(D) Frank Key's History of Water Skiing

200. What is implied about the book reviewed by Mr. Wang?

(A) It was rewritten for Australian readers.

(B) It is suitable for people who build their own boats.

(C) It was written by a client of Ms. Tran's.

(D) It has been discounted.

Questions 147-148 refer to the following notice.

Help Wanted

❶Pollex Industries is seeking a full-time technician with experience in the repair and servicing of devices used in the manufacturing industry. We specialize in the production of automobile parts. However, applicants with experience in other kinds of manufacturing are also encouraged to apply. While relevant training will be provided, ❷it is important that the applicants be electricians certified with the state licensing board. Working hours are Monday through Friday from 9:00 A.M. to 5:00 P.M. From time to time, the successful applicant may be required to work on Saturdays and Sundays. Apply by sending an e-mail with a résumé and cover letter attached to hr@pollexindustries.com.

設問147-148は次のお知らせに関するものです。

従業員募集

Pollex Industries社は製造業で使われる機器の修理や点検サービスの経験を持つ常勤の技術者を探しています。弊社は自動車部品の製造に特化しています。しかしながら、他の製造業での経験がある方のご応募もお待ちしています。関連した研修は行いますが、応募者は州政府の免許委員会に認定された電気技師であることが重要です。勤務時間は月曜日から金曜日の午前9時から午後5時までです。採用された方は時折、土日の勤務を求められることもあります。履歴書と添え状を添付したメールを hr@pollexindustries.com までお送りいただき、ご応募ください。

語句 □ Help Wanted 従業員募集（求人募集の慣用表現）　□ seek ～を求める
□ full-time 常勤の、フルタイムの　□ specialize in ～ ～に特化する
□ applicant 応募者　□ other kinds of ～ 他の種類の～　□ relevant 関連した
□ certified 認定された　□ licensing board 免許委員会　□ working hours 勤務時間
□ from time to time 時々　□ be required to do ～することを求められる
□ résumé 履歴書　□ cover letter （書類送付時の）添え状　□ attach ～を添付する

147.

What is the purpose of the notice?	お知らせの目的は何ですか。
(A) To promote a repair service	(A) 修理サービスを宣伝すること
(B) To advertise automobile supplies	(B) 自動車用品を広告すること
(C) To recruit a professional mechanic	(C) 専門の機械技術者を募集すること
(D) To introduce training courses	(D) 研修を導入すること

正解 (C)

解説 お知らせの目的が問われています。❶に「Pollex Industries 社は製造業で使われる機器の修理や点検サービスの経験を持つ常勤の技術者を探している」とあることから，機械技術者の採用に関するお知らせだとわかります。以上より正解は(C)となります。文書の目的を問われたときは冒頭部分をよく読むことが大事です。しっかり読んで確実に解きましょう。

語句 □ automobile supplies 自動車用品　□ recruit ～を募集する

148.

What is a requirement for the position?	その職の必須要件は何ですか。
(A) Possession of an electrician's certificate	(A) 電気技師資格を持っていること
(B) Experience in leading a team of workers	(B) 作業者チームを牽引した経験
(C) Availability to work at night	(C) 夜間働くことが可能であること
(D) Willingness to travel internationally	(D) 海外出張をいとわないこと

正解 (A)

解説 募集している職の必須要件は何か問われています。❷に「応募者は州政府の免許委員会に認定された電気技師であることが重要」とあるので，「電気技師資格を持っていること」と言い換えた(A)が正解です。

語句 □ possession 保有，所持　□ certificate 免許証，証明書
□ availability to *do* ～するのが可能なこと　□ willingness to *do* 快く～すること
□ internationally 国際的に

Questions 149-150 refer to the following text-message chain.

Takanori Ueyama　　　8:50 A.M.
I'm having a party at my home on Saturday. Do you think you can come?

Andie Wilde　　　8:51 A.M.
❶Thanks for the invite. ❷I have to check with my family before I answer.

Takanori Ueyama　　　8:53 A.M.
No problem. Let me know whenever you can.

Andie Wilde　　　9:00 A.M.
It looks like I'm free.

Takanori Ueyama　　　9:01 A.M.
Great news! I live at 34 Maxwell Drive in Hansford.

Andie Wilde　　　9:06 A.M.
OK. What time is the party?

Takanori Ueyama　　　9:09 A.M.
We're starting at around 4:00 P.M. ❸You can leave your car on the street in front of my house, if you like.

Andie Wilde　　　9:10 A.M.
OK. I'll see you on Saturday.

設問149-150は次のテキストメッセージのやりとりに関するものです。

Takanori Ueyama	午前8時50分
土曜日に僕の家でパーティーをやるんだ。来られるかい？	
Andie Wilde	午前8時51分
お誘いありがとう。返事をする前に家族に確認しなきゃ。	
Takanori Ueyama	午前8時53分
いいよ。わかったら知らせて。	
Andie Wilde	午前9時00分
私は空いているみたい。	
Takanori Ueyama	午前9時01分
それは良かった！　うちの住所はHansfordのMaxwell通り34番地だよ。	
Andie Wilde	午前9時06分
わかったわ。パーティーは何時なの？	
Takanori Ueyama	午前9時09分
午後4時ごろから始めるつもりだよ。良かったら，僕の家の前の通りに車を止めてもいいよ。	
Andie Wilde	午前9時10分
了解。じゃあ土曜日にね。	

語句　□ in front of ～　～の前に

149.

At 9:00 A.M., what does Ms. Wilde mean when she writes, "It looks like I'm free"? (A) She has checked her work schedule. (B) She does not have any family commitments. (C) She is willing to help Mr. Ueyama. (D) She does not have to pay an admission fee.	午前9時00分に, Wildeさんが "It looks like I'm free" と書いているのは何を意図していますか。 (A) 自分の仕事の予定を調べた。 (B) 家庭の用事がない。 (C) 喜んでUeyamaさんを手伝おうと思っている。 (D) 入場料を支払う必要がない。

正解 (B)

解説 意図問題です。Wildeさんはまず❶でパーティーへの招待に対するお礼を述べ, ❷で家族に確認すると書いてから, この発言をしています。つまり, このfreeは「(家族との予定がないので) 時間が空いている」という意味で使われているので,「家族との予定」を family commitmentsと表した(B)が正解です。

語句 □ family commitment 家庭の用事　□ admission fee 入場料

150.

What does Mr. Ueyama suggest that Ms. Wilde do? (A) Bring a friend to his party (B) Check his address on a map (C) Park her car near his home (D) Contact a colleague	Ueyamaさんは Wildeさんに何をするように勧めていますか。 (A) 友人をパーティーに連れてくる (B) 地図で彼の住所を確認する (C) 彼の家の近くに車を止める (D) 同僚に連絡する

正解 (C)

解説 UeyamaさんがWildeさんに勧めていることが問われています。❸でUeyamaさんは「僕の家の前の通りに車を止めてもいい」と書いているので, それを言い換えた(C)が正解です。

Questions 151-152 refer to the following information.

Giordano Event Management Presents
the Convention for Unexplored Programming Opportunities

❶There is a huge separation between people in the programming industry and those in other fields. This means that there are hundreds, if not thousands, of important time-saving applications that never get made. Programmers are simply unaware of the necessity of them and potential users have no access to people with programming knowledge with whom to discuss their ideas.

❷The Convention for Unexplored Programming Opportunities seeks to bridge that divide. Giordano Event Management has sent its staff to survey people in hundreds of companies in dozens of industries to learn what kind of software they need. We have come up with more than a hundred potential products that are presently unavailable to consumers despite their high demand. At the convention, we will be discussing these needs in a series of presentations. ❸Industry representatives will also be on hand to discuss their members' needs with programmers.

This is an event you cannot afford to miss.

Date: August 18 and August 19
Time: 9:00 A.M. to 5:00 P.M. (Both days)
Location: Parton Convention Center, Dallas, Texas
Price: $750
Reservations can be made on the Web site at www.giordanoem.com.

設問 151-152 は次の案内に関するものです。

Giordano Event Management 社が提供する
未開拓のプログラミング機会に関する会議

プログラミング業界の人々と他の業界の人々との間には大きな隔たりがあります。このことは, 何千とは言わないまでも, 何百もの決して作られることのない重要な時間節約のアプリがあることを意味します。プログラマーの方々は単純にそれらの必要性に気付いておらず, 潜在的なユーザーは自分たちのアイデアについて話せるようなプログラミングの知識を持つ人たちと知り合うすべがありません。

未開拓のプログラミングの機会に関する会議はその隔たりに橋を架けることを目指します。Giordano Event Management 社はスタッフを派遣して, 多くの業界の何百という会社の人々がどんなソフトウエアを必要としているのか調査しました。我々は, 高い需要にもかかわらず, 現在消費者が手にしていない100以上もの潜在的な製品を考案するに至っています。会議では, 一連のプレゼンの中でこれらのニーズについて話し合う予定です。業界を代表する方々も出席し, 各業界

のニーズについてプログラマーの方々と話し合います。

これは見逃すことのできないイベントです。

日付：8月18日，8月19日
時間：午前9時〜午後5時（両日とも）
場所：Parton コンベンションセンター，Texas州Dallas市
費用：750ドル
ウェブサイトwww.giordanoem.comにてご予約いただけます。

語句 □ unexplored 未開拓の　□ separation 隔たり，分離
　　□ hundreds, if not thousands, of 〜 何千とは言わないが，何百もの〜
　　□ be unaware of 〜 〜に気付いていない　□ potential 潜在的な
　　□ bridge 〜に橋を架ける　□ divide 分断　□ be on hand 出席している

151.

選択肢照合型問題

What is indicated about the event?
(A) It is held at the same location every year.
(B) It will supply refreshments to participants.
(C) It will introduce programmers to new markets.
(D) It has been promoted in industry publications.

イベントについて何が述べられていますか。
(A) 毎年同じ場所で開催される。
(B) 参加者に軽食を提供する。
(C) プログラマーたちに新たな市場を紹介する。
(D) 業界の刊行物で宣伝されている。

正解 (C)

解説 イベントについて述べられていることが問われています。❶に「プログラミング業界の人々と他の業界の人々の間には隔たりがあり，これをつなぐ方法がない」とあり，❷で「今回のイベントはその隔たりに橋を架ける」と述べています。つまりこのイベントは，プログラマーに新たな業界，市場を紹介するためのものなので，これを表した(C)が正解です。

語句 □ refreshments 軽食

152.

詳細を問う問題

What will be available to participants?
(A) Access to the raw data collected from surveys
(B) A chance to download applications
(C) Information about job opportunities at programming companies
(D) Opportunities to speak with people from a variety of industries

参加者は何を得られますか。
(A) 調査で集められた生のデータへのアクセス
(B) アプリをダウンロードする機会
(C) プログラミング会社の求人に関する情報
(D) さまざまな業界の人と話す機会

正解 (D)

解説 イベント参加者が得られるものが問われています。❸に「業界を代表する方々も出席し，各業界のニーズについてプログラマーの方々と話し合う」とあるので，それを「話す機会」と表した(D)が正解です。

語句 □ raw data 生のデータ　□ a variety of 〜 さまざまな〜

簡単な案内・お知らせ　♪ 088

NOTICE:

This is a shared area for ❶all users of the Clement Camping Grounds.

The bathroom and kitchen facilities have been provided by the National Parks and Wildlife Department to promote the use of the park in a way that does not harm the natural environment.

❷It is the responsibility of all users to keep the area clean and to use the facilities carefully to ensure that others can enjoy the same convenience.

❸The National Parks and Wildlife Department is able to maintain this service due to funding from the general public. ❹If you are able to contribute funds, please visit our Web site and click the donate button at the bottom of the page. Every little bit counts.

If you would like to report any damage or misuse of the facilities, please call the Clement National Park Rangers Office at 555-8342.

設問 153-154 は次のお知らせに関するものです。

お知らせ：
ここは Clement キャンプ場利用者の皆さまの共有エリアです。

トイレと台所設備は国立公園野生生物省によって提供されており，自然環境を害さずに公園を利用することを奨励しています。

このエリアをきれいに保ち，施設を大切に使って他の人も同じように便利に使えるようにするのは利用者の皆さま全員の責任です。

国立公園野生生物省は一般の方々からの資金提供によってこのサービスを維持できています。もしご寄付いただけるようでしたら，ウェブサイトにアクセスしてページ下の「寄付する」ボタンをクリックしてください。少しであっても助かります。

もし施設の破損や誤用などについてご連絡いただく場合は，Clement 国立公園管理事務所 555-8342 までお電話ください。

語句　□ shared area 共有場所　□ bathroom トイレ，（トイレ付きの）浴室　□ harm ～に害を及ぼす　□ natural environment 自然環境　□ carefully 注意深く　□ ensure that ～確実に～するようにする　□ maintain ～を維持する　□ due to ～ ～により　□ funding 資金提供，基金　□ general public 一般の人々　□ donate （～に）寄付する　□ every little bit ごく少しずつの全て　□ count 重要である　□ misuse 誤用

153.

For whom is the notice most likely intended?
(A) Park rangers
(B) Campers
(C) Cleaning staff
(D) Business owners

お知らせはおそらく誰に宛てられたものですか。
(A) 公園管理者
(B) キャンプをする人
(C) 清掃作業者
(D) 会社経営者

正解 (B)

解説 このお知らせが誰宛てのものか問われています。❶に「キャンプ場利用者の皆さま」，❷に「きれいに保ち，施設を大切に使うのは利用者の皆さま全員の責任」とあるので，ここから「キャンプ場利用者」を表す(B)が正解だとわかります。

語句 □ park ranger 公園管理者

154.

What are readers of the notice encouraged to do?
(A) Take a tour
(B) Read a manual
(C) Donate money
(D) Carry out repairs

お知らせの読み手は何をするよう奨励されていますか。
(A) 見学をする
(B) マニュアルを読む
(C) お金を寄付する
(D) 修復を行う

正解 (C)

解説 読み手は何をするよう奨励されているか問われています。❸に「トイレや台所などの設備は基金により維持できている」とあり，続く❹に「寄付のお願いと方法」が書かれていることから，(C)が正解だとわかります。

語句 □ carry out ～ ～を行う，実行する

メモ　♪ 089

❶You are required to leave a note with your contact number when the recipient is not home to receive a parcel. ❷Parcels should only be left unattended if the sender has stipulated that course of action in their instructions. You can check these instructions by inputting the tracking number into the tablet computer you have been provided. If you are instructed to leave a parcel unattended, please take a photograph of the parcel at the delivery address as proof of delivery. ❸Failure to follow these instructions may result in damage or loss of parcels, for which Dalton Logistics could be held responsible. ❹Our insurance only covers us when you have complied with the above instructions.

If for any reason you believe that there is a high risk that a parcel will be damaged or lost due to unforeseen circumstances, do not leave it unattended. Leave a note for the recipient explaining the situation. Depending on the time of day, you may return later or suggest that the recipient come to our distribution center to pick up the parcel. ❺Each district follows slightly different procedures. In such cases, you should discuss the situation with your district manager.

設問155-157は次の指示書に関するものです。

受取人がご自宅に不在で荷物を受け取れない場合は，連絡先電話番号を書いた連絡票を残しておく必要があります。送り主がそうするよう指示書に明記している場合に限り，荷物をそのまま置いておくようにしてください。送り主の指示については，支給されたタブレット型パソコンに追跡番号を入力すれば確認できます。荷物をそのまま置いておくよう指示された場合は，配達証明として配送先住所で荷物の写真を撮影してください。これらの指示に従わなければ荷物の破損や紛失につながるかもしれず，それに対してDalton Logistics社が責任を負う可能性があります。当社の保険は上記の指示に従った場合にしか適用されません。

何らかの理由で，荷物が予期せぬ状況下で破損または紛失するリスクが高いと思われる場合は，荷物を放置しないでください。受取人にその状況を説明する連絡票を残してください。時間帯によって，後で再配達するか，受取人の方に配送センターに荷物を取りに来てもらうよう提案することになるかもしれません。地区ごとに微妙に異なる手順に従っています。そのような場合は，自分の地区の責任者に状況について相談してください。

語句　□ be required to *do* ～することが必要とされる　□ note メモ　□ recipient 受取人
□ parcel 荷物，小包　□ unattended 放置された　□ sender 送り主
□ stipulate ～を明記する，規定する　□ course of action 一連の行動
□ tracking number 追跡番号　□ tablet computer タブレット型パソコン

□ be instructed to *do* ～するよう指示される　□ proof 証拠，証明
□ failure（～を）しないこと，不履行　□ insurance 保険　□ due to ～ ～のために
□ unforeseen 予期しない　□ circumstances 状況　□ depending on ～ ～によって
□ district 地区　□ procedure 手順

155.

情報をもとに推測する問題

For whom are the instructions most likely intended?	指示書はおそらく誰に宛てられていますか。
(A) Insurance company employees	(A) 保険会社の社員
(B) Online store owners	(B) ネットショップのオーナー
(C) Delivery staff	(C) 配送員
(D) Recipients of parcel deliveries	(D) 宅配物の受取人

正解 (C)

解説 この指示書が誰宛てのものか問われています。❶に「受取人が配達の際に自宅に不在の場合は連絡票を残すこと」，❷に「送り主の指示がある場合に限り，荷物を置いておくこと」とあることから，宅配物配送員への指示と推測できます。以上から正解は(C)となります。

156.

選択肢照合型問題

What is implied about Dalton Logistics?	Dalton Logistics社について何が示唆されていますか。
(A) It provides ongoing training for its employees.	(A) 従業員に継続した教育を行っている。
(B) It encourages employees to purchase tablet computers.	(B) 従業員にタブレット型パソコンの購入を推奨している。
(C) It offers discounts to repeat customers.	(C) リピート客に割引を提供する。
(D) It pays compensation for certain damages.	(D) 一定の破損に対して補償する。

正解 (D)

解説 Dalton Logistics社について何が示唆されているか問われています。❸に「これらの指示に従わない場合，荷物の破損や紛失を招くかもしれず，それに対してDalton Logistics社が責任を負う可能性がある」，❹に「保険は上記の指示に従ったときのみ適用」とあります。ここから，指示に従わずに荷物が破損・紛失した場合にはDalton Logistics社自体が補償すると考えられるので，(D)が正解です。

語句 □ ongoing 継続した，現在行われている　□ repeat customer リピート客
□ pay compensation for ～ ～について補償する

157.

According to the instructions, why might a
staff member contact a district manager?

(A) To get an update on the location of a parcel
(B) To ask for assistance finding an address
(C) To notify colleagues about traffic conditions
(D) To request information about local policies

指示書によると、職員はなぜ地区の責任者に連絡する可能性がありますか。

(A) 荷物の所在位置に関する最新情報を得るため
(B) 住所を見つけるのに協力を求めるため
(C) 同僚に交通状況について知らせるため
(D) 地区の方針についての情報を求めるため

正解 (D)

解説 職員（＝配送員）が地区の責任者に連絡する場合の理由について問われています。❺に「地区により手順が微妙に異なるため、状況について地区の責任者に相談するように」とあります。ここから、地区の方針について尋ねるという(D)が正解だとわかります。

語句 □ notify（人）に知らせる

Questions 158-160 refer to the following article.

Hampton—❶In just two months, Hampton will be getting a new youth center, which will provide young people with a much-needed place to train for a variety of athletic events. With the announcement that Hampton will host the National Youth Athletics Meet in two years' time, city leaders have decided to invest in youth sports to ensure proper representation by local athletes. ❷The center, to be known as the Joel Whittaker Memorial Youth Center, will have its grand opening on September 21. ❸The date was chosen to coincide with the Hampton City to Bay Fun Run, and the new youth center will be used as the starting point.

❹The former mayor for whom the center was named will be in attendance to open the center and fire the starting pistol. If you would like to take part in the run, you can learn more about it by visiting the Web page at www. hamptonfr.org. As yet, the youth center does not have a Web site of its own. However, you can see the plans at Hampton City Hall and talk about opportunities for local youth groups by setting up an appointment with Fran Sanders, the city's director of youth welfare. Contact her office at 555-9392.

設問158-160は次の記事に関するものです。

Hampton市—ちょうど2カ月後にHampton市には新しい青少年センターができ，若者たちにさまざまな運動競技イベントに向けてトレーニングをするための待望の場所を提供することになる。Hampton市は2年後のNational Youth Athletics Meetの開催を発表し，市の指導者たちは地元のスポーツ選手が確実にしかるべき代表になれるよう，青少年のスポーツに投資することを決めた。センターは，Joel Whittaker記念青少年センターとして知られることになるが，9月21日にグランドオープンを迎える。この日程はHampton City to Bay市民マラソンに合わせて設定され，新青少年センターはスタート地点として使用される。

このセンターの名前の由来となっている前市長がセンターのオープンとスタートの号砲を鳴らすために出席する予定だ。マラソンへの参加を希望する人は，ウェブページ www. hamptonfr.org にアクセスすればさらに情報が得られる。今のところ，青少年センターには自身のウェブサイトがない。しかしHampton市役所でセンターの計画を閲覧し，市の青少年福祉部長Fran Sanders氏との面会の予約を取って地元の若者グループのための機会について話し合うことができる。連絡は氏の執務室555-9392まで。

語句　□ youth center 青少年施設　□ much-needed 待望の，切望された
□ athletic 運動競技の　□ in ～ years' time ～年後に　□ invest in ～ ～に投資する
□ proper 適切な　□ representation 代表　□ grand opening グランドオープン
□ coincide with ～ ～と同時に起こる　□ fun run 市民マラソン
□ starting point スタート地点　□ former 前の　□ be in attendance 出席している
□ fire ～を発砲する　□ take part in ～ ～に参加する

□ as yet これまでのところは（通常否定文で用いる） □ set up ～ ～を設定する
□ welfare 福祉

158.

According to the article, what will soon be available in Hampton?	記事によると，Hampton市では間もなく何が利用可能になりますか。
(A) An office to coordinate volunteer activities	(A) ボランティア活動を調整する事務所
(B) A college course for mature students	(B) 成人学生用の大学講座
(C) A new performing arts center	(C) 新しい舞台芸術センター
(D) A public sports facility	(D) 公共スポーツ施設

正解 (D)

解説 Hampton市でもうすぐ利用可能になるものが問われています。❶に「2カ月後に新しい青少年センターができ，若者たちにさまざまな運動競技イベントに向けてのトレーニングをする場所を提供する」とあることから，(D)が正解です。センターが多目的に使用される可能性はありますが，(A)，(B)，(C)についての具体的な記載はないので不正解です。

語句 □ coordinate ～を調整する □ mature student 成人学生
□ performing arts 舞台芸術

159.

What event will be held in September?	9月にどんなイベントが開催されますか。
(A) An athletic event	(A) 運動競技のイベント
(B) A riverside cleanup	(B) 川辺の清掃
(C) A cultural festival	(C) 文化祭
(D) A local election	(D) 地方選挙

正解 (A)

解説 9月に開催されるイベントについて問われています。❷に「センターは9月21日にオープン予定」，❸に「この日程は市民マラソンに合わせて設定」とあるので，9月に運動競技のイベントであるマラソン大会が行われることがわかります。以上から，正解は(A)となります。

語句 □ cultural festival 文化祭

160.

Who most likely is Joel Whittaker?	Joel Whittakerさんとはおそらく誰ですか。
(A) An athlete	
(B) A newspaper journalist	(A) スポーツ選手
(C) An event organizer	(B) 新聞ジャーナリスト
(D) A politician	(C) イベント企画者
	(D) 政治家

正解 (D)

解説 Joel Whittakerさんが誰か問われています。❷の「新設のセンターは，Joel Whittaker記念青少年センターという名前になる」ということと，❹の「前市長がこのセンターの名の由来」ということから，Joel Whittakerさんは前のHampton市長だとわかります。以上からmayor（市長）をpolitician（政治家）と言い換えた(D)が正解です。

Questions 161-163 refer to the following advertisement.

The freshest ingredients to your door daily

❶ Nutriplus provides daily deliveries of perfectly measured ingredients for our ultra-healthy menus for less than you would spend at the supermarket. — [1] —. ❷ What's more, all of our meals are designed by renowned chef and qualified nutritionist, Renee Strahovski. ❸ Every day, our delivery drivers drop off a refrigerated container at our customers' front doors. Inside is an easy-to-follow recipe and all the ingredients you need to make it. ❹ There are even online videos you can watch to learn from our expert chefs. — [2] —. Visit our Web site, input your dining preferences, and get your first meal for free. It's that easy. ❺ We are extending our reach every month. To find out whether or not your address is covered, call one of our friendly customer service representatives at 555-8348. — [3] —. They are waiting to take your call.

With Nutriplus, you will reduce your cooking time, spend less money, and enjoy the healthiest meals. — [4] —. You can't go wrong.

www.nutriplus.com

設問161-163は次の広告に関するものです。

Nutriplus社
新鮮な材料を毎日あなたの玄関へ

Nutriplus社は，超健康的なメニューのために完璧に計量された材料を，スーパーで支払う金額よりも安いお値段で毎日お届けします。—[1]— さらに，わが社の食事は全て有名なシェフであり認定栄養士のRenee Strahovski氏によって考案されたものです。毎日，わが社の配送ドライバーがお客さまの玄関の前に冷蔵容器を置いていきます。その中には，わかりやすいレシピとそれを調理するために必要な全ての材料が入っています。わが社の熟練シェフたちから見て学べるオンラインの動画もございます。—[2]— ウェブサイトにアクセスし，食事の好みを入力して，無料で初回の食事を手に入れてください。とても簡単です。わが社は毎月対象地域を拡大しています。お客さまのご住所が対象地域に含まれるかどうかを調べるには，私どもの気さくなお客さま担当者宛てに555-8348までお電話ください。—[3]— 皆さまからのお電話をお待ちしています。

Nutriplus社のご利用によって，調理時間を減らし，支出を抑え，そして最高に健康的な食事を楽しめます。—[4]— これで間違いなしです。

www.nutriplus.com

語句 □ ingredient 材料　□ measured 計量された　□ ultra-healthy 超健康的な
□ renowned 有名な　□ qualified 認定された，有資格の　□ nutritionist 栄養士
□ refrigerated 冷蔵された　□ easy-to-follow わかりやすい　□ recipe レシピ，調理法
□ dining preference 食事の好み　□ extend ～を伸ばす　□ reach（届く）範囲
□ whether or not ～ ～か否か　□ You can't go wrong. それなら間違いなしだ。

161.　　　　　　　　　　　　　　　選択肢照合型問題

What is indicated about Ms. Strahovski?
(A) She helps customers choose a plan.
(B) She represents a supermarket chain.
(C) She has published a book on nutrition.
(D) She creates recipes for Nutriplus.

Strahovskiさんについて何が述べられていますか。
(A) 顧客がプランを選ぶのを助ける。
(B) スーパーマーケットチェーンの代表である。
(C) 栄養学に関する本を出版した。
(D) Nutriplus社のレシピを作成している。

正解 (D)

解説 Strahovskiさんについて述べられていることが問われています。❷に「全ての食事は有名なシェフであり認定栄養士のRenee Strahovski氏が考案」とあることから，Strahovskiさんは料理人かつ栄養士で，この会社が提供するメニューを考案していることがわかるので，それを言い換えた(D)が正解です。顧客が選択するのを助けるという(A)や，(B)の本の出版，(C)のスーパー経営というような記述はありません。

語句 □ nutrition 栄養学

162.

What is NOT mentioned about Nutriplus? (A) It will negotiate on price. (B) It provides home delivery. (C) It is broadening its service area. (D) It offers instructional videos.	Nutriplus社について述べられていないことは何ですか。 (A) 価格について交渉する。 (B) 自宅配送をする。 (C) 営業エリアを拡大している。 (D) 指導用の動画を提供している。

正解 (A)

解説 NOT問題で，Nutriplus社について述べられていないことが問われています。❸の「玄関前にドライバーが冷蔵容器を置いていく」が(B)と，❹の「見て学べるオンライン動画」が(D)と，❺の「対象地域の拡大」が(C)と合致するので，残った(A)が正解です。❹の直後に初回の食事が無料というサービスについて述べられていますが，これは価格を下げるなどの交渉には当たらないため，(A)は本文に述べられていることには該当しません。

語句 □ negotiate on price 価格交渉をする　□ home delivery 自宅配送，宅配
□ broaden 〜を拡大する　□ instructional 指導の，教育用の

163.

In which of the positions marked [1], [2], [3], and [4] does the following sentence best belong? "This means there is no waste, little trash, and only minimal cleaning required." (A) [1] (B) [2] (C) [3] (D) [4]	以下の文は[1]，[2]，[3]，[4]のどの位置に入るのが最も適していますか。 「これは無駄がなく，ごみもほとんど出ず，最小限の洗浄だけで済むということです」 (A) [1] (B) [2] (C) [3] (D) [4]

正解 (A)

解説 文挿入位置問題です。この文書は，家庭での調理用に計量された食材を宅配するという広告で，挿入する文は「無駄がなく，ごみもほとんど出ず，最小限の洗浄だけで済む」と「食材」について説明していると考えられます。その観点で本文を見ると，❶の「超健康的なメニューのために完璧に計量された材料を届ける」という文で「食材」に触れているので，この❶の直後に入れると文意が通ります。以上から正解は(A)となります。

語句 □ trash ごみ　□ minimal 最小限の

Questions 164-167 refer to the following e-mail.

To:	Dolly Holland <dholland@sybiotech.com>
From:	Greg Simon <gsimon@sybiotech.com>
Subject:	Welcome back
Date:	September 16

Dear Ms. Holland,

I am pleased to welcome you back from your holiday. ❶The fact that Sybiotech allows us to take these extended holidays after 10 years of service is one of my favorite aspects of the job. I am looking forward to taking advantage of the arrangement again myself next year.

❷I'd like to inform you that Mr. Patel retired in your absence and he has been replaced by me. ❸One of my first decisions as section supervisor was to make some changes to improve efficiency. ❹I regret that I was unable to consult with you before rearranging your schedule, but I trust you will find the new situation advantageous.

In previous years, you have spent Mondays and Fridays at the factory in Maine and the rest of the week at the head office. When you return to work, you will be required to spend Mondays and Tuesdays in Maine. You can spend the night at a hotel there. ❺The reduced number of trips will help us save on transportation costs.

I look forward to discussing the arrangements with you in detail when you get back on Monday morning.

Sincerely,

Greg Simon

設問164-167は次のEメールに関するものです。

宛先：Dolly Holland <dholland@sybiotech.com>
送信者：Greg Simon <gsimon@sybiotech.com>
件名：お帰りなさい
日付：9月16日

Holland様

休暇から戻って来てくれてうれしいです。Sybiotech社が勤続10年でこの長期休暇を取らせてくれるという事実は，私がこの仕事で好きな点の1つです。来年私も再度その制度を利用できるのを楽しみにしています。

Patelさんがあなたのいない間に引退し，私がそのポジションを引き継いだことをお知らせします。部門長として私が最初に決めたことの1つは，効率を上げるためにいくつかの変更を行うことでした。あなたの予定を組み直す前にあなたに相談できなくて申し訳ないのですが，新しい体制は好都合だと理解してもらえると思います。

過去数年間，あなたは月曜日と金曜日をMaineの工場で過ごし，残りの曜日を本社で勤務してくれましたね。仕事に復帰したら，月曜日と火曜日にMaineに行ってもらうことになります。夜はあちらのホテルに泊まることができます。移動の回数が減ることは，旅費削減に寄与します。

月曜日の朝あなたが戻って来たときに，詳しいことについて調整させていただければと思います。

敬具

Greg Simon

語句 □ extended holiday 長期休暇 □ arrangement 取り決め，調整 □ absence 不在
□ replace 〜に取って代わる □ efficiency 効率 □ consult with 〜 〜と相談する
□ rearrange 〜を再調整する □ advantageous 好都合な
□ transportation costs 交通費 □ in detail 詳細に，詳しく

164.

What is suggested about Ms. Holland?	Hollandさんについて何が示されていますか。
(A) She has recently acquired a new qualification.	(A) 最近新たな資格を取った。
(B) She was hired before Mr. Simon.	(B) Simonさんより前に採用された。
(C) She has been with Sybiotech for over a decade.	(C) 10年以上Sybiotech社に勤務している。
(D) She has been asked to run a training workshop.	(D) 教育研修を指揮するよう依頼された。

正解 (C)

解説 Hollandさんについて何が示されているか問われています。メールの冒頭で休暇から戻って来たHollandさんに歓迎の意を示した後、❶で「Sybiotech社は勤続10年ごとにこの長期休暇を取らせてくれる」と書いていることから、Hollandさんは勤続10年の社員に与えられる長期休暇を取っており、この会社で10年以上働いているとわかります。また、(A)、(B)、(D)の内容については文書中に記載がありません。よって、正解は(C)となります。decadeは「10年」という意味ですが、この語はPart 7によく登場するので確実に覚えておきましょう。

語句 □ qualification 資格　□ run（業務など）を指揮する

165.

Why did Ms. Holland receive the e-mail?	Hollandさんはなぜメールを受け取ったのですか。
(A) Her work schedule has been changed.	(A) 彼女の仕事の予定が変更された。
(B) She will be given a promotion.	(B) 彼女は昇進することになる。
(C) Her office will be relocated.	(C) 彼女の職場が移転することになる。
(D) She is planning to retire.	(D) 彼女は引退する予定だ。

正解 (A)

解説 Hollandさんがメールを受け取った理由が問われています。第2段落の❹から「SimonさんはHollandさんの仕事の予定を組み直した（＝Hollandさんにとっては予定が変更された）」ということがわかるので、これを言い換えた(A)が正解です。続く第3段落に変更の詳細が書かれています。

語句 □ promotion 昇進

166.

Who most likely is Mr. Patel?	Patelさんとはおそらく誰ですか。
(A) A company president	(A) 会社の社長
(B) A former supervisor	(B) 以前の監督者
(C) A human resources officer	(C) 人事担当役員
(D) A maintenance worker	(D) 整備作業員

正解 (B)

解説 Patelさんがおそらく誰か問われています。第2段落の❷に「Hollandさんの休暇中にPatelさんが引退し，私（＝送信者のSimonさん）がそのポジションを引き継いだ」，❸に「部門長として私が最初に決めた…」とあるので，ここから(B)が正解だとわかります。

語句 □ former 前の

167.

What is the reason that Mr. Simon made the change?	Simonさんが変更した理由は何ですか。
(A) To reduce air pressure	(A) 空気圧を減らすため
(B) To cut down on expenditures	(B) 支出を減らすため
(C) To better understand clients' needs	(C) 顧客のニーズをよりよく理解するため
(D) To accommodate additional employees	(D) 追加の従業員を収容するため

正解 (B)

解説 Simonさんが変更を行った理由が問われています。Simonさんは第3段落でHollandさんのMaineでの勤務日程の変更について述べており，❺で「移動の回数が減ることは，旅費削減に寄与する」と述べているので，これを「支出を減らす」と言い換えた(B)が正解です。

×

Sam Cole　　　　　3:30 P.M.:
❶Who saw the advertisement for Carleton Window Dressings last night?

Rhod Harps　　　　3:31 P.M.:
I did. ❷The prices they were offering on drapes were even lower than what we pay our supplier.

Leanne Milton　　　3:31 P.M.:
Right. I don't know how they are doing it. ❸It's going to be almost impossible for us to compete.

Sam Cole　　　　　3:33 P.M.:
That's what I thought. ❹I've asked our supplier to come in and discuss the issue tomorrow afternoon. As we're all partners in the business, I think we should all try to attend.

Rhod Harps　　　　3:35 P.M.:
I have an appointment at Haddonfield Public Hospital from 2:00 P.M.

Aina Rashid　　　　3:35 P.M.:
I'll be out until 3:30 P.M. I have to show some samples to an interior decorator in Cork.

Rhod Harps　　　　3:37 P.M.:
❺I'll be back at around 4:00 P.M., I suppose.

Sam Cole　　　　　3:45 P.M.:
❻That's when we will have to ask him to come, then.

Leanne Milton　　　3:46 P.M.:
❼I have a dinner reservation at 7:00 P.M. tomorrow night. Do you think I should reschedule?

Sam Cole　　　　　3:49 P.M.:
❽It should be fine. We'll be done by 5:00 P.M.

設問168-171は次のオンラインチャットの話し合いに関するものです。

Sam Cole [午後3時30分]:
誰か昨夜のCarleton Window Dressings社の広告を見たかい？

Rhod Harps [午後3時31分]:
見ましたよ。カーテンの販売価格は当社が供給業者に支払う額よりも安いくらいでした。

Leanne Milton [午後3時31分]:
そうですよね。彼らはどうやっているのかしら。私たちが競合するのはほぼ不可能になりそうだわ。

Sam Cole [午後3時33分]:
私もそう思った。明日の午後，供給業者にこの件について打ち合わせに来てもらうように頼んだよ。我々は皆ビジネスパートナーだから，全員出席できるようにすべきだと思うのだが。

Rhod Harps [午後3時35分]:
私は午後2時からHaddonfield公立病院で予約があります。

Aina Rashid [午後3時35分]:
私は午後3時30分まで外出する予定です。Corkの室内装飾家にサンプルを見せなくてはいけなくて。

Rhod Harps [午後3時37分]:
私は午後4時ごろには戻れると思います。

Sam Cole [午後3時45分]:
それでは，そのころに業者に来てもらうように頼めばいいね。

Leanne Milton [午後3時46分]:
私は明日の夜7時にディナーの予約があるんですが，予定を変更したほうがいいですか。

Sam Cole [午後3時49分]:
大丈夫だよ。午後5時までには終わるだろう。

語句 □ drapes（厚手の）カーテン □ even さらに，一層
□ That's what I thought. 私もそう思った。 □ interior decorator 室内装飾家
□ that's when ～ ～するのはその時だ

168.

詳細を問う問題

Where do the writers work?	書き手たちはどこで働いていますか。
(A) At a fashion house	(A) 服飾会社
(B) At a catering company	(B) ケータリング会社
(C) At a curtain store	(C) カーテン店
(D) At a medical facility	(D) 医療施設

正解 (C)

解説 この話し合いをしている人たちが働いている場所が問われています。❶，❷のやりとりで「Carleton Window Dressings社の広告」について取り上げ，「彼らのカーテンの販売価格は当社の仕入れ値よりも安い」と述べていることから，書き手たちはカーテンを取り扱っている会社の社員だとわかります。以上から正解は(C)となります。

語句 □ catering ケータリング，仕出し □ medical facility 医療施設

169.

What will the writers most likely discuss with the supplier?	書き手たちはおそらく何について供給業者と打ち合わせをしますか。
(A) Improving production times	(A) 製造時間の改善
(B) New design ideas	(B) 新しいデザイン案
(C) Changing delivery routes	(C) 配送経路の変更
(D) A price reduction	(D) 価格の値下げ

正解 (D)

解説 書き手たちが供給業者と何について打ち合わせるか問われています。❷、❸、❹で「他社のカーテンの販売価格は当社仕入れ値よりも安い」「私たちは競合できないのではないか」「業者に来てもらってこの件について打ち合わせを」というやりとりがあるので、他社と競合できるよう業者に仕入れ値を下げてもらえないか交渉するだろうと推測できます。以上から、正解は(D)となります。

語句 □ production time 製造時間　□ delivery route 配送経路　□ price reduction 値下げ

170.

What time will the meeting most likely take place?	打ち合わせはおそらく何時に行われますか。
(A) At 2:00 P.M.	(A) 午後2時
(B) At 3:30 P.M.	(B) 午後3時30分
(C) At 4:00 P.M.	(C) 午後4時
(D) At 4:30 P.M.	(D) 午後4時30分

正解 (C)

解説 打ち合わせを行う時間が問われています。まず、Coleさんが❹で明日の午後と指定し、その後各自が予定を言い合いながら、❺でHarpsさんが「私は午後4時ごろ戻れると思う」と書くと、Coleさんが❻で「そのころに業者に来てもらうように頼めばいいね」と提案しています。それ以降、異論は出ていないので、(C)が正解です。オンラインチャットの話し合いには複数の人物が登場するので、点在する情報をよく整理しましょう。

171.

At 3:49 P.M., what does Mr. Cole mean when he writes, "We'll be done by 5:00 P.M."?

(A) Employees will not need to work overtime.
(B) Ms. Milton does not need to change her plans.
(C) They can avoid rush hour traffic.
(D) A meeting will be shorter than planned.

午後3時49分に、Coleさんが"We'll be done by 5:00 P.M."と書いているのは何を意図していますか。

(A) 従業員は残業する必要がない。
(B) Miltonさんは予定を変更する必要はない。
(C) ラッシュアワーの交通を避けることができる。
(D) 打ち合わせは予定していたよりも短くなる。

正解 (B)

解説 意図問題です。問われている文は話し合いの最後に出てくるので、その直前を見てみると、❼「午後7時のディナーの予約を変更したほうがいいか」→ ❽「大丈夫」という流れになっており、その後に「午後5時までには終わる」と続いています。つまり問われている意図は「打ち合わせは5時に終わるので、7時からのディナーの予約を変更する必要はない」ということなので、正解は(B)となります。

語句 □ work overtime 残業する　□ rush hour ラッシュアワー、混雑する時間帯

メモ ♪ 094

To: All office staff
From: Todd Nugent
Subject: Annual Somersby Riverbank Cleanup Day
Date: Wednesday, August 21

❶In order to improve our profile in the community and attract more local clients, I would like as many employees as possible to take part in the Annual Somersby Riverbank Cleanup Day this year. It will be held on Sunday, September 15 and it starts at 7:00 A.M. It is generally over by noon and everyone who contributes is invited to enjoy a barbecue lunch provided by the city council. — [1] —. ❷I have attended as a volunteer for the last five years and noticed that many local businesses were sending teams. They were all wearing specially printed T-shirts which showed what business they worked for. They seem to attend every year, so they must be experiencing some benefits. — [2] —.

I'll be ordering T-shirts, so ❸please let me know whether or not you will be able to attend. ❹I also need to know whether you'd like a small, medium, or large. — [3] —. I have come up with a design for the T-shirts. Please take a look at it and give me your input. ❺I've posted it on the notice board in the break room. You'll find a signup sheet there also. — [4] —. I hope you will be able to take part, but you should not feel overly pressured, as this will not be taken into account for your upcoming employee evaluation.

設問172-175は次のメモに関するものです。

宛先：事務所全スタッフ
差出人：Todd Nugent
件名：年次Somersby Riverbankクリーンアップデー
日付：8月21日（水）

地域社会における当社の印象を良くして，もっと多くの地元のお客さまを引き付けるため，今年はできるだけ多くの従業員に年次Somersby Riverbankクリーンアップデーに参加してほしいと思います。それは9月15日（日）に開催される予定で，午前7時から始まります。大体正午までには終了し，参加した人は全員，市議会の提供するバーベキューランチに招待されます。―[1]― 私はここ5年間ボランティアとして参加してきましたが，たくさんの地元の会社がチームを送り込んでいるのに気付きました。彼らは皆どこの会社で働いているかを示す特注のTシャツを着ていました。彼らは毎年参加しているようなので，何らかの恩恵を享受しているのでしょう。―[2]―

Tシャツを注文する予定なので，参加できるかどうかを私に知らせてください。またS，M，Lのどのサイズが希望かも知る必要があります。―[3]― 私はTシャツのデザインを考案しました。それを見て，皆さんの意見を聞かせてください。休憩室の掲示板に張ってあります。そこには登録用紙もあります。―[4]― 皆さんが参加してくれることを願っていますが，今回の件は来る従業員評価には考慮されないので，過度にプレッシャーを感じないでください。

語句 □ cleanup 掃除，清掃　□ in order to *do* 〜するために　□ profile 印象，イメージ
□ community 地域社会　□ take part in 〜 〜に参加する　□ contribute 貢献する
□ city council 市議会　□ whether or not 〜 〜か否か
□ come up with 〜 〜を考案する　□ input 意見，考え　□ notice board 掲示板
□ break room 休憩室　□ signup sheet 登録用紙　□ overly 過度に
□ take 〜 into account 〜を考慮に入れる　□ upcoming 来る
□ employee evaluation 従業員評価

172.

目的・テーマを問う問題

What is the purpose of the memo?	メモの目的は何ですか。
(A) To encourage attendance at an event	(A) イベントへの参加を奨励すること
(B) To announce the end of a campaign	(B) キャンペーン終了を知らせること
(C) To thank people for contributing funds	(C) 資金を提供した人に感謝すること
(D) To recommend a local business	(D) 地元企業を推薦すること

正解 (A)

解説 メモの目的が問われています。❶に「地元における当社のイメージアップのためにできるだけたくさんの社員にクリーンアップデーに参加してほしい」とあることから，このイベントへの参加を促すのが目的だとわかります。以上から，(A)が正解です。

語句 □ attendance 参加，出席　□ funds 資金

173.

What does Mr. Nugent claim to have done?	Nugentさんは何をしたと主張していますか。
(A) Taken part in a fun run	(A) 市民マラソンへの参加
(B) Contacted an advertising agency	(B) 広告代理店への連絡
(C) Volunteered in the community	(C) 地域社会でのボランティア活動
(D) Completed an employee evaluation	(D) 従業員評価の完了

正解 (C)

解説 Nugentさんがしたと主張していることについて問われています。❷に「ここ5年間ボランティアとして参加してきました」とあるので，それを言い換えた(C)が正解です。

語句 □ claim ～を主張する　□ fun run 市民マラソン

174.

What information does Mr. Nugent require from participants?	Nugentさんはどんな情報を参加者に求めていますか。
(A) Their T-shirt size	(A) Tシャツのサイズ
(B) Their home address	(B) 自宅住所
(C) Their telephone number	(C) 電話番号
(D) Their cleaning schedule	(D) 清掃のスケジュール

正解 (A)

解説 メモの書き手であるNugentさんがイベント参加者に求めている情報が問われています。❸でまず「参加の可否」について知らせてほしいと述べた後，❹で「サイズはS，M，Lのどれがいいか」と注文するTシャツのサイズを聞いているので，(A)が正解です。

175.

In which of the positions marked [1], [2], [3], and [4] does the following sentence best belong?

"Just write your name in the space provided and I will take care of the registration process."

(A) [1]
(B) [2]
(C) [3]
(D) [4]

以下の文は [1]，[2]，[3]，[4] のどの位置に入るのが最も適していますか。

「所定の欄に記名してください。そうすれば私の方で登録手続きをします」

(A) [1]
(B) [2]
(C) [3]
(D) [4]

正解 (D)

解説 文挿入位置問題です。挿入する文は「記名のお願いとその後の登録手続きの流れ」について述べています。つまり，この文の直前には，名前を書き込むべき何らかの用紙（申込書など）についての情報があると思われます。挿入箇所候補それぞれの前の文を見ると，❺に「（Tシャツのデザイン案を）休憩室の掲示板に張った。そこに登録用紙もある」とあるので，この登録用紙に記名すると考えれば文脈がつながります。以上から正解は (D) となります。

語句 □ the space provided 所定の欄　□ registration process 登録手続き

Questions 176-180 refer to the following memo and schedule.

MEMO

To: All Baxter Pools Staff
From: Steven Baxter
Subject: NPS
❶Date: Monday, April 3

❷I am sure many of you have already heard that we are in the process of purchasing Nolte Pool Services (NPS). NPS was advertised for sale last month and we have been negotiating with its owners. ❸We expect to sign an agreement the day after tomorrow.

❹Through this arrangement, we should be able to save money by sharing some expenses such as bookkeeping, customer service, and advertising. Unfortunately, we do not have sufficient room in our current building to accommodate the staff and equipment of NPS. ❺Therefore, we are planning an addition to the building, which should be completed at the end of July. ❻At present, NPS is a little short-staffed but rather than hiring someone new on a temporary basis, I will be asking some of our staff to help out there for a few days a week. ❼We need someone with a hazardous chemical handling certificate. If you are suitably qualified and willing to spend a couple of days at Hazlehurst every week until the construction is complete, please send me an e-mail at sb@baxterpools.com.

Roster for Baxter Pools Employees to Work at NPS (Hazlehurst)
❽The relocation is scheduled for September 9. Staff members whose names appear on the roster for that day are required to help with the office relocation.

Sunday	Monday	Tuesday	Wednesday	Thursday	Friday	Saturday
27	28 ❾Trevor Lowry	29	30 Trevor Lowry	31 Valerie Singh	1 (September)	2
3	4 Trevor Lowry	5	6 Trevor Lowry	7 Valerie Singh	8	9 Peter Sanchez Bruce Tilley

設問176-180は次のメモと日程表に関するものです。

メモ

宛先：Baxter Pools社全従業員
差出人：Steven Baxter
件名：NPS
日付：4月3日（月）

皆さんの多くはすでに，わが社がNolte Pool Services社（NPS）の買収を進めていることを聞いていると思います。NPSは先月売却の告示が出され，我々は先方の所有者と交渉してきました。明後日には合意文書に署名する見込みです。

この協定を通じて，我々は簿記，顧客サービス，広告などにかかる支出を共にすることによって経費を節減することができるはずです。残念ながら，わが社の現在のビルにはNPSの従業員と設備を収容する十分なスペースがありません。そこで，ビルを増築する計画を立てており，7月末に完工する見込みです。現在のところ，NPSは若干人材が不足していますが，期限付きで新しい人を雇うのではなく，当社から何人かの人に1週間のうち何日間かNPSに手伝いに行ってもらいたいと思います。危険化学物質の取扱資格を持っている人が必要です。ふさわしい資格を持っていて，完工までの毎週2，3日をHazlehurstで過ごしてもよいという人は，私宛てにsb@baxterpools.comまでメールを送付してください。

語句 □ negotiate 交渉する □ expect to *do* ～する見込みである □ agreement 同意書
□ the day after tomorrow 明後日 □ arrangement 協定，合意
□ bookkeeping 簿記 □ sufficient 十分な □ accommodate ～を収容する
□ equipment 設備，装置 □ short-staffed 人手不足の
□ rather than ～ ～よりむしろ □ on a temporary basis 臨時に，期限付きで
□ hazardous chemical 危険化学物質 □ qualified 資格のある
□ be willing to *do* ～する気がある

NPS（Hazlehurst）でのBaxter Pools社従業員業務当番表
移転は9月9日の予定。当日，当番表に名前のある従業員は
オフィスの移転を手伝う必要があります。

日曜日	月曜日	火曜日	水曜日	木曜日	金曜日	土曜日
27	28	29	30	31	1	2
	Trevor Lowry		Trevor Lowry	Valerie Singh	（9月）	
3	4	5	6	7	8	9
	Trevor Lowry		Trevor Lowry	Valerie Singh		Peter Sanchez Bruce Tilley

---

語句 □ roster 当番表 □ relocation 移転 □ be required to *do* ～する必要がある

176.

What is one purpose of the memo?	メモの目的の1つは何ですか。
(A) To announce the acquisition of another company	(A) 他の会社の買収を知らせること
(B) To request assistance in arranging an industry event	(B) 業界イベントの企画に当たり援助を要請すること
(C) To suggest a change in company policy	(C) 会社方針の変更を提案すること
(D) To recommend swimming exercise	(D) 水泳トレーニングを推奨すること

正解 (A)

解説 メモの目的の1つが何か問われています。❷、❸に「現在NPSの買収を進めている」「明後日には合意できる見通し」とあるので、「買収を知らせる」という内容の(A)が正解です。

語句 □ acquisition 買収　□ industry event 業界イベント

177.

When will the agreement with the owners of NPS probably be finalized?	NPSの所有者との合意はおそらくいつまとまりますか。
(A) On April 3	(A) 4月3日
(B) On April 4	(B) 4月4日
(C) On April 5	(C) 4月5日
(D) On April 6	(D) 4月6日

正解 (C)

解説 NPSの所有者との合意はいつまとまるか問われています。❶の「メモの日付」は4月3日で、❸に「明後日に合意の見込み」とあることから、メモが書かれた4月3日の2日後である(C)が正解だとわかります。時系列を問う問題はよく出題されるので、メモやメールの日付は必ずチェックするようにしましょう。

178.

Which of the following expenses is NOT mentioned in the memo?	次の支出のうちメモの中で述べられていないものは何ですか。
(A) Marketing	(A) マーケティング
(B) Accounting	(B) 会計
(C) Insurance	(C) 保険
(D) Customer service	(D) 顧客サービス

正解 (C)

解説 メモの中で述べられていない支出はどれか問われています。❹にNPSと分担する経費の項目として「簿記、顧客サービス、広告」が挙げられており、それぞれ(B)、(D)、(A)に相当します。以上より残った(C)が正解です。

語句 □ insurance 保険

179.

What is suggested about Trevor Lowry?	Trevor Lowryさんについて何が示され
(A) He will assist with the office relocation.	ていますか。
(B) He is certified to handle unsafe substances.	(A) オフィスの移転を手伝う。
(C) He has worked at NPS in the past.	(B) 危険物質を扱う資格がある。
(D) He is a member of senior management.	(C) 過去にNPSで働いたことがある。
	(D) 経営幹部の1人である。

正解 (B)

解説 Trevor Lowryさんについて示されていることが問われています。Lowryさんの名前は当番表の❾に出てきます。メモの❻, ❼に「当面Baxter Pools社から何人かNPSに手伝いに行ってほしい」「危険化学物質取扱資格を持っている人が必要」とあります。つまりLowryさんはBaxter Pools社から派遣される，危険物取扱資格を持つ応援スタッフだとわかります。以上から(B)が正解です。ある人物について問われた場合は，まず文書の中でその人物がどこに出てくるかを確認し，前後の文脈から判断して正解を選ぶことになります。今回はメモの内容を把握した上で当番表を見れば，Lowryさんが危険物取扱資格を持っていることはすぐに判断できます。(A)で迷った人もいるかもしれませんが，オフィスの移転を手伝う必要があるのは，移転当日の9月9日に名前のある人なので，Lowryさんは該当しません。

語句 □ be certified to *do* ～する資格がある　□ unsafe 安全でない，危険な
□ substance 物質　□ senior management （会社などの）最高幹部，経営陣

180.

What is implied about the construction work?	建築工事について何が示唆されていますか。
(A) It will be paid for by NPS.	(A) NPSが費用を負担する。
(B) It cost more than originally planned.	(B) 当初の予定より費用がかかった。
(C) It does not provide enough room.	(C) 十分なスペースを与えてくれない。
(D) It is behind schedule.	(D) 計画より遅れている。

正解 (D)

解説 建築作業について示唆されていることが問われています。メモの❺に「（従業員と設備を収容するスペースがないことを受けて）ビルに増築を行う計画を立てており，7月末に完工する見込みだ」と書いています。次に日程表を見ると，❽に「移転は9月9日」とあることから，7月末に完工する予定が少しずれ込んでいることが推測できるので，これを言い換えた(D)が正解です。参考までに「予定より遅れて」はbehind schedule，「予定通りに」はon schedule，「予定より早く」はahead of scheduleと言います。

語句 □ than originally planned 当初計画されたよりも

広告・宣伝／プレスリリース　♪ 097

Brighton Technology District (BTD)

The Brighton Technology District is an area of reclaimed land by Lake Hawke. It has been designated for use by businesses in the technology sector. ❶There are many advantages to locating a business here. ❷The most compelling of these is the extremely low rent. ❸Thanks to a generous subsidy from the local government, rent in the BTD is around half that of comparable offices elsewhere.

❹Another significant benefit is free electricity from the BTD Solar Power System. ❺Businesses can also take advantage of agreements with the Brighton University of Technology, which is a private institution also located in the BTD. ❻These agreements include access to their excellent internship program and assistance with research and development. The relationship also means that businesses in the BTD tend to recruit many of the university's top students.

There are some conditions which must be met in order to qualify as a tenant in the BTD. ❼One is that businesses must generate their principal income from computer programming. Another is that businesses must employ at least one graduate of the Brighton University of Technology.

So far, the BTD has helped several of the nation's top technology companies get started. These include Geovech, Biowave, and Dolphware, all of which have had huge success both here and abroad. For more information about the BTD or if you would like to apply to be a tenant, please contact the BTD Administrator's Office at 637-555-3923.

フォーム　♪ 098

Parking Permit for Tenants
in the Brighton Technology District

Vehicle Registration:　733YTU

❽**Vehicle Owner:**　Todd Masterson

❾**Employer:**　Velocidyne

Valid for 12 months from:　12 June

This pass must be affixed to the front windshield of your vehicle. ❿Vehicles displaying valid parking permits are entitled to park in any parking space within the BTD.

設問181-185は次の案内と駐車許可証に関するものです。

Brighton科学技術地区（BTD）

Brighton科学技術地区はHawke湖そばの埋め立て地域です。科学技術分野の企業による使用を指定されています。ここに会社を定めることには多くの利点があります。最も魅力的なのは賃料が極めて安いということです。地方自治体からの潤沢な補助金のおかげで，BTDにおける賃料は他の場所にある同等物件の約半額です。

もう1つの大きなメリットはBTD太陽光発電システムから無料で電気が供給されることです。また企業は，BTD内にある私立教育機関であるBrighton工科大学との協定を活用することもできます。これらの協定にはBrighton工科大学の素晴らしいインターンシップ制度を利用できることや研究開発における支援も含まれています。その関係はまた，BTD内の企業がこの大学の最も優秀な学生の多くを採用する傾向にあることを意味します。

BTDのテナントになる資格を得るためには満たさなくてはならない条件がいくつかあります。1つは企業がコンピュータープログラミングによって主な収益を上げる必要があることです。もう1つは企業がBrighton工科大学の卒業生を少なくとも1人は雇用しなければならないということです。

これまで，BTDは国内の大手科学技術企業のいくつかが起業するのを支援してきました。その中には，Geovech社，Biowave社，そしてDolphware社といった国内外で大きな成功を収めた企業が含まれます。BTDについてさらに詳しくお知りになりたい場合，もしくはテナントにご応募される場合は，BTD管理事務所の637-555-3923までご連絡ください。

語句　□ district 地区，区域　□ reclaimed land 埋め立て地　□ designate ～を指定する
□ sector 部門　□ compelling 説得力のある，強制的な　□ extremely 極めて
□ low rent 低家賃　□ thanks to ～ ～のおかげで　□ generous たくさんの，寛大な
□ subsidy 補助金　□ comparable 同等の　□ elsewhere 他の場所で
□ significant かなりの　□ private institution 私立の（教育）機関
□ access to ～ ～の利用　□ internship program インターンシップ制度
□ research and development 研究開発　□ tend to *do* ～する傾向にある
□ recruit ～を採用する　□ condition 条件　□ meet （条件）を満たす
□ qualify 資格がある　□ tenant テナント，賃借人　□ generate ～を生み出す
□ principal income 主な収入　□ so far これまでのところ
□ get started 始める，起業する

テナント向け駐車許可証
Brighton科学技術地区

車両登録番号：733YTU
車両所有者：Todd Masterson
雇用主：Velocidyne社
以下の日付より12カ月有効：6月12日
この許可証は車両のフロントガラスに添付しておくこと。有効な駐車許可証を掲示している車両はBTD内のどの駐車場でも駐車することができます。

語句　□ vehicle registration 車両登録　□ valid 有効な　□ pass 許可証
□ affix ～を添付する，張る　□ windshield （自動車などの）フロントガラス
□ be entitled to *do* ～する権利がある

181.

What is a benefit of having a company in the BTD?	BTD内に会社を持つメリットは何ですか。
(A) Central location	(A) 中心地にあること
(B) Subsidized rent	(B) 補助金を受けた賃料
(C) Discount solar panels	(C) 値引きされた太陽光パネル
(D) Excellent views	(D) 素晴らしい眺め

正解 (B)

解説 BTD内に会社を持つメリットが問われています。案内の❶に「BTD内に会社を定めることには多くの利点がある」、❷に「最も魅力的なのは低賃料」、❸に「自治体からの補助金で他のエリアの半額」という記載があることから、(B)が正解だとわかります。

語句 □ subsidize 〜に補助金を与える　□ solar panel 太陽光パネル

182.

What is implied about the Brighton University of Technology?	Brighton工科大学について何が示唆されていますか。
(A) Its advertisements have appeared on television.	(A) 広告がテレビに出た。
(B) Its students may park anywhere in the BTD.	(B) 学生はBTD内のどこにでも駐車してよい。
(C) It has recently expanded its campus.	(C) 最近、キャンパスを拡張した。
(D) It receives free electricity.	(D) 無料の電気を受け取る。

正解 (D)

解説 Brighton工科大学について何が示唆されているか問われています。案内の❹に「(BTDの) もう1つのメリットは電気代が無料であること」とあり、❺に「Brighton工科大学はBTD内にある」とあります。ここからBTD内にあるBrighton工科大学でも電気代が無料だと推測できるので、(D)が正解です。2つ目の文書である駐車許可証には「有効な許可証を掲示した車両のみどの駐車場でも使える」とあり、学生が自由に駐車できるわけではないので(B)は不正解です。

語句 □ appear 出現する　□ expand 〜を拡大 [拡張] する

183.

How does the Brighton University of Technology assist businesses in the BTD?	Brighton工科大学はどのようにBTD内の企業を支援していますか。
(A) By offering its rooms for use	(A) 使用できる部屋を提供することで
(B) By helping with research projects	(B) 研究プロジェクトを支援することで
(C) By arranging visits by industry experts	(C) 業界の専門家の訪問を手配することで
(D) By providing free staff training	(D) 無料の社員教育を提供することで

正解 (B)

解説 Brighton工科大学がBTD内の企業を支援する方法について問われています。案内の❺、❻に「BTD内の企業はBrighton工科大学と協定を結んでいる」「協定にはBrighton工科大学の研

究開発への支援が含まれる」とあります。research and development を research projects と言い換えた(B)が正解です。

語句 □ industry expert 業界の専門家

184.

クロスリファレンス問題

What is probably true about Velocidyne?	Velocidyne社についておそらく何が正しいですか。
(A) It is in the software industry.	
(B) It has been in business for less than 12 months.	(A) ソフトウエア業界に属している。
(C) It occupies offices previously used by Dolphware.	(B) 事業期間は12カ月に満たない。
(D) It only hires graduates of the Brighton University of Technology.	(C) Dolphware社が以前使用していた事務所を占有している。
	(D) Brighton工科大学の卒業生しか採用しない。

正解 (A)

解説 Velocidyne社について正しいことは何か問われています。BTDのテナントになるための条件の1つに❼「企業がコンピュータープログラミングによって主な収益を上げる必要がある」とあります。また，駐車許可証を見ると，❾の雇用者がVelocidyne社となっています。つまり，Velocidyne社はBTD内にある会社で，コンピュータープログラミング事業を行っていることがわかるので，それを言い換えた(A)が正解です。

語句 □ occupy ～を占有する

185.

選択肢照合型問題

What is suggested about Mr. Masterson?	Mastersonさんについて何が示されていますか。
(A) He has not been assigned a specific parking space.	(A) 特定の駐車スペースは割り当てられていない。
(B) He usually relies on public transportation.	(B) たいてい公共交通機関に頼っている。
(C) He received a parking permit with his rental agreement.	(C) 賃貸契約とともに駐車許可証を受け取った。
(D) He previously worked at Geovech.	(D) 以前Geovech社で働いていた。

正解 (A)

解説 Mastersonさんについて示されていることが問われています。Mastersonさんは❽から駐車許可証の保持者であることがわかります。❿に「有効な許可証を示せばBTD内のどの駐車場でも駐車することができる」とあり，特に駐車スペースが指定されているわけではないと推測できます。駐車許可証を持っていることから(B)は不適切，また(C)(D)についても本文に言及はないので，正解は(A)となります。

語句 □ assign ～を割り当てる □ rely on ～ ～に頼る，依存する
□ public transportation 公共交通機関 □ rental agreement 賃貸契約

記事　♪ 099

The Byron Bay Coffee Festival

Byron Bay (10 August)—❶The Byron Bay Farmers' Association, led by Gloria Waters, has managed to convince the city council to host Byron Bay's first-ever coffee festival. Coffee is one of the region's main industries and even though it exports coffee to North America and Europe, it is relatively unknown here in Australia. "Depending on the success of this year's festival, this may become an annual event" explained Terry Davis, one of the event organizers.

❷The festival will be held from 10 November to 14 November, during which time there will be a street parade as well as other events such as contests, farm tours, and cooking workshops. The council hopes to attract tourists to the area to boost the local economy. ❸Gloria Waters explained that her members were more interested in gaining exposure so that they can sell more of their product domestically.

❹One business with a vested interest in the festival's success is the Steele Coffee Processing Plant. The company's owner Helena Barkworth is a major sponsor of the event. Her company is Byron Bay's only processing plant and it has recently expanded its operations in anticipation of increased demand.

Eメール・手紙　♪ 100

To:	Terry Davis <tdavis@byronbaycc.org>
From:	Norma Harris <nharris@novacrane.com>
Date:	November 16
Subject:	Byron Bay Coffee Festival

Dear Mr. Davis,

I am writing with regard to the Byron Bay Coffee Festival. I thought it was a wonderful event and you and the other organizers should be commended. ❺I particularly enjoyed visiting the coffee processing plant. The guide who showed us around was very knowledgeable and entertaining. Unfortunately, there was little activity at the plant as the harvesting is mostly finished by November. ❻I suggest holding the festival in mid-October next year so that we can see the plant when it is at peak production.

Norma Harris

設問186-190は次の記事，Eメール，チラシに関するものです。

Byron Bay コーヒー祭り

Byron Bay市（8月10日）— Gloria Waters氏率いるByron Bay農業協同組合は，Byron Bay市初のコーヒー祭りを開催するよう市議会を説得することができた。コーヒーはこの地域の主要産業の1つであり，北アメリカやヨーロッパに輸出しているにもかかわらず，ここオーストラリアでは比較的知られていない。「今年の祭りの成功次第では，毎年恒例のイベントになるかもしれない」とイベント主催者の1人であるTerry Davis氏は言う。

祭りは11月10日から11月14日まで開催され，その間，コンテストや農場見学，料理教室といったイベントはもちろん，街頭パレードも行われる。市議会では地元経済を活性化するために観光客を呼び込むことを期待している。組合員たちは，自分たちの製品の国内での販売量を増やすために公の目に触れることにもっと関心を持つようになってきているとGloria Waters氏は述べた。

この祭りの成功に強い関心を持つ会社の1つは，Steeleコーヒー加工工場である。経営者であるHelena Barkworth氏はこのイベントの主要スポンサーである。Steele社はByron Bay市唯一の加工工場であり，需要の増加を見込んで最近操業を拡大している。

語句　□ association 協会，組合　□ led by ～ ～に導かれた　□ manage to *do* 何とか～する
　　　□ convince ～を説得する　□ city council 市議会　□ first-ever 史上初の
　　　□ industry 産業　□ even though ～ たとえ～でも　□ export ～を輸出する
　　　□ relatively 比較的　□ depending on ～ ～によって，応じて　□ organizer 主催者
　　　□ street parade 街頭パレード　□ boost（景気）を押し上げる
　　　□ gain exposure 露出する，公の目に触れる　□ domestically 国内で
　　　□ vested interest（既得権益に基づく）関与　□ processing plant 加工工場
　　　□ in anticipation of ～ ～を見込んで　□ increased demand 増加した需要

宛先：Terry Davis <tdavis@byronbaycc.org>
送信者：Norma Harris <nharris@novacrane.com>
日付：11月16日
件名：Byron Bay コーヒー祭り

Davis様，

Byron Bay コーヒー祭りの件で，これを書いています。それは素晴らしいイベントで，あなたと他の主催者の方々は称賛に値すると思います。私は特に，コーヒー加工工場の見学が楽しかったです。私たちを案内してくれたガイドの方はとても博識で，かつ楽しませてくれました。残念ながら，11月までには収穫がほとんど終わっていたため，工場での活動がほとんどありませんでした。来年は生産の最盛期に工場見学ができるよう，10月中旬にこのお祭りを開催することを提案します。

Norma Harris

語句　□ with regard to ～ ～の件で，～に関して　□ commend ～を褒めたたえる
　　　□ particularly 特に　□ knowledgeable 知識のある，聡明な
　　　□ entertaining（人を）楽しませる，面白い　□ harvesting 収穫
　　　□ peak production 生産の最盛期

The Second Annual Byron Bay Coffee Festival
15 to 18 October

Event	Location	Date and Time
Cooking with Coffee — Expert chef Tina Day leads a free practical workshop.	Day School of Cooking	10:00 – 11:30 A.M. 15 and 17 October
Street Parade — Colorful floats sponsored by the various local growers and cafés pass along Main Street.	Main Street	4:00 – 5:00 P.M. 17 October
Best of the Fest — Festivalgoers can try the different blends of coffee that have been entered for the annual brewing contest.	Main Tent at Caulfield Park	10:00 A.M. – 7:00 P.M. 15 to 18 October
Coffees of Byron — A documentary film on the Byron Bay coffee industry	Byron Bay Community Hall	7:00 – 9:00 P.M 15 to 18 October

More information about special offers and events by local businesses is available from the Web site at www.byroncoffeefest.org.

第2回年次 Byron Bay コーヒー祭り
10月15日〜18日

イベント	場所	日時
コーヒーを使った料理 — 料理のエキスパート Tina Day 氏が無料実践講習会を担当します。	Day 料理学校	10月15日，17日 午前10時〜11時30分
街頭パレード — 多くの地元の栽培業者や喫茶店が出資した色とりどりの山車が大通りを進みます。	大通り	10月17日 午後4時〜5時
祭りのNo.1 — 祭りの参加者は恒例のコーヒーを入れるコンテストにエントリーしたいろいろなブレンドコーヒーを試飲できます。	Caulfield公園のメインテント	10月15日〜18日 午前10時〜午後7時
Byronのコーヒー — Byron Bay 市のコーヒー産業に関するドキュメンタリー映画	Byron Bay コミュニティーホール	10月15日〜18日 午後7時〜9時

地元企業による特典やイベントに関するさらなる情報はウェブサイト www.byroncoffeefest.org から入手可能です。

語句 □ expert 腕のよい，プロの □ practical 実践的な □ float 山車，パレード車両 □ various たくさんの，さまざまな □ grower 栽培者 □ festivalgoer 祭りに行く人 □ brewing （コーヒーを）入れること，醸造

186.

目的・テーマを問う問題

What is the purpose of the article?	記事の目的は何ですか。
(A) To announce an event	(A) イベントについて知らせること
(B) To discuss an economic trend	(B) 経済の動向について議論すること
(C) To introduce a local club	(C) 地元のクラブを紹介すること
(D) To profile a local politician	(D) 地元の政治家を紹介すること

正解 (A)

解説 記事の目的が問われています。❶に「Byron Bay市初のコーヒー祭りを開催」とあり，❷に「コーヒー祭りの日程と各種イベント」についての告知があるので，これから行われるイベントの開催を知らせていることがわかります。以上から，正解は(A)となります。記事のタイトルに「Byron Bayコーヒー祭り」とあることからも，正解が推測できる問題です。

語句 □ economic trend 経済の動向　□ profile ～を紹介する

187.

詳細を問う問題

What does Ms. Waters mention that her members want to do?	Watersさんは会員が何をしたがっていると述べていますか。
(A) Attract investors to their business	(A) 自分たちの事業に投資家を引き付ける
(B) Launch a new Web site	(B) 新しいウェブサイトを立ち上げる
(C) Find new production methods	(C) 新しい製造方法を見つける
(D) Raise the profile of a local product	(D) 地元の製品の注目度を高める

正解 (D)

解説 会員がしたいと思っていることについてWatersさんは何と述べているか問われています。記事を見ると，❸でWatersさんは「組合員たちは自分たちの製品の国内販売量を増やすために公の目に触れることにもっと関心を持つようになってきている」と述べているので，製品の認知度を上げたいことがわかります。以上から，それを言い換えた(D)が正解です。

語句 □ investor 投資家　□ launch ～を立ち上げる　□ production method 製造方法
□ raise the profile of ～ ～の認知度を上げる

188.

What is indicated about Ms. Harris?
(A) She is not a resident of Byron Bay.
(B) She visited Ms. Barkworth's business.
(C) She took a tour of local growers.
(D) She was a judge in the brewing contest.

Harrisさんについて何が述べられていますか。
(A) Byron Bay市の住人ではない。
(B) Barkworth氏の会社を訪問した。
(C) 地元の栽培業者を見学して回った。
(D) コーヒーを入れるコンテストの審査員だった。

正解 (B)

解説 メールの書き手であるHarrisさんについて述べられていることは何か問われています。Harrisさんは❺で「コーヒー加工工場の見学が楽しかった」と述べています。また，記事の❹に「コーヒー祭りの成功に強い関心を持っているのはSteeleコーヒー加工工場」「経営者はHelena Barkworth氏」「Steele社はByron Bay市唯一の加工工場」とあります。以上から，Harrisさんが訪れたコーヒー加工工場はBarkworth氏の会社ということがわかるので，(B)が正解です。

語句 □ resident 住人　□ take a tour of ～ ～を見学して回る

189.

What is implied about Mr. Davis?
(A) He took Ms. Harris' advice.
(B) He will attend the cooking event.
(C) He left the organizing committee.
(D) He is collecting data on local tourism.

Davisさんについて何が示唆されていますか。
(A) Harrisさんのアドバイスに従った。
(B) 料理のイベントに参加する予定だ。
(C) 組織委員会を離れた。
(D) 地域観光に関するデータを集めている。

正解 (A)

解説 Davisさんについて示唆されていることは何か問われています。Harrisさんはメールの❻で祭りの主催者の1人であるDavisさんに「来年はお祭りを10月中旬に開催してはどうか」と提案しています。次にチラシの❼を見ると「(第2回Byron Bayコーヒー祭りは) 10月15日から18日まで」と10月中旬に開催されることがわかります。つまり，DavisさんはHarrisさんのアドバイスに従って開催日を10月中旬にしたと判断できるので，正解は(A)となります。このように「提案・要望→その結果」はクロスリファレンス問題でよく出題されるポイントの1つです。

語句 □ organizing committee 組織委員会　□ local tourism 地域観光

190.

Where will the coffee tasting be held?
(A) At the Day School of Cooking
(B) On Main Street
(C) At Caulfield Park
(D) At Byron Bay Community Hall

コーヒーの試飲はどこで行われますか。
(A) Day料理学校
(B) 大通り
(C) Caulfield公園
(D) Byron Bayコミュニティーホール

正解 (C)

解説 コーヒーの試飲が行われる場所が問われています。チラシを見ると，❽にいろいろなブレンドのコーヒーの試飲ができるイベントについて示されており，❾からその場所がCaulfield公園だとわかります。よって(C)が正解です。

語句 □ community hall 公民館

Questions 191-195 refer to the following Web page, survey, and e-mail.

ウェブページ ♪ 102

×

www.sweetridecarrental.com/springspecials

Sweetride Car Rental

Welcome back, Martin Mullholland

❶ You have reached this page by clicking a link in our members' e-mail for spring. Below, you will find spring special offers available only to our customers who have agreed to receive periodic e-mails.

People renting vehicles for seven days or more during March, April, or May can select one of the following four options.
(1) A 10 percent discount on your total rental rate
(2) A free vehicle upgrade
(3) A free GPS system
❷ (4) A free tank of fuel

Please let the reservation staff know which option you choose when you make your reservation.

フォーム ♪ 103

Customer Survey

Thank you for renting a quality vehicle from Sweetride Car Rental. Please take a couple of minutes to fill out this survey to let us know about your rental experience.

❸ **Name:** Martin Mullholland ❹ **Booking Reference:** H83923NM

❺ What was the purpose for renting this vehicle? Business / Pleasure

Do you intend to rent a vehicle from Sweetride again? Yes / No

Comment:

❻ I forgot about the spring special and filled the tank just before I returned the car. As a result, I was unable to take advantage of the offer I chose. I asked the person operating the returns counter to change my selection to the 10 percent discount, but I was informed that that would not be possible. I think that Sweetride should be more understanding in this regard and not use this as an opportunity to make additional profit.

設問191-195は次のウェブページ，アンケート，Eメールに関するものです。

---

www.sweetridecarrental.com/springspecials
Sweetride Car Rental社

お帰りなさい，Martin Mullhollandさん

あなたは春の会員さま向けメール内のリンクをクリックしてこのページにアクセスされました。以下に，定期的なメールの受信に同意していただいたお客さまのみご利用いただける春の特典がございます。

3月，4月，5月の間に7日間以上車両をレンタルされた方は，以下の4つの選択肢から1つお選びいただけます。
(1) レンタル料の合計金額より10パーセント割引
(2) 車両の無料アップグレード
(3) 無料のGPSシステム
(4) ガソリン1タンクの補充無料

ご予約の際にどれをお選びになるか，弊社予約係にお知らせください。

語句 □ click ～をクリックする □ periodic 定期的な □ following 以下の
□ option 選択肢 □ rental rate レンタル料金
□ GPS 全地球測位システム（GPSはGlobal Positioning Systemの略）
□ a tank of fuel タンク満タンの燃料

お客さまアンケート

Sweetride Car Rental社にて高品質の自動車をレンタルしていただきありがとうございます。少しお時間を割いてアンケートにご記入いただき，レンタルの体験談をお聞かせください。

氏名：Martin Mullholland様　　**ご予約照会番号**：H83923NM

この車をレンタルされた目的は何ですか。(仕事)/ プライベート

またSweetride社でレンタルしていただけますか。 はい /(いいえ)

コメント欄：
春の特典のことを忘れていて，車を返却する直前にガソリンを満タンにしてしまいました。その結果，自分が選んだ特典を利用することができませんでした。返却カウンターの担当者に10パーセント割引に変更してほしいとお願いしましたが，それはできないと言われました。Sweetride社にはこういう場合もっと融通を利かせてほしいですし，これを追加の利益を得る機会として利用しないでほしいと思います。

語句 □ quality 高品質の □ fill out ～ ～に記入する □ reference 照会番号
□ Business / Pleasure 仕事／遊び，娯楽（などプライベートを指す）
□ intend to do ～するつもりである □ fill the tank 満タンにする
□ as a result その結果 □ take advantage of ～ ～を利用する
□ be informed that ～ ～ということを知らされる □ in this regard この件について
□ make a profit 利益を上げる，もうける

To:	Martin Mullholland <mmullholland@betatrading.com>
From:	Veronica Holden <vholden@sweetridecr.com>
Date:	June 27
Subject:	Spring specials

Dear Mr. Mullholland,

❼Regarding your desire to change your spring special selection, I am happy to inform you that we can accommodate your request. I regret that the clerk at the counter was not able to resolve the issue for you immediately. ❽Yours was a rare case and the clerk had not been trained on how to deal with it.

If you check your next credit card statement, you will see that you have been refunded the appropriate amount.

Sincerely,

Veronica Holden
Customer Service, Sweetride Car Rental

宛先：Martin Mullholland <mmullholland@betatrading.com>
送信者：Veronica Holden <vholden@sweetridecr.com>
日付：6月27日
件名：春の特典

Mullholland様

春の特典の変更ご希望の件につきまして, お客さまのご要望にお応えできますことを喜んでお知らせいたします。カウンターにいた担当者がすぐにこの件について処理することができず, 申し訳ありませんでした。お客さまの件はまれなケースで, 担当者はそれに対する対処の方法を教育されていませんでした。

次回のクレジットカード明細をご覧いただくと, 適切な金額が返金されているのをご確認いただけます。

敬具

Veronica Holden
Sweetride Car Rental社お客さま担当

語句　□ regarding ～に関して　□ desire 要望, 願望　□ accommodate （要求）を受け入れる
□ regret ～を残念に思う　□ train （人）を教育する
□ credit card statement クレジットカード明細書　□ refund *A B* AにBを返金する
□ appropriate 適切な, 正しい

191.

選択肢照合型問題

What is implied about Mr. Mullholland?
(A) He rented a car during winter.
(B) He is an employee of Sweetride Car Rental.
(C) He subscribed to a mailing list.
(D) He updated the company Web site.

Mullhollandさんについて何が示唆されていますか。
(A) 冬の間に車を借りた。
(B) Sweetride Car Rental社の従業員である。
(C) メーリングリストに登録した。
(D) 会社のウェブサイトを更新した。

正解 (C)

解説 Mullhollandさんについて示唆されていることが問われています。ウェブページの❶に「春の会員さま向けメール内のリンクからこのページにアクセスした」「定期的なメールの受信に同意した顧客のみ利用できる春の特典がある」とあります。ここから、正解は(C)です。Mullhollandさんはアンケートで特典使用についての苦情を述べていることからも、定期的にメールを受け取っている顧客と判断できます。

語句 ☐ subscribe to ～ ～に登録する　☐ mailing list メーリングリスト

192.

クロスリファレンス問題

Which spring special option did Mr. Mullholland choose when he made the reservation?
(A) Option 1
(B) Option 2
(C) Option 3
(D) Option 4

Mullhollandさんは予約した際に、どの春の特典オプションを選びましたか。
(A) オプション1
(B) オプション2
(C) オプション3
(D) オプション4

正解 (D)

解説 Mullhollandさんがレンタカーを予約した際にどの特典を選んだか問われています。アンケートの❻に「春の特典のことを忘れて、ガソリンを満タンにした」「この特典を利用することができなかった」とあります。この後に「10パーセント割引に変更を希望した」と別のオプションについての言及がありますが、予約の時点で選んだのはウェブページの❷にある「(4) ガソリン1タンクの補充無料」だと考えられるので、正解は(D)です。特典でオプションが複数示された文書の場合、別の文書でどれを選ぶかが示され、この点を問うクロスリファレンス問題の質問が出題される場合が多いです。オプションがあった場合は「両文書参照型かな？」と想定して読み進めましょう。

193.

What information is NOT required in the survey?	アンケートで要求されていないのはどの情報ですか。
(A) The customer's name	(A) お客さま氏名
(B) The vehicle preference	(B) 車の好み
(C) The reservation code	(C) 予約番号
(D) The renter's purpose	(D) 借りた人の目的

正解 (B)

解説 NOT問題で，アンケートで要求されていない情報はどれか問われています。アンケートの記入欄にある❸「お客さま氏名」，❹「予約番号」，❺「レンタルの目的」がそれぞれ(A)，(C)，(D)に一致しており，残った(B)の「車の好み」については聞かれていないので，(B)が正解です。referenceとpreferenceのようにつづりの似た語を混同しないよう注意しましょう。

語句 □ preference 好み，嗜好

194.

What is suggested about Ms. Holden?	Holdenさんについて何が示されていますか。
(A) She read Mr. Mullholland's survey response.	(A) Mullhollandさんのアンケートの回答を読んだ。
(B) She is the president of Sweetride Car Rental.	(B) Sweetride Car Rental社の社長である。
(C) She is in charge of training new employees.	(C) 新入社員教育を担当している。
(D) She works at a credit card company.	(D) クレジットカード会社で働いている。

正解 (A)

解説 メールの書き手であるHoldenさんについて何が示されているか問われています。Holdenさんは❼で「春の特典の変更ご希望の件について，お客さまのご要望にお応えできる」と伝えています。ここから，このメールはHoldenさんがMullhollandさんのアンケートのコメントを読んで対応しているものと判断できるので，(A)が正解です。❽で社員の教育について触れていますが，Holdenさん自身が教育担当かどうかは書かれていないので，(C)は不正解です。

語句 □ in charge of ～ ～を担当して

195.

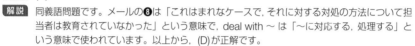

In the e-mail, the phrase "deal with" in paragraph 1, line 4, is closest in meaning to	Eメールの第1段落・4行目にある "deal with" に最も意味が近いのは
(A) advise	(A) ～に助言する
(B) concern	(B) ～に心配させる
(C) record	(C) ～を記録する
(D) process	(D) ～を処理する

正解 (D)

解説 同義語問題です。メールの❽は「これはまれなケースで,それに対する対処の方法について担当者は教育されていなかった」という意味で,deal with ～ は「～に対応する,処理する」という意味で使われています。以上から,(D)が正解です。

Questions 196-200 refer to the following order confirmation, text message, and review.

リスト 🎵 105

Fennville Bookstore Online Order Confirmation

Thank you for shopping at Fennville Bookstore. We do not provide paper receipts. Please print out and keep this document for your records.

Customer: ❶Ms. Paula Tran

Ship to: Clarkson Brothers

Address: 234 Nautical Way, Miami, QLD

Contact telephone: 555-3489

Date: 11 June

Order number: Y634623

Item	Quantity	Price
Sailing Solo Around the World	1	$39.00
❷Power Boat Maintenance for Beginners	1	$78.00
❸Buying and Selling Boats for Profit	1	$48.50
Fishing Around Fraser Island	1	$45.00
Frank Key's History of Water Skiing	1	$11.00
❹Shipping and handling		$0.00
❺Total:		$221.50

Orders may be shipped separately in order to meet weight requirements or if certain titles are out of stock. ❻Shipping is free for members of our customer rewards program. Membership in the program is exclusive to customers who have spent more than $200 and completed a registration form at one of our physical stores. ❼If you require a return or a replacement, please quote the order number when making your request.

テキストメッセージ・チャット 🎵 106

To: Paula Tran

From: Steve Prince

Date: 20 June

Paula, I see that you've purchased some books for the waiting room. ❽I think it is a great idea as it can often take a long time to retrieve clients' boats for them. This is especially true when we have been asked to keep them in the long-term warehouse. It is nice to keep people occupied so that they do not feel like they've been waiting for a long time. ❾Nevertheless, I would like to ask you to return the one about taking care of speedboats. It is unlikely to be of interest to our clients and it is over the maximum spending limit of $50.

設問196-200は次の注文確認書，テキストメッセージ，レビューに関するものです。

Fennville 書店オンライン注文確認書

Fennville 書店でお買い求めいただきありがとうございます。当店では紙のレシートを
発行していません。この文書を印刷し，記録として保管してください。

お客さま氏名：Paula Tran 様　　　　　　　**日付**：6月11日
送付先：Clarkson Brothers 社　　　　　　　**注文番号**：Y634623
住所：Queensland 州 Miami 市 Nautical 通り 234 番地
連絡先お電話番号：555-3489

品目	数量	価格
世界を単独で航海する	1	39.00 ドル
初心者向けモーターボートのメンテナンス	1	78.00 ドル
利益の出るボートの売買	1	48.50 ドル
Fraser 島周辺での釣り	1	45.00 ドル
Frank Key の水上スキーの歴史	1	11.00 ドル
送料及び手数料		0.00 ドル
合計：		221.50 ドル

重量制限を満たすため，または在庫切れの本がある場合は別送になることがあります。お客さま特典プログラムの会員は送料無料です。このプログラムへの入会は 200 ドル以上ご購入いただき，いずれかの実店舗で登録用紙に記入されたお客さまに限らせていただいております。返品もしくは交換をご希望の場合，ご依頼時に注文番号をお知らせください。

語句 □ order confirmation 注文確認書　□ paper receipt 紙のレシート　□ solo 単独で
□ for profit 利益が出るための　□ shipping and handling 送料及び取扱手数料
□ separately 分けて，別々に　□ weight requirements 重量制限
□ rewards program （ポイント制などの）特典プログラム
□ registration form 登録用紙　□ physical store （オンラインショップに対して）実店舗
□ quote 〜を引き合いに出す

宛先：Paula Tran
差出人：Steve Prince
日付：6月20日

Paula さん，待合室に置くための本を数冊購入したんですね。お客さまのボートを取ってくるのに相当時間がかかることも多いので，とてもいいアイデアだと思います。長期間用の倉庫に保管するよう依頼されていた場合は，特にそうです。お客さまが長時間待っていると感じないように，何かしてもらうようにするというのはいいですね。ただし，高速モーターボートの整備に関する本は返品してほしいと思います。当社のお客さまの興味を引くとは思えないし，50 ドルの支出上限を超えてしまっています。

語句 □ retrieve 〜を取ってくる　□ keep 〜 occupied 〜を忙しくさせておく
□ be of interest 関心のある，興味深い

Reviews of *Buying and Selling Boats for Profit*

Reviewed by: Roger Wang　　　**Date:** 12 August

I ordered this book from a seller in the United States as I was preparing to sell my boat. Unfortunately, I think that much of the advice is only applicable to selling boats in the United States. ⑩The rules and regulations in Australia are very different, so I don't really think it was worth the $20 I paid. There was, however, some good advice about buying boats that I wish I had read before I made my purchase.

『利益の出るボートの売買』のレビュー

投稿者：Roger Wang　　　日付：8月12日

私はボートを売却する準備をしていたので，この本をアメリカ在住の売り手に注文しました。残念ながら，本のアドバイスの大半はアメリカ国内でボートを売却する場合にのみ適用するものだと思います。オーストラリアの規定はかなり異なっているので，私が支払った20ドルの価値があるとは思えません。でも，ボート購入に関してはいいアドバイスがあったので，ボートを買う前に読んでいたらなあと思います。

語句　□ applicable 適用［応用］される　□ worth ～の価値がある

196.

情報分散型問題

What is most likely true about Ms. Tran?
(A) She bought the books as a present.
(B) She has visited a Fennville Bookstore in person.
(C) She got approval for the purchase in advance.
(D) She receives a corporate discount from Fennville Bookstore.

Tranさんについておそらく何が正しいですか。
(A) プレゼントとして本を購入した。
(B) 直接Fennville書店に行った。
(C) 事前に購入許可をもらった。
(D) Fennville書店から法人割引を受けている。

正解　(B)

解説　Tranさんについて正しいことを選ぶ問題です。注文確認書の❶からTranさんは本を発注した本人であることがわかります。❻に「お客さま特典プログラムの会員は送料無料」「200ドル以上購入して実店舗で登録すれば特典プログラムの会員になれる」とあります。❹のShipping and handlingの欄が「0ドル」となっていること，❺のTotalが221.50ドルであることから，Tranさんは200ドル以上購入し，実店舗で特典プログラムの会員登録を行ったと考えられます。よって，正解は(B)です。

語句 □ in advance 事前に

197.

According to the order confirmation, when are customers required to provide their order number?

(A) When sending back an item
(B) When confirming a delivery date
(C) When checking on the warranty status
(D) When canceling a subscription

注文確認書によると、いつ顧客は注文番号の提示を求められますか。

(A) 商品を返品するとき
(B) 配送日を確認するとき
(C) 保証の状況を確認するとき
(D) 予約購入を取り消すとき

正解 (A)

解説 注文確認書から、顧客が注文番号の提示が必要な場合がいつか答える問題です。備考欄の❼に「返品もしくは交換をご希望の場合、ご依頼時に注文番号をお知らせください」という記載があるので、そのうちのreturn「返品」をsend backと言い換えた(A)が正解です。

語句 □ send back ~ ~を返送する、送り返す　□ subscription 予約購入

198.

Where do Ms. Tran and Mr. Prince most likely work?

(A) At a bookstore
(B) At a travel agency
(C) At a boat storage facility
(D) At a fishing tour company

TranさんとPrinceさんはおそらくどこで働いていますか。

(A) 書店
(B) 旅行代理店
(C) ボート保管施設
(D) 釣り旅行の会社

正解 (C)

解説 TranさんとPrinceさんがどこで働いているか問われています。テキストメッセージの❽に「お客さまのボートを取ってくる」「お客さまが長期間用の倉庫に保管を依頼する」とあるので、ボートの保管に関連した仕事であることが推測できます。以上から正解は(C)となります。

語句 □ travel agency 旅行代理店　□ storage 保管

199.

Which item is Ms. Tran asked to return?
(A) Sailing Solo Around the World
(B) Power Boat Maintenance for Beginners
(C) Fishing Around Fraser Island
(D) Frank Key's History of Water Skiing

Tranさんはどの本を返品するよう頼まれていますか。
(A) 世界を単独で航海する
(B) 初心者向けモーターボートのメンテナンス
(C) Fraser島周辺での釣り
(D) Frank Keyの水上スキーの歴史

正解 (B)

解説 Tranさんが返品するように頼まれた本はどれか問われています。Princeさんはテキストメッセージの❾で「高速モーターボートの整備に関する本は返品するように」「お客さまの興味を引くとは思えないし、50ドルの支出上限を超えている」と述べています。ここで注文確認書を見ると、モーターボートの整備に関連する本で、かつ50ドルの上限を超えているのは❷なので、正解は(B)です。ここではtaking care of speedboatsという表現とPower Boat Maintenanceを結び付けて解答できるかどうかが鍵になっていますが、このような問題は時折出題されるので、本や映画のタイトルもある程度意味が取れるようにしておきましょう。

200.

What is implied about the book reviewed by Mr. Wang?
(A) It was rewritten for Australian readers.
(B) It is suitable for people who build their own boats.
(C) It was written by a client of Ms. Tran's.
(D) It has been discounted.

Wangさんがレビューした本について何が示唆されていますか。
(A) オーストラリアの読者用に書き直された。
(B) 自分でボートを製作する人向けである。
(C) Tranさんの顧客によって書かれた。
(D) 割引されていた。

正解 (D)

解説 Wangさんがレビューした本について示唆されていることが問われています。Wangさんは購入したBuying and Selling Boats for Profitについてレビューの❿に「オーストラリアの規定はかなり違うので、支払った20ドルの価値があるとは思えない」と書いているので、Wangさんはこの本を20ドルで購入したことがわかります。次に注文確認書を見ると、❸からこの本の定価は48.50ドルだとわかります。つまり、Wangさんが買ったこの本は、中古品あるいは別の理由で割引されていたと推測できるので、正解は(D)となります。

語句 □ rewrite 〜を書き直す

Final Test 解答一覧

設問番号	正解	設問番号	正解	設問番号	正解
147	C	172	A	197	A
148	A	173	C	198	C
149	B	174	A	199	B
150	C	175	D	200	D
151	C	176	A		
152	D	177	C		
153	B	178	C		
154	C	179	B		
155	C	180	D		
156	D	181	B		
157	D	182	D		
158	D	183	B		
159	A	184	A		
160	D	185	A		
161	D	186	A		
162	A	187	D		
163	A	188	B		
164	C	189	A		
165	A	190	C		
166	B	191	C		
167	B	192	D		
168	C	193	B		
169	D	194	A		
170	C	195	D		
171	B	196	B		

♪ ナレーター一覧

★…アメリカ（男性）　☆…アメリカ（女性）　○…イギリス（女性）

トラック番号	ナレーター	トラック番号	ナレーター	トラック番号	ナレーター	トラック番号	ナレーター
001	☆	028	☆	055	☆	082	★
002	★／○	029	○	056	★	083	○
003	○	030	☆	057	☆	084	★
004	★	031	★	058	★	085	☆
005	☆	032	★／☆	059	○	086	★／○
006	★	033	★／○	060	☆	087	☆
007	☆	034	☆	061	★	088	★
008	○	035	★	062	★	089	☆
009	★	036	☆	063	○	090	★
010	★／☆／○	037	○	064	☆	091	○
011	☆	038	★	065	☆	092	★
012	○	039	★	066	★	093	★／☆／○
013	★	040	★	067	☆	094	★
014	☆	041	☆	068	★／☆	095	★
015	○	042	☆	069	★／○	096	○
016	☆	043	○	070	★／☆	097	☆
017	★	044	○	071	○	098	★
018	☆	045	★	072	☆	099	○
019	★	046	☆	073	★	100	☆
020	○	047	★	074	☆	101	★
021	☆	048	☆	075	☆	102	○
022	★	049	★	076	○	103	★
023	★	050	○	077	★	104	☆
024	○	051	★	078	☆	105	○
025	☆	052	☆	079	○	106	★
026	★	053	○	080	☆	107	★
027	○	054	★	081	★		